To Miss Mary Davis
with appreciation and
best wishes
W. T. Young

Application of Science in Examination of Works of Art

Application of Science

in Examination

of Works of Art

Editor: William J. Young

Proceedings of the Seminar:

June 15—19, 1970

conducted by the Research Laboratory

Museum of Fine Arts

Boston, Massachusetts

All Rights Reserved by Museum of Fine Arts, Boston, 1973
SBN 0-87846-071-3
Library of Congress Catalogue Card No. 73-79826
Printed in West Germany by Brüder Hartmann, Berlin
Designed by Carl F. Zahn, Museum of Fine Arts, Boston

Foreword

This third international seminar to be conducted by the Research Laboratory of the Museum of Fine Arts was eminently successful in that it effectively provided both the arena and the atmosphere necessary for the free exchange of ideas and findings on the study and application of science to art. The integration of science with art is a vital factor in attaining future technological goals in regard to art. For as art has become more popular — as witnessed by the tremendous influx of museum visitors — there is necessarily a greater demand for better exhibition presentation. This in itself tends to create serious problems in the conservation and preservation of works of art. A museum is essentially a repository for art objects, and its ultimate objective is to hand down objects to the future generation in as stable a condition as possible. The environment in which a work of art is exposed greatly affects its future aging process. Thus the study of conservation and preservation of art through science should be one of a museum's first priorities. It is hoped that the seminar and this book that is its outgrowth will contribute to that aim.

GEORGE C. SEYBOLT
President

Introduction

The third seminar under the title *Application of Science in the Examination of Works of Art* was organized in 1970 on an international scale with the intention of presenting an opportunity by formal lectures and informal discussions for the exchange of knowledge concerning new advances in science as applied to art since the last seminar, which took place in 1965. The seminar was also planned to celebrate the museum's centennial year and the opening of the new Research Laboratory in the new George Robert White wing of the museum. Trustees and many friends of the research laboratory enthusiastically collaborated by entertaining small groups of delegates and providing an atmosphere which encouraged personal contact. The seminar was made financially possible only through the generosity of Dr. Edmundo Lassalle and Mr. Paul Bernat.

A museum scientist not only is obligated to conserve works of art for the study and enjoyment of the future generation but is also obligated to record new technological approaches in the study of works of art. The publication of this book was made possible by a generous grant of the Alfred P. Sloan Foundation. It is only by continued interest of foundations and friends of the museum that such important studies can be undertaken and recorded through literature for future scholars.

W. J. YOUNG
Head of the Research Laboratory

Table of Contents

ADON A. GORDUS

Neutron Activation Analysis of Streaks from Coins and Metallic Works of Art

Introduction

The ore-refining techniques used in ancient and medieval times were relatively crude. As a result metalware and coins from these periods contain detectable amounts of various impurities. For example, gold, lead, antimony, arsenic, and frequently also zinc, tin, bismuth, and iron are usually associated with silver. Some of these impurities, such as gold, may have been contained in the original silver; others, such as antimony and arsenic, may arise principally as impurities in the copper used to alloy or debase the silver; the lead impurity, on the other hand, probably was mainly introduced during lead-cuppelation processing of silver.

It appeared to us that it might be possible to use information on the level of impurities in silver coins and art objects to assist in the authentication and the identification of the region and period of manufacture of the art objects. Described here are studies we have performed of one of the impurities, gold, which seems to provide particularly useful information.

Two nondestructive analytic methods were devised and perfected. Emphasis in both methods was on the speed of analysis, since we wanted data for a large enough number of coins and art objects to yield statistically relevant results. The bulk of the coins and art objects we have analyzed by both methods are Near Eastern in origin, and examples will be given mainly of data derived from Sasanian (Persia: A.D. 224–651) and early Islamic coins and metalwork.

Howitzer Coin Analysis

Howitzer coin analysis has been described in detail in previous publications.[1–3] It consists of irradiating a coin for one minute in a low-intensity neutron source (fig. 1) followed by a one minute analysis of the induced silver radioactivity. The activity in the coin is dissipated in 10 to 15 minutes, and it is possible to perform repeat analyses, thus improving the statistics. In using this method we have been able to determine the silver fineness of a coin to ±1 to 1.5%.

We have analyzed over 3500 ancient and medieval coins by this method of activation. Shown in fig. 2 are silver fineness data for over 400 Sasanian coins. Alternating open and closed circles are used to assist in the visual correlation of the data with the ruling monarch issuing the coins. Beginning with the reign of Kavad I, coins have inscribed on them the year of issue, and the data in fig. 2 are arranged in accordance with these dates. Prior to these analyses, many historians had assumed that, except for some obviously debased issues of Shapur I, all other Sasanian drachms were more than 90% silver.

Streak Analysis Method

The oxidized surface of a coin or metallic art object and the

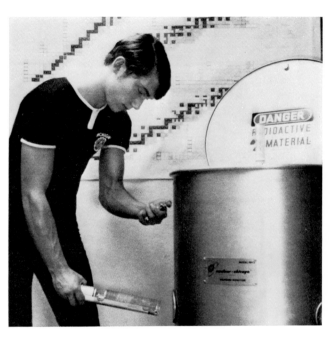

1. A student inserting into the neutron Howitzer a cartridge containing the coin to be irradiated.

nontarnished portion in immediate contact with the corrosion layer generally have a composition quite different from that in the interior of the coin.[4, 5] This results from the fact that the more reactive elements, such as copper, are oxidized and lost from the surface more readily than the less reactive elements, silver and gold. Because of this surface-depletion effect it is necessary to be certain that samples are taken at a depth where the composition is that of the original coin. For extremely heavily corroded coins or coins corroded throughout, it is important to emphasize that no method of analysis, including destructive chemical analysis, will yield composition data indicative of the original coin.

Our procedure involves first removing the corrosion layer on a tiny area on the edge of the coin or art object by stroking the edge with fine-grained emery paper. A few extra strokes with the emery paper remove about 0.01 inches of metal. A small, cleaned piece of roughened quartz tubing is then rubbed on the brightened area of the coin edge (fig. 3), producing a streak on the quartz tubing weighing less than about 0.0001 gm. Usually one or two additional pieces of quartz are also streaked in the same spot and used for confirmatory analyses.

Typically 40 to 50 streaks from coins plus 5 streaks from alloys of known composition are individually sealed in polyethylene and irradiated together in a nuclear reactor for two hours at a neutron intensity of 3×10^{13} neutrons x cm^{-2} x sec^{-1}.

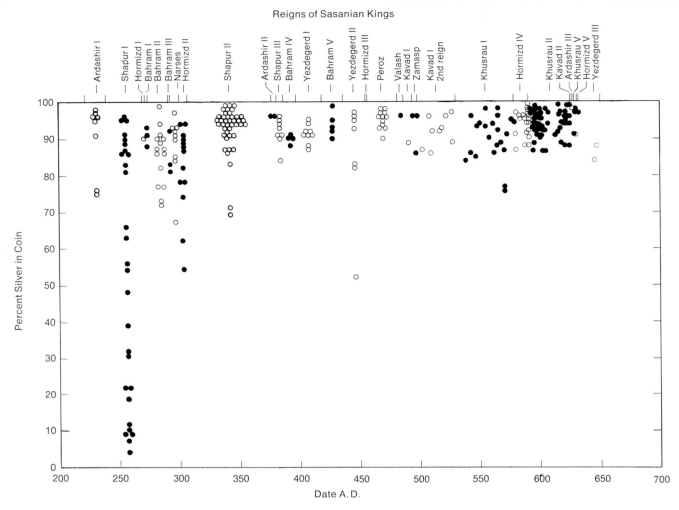

Reigns of Sasanian Kings

2. Silver contents of Sasanian coins as determined by the Howitzer irradiation method of analysis.

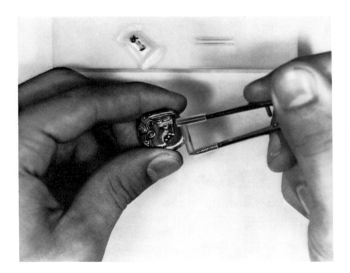

3. Method of streaking a coin.

4. Gamma-spectra analysis using the multichannel pulse-height analyzer.

The irradiated streaks are then mounted separately on cards and analyzed for their silver, gold, copper, zinc, arsenic, and antimony radioactivity. A multichannel pulse-height analyzer coupled to a high-resolution Ge(Li) detector is used for the analysis (fig. 4). Since the streaks are not weighed the radio-activity levels in the streaks are compared with those in the standard-alloy streaks and the ratios %Cu/%Ag, %Au/%Ag, %Zn/%Ag, %Sb/%Ag, and %As/%Ag are calculated.

Published chemical analyses of ancient and medieval silver coins and art objects indicate that, in almost all cases, silver and copper account for over 95% of the metallic content. Some having high copper contents may also have more than 1% tin or zinc, but in most cases the lead, gold, silver, and copper percentage sum is about 99%. Our method of streak analysis does not permit us to determine the presence of tin or lead. Hence, we assume that the %Ag + %Cu + %Zn + %Ag + %Sb + %Au = 100. For almost all of the coins and art objects discussed below the %Zn + %As + %Sb is much less that 1%. Our approximation, therefore, reduces to: %Ag + %Cu + %Au = 100 and data are reported here in two forms, %Ag + %Au and 100 x (%Au/%Ag). The latter term, as discussed below, is indicative of the %Au impurity in the silver.

It was apparent early in our studies that the gold being detected was associated almost entirely with the silver in a coin. For instance, data for 40 coins of Shapur I are arranged in decreasing order of the %Ag contents on the upper graph of fig. 5. The lower graph of this figure illustrates that the gold-to-silver ratio for these coins is quite constant irrespective of the amount of silver in the coin. What the data on the lower graph also suggest is that certain gold-silver ratios exist. There are data clusters at about 0.3, 0.4–0.5, 0.55, and 0.65. This must mean that as many as four separate sources of silver were being used by minters during the reign of Shapur I.

Apparently the ancient minters did not know that the silver they were using contained up to 1% gold impurity and, therefore, did not attempt to remove it. Since gold and silver are chemically similar, the gold impurity level would not be changed appreciably in the silver refining process. As a result, the percent gold impurity level of silver in a coin is an indication of the level existing in the original silver ore. Of course, there was some reuse of old coins, and if coins made from different silver sources are remelted together an averaging of gold levels would result. The composite data for a series of coins from a given period or even from a single mint during a given period will not necessarily show distinct levels but instead will show general clusterings. More randomness would be expected for those mint cities that relied on a number of silver sources. Similarly, cities that were on principal trade routes and might receive coins from other mints might then remelt these coins for their own use; these cities would have

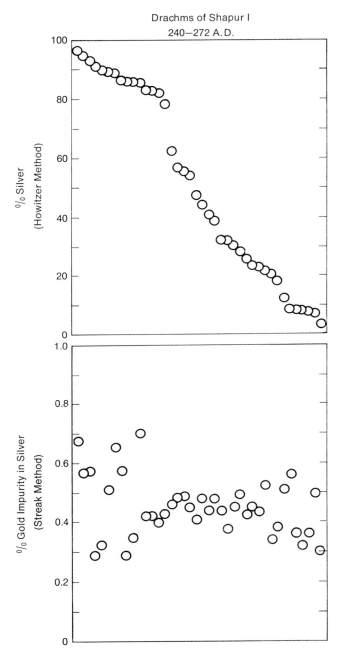

5. Silver content and gold-impurity levels for 40 coins of Shapur I arranged in order of decreasing silver fineness.

also issued coins that showed greater randomness in their gold levels. The most uniform levels of gold impurity would be expected for coins issued by small mint cities adjacent to silver sources.

The data of fig. 6 for coins from the reigns of six Sasanian kings indicate either that the same silver sources were not being exploited for prolonged periods of time or, if they were, that the gold levels changed as the mines were being worked. In any case, the coins from each time period tend to have separate overall gold-impurity patterns. In plotting this and other bar graphs of gold levels we have chosen to use an arbitrarily divided logarithmic scale. The listing in table I indicates the gold-impurity ranges used in constructing these graphs.

The gold levels from over 1000 Sasanian coins are shown in fig. 7. The latter years were characterized by some use of silver with relatively low gold levels. Of interest in fig. 7 are the data given by open squares. These all represent modern fakes. Some modern fake silver coins can be even more readily identified, since they contain less than 0.001% gold impurity, which is characteristic of modern highly refined silver. The fact that the gold is associated with the silver as an impurity means that the analyzed gold content should be added to that of the silver content in determining the intended silver fineness of a coin. In addition, lead, which probably remains from the silver-ore refining process, should also be included in calculating the intended fineness.

Caley, in 1957, published a series of chemical analyses of eight Umayyad dirhems.[6] His data are given in table II as the top row of values for each coin. Also given are his %Ag + Au + Pb data, which we have taken as the intended silver fineness. The second row contains his data normalized for %Ag + Cu + Au = 100%, which is the equation we use here for reporting our data. It is important to note that the adjusted %Ag + Au values are generally within 0.1 to 0.2% of the experimentally observed intended silver fineness. Thus, our method of reporting the data, even though we do not detect lead or tin or iron, results in data which very closely approximate the answer to the question being asked: "What did the ancient minter intend as the fineness of the coin?" Our data for the silver content using the streak method will generally be a few percentage points higher than the actual silver content, as is seen by the comparison of the two sets of %Ag values for each coin in table II. We also observe this small difference when comparing the streak %Ag with the actual %Ag as found by the Howitzer method.

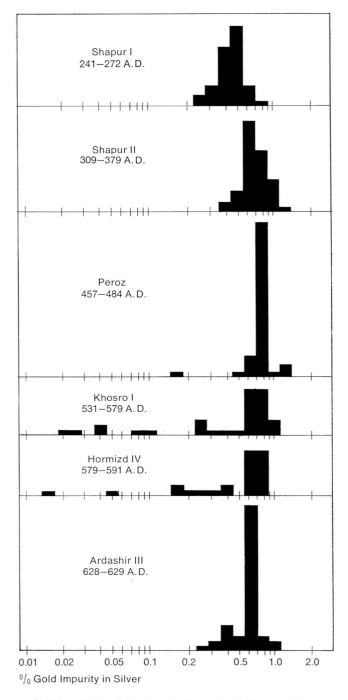

6. Gold-impurity level data for coins issued by six Sasanian kings. Logarithmic ranges used in preparing graphs are given in table I.

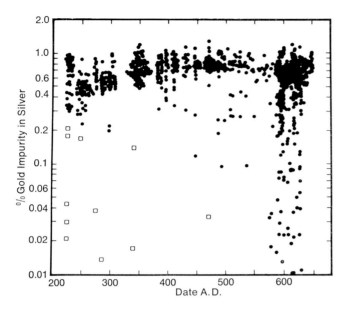

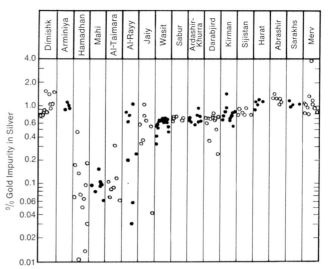

7. Gold-impurity level data for over 1000 Sasanian coins. Open squares are data for modern fake Sasanian coins.

8. Gold-impurity level data for Umayyad coins from 17 mints for the period AH 90—98/A.D. 708—717.

Table I

Logarithmic gold-impurity ranges used in constructing bar graphs

% Gold	Range	% Gold	Range
	1		
0.011		0.114	
	2		12
0.014		0.142	
	3		13
0.018		0.180	
	4		14
0.023		0.225	
	5		15
0.029		0.288	
	6		16
0.036		0.360	
	7		17
0.045		0.450	
	8		18
0.057		0.567	
	9		19
0.072		0.715	
	10		20
0.090		0.900	
	11		21
0.114		1.140	
			22

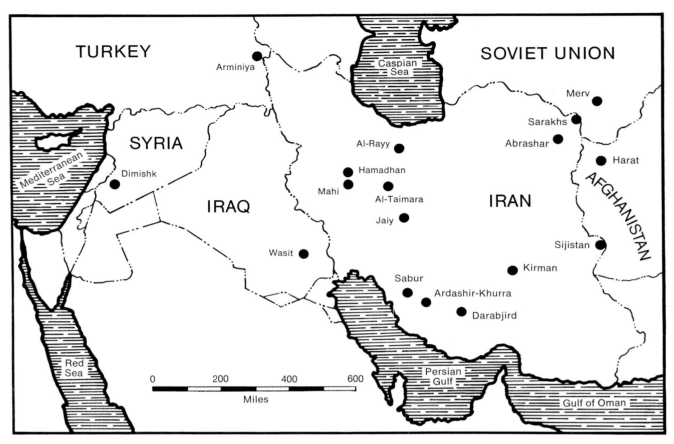

9. Location of Umayyad mint cities listed in fig. 8.

Umayyad Dirhems

Shown in fig. 8 are the gold-impurity data for Umayyad dirhems issued at 17 mints during the nine year period: A.H. 90—98/ 708—717 A.D. The mint locations are shown in fig. 9. It is clear from fig. 8 that a number of silver sources were being used during this period. One silver source, used mainly for coins issued at Hamadhan, Mahi, and al Taimara, had about 0.05 to 0.20 % gold. Another source, used mainly by Wasit, but also by Sabur, Ardashir-Khurra, and Darabjird, had about 0.6 to 0.8 % gold impurity. Sijistan used silver with about 0.8 to 1.0 % gold, whereas Harat, Abrashar, Sarakhs, and to some extent Merv relied heavily on silver with about 1.0 to 1.3 % gold. The occasional points in the range of 0.3 to 0.4 % gold in fig. 8 could be the result of silver mixtures or could represent the occasional use of silver from yet another source. This latter hypothesis is a distinct possibility, since a large number of later-dated Islamic coins have this level of gold impurity. Because of the distance from Abrashar, and the small use of silver having about 1% gold at Rayy, it would appear that the silver used at Arminiya having about 0.9 to 1.2 % gold is from a separate source. Perhaps part of the silver used at Dimishk derives from the same source being utilized by Arminiya.

Data such as those given in fig. 8 can be used in a variety of ways.

1. In some cases, the location of particular mint cities may be unknown. For instance, Walker[7] states that the mint city of Mahi may be either near Merv or near Hamadhan. The data of fig. 8 clearly indicate that the latter is the correct choice.

2. Knowledge of the amounts and types of silver being used in manufacturing coins in a given city might indicate the degree of importance of that city as a trade center.

3. By determining which mints use which types of silver it is possible to approximate the locations of silver sources and to suggest the silver trade-route patterns. For example, a silver source must have existed in the vicinity of Hamadhan-Mahi-al Taimara.

4. As we have discussed elsewhere,[3] the gold-impurity data can assist in deciphering some of the Sasanian mint names which are inscribed in the ancient Pehlevi script.

5. The gold-impurity levels found in silver art objects can be compared with the levels found in coins to suggest periods or regions of manufacture of the art objects.

6. When an art object is clearly of a design indicative of a given period and region of manufacture, yet has a grossly different gold level (generally lower) compared with authentic coins of the same period and region, this can frequently be taken as evidence that the art object is a modern forgery.

7. Similarly, modern fakes of ancient coins can frequently be detected by their having gold levels different from those of authentic coins.

Sasanian Art Objects

The largest collection of silver Sasanian-style art objects is in the Hermitage Museum, Leningrad. We have been able to ob-

tain streaks from their entire collection as well as from Sasanian-styled silver art housed in other major museums and in certain private collections throughout the world.

In examining data from these objects it is first necessary to consider which of the objects might be incorrectly attributed to the Sasanian period and which might be fake. The Sasanian coin analysis data can aid in this task, since the silver used by the Sasanian metalworker most probably was derived from the same mines as that used in minting coins. The data of fig. 7 indicate that, except for the first two reigns, Ardashir I and Shapur I (A.D. 224–272), over 90 % of the Sasanian coins have between 0.50 and 1.00 % gold impurity. Therefore, we would also expect most of the Sasanian silver art to have gold levels in this range.

The gold-impurity level data from the Sasanian-labeled museum objects are given in fig.10, and the data from objects in private collections are given in fig.11. In both figures the graphs are plotted using the log ranges defined in table I.

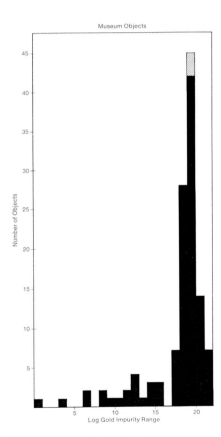

10. Distribution of gold-impurity levels for Sasanian-style silver art objects in museum collections. Refer to table I for log ranges. Cross-shaded data points are for plain oval bowls.

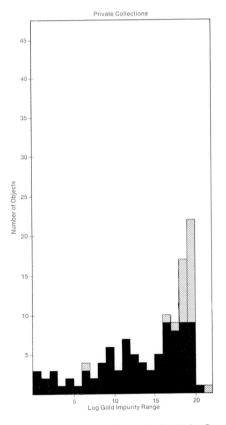

11. Distribution of gold-impurity levels for Sasanian-style objects in private collections.

Museum Objects

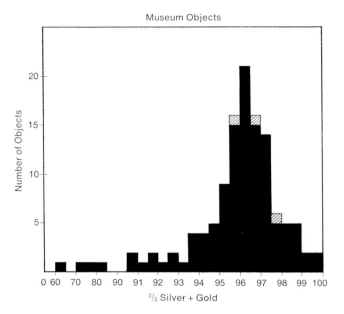

12. Distribution of %Ag + Au data for Sasanian-style silver art objects in museum collections. Refer to table I for log ranges. Cross-shaded data points are for plain oval bowls. Note x 10 scale used between 60 and 90 % and x 60 scale below 60 %.

Private Collections

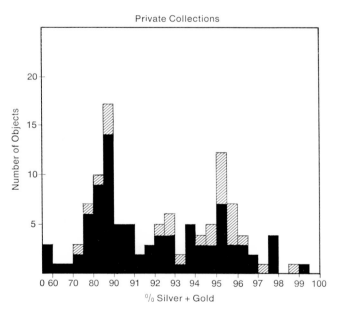

13. Distribution graph similar to fig.12 but for Sasanian-style objects in private collections.

Of the 122 museum objects labeled Sasanian, 28 have gold-impurity levels less than 0.56 % (ranges 1—18). Of these, 23 are either modern fakes or of a design and style that some art historians would identify as non-Sasanian. Included in the former group is a 19th century copy[8] of the Bahram V plate, which is part of the Oxus treasure in the British Museum. Of the 73 objects in ranges 19 and 20 only 1 may be fake and 6 may be misattributed. Of the 21 objects in ranges 21 and 22, 11 might be non-Sasanian. Seven of the 10 objects in these two highest ranges that are probably Sasanian have gold levels less than 0.95 %. This range of 0.56 to 0.95 % gold therefore includes 73 of the 81 objects that many art historians would label Sasanian. This is in good agreement with the distributions found for Sasanian coins.

The comparison between the gold levels in art objects and in coins can be illustrated by examining the data for museum objects which portray a Sasanian king. For example, two plates from the Hermitage[9] with Shapur II as well as the large head of Shapur II at the Metropolitan Museum of Art in New York have gold levels of 0.95, 0.69, and 0.67 %, respectively. This fits very well with the data of fig. 6 for this monarch. A Hermitage plate with Peroz[10] has 0.77 % gold impurity; another Peroz plate at the Metropolitan Museum of Art has 0.84 % gold. Both are in agreement with the data for Peroz coins. There are a few exceptions, however. The most notable is another Hermitage plate[11] with Shapur II having only 0.18 % gold impurity — clearly outside the range for this king. This plate, for which there is no reason to question its authenticity, must have been constructed in a non-Sasanian geographical region or, perhaps more likely, must have been made in a later, perhaps post-Sasanian period.

The data for samples taken from 115 privately owned Sasanian-style art objects reveal a different pattern of gold levels (fig.11). Of the 74 objects having less than 0.56 % gold, 72 are probably modern fakes and 2 may be misattributed. Of the 41 objects in ranges 19—22, a total of 34 are possibly authentic, including the 21 plain oval bowls; 3 are probably fake; and 4 are probably misattributed. It is also possible to examine the objects in terms of the %Ag + Au data, as shown in figs.12 and 13. As is seen in fig.12, most of the museum objects have %Ag + Au values greater than 93.5 %, whereas the privately owned objects, most of which are probably modern fakes, generally are made of more debased silver.

The museum objects that may be misattributed can now be examined in relation to data for gold, silver, and other elements from Parthian and Islamic coins, and from these comparisons it is possible to suggest periods and regions of manufacture. The complete data for over 400 silver art objects including Sasanian, Greco-Bactrian, Hellenistic, Achaemenid, Parthian, Islamic, and Central Asian objects will be published separately.

Table II

Original and adjusted chemical analysis data of E. Caley*

Umayyad Mint	Date AH	% Ag	% Cu	% Au	% Pb	% Sn	% Fe	Total	% Ag+ Au+ Pb	% Ag +Au
Wasit	AH–85	91.49	6.16	0.62	1.58	0.05	0.05	99.95	93.69	
		93.10	6.27	0.63	–	–	–	100.00		93.73
Darabjird	AH–92	92.73	4.25	0.66	1.85	0.12	0.18	99.79	95.24	
		94.97	4.35	0.68	–	–	–	100.00		95.65
Kirman	AH–95	94.15	3.56	0.67	1.48	0.10	0.10	100.06	96.30	
		95.70	3.62	0.68	–	–	–	100.00		96.38
Al-Basra	AH–100	91.17	6.36	0.42	1.63	0.10	0.09	99.77	93.22	
		93.08	6.49	0.43	–	–	–	100.00		93.51
Dimishk	AH–100	95.58	2.24	1.35	0.68	0.07	0.07	99.99	97.61	
		96.38	2.26	1.36	–	–	–	100.00		97.74
Ifriqiyyah	AH–112	98.06	0.84	0.70	0.42	0.10	0.05	100.17	99.18	
		98.45	0.85	0.70	–	–	–	100.00		99.15
Al Andalus	AH–118	94.21	3.96	0.60	1.10	0.05	0.06	99.98	95.91	
		95.48	4.01	0.61	–	–	–	100.00		95.99
Wasit	AH–124	98.46	0.23	0.06	1.10	0.01	0.04	99.90	99.62	
		99.70	0.23	0.06	–	–	–	100.00		99.77

* Am. Num. Soc. Museum Notes, 7 (1957), 211.

Acknowledgments

None of these studies would have been possible without the willing cooperation of curators at the Hermitage Museum, Tehran Archaeological Museum, Istituto Italiano de Medio e Estremo Oriente (Rome), Bibliothèque Nationale (Paris), Louvre, British Museum, Ashmolean Museum, Metropolitan, Boston, and Cleveland museums of fine art, and the Freer Gallery, as well as numerous private collectors. Financial support for the development of these analysis techniques was received from the University of Michigan-Memorial Phoenix Project and from the U.S. Atomic Energy Commission, Division of Research. This is publication COO-912-24.

References

1. Gordus, A. A. *Archaeometry,* 10 (1967) 78.

2. Gordus, A. A. chapter 10, "Rapid Nondestructive Activation Analysis of Silver in Coins," in *Science and Archaeology,* R. Brill, ed. Cambridge, Mass., M.I.T. Press, 1971.

3. Gordus, A. A. "Neutron Activation Analysis of Coins and Coin Streaks" in Symposium on the Analysis of Ancient and Medieval Coins in E. T. Hall and D. M. Metcalf, eds., Royal Numismatic Society, Special Publication no. 8, London, 1972, pp. 127–148, plate xv, figs. 1–7.

4. Condamin, J., and Picon, M. *Archaeometry,* 7 (1964) 98.

5. Carter, G. F. *Archaeometry,* 7 (1964) 106.

6. Caley, E. *Am. Num. Soc., Museum Notes,* 7 (1957) 211.

7. Walker, J. *A Catalog of Arab-Byzantine and Post-Reform Umaiyad Coins,* London, Oxford University Press, 1956.

8. Orbeli, J., and Trever, C. *Orfèvrerie Sassanide,* Moscow and Leningrad, 1935, fig.10.

9. Lukonin, V. G. *Archaeologia Mundi: Persia II,* Geneva, Nagel Publishers, 1967, figs.139 and 140.

10. Ibid., fig. 143.

11. Ibid., fig. 138.

VICTOR F. HANSON

The Curator's Dream Instrument

The eternal dream of the curator has been to have access to an instrument which is capable of determining the following characteristics of his priceless object: (1) When was it made? (2) Who made it? (3) Where was it made? (4) How was it made? (5) Of what material was it made?

You have all heard reports at meetings of how the probing mind and the ingenious scientist and historian have teamed together and pieced bits of evidence together to answer at least some of these questions. Before arriving at even an elementary answer, the scientist typically says that he must take a sample from a prominent part of the object. He would like a large sample so that his analytical method can be carried out with high accuracy. He furthermore contends that his professional integrity requires samples from many points so that data having high statistical significance can be presented. At this point in time, the curator develops a strong loathing at the mere sight of the scientist. He lays down the following rules of conduct in the process of characterizing the priceless irreplaceable objects of his collection: (1) You must not deface it! (2) If you *must* take a sample for analyzing it must be taken from a spot that is never seen by the viewing public. (3) No matter how obscure the sampling point, it must have a composition typical of the object as a whole. (4) You can take as large a sample as you wish as long as it is a fraction of a milligram. (5) You can take as long as you wish to make the analysis provided the final results are available within an hour. Such refractory requirements have alienated the affection of museum scientists for curators.

The advent of the energy-dispersive X-ray fluorescence analyzer has changed all of this. It has restored the mutual admiration of curator and scientist, and it has solved many problems of long standing. It has created more problems, however, than you ever dreamed of. I will discuss this point later.

Analysis by X-Ray

I will discuss briefly how X-ray technology is employed as an analytical method. Avoiding the sticky technical details, we may say that electromagnetic radiation — X-rays, ultraviolet, visible, and infrared light, and even radio waves after "contacting" matter — are reflected, absorbed, or scattered. If they are absorbed, they are largely converted to heat. A small fraction interacts with the electrons in the atoms and is remitted later at a longer wavelength by processes known as fluorescence or phosphorescence. A familiar example in the visible region is the color TV tube, in which atoms from carefully selected elements are excited by a common beam of electrons, giving three primary colors which in combination produce white light. Actually there are at least 10 kinds of atoms involved, which produce 10 different colors which are in turn mixed in the proper proportion to provide an acceptable color.

This same process occurs in the X-ray region and has been employed for many years to analyze materials for the kinds of atoms present. X-ray fluorescence spectrometers of this type have employed the familiar electronic X-ray tubes, generally one with a copper target. While we speak of an X-ray "beam," the X-rays are emitted in all directions. An explanation is easier if we pretend that there is a beam that has parallel rays that can be focussed on a small area of an object to be analyzed. Fluorescing rays are reemitted from the individual atoms in the object, again in all directions. Here again we take a few rays in a "beam" and disperse them into their various energies in much the same fashion that we separate light by a refracting prism or a diffraction grating in a spectrometer. The diffracting element is mounted so that it can be moved periodically allowing rays of specific wavelengths to enter a geiger counter. An electrical pulse is produced whenever an X-ray is absorbed by the gas in the geiger tube (fig.1).

The wavelength measurement is determined by the position of the refractor. The counter, which responds to all wavelengths, records the number of counts produced in a fixed time interval. This is related to the number of atoms of a specific element which are present. While this technique has been employed for many years for qualitative analysis, techniques are now available to make it a highly quantitative instrument.

The fairly large (half gram) sample to be analyzed is mounted in an evacuated chamber, and the time required to make an analysis is typically measured in terms of hours or days, depending on the sample size, the number of elements to be determined, and the accuracy required.

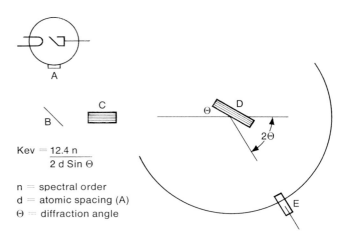

$$Kev = \frac{12.4\,n}{2\,d\,Sin\,\Theta}$$

n = spectral order
d = atomic spacing (A)
Θ = diffraction angle

Flat crystal spectrometer geometry: (A) X-ray tube, (B) specimen, (C) collimator, (D) analyzing crystal, (E) detector.

1. Wavelength-Dispersive X-Ray Fluorescence Spectrometer.

Energy-Dispersive X-Ray Fluorescence Analyzer

A radical improvement in this method of analysis was the result of developments in atomic energy and space age research. Physicists discovered an X-ray detector which produced electrical pulses whose heights were proportional to the energy of the X-rays which produced them. This eliminated the need for the dispersive element that I described previously. Furthermore these detectors have been improved so that they are extremely efficient in the energy region of interest to the X-ray fluorescence spectroscopist, i.e., 0—30 keV.

The needs of the space age led to the development of reliable compact electronic analyzers and memory systems which are capable of sorting out the pulses and storing them in memory banks whose contents can be continuously displayed on a cathode ray oscilloscope. The stored information can be treated mathematically in many ways and read out on graphic recorders or as digital information on punched tape, numerical registers, or on a teletypewriter. These data can subsequently be fed into a computer for further processing if this is required.

The high selectivity of the lithium-doped silicon detector and the associated critical electron circuitry is achieved in part by keeping them at a very low temperature. A dewar or giant "Thermos" bottle contains liquid nitrogen, which keeps the critical elements at about –320° by means of a copper bar which conducts the heat of the working parts down the rod, which loses its heat by boiling the liquid nitrogen refrigerant. The dewar uses about 10 liters of liquid nitrogen per week.

A radioactive source mounted in a lead-lined holder is mixed with an element which acts in the same fashion as the

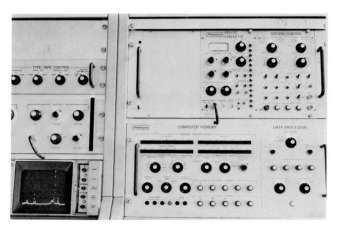

3. Computer Memory, Data Programming, and Visual Display systems.

target in an X-ray tube. The source that we use for silver analysis is cadmium 109 — a man-made isotope which produces silver 47 X-rays after decaying from Cd-109. The silver 47 excites the atoms of the sample, which is placed about 2 cm above it. A small opening in the holder permits fluorescent rays from the sample to pass through a thin beryllium window to the refrigerated detector, which is maintained in a high vacuum.

Pulses from the detector are amplified and processed in several ways which I will not discuss at this time. In our instrument the pulses are sorted and stored up in 512 channels according to their pulse height, which is related to the energy of the X-ray which produced the pulse. This energy in turn is uniquely related to the element which produced the X-ray. Our instrument, shown in fig. 3, has two groups of storage 512 channels, which enables us to store the spectrum of a "known" or reference standard in one storage group and use it for visual comparison to an "unknown" at any time. Believe it or not, this enables one to tell within 30 seconds if the unknown has elements not contained in the standard. It also permits one to tell at a glance how the content of both major and minor elements of the unknown are related to the standard.

Development of Quantitative Techniques

Since installing the equipment shown in fig. 4 in late March 1970, at Winterthur we have devoted much of our effort to determine the reproducibility of the instrument on a day-to-day basis. We are developing techniques to obtain quantitative results which I will define later when I describe some of our results. I indicated earlier that while this instrument has solved some problems, it has created many more. One of the new problems arises from the fact that the analytical results are

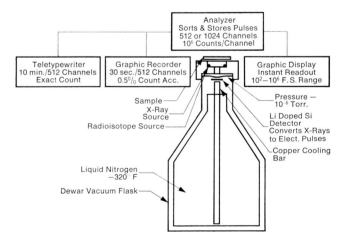

2. Schematic Diagram Energy-Dispersive X-Ray Analyzer System.

4. Winterthur's Kevex-Packard Energy-Dispersive Analyzer System. The unit on the right analyzes silver routinely. The one on the left, which has a computer-operated direct read-out, is used for glass, ceramics, paints, and various metallic objects.

practically instantly available, so the tendency has been to examine all kinds of objects, including those in the pockets of our many visitors. This leaves little time to analyze the results.

We have made spectra of the most important chemical elements, some of which are shown in fig. 5, so that we can quickly "home in" on a strange peak and identify it unequivocally. We have prepared reference standards of silver-copper alloys so that we can make a scholarly study of the metallurgical and fabrication practices of the early silversmiths. I will show the results to date of these studies later.

In addition to the vexing problem associated with collecting so much data that we do not have time to analyze them, is another problem that should be of special interest. The X-rays employed in this instrument are very soft — in the range of 1 to 30 kV, so that their depth of penetration is small. The analytical data are, therefore, related to the materials very close to the surface. I speak of this as a problem, whereas in reality it presents us with great opportunities to obtain information that is obscured on analytical results that are based on average values of the composition of an object. The "problem" that

I refer to is that the analytical result will not necessarily be the same as that obtained by other methods. The results obtained by both methods can be valid and highly informative. This situation reinforces the pleas made by such authorities as Dr. Gettens and Dr. Organ to be specific and explicit in describing the analytical method, the standards employed, and the points from which the sample or measurements were taken.

The "opportunity" that I mentioned based on the shallow depth of penetration of the soft X-rays is that in art objects the greatest interest to the viewers is what is at or near the surface that affects its appearance. Another opportunity resulting from the softness of the X-rays and their low penetration which I did not discuss earlier is that their penetration is greater for elements of the lower atomic numbers. These low atomic number elements, which include hydrogen, oxygen, chlorine, sulphur, calcium, aluminum, carbon, and nitrogen, are the elements normally appearing on the surface of objects due to corrosion, oxidation, dirt accumulation, or from protective coatings applied to minimize these deposits. The analyzing X-rays go through these deposits as though they were not there. We obtained spectra of old brass that was so heavily coated with deposits from being in the ground that the surface gave no indication that it was brass at all. The spectra obtained through the deposit were practically identical with those of the object after the deposit was off.

I will demonstrate for you later how we were able to identify the composition of some pewter candle reflectors that were enclosed in a wood case. This measurement required less than a minute to prove that these reflectors were of a tin-lead alloy and that the high reflectivity was due to the earlier solidification of pure tin on the cold mold surface and not due to a surface deposit of mercury or silver that had been surmised.

Analysis Program — Metal Objects

The creation of the laboratory building (fig. 6) at Winterthur was due in part or certainly influenced by a study that was initiated by Charles Montgomery and Charles Hummel in co-operation with the University of Delaware. The aim of this

program was to determine if the composition of silver and brass objects of the Winterthur collection could be related to the period and place of origin. Without going into details, I will say that the results are confusing but promising. They were sufficiently promising that the new Louise du Pont Crownin-shield building included substantial laboratory space and the Longwood Foundation provided a grant to equip the laboratory.

We set as our goal the development of equipment and techniques to characterize objects of the collection by *nondestructive* methods. Since we have one of the most important collections of American silver in the country — several thousand pieces — we decided to analyze all of these pieces and catalogue their composition in sufficient detail that future scholars could get a better understanding of the silversmith's practices. We also hope to provide information on the trace element content that might provide clues to the origin of the ores from which the metals were extracted.

5. Sensitivity of analyzer in counts per second for various elements in the region from 7.5 to 15 Kev with Cd 109 excitation.

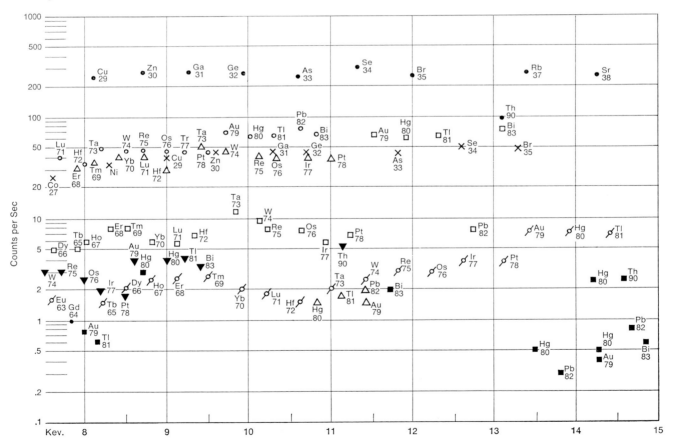

6. Louise du Pont Crowninshield Research Building of the Winterthur Museum.

After considering emission spectroscopy, wet-chemical methods, electrolytic methods, atomic absorption X-ray fluorescence, and several others, we concluded that the recently developed nondispersive X-ray fluorescence equipment had the best long-range potential to fulfill our needs. We contracted several makers of this equipment and selected the Kevex instrument with Packard analyzer and control gear. While the selection of these particular components was somewhat arbitrary, they appeared to have sufficient flexibility to meet our needs. The equipment performance far exceeded our expectations. It has operated without fault since the day it was turned on.

The development of quantitative methods depends completely on having reference standards of known composition. We contacted Dr. Charles Coxe of Handy and Harman, who kindly prepared silver and brass coupons about 10 x 25 x 35 mm having the following ingredients.

Table I
Silver series reference standards*

Ref. no.	% weighed in			Analyzed values chilled side			Analyzed values top side		
	Ag	Cu	Au	Ag	Cu	Au	Ag	Cu	Au
47.1	92.5	7.5	0.00	92.2	7.7	0.00	93.4	6.6	0.00
47.2	92.5	7.4	0.10	92.5	7.3	0.08	93.8	6.0	0.05
47.3	92.5	7.3	0.20	92.4	7.4	0.14	93.7	5.8	0.16
47.4	92.5	7.0	0.50	92.5	7.0	0.50	93.8	5.3	0.45
47.5	90.0	10.0	0.00	88.4	12.1	0.00	89.5	11.8	0.00
47.6	95.0	5.0	0.00	94.5	5.6	0.00	95.8	4.1	0.00
47.7	85.0	15.0	0.00	81.5	18.6	0.00	87.4	12.6	0.00

* Analysis results from Kevex-Packard X-ray fluorescence analyzer of "Reference Standards" cast blocks. The chilled side of 47.4 was selected as the arbitrary reference standard. Note that the copper content at the top side of the coupons is lower than that of the chilled side of the base. Such "segregation" is carried through subsequent rolling operations even in a minted U.S. half dollar.

1944 U.S. silver half dollar

	Ag	Cu	Au
Specifications	90	10	0.00
Heads	90.4	9.22	0.00
Tails	89.8	9.89	0.00

Table II
Brass series reference standards*

Ref. no.	% weighed in			Analyzed values, chilled side			Analyzed values, top side		
	Cu	Zn	Ag	Cu	Zn	Ag	Cu	Zn	Ag
29.1	80.0	20.0	0.00	80	20.2	0.00	82.0	18.6	0.004
29.2	70.0	30.0	0.00	71.1	28.9	0.005	71.0	29.6	0.006
29.3	60.0	40.0	0.00	60.5	38.5	0.006	62.0	37.0	0.010
29.4	75.0	25.0	0.00	73.4	25.3	0.010	77.5	22.9	0.008
29.5	75.0	24.9	0.10	75.8	24.0	0.105	77.5	22.9	0.160
29.6	75.0	24.8	0.20	76.8	23.6	0.202	78.0	22.4	0.155
29.7	75.0	24.5	0.50	75.0	24.5	0.50	77.2	23.1	0.400
29.7**				74.5	25.2	0.47			
29.7***				75.5	25.0	0.42			

* Analysis results from Kevex-Packard X-ray fluorescence analyzer of "Reference Standards," 25 x 32 x 12 mm cast brass blocks. The chilled face of ref. 29.7 was selected to be the arbitrary reference standard. A slice 8 mm from the chilled face was cut by a hacksaw. The analysis of the intermediate face is given in the second from the bottom row, and values from 32 mg of the cuttings are given in the bottom row. Note that here too there is segregation. The zinc solidifies faster than the copper, leaving the top, which is the last part to solidify, low in zinc. This illustrates the fallacy of analyzing one part of a casting and presuming that all parts will be the same.

** Section 8 mm from chilled face.

*** 32 mg chips from interface.

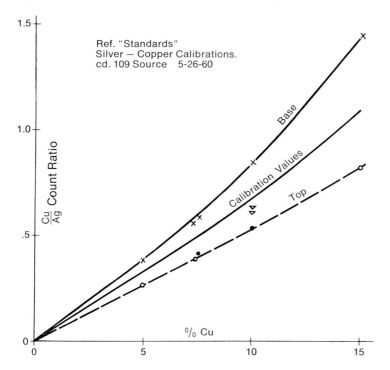

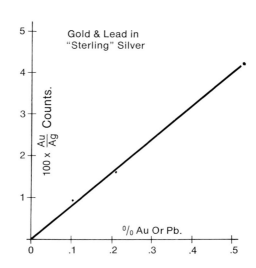

7. Ratios of copper to silver counts of cast silver-copper-gold alloy coupons on the left. The ratio of gold and lead to silver counts is shown on the right. Note the differences in copper concentration on the two sides of a 1963 silver half dollar designated by the triangles at the 10% level.

Dr. Coxe knowingly and wisely agreed to supply us only with the as-cast coupon, leaving the calibration up to us. We had previous knowledge of the problems resulting from the segregation of the various elements in the coupon as it solidified from the melt. The thing that we did not appreciate was the magnitude of the effect of this segregation. These effects were described by W. R. Myers at a February scientific advisory committee meeting. Tables I and II show the differences between the top and the bottom of the coupons as received from Handy and Harman. This striking difference made it clear to us why Dr. Coxe declined to "prove" the calibration of the sources. It also makes it amply clear why analytical results reported by various analysts vary so much. It also provides a bit of comfort to the analyst when he is questioned by the curator for the lack of reproducibility of results. What is of greatest significance for this group of scientists today is that it points out that the analysis of a sample taken from below the base of a statue will probably not be even close to that of a more prominent part of the piece. This is the nature of one of the newly created problems that I alluded to earlier. I do not have the answer to this dilemma, but I assure you that these effects are real and that they are going to perplex us for a long time.

As I said earlier, we recognized that segregation in our reference specimens would be a problem. We planned to machine off small layers from the top and bottom until we reached a point where both sides gave the same count. Fortunately, we had a spare specimen of Reference 1. We boldly removed 5 mills from both sides and were embarrassed to find that we overshot the mark on the basis of comparison with measurements on modern silver which we know to be carefully controlled.

This created a dilemma which really worried me until I had a really brilliant idea — not quite of Nobel Prize stature but brilliant in its own right. I speculated that the United States mint was an impeccable agency which would maintain extremely close metallurgical control on the coin of the realm. I figured that measurements made on a coin would provide me with a calibration point that even Dr. Gettens could not question. After establishing this point, I would draw a curve and adjust my standards until they fell on this curve.

I purloined a 1963 fifty-cent piece from my wife's coin collection and measured the copper-silver count ratio several times and decided that this would establish the base datum point. To this day I do not know why I did it, but I did. I turned the coin over and repeated the measurement. Imagine my sinking feeling when I realized that the Nobel Prize was beyond my reach because there was a difference of 6% in the absolute concentration of the copper count on the two sides of the coin. These points are shown by the triangles on the graph. I found comparable differences with other coins. I will mention in passing that this is another illustration of how segregation of the elements in the cooling of billet is carried through the subsequent rolling operations and appears in the final product. One would never even suspect this by making an analysis from drillings taken from an object. One could find these small differences by careful analysis of scrapings, as I will show later.

At this point in time I become painfully aware of my promise to Dr. Young for a paper containing all the answers to all the questions that were outlined in my introduction. At this point I had only new questions and no answers to old questions. I decided to live with my reference standards, which after a light dressing, were consistent with each other and in close agreement with the values measured on silver marked "sterling" c. 1930.

Analytical Results

The data that I am about to present are intended to illustrate the capability of the energy-dispersive X-ray fluorescence analyzer to rapidly and continually provide analytical data within the limits I have described previously. It is premature to attempt to draw too many rigorous conclusions from the limited number of specimens that we have examined to date. We are proceeding with our study, and we hope to present more comprehensive results at a later date.

We have analyzed about 100 silver objects of British origin classified at 50-year intervals between 1700 and 1900 and about 100 objects of American origin covering the same period (shown in fig. 7). The arrow indicates the 92.5 % silver level of the present sterling standard. It is important to note that the British maintained the silver content above this value consistently even back into the 17th century. The American silversmiths did not exercise very close control of the silver alloy composition until late in the 19th century. Many interesting speculations can be derived from these data. In the 18th century the silver assaying above 92 % silver was probably obtained from England, since the composition pattern is similar to the British silver. The objects analyzing about 90 % silver content might have been made from coin. The American silversmiths of the 19th century picked up a few extra dollars by watering down the silver with copper, but not nearly as much as the U.S. government achieved in making the present popular sandwich coins, which the instrument shows to contain little if any silver.

Minor Elements

Two minor elements of interest in early silver are lead and gold, which are present in varying amounts. We plan a study of U.S., British, and Spanish coins which may provide clues as to the origin of the silver on the basis of the gold and lead content. There are many more minor elements present which we have not attempted to measure at this time. Our tabulated data can be used at a later date to determine the amounts of these elements present.

8. "N. & S. Richardson" tankard no. 64.52. Unfortunately the absence of gold and lead in the body as noted in table III confirms that this "antique" piece was assembled in the 20th century.

Composite Silver Objects

Winterthur Museum recently acquired a coffeepot made by Nathaniel and Joseph Richardson in the period between 1771 and 1791. Our "study collection" is composed largely of pieces that look authentic to the layman but lack the attributes which convince the connoisseur that the alleged maker ever saw the piece. These are used in curatorial studies to teach neophytes to be wary. Included in this study collection is what is known as a "new and improved" Richardson tankard. We thought that it would be interesting to compare this with other Richardson pieces that were available for study.

If we first look at the results from the coffeepot study given in table III we find in Runs 80 to 85 that the rim of the base and the casting at the base of the handle were probably cast from the same batch of metal. The top and the side of the pot had identical lead and gold contents, but the copper content of the side was 0.9 % higher than the top. The measurement that was of greatest interest was the fact that the inside of the base was 3.2 % richer in silver than the outer rim of the same casting. I remembered the segregation theory and its implications, but I was not convinced that such a great difference could be the result of segregation. I thought it must be due to an error in the

Table III

Composite Silver Objects — American*

Piece	Run	Analysis point	Analysis data, %			
			Silver	Copper	Lead	Gold
Coffeepot, G70–19,	80	Side of pot	91.2	8.5	0.17	0.09
N & S Richardson,	81	Top	92.2	7.6	0.15	0.08
Philadelphia, 1771–1791	82	Inside base	97.6	2.0	0.20	0.18
	83	Rim of base	94.6	5.2	0.14	0.10
	84	Spout	95.1	4.6	0.20	0.10
	85	Handle bottom	94.5	5.2	0.20	0.07
	112	Inside base	97.6	2.2	0.18	0.18
	113	Scraped 0.006 mm.	96.3	3.3	0.20	0.15
	114	Scraped 0.010 mm.	94.8	4.8	0.20	0.18
	115	Scraped 0.014 mm.	93.8	5.8	0.20	0.16
Sugar tong, N & S Richardson,	99	Tong	93.0	6.2	0.60	0.16
Philadelphia, 1771–1791						
Covered sugar urn, N & S Richardson,	90	Inside cover	95.0	4.4	0.20	0.35
Philadelphia, 1771–1791	91	Finial	96.4	3.1	0.16	0.33
	92	Side of bowl	93.0	6.1	0.60	0.30
	93	Underside of bowl	96.5	2.6	0.60	0.30
	94	Gallery	94.1	5.0	0.50	0.40
	95	Top of base	94.1	5.1	0.50	0.30
Creamer, N & S Richardson,	96	Underside of base	97.1	2.2	0.36	0.30
Philadelphia, 1771–1791	97	Top of base	96.1	3.3	0.40	0.15
	98	Side of bowl	96.8	2.6	0.35	0.16
Tankard, 64.52,	116	Bottom	94.9	4.5	0.50	0.07
"N & S Richardson," date?	117	Side	92.8	7.2	0.00	0.00
	118	Top	93.4	6.4	0.06	0.18
	119	Handle	94.8	4.7	0.44	0.07
	120	Top hinge	94.4	5.2	0.36	0.06
	121	Bottom rim	93.4	6.0	0.52	0.07
	122	Top rim	94.4	5.1	0.40	0.12

* Analyses of N. & S. Richardson holloware pieces. The tankard, No. 64.52, is a well-known fake piece. Run 117 made on the side of the tankard lacks the gold and lead found in old silver. The other parts of the tankard were of old silver.

Table IV

Composite silver objects — British*

Piece	Run	Analysis point	Analysis data, %			
			Silver	Cop-per	Lead	Gold
Coffeepot, OC21–2Q706,	242	Side	93.1	6.8	0.05	0.02
London, c. 1860	243	Top	93.4	6.4	0.16	0.03
	244	Bottom	93.9	6.0	0.01	0.00
Candlestick, OC19.2–2Q118,	245	Base	94.8	4.8	0.30	0.10
Wm. Cafe, London, 1767	246	Stick	93.1	6.5	0.30	0.11
Standing cup, OC24–2Q262,	235	Edge of base	91.8	7.3	0.55	0.34
J. Laughlin, Dublin, 1740	236	Side of cup	92.6	7.0	0.25	0.16
	237	Left handle	92.2	7.3	0.27	0.25
	238	Right handle	92.4	7.2	0.22	0.20
Server, OC4–2Q512,	273	Pan	93.2	6.7	0.10	0.02
London, c. 1860	274	Handle	93.2	6.6	0.18	0.02
Tray, 2Q1355,	286	Bottom	93.8	5.3	0.75	0.16
Eben Coker, London, 1772	287	Rim	93.3	5.7	0.85	0.20
	288	Foot	94.5	5.0	0.30	0.16
Tray, 2Q1359,	289	Bottom	93.1	6.3	0.44	0.13
R. Alexander, London, 1741	290	Rim	93.1	6.3	0.45	0.14
	291	Foot	93.1	6.3	0.45	0.14
Tray, 2Q1357, England, 1723	296	Bottom	96.4	3.6	0.10	0.00
	293	Rim	94.3	5.3	0.29	0.07
	294	Foot	87	12**	0.35	0.25
	295	Top	96.4	3.5	0.10	0.04
Tray, 2Q1362, J. Tuile, London, 1737	296	Bottom	92.9	6.5	0.53	0.10
	297	Rim	93.3	6.1	0.51	0.10
	298	Leg	93.8	5.7	0.35	0.13
Coffeepot, J. Swift, London, 1762	299	Side	93.1	6.6	0.20	0.10
	300	Top	93.1	6.6	0.21	0.12
	301	Edge of base	93.3	6.2	0.27	0.13
	302	Spout	93.9	5.7	0.30	0.11
	303	Handle base	93.5	6.0	0.35	0.11
	304	Handle top	94.8	7.5	0.33	0.26

* Analysis of various parts of 9 pieces of 18th century holloware.
Note the uniformity of analysis of the various parts compared with
comparable American pieces given in table III.

** Silver solder.

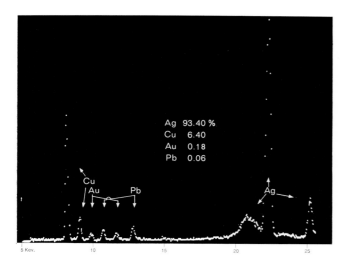

9. Spectrogram of "Richardson" tankard top of Run 118 listed in table III. Note gold and lead peaks which are characteristic of "old" silver.

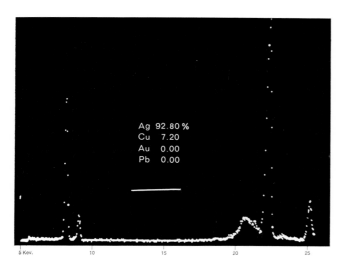

10. Spectrogram of side of "Richardson" tankard listed as Run 117 of table III. The absence of gold and lead confirms that this part of the tankard was made of 20th century silver.

measurement, so I repeated it and got the same result. I discussed the result with our curator, and he pointed out that it was the practice of silversmiths to dip their finished product in acid to remove scale and other discoloring materials. He also pointed out that the inside of the base was concave and difficult to get at. Since it was out of sight, no one ever bothered to polish it, whereas the outside, which had been polished repeatedly, had lost the thin copper-free layer which was the result of the acid etch. I told our curator that if he really believed this theory he should allow me to scrape the inside of the base until I reached metal having the same composition as the outside rim values of Run 83. I rushed back to the laboratory before he had an opportunity to change his mind and scraped a circular area of about one-inch diameter. I weighed the scrapings and calculated that I had removed 0.006 mm. Run 113 shows that the copper content jumped from 2.2 to 3.3 % in the process. Another 0.004 mm increased the copper content to 4.8 % and another 0.004 mm brought it up to 5.8 %, which was higher than the outside of the rim. This had inspired me to embark on new adventures to account for this difference, when the curator arrived and snatched the piece from my hands. We may never know how much metal must be removed from the rim to bring it up to the –0.014 mm level of the inside of the base. Furthermore, we may never know if the higher silver content of the top over that of the side was the result of an overzealous silver polisher or whether the top was actually made from a different batch of metal than the body.

The measurements of the various parts of the "new and improved" Richardson tankard (fig. 8) are also given in table III. The gold content was slightly lower than that of the coffeepot, and the lead content was comparable with other Richardson pieces. The side or body of the tankard, however, had the exact composition of sterling silver *c.* 1930. It had a trace neither of lead nor of gold, which has been found in every piece measured so far that was made before 1890. The spectrograms, which were each obtained in two minutes, are shown in figs. 9 and 10.

Finally I wish to call to your attention the wide variation in alloy composition of all the parts from the four authentic Richardson pieces. Contrast this variation with the close control that is found in measurements made on British pieces of a comparable period shown in table IV. One additional interesting speculation of the reason for the differences which appear in the British and the American composite pieces is that the British shops not only exercised closer control of their alloy but also made their alloys in larger batches and cast many parts from the same batch of metal. Maybe the American silversmith had to wait until his wife was out of sight so that he, too, could purloin a few of the family coins to make up a new casting for a piece in his shop.

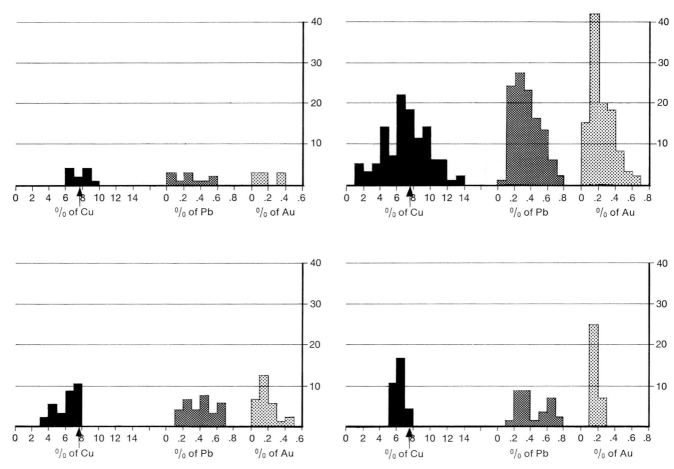

11. Bargraphs of copper, lead, and gold content of 18th century British and American silver. The vertical scale represents the number of objects analyzed having the concentration given in the horizontal scale. The arrows indicate the value of the modern sterling standard. First half century is at left, second half at right. American silver, above, British below.

Silver Polish Experiments

Last winter, just before our semiannual scientific advisory committee meeting at Winterthur, the museum curator received several inquiries from other museums regarding the best polish to use on silver. One of these stated that the writer had received five different recommendations from five different museums. Furthermore, he pointed out that the recommendations from the five museums were strongly expressed in each case.

On the spur of the moment we decided to try to determine how much metal was removed by employing various polishes. We bought one of each brand available at our local supermarket, which, together with samples of the brands employed at my home and at Winterthur, totalled 13 brands (table V). We cut a one-inch square opening in a piece of pressure sensitive tape and placed this on a well-tarnished object. Two drops of polish placed on a double "Hoopes" 22-caliber rifle cleaning patch were rubbed in a circular motion until the tarnish was removed and the silver had an acceptable luster. The number of rubbing cycles was recorded and the silver pick-up on the patch was measured by the number of silver counts appearing in 10 seconds. The process was repeated, with rubbing carried on in the same area for 100 cycles. The pick-up was again measured by the silver count accumulating in 10 seconds. In the meantime we prepared a silver nitrate solution containing 0.1 mg of silver per drop. One, 2, and 4 drops applied to similar

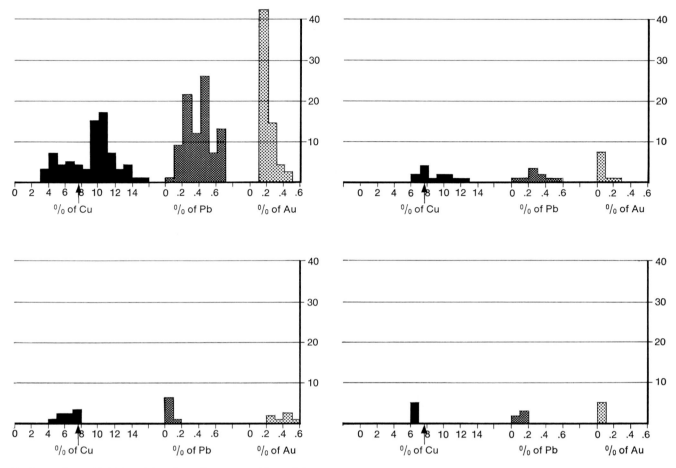

12. Comparison of British and American silver compositions of the 19th century. Vertical scale same as fig. 9.

patches provided us with calibration data so that we could show the actual amount of silver that was removed by the various polishes to achieve a certain luster. We were also able to show how much metal can be removed by overzealous silver polishers.

These tests, listed in table V, indicated silver removal rates that differed by a factor of four between some of the polishes. The test was only intended to demonstrate the feasibility of the method. We have on order some sheets of sterling silver which we will allow to tarnish, and we will repeat the tests with a group of experienced silver polishers and some novices. We will again measure silver losses and the time that elapses before the various strips show evidence of tarnishing. We are

not yet certain how or where to present our results, but I hope that they can be made available if the tests prove definitive.

I have described the principles of operation of our recently acquired Kevex X-ray fluorescence analyzer. I have described our experiences in developing reference standards to make possible quantitative determinations. The effect of shallow penetration of the soft X-rays employed was described. These effects produce different analytical results than those obtained by "in-depth" sampling. These effects also make possible the characterizing of objects by their near-to-surface composition — these are the characteristics that greatly influence the appearance of the object. I have attempted to describe the ease and speed with which measurements can be made. I gave an

Table V

Silver polish tests*

Item	Passes to clean			100 Passes	
	Number	Counts	Milligrams	Counts	Milligrams
1	28	46	0.11	38	0.1
2	12	32	0.08	60	0.15
3	6	15	0.04	15	0.03
4	17	28	0.07	245	0.6
5	70	28	0.07	3	0.007
6	20	46	0.11	120	0.3
7	40	45	0.11	38	0.1
8	26	55	0.14	75	0.2
9	23	32	0.08	17	0.04
10	28	26	0.07	68	0.16
11	35	35	0.09	5	0.012
12	62	19	0.05	3	0.01
13	55	45	0.11	97	0.25

* Preliminary tests results of experiments with 13 proprietary silver polishes. These experiments will be repeated at greater depth at a later date.

Polishes tested

Gorham Cream	Silvo
Hagerty Silversmiths Polish	Goddards Long Shine
Goddards Silver Dip	Hagerty Silver Foam
Tarnish Shield	Tests Systems Metal Polish
Test Systems Brass and Bronze	Goddards Silver Care
Goddards Tarnish Preventative	Noxon Quick Dip Silver

References

Bowman, Hyde, Thompson, and Jared. "Application of High-Resolution Semiconductor Detectors in X-ray Emission Spectrography," *Science,* 151 (February 4, 1966), 562.

Young, W. J. *Recent Advances in Conservation: Contributions to the IIC Rome Conference, 1961.* London: Butterworths, 1963.

Gettens, Rutherford J., and Stout, George L. *Painting Materials: A Short Encyclopaedia.* New York: Dover Publications, 1942.

Organ, R. M. *Design for Scientific Conservation of Antiquities,* Washington, D.C., Smithsonian Institution Press, 1968.

Myers, Ward R. "Metallurgical Problems in Identifying Objects of Silver and Copper Alloys," *Bulletin of the American Group — The International Institute for Conservation of Historic and Artistic Works.* 10, no. 2 (1970), 15—24.

Frankel, R. S. "Nondispersive X-ray Spectrometers," *American Laboratory,* 50 (May 1969).

example to illustrate this point. The experiments on silver polishes were carried out in one afternoon by a technician who had not seen the instrument before noon of that day.

We have also had excellent results in analyzing paint samples. We obtained a spectrum from 0.3 mg sample which showed the presence of lead and iron and no tin nor titanium. We have found significant differences between some new and old glass objects of similar appearance. We have found clues that help differentiate between new and old brass.

Acknowledgments

Among those who have been helpful in the conduct of this study are the Winterthur staff, who have supplied those objects which would be most appropriate for the preparation of this paper. David Stockwell was most generous in loaning us priceless British pieces dating back to the 17th century so that we could compare the analyses obtained from those pieces with American objects from the Winterthur collection of the same period. Dr. Charles D. Coxe of the Handy and Harman Company was most helpful in his discussion of the problems associated with the preparation of reference standards and for making up the initial lot that I have described here.

MAURICE E. SALMON

An X-Ray Fluorescence Method for Micro Samples

X-ray fluorescence spectrography is a relatively common method in museum laboratories for the analysis of artifacts. The technique most commonly used involves the exposure of unprepared or minimally prepared surfaces to the X-radiation. The method is nondestructive. However, major errors can be present in these results if the surface of the area exposed to the beam of X-rays is insufficiently flat. Further error is introduced when there are variations in composition between interior and surface layers, caused by the manufacturing process or by preferential dissolution and corrosion prior to recovery. The lack of adequate solid standards is another serious problem of this method. Ideally, these should have the same physical condition as found in the artifact and should have approximately the same composition in order to permit accurate calibration curves. Most of these difficulties can be circumvented by the method to be described.

Inhomogeneity of the artifact need not result in major errors of analysis if the material is sampled. Careful sampling can be made almost nondestructively. The drilling-out of a minute sample provides material which is more nearly representative of the inconstant composition of the usual object. Furthermore, the sample can then be manipulated and prepared in a constant manner in order to yield a flat surface, homogeneous and representative in composition of the bulk of the material, ready for exposure to the beam of X-rays. Finally, the drilled-out hole may be filled so that the restored sample-site is virtually undetectable. An additional advantage of the micro-method of analysis to be described is that a series of samples can be taken from an object, thus yielding a statistical estimate of the bulk composition of the object.

The method had its origin in studies by Rose, Cuttitta, and Larson.[1] They showed that it is feasible to dissolve milligram amounts of silicates in an appropriate reagent and then to absorb the resulting solution in powdered chromatographic paper. The resulting pulp can then be dried, formed into a disc-shape (pellet) under pressure between polished parallel faces of a die, and exposed to the X-ray beam in that form. This method of preparation results in a homogeneous distribution of the sample in a bulk matrix of cellulose. In consequence, the nature of the major elements becomes relatively unimportant — matrix effects are minimized because of the dilution. Furthermore, the standards required can be prepared easily by adding solutions of elements to cellulose powder, drying the standard sample, and forming it into a pellet in a standardized manner.

Rose et al. found detection limits of their method to be in the microgram and sub-microgram range, thus permitting detection of 0.1% of an element or less in a 1mg sample. Furthermore, the calibration curves were found to be linear, so long as the pellet thickness remained constant. However, selection of a different reagent for dissolution can result in significant change in effective thickness of the pellet. For this reason the method and a single set of standards can only serve for samples that are completely soluble in a single selected reagent.

By design, the pellets are made thinner than the critical thickness, as defined by Glocker and Schreiber[2] (while thin, the intensity of emergent characteristic radiation still varies with the thickness of pellet. Above the critical thickness, intensity is independent of thickness, although the weight of element sought may vary considerably, an effect caused by self-absorption). It is always possible to ensure that the sample pellets are thinner than the critical thickness simply by reducing the weight of absorbent paper used.

Direct adaptation of this method to estimation of metallic elements in alloys resulted in an unexpected difficulty. The first alloy-system to which the method was applied experimentally and satisfactorily contained only silver and copper, but samples taken from actual antiquities were found to contain appreciable quantities of gold. In the quantities found (about 2%) this metal failed to dissolve completely in the reagents chosen and potassium cyanide was added to complex the gold and permit dissolution. This addition of nonvolatile material changed the X-ray absorption characteristics of the pellets. The desirable linear relation between intensity and elemental content no longer prevailed. A method of compensation for this variable was now sought.

One possible method of correcting for absorption caused by the presence of variable amounts of potassium cyanide absorbent and by variation in pellet thickness involves measurement of intensity of the emergent radiation under three successively different conditions: (1) from the pellet alone; (2) from the pellet backed by an "infinitely" thick disc of a material containing the element being estimated; (3) from the "infinitely" thick disc alone.

Carr-Brion[3] used essentially this method to analyze mineral powders. He dispersed them in wax, at constant dilution, and formed the mixture into a film, of constant thickness, which he placed over an "infinitely" thick disc of the pure element being sought. He found that even if the films were thick, provided they were thinner than the critical thickness, then there is little loss in sensitivity and it remains possible to excite and detect the characteristic X-rays from a massive metallic sample placed behind the mineral-loaded film.

This method was now tested experimentally. With the data-reduction scheme presented by Carr-Brion it was found that when our standard pellets were used the results were imprecise and that their imprecision varied with dilution of the sample and thickness of the pellet. Investigation of this anomaly resulted in a generalized scheme of data-reduction which is independent of the effects of variable thickness and matrix-absorption characteristics. The argument is as follows.

The Limiting Case

The intensity $I\infty$ of the characteristic (secondary) X-rays emitted by an "infinitely" thick sample containing a given concentration of an element, when excited by an incident (primary) beam of monochromatic X-rays of wavelength λ_p is given by:

$$I\infty = \frac{K}{(\mu_p \csc \theta_p + \mu_s \csc \theta_s)\dfrac{W}{Ad}} \tag{1}$$

were K is a proportionality constant, a measure; (1) of the intensity of the incident beam; (2) of the absorption of incident (primary) radiation by the sample; (3) of the excitation efficiency; and (4) of the concentration of the element which is the source of the characteristic radiation being measured.

μ_p and μ_s are the mass absorption coefficients for the incident and characteristic wavelengths (λ_p and λ_s) respectively.

$\dfrac{W}{Ad}$ is the density of a sample pellet of weight W(gram), area A (sq.cm) and thickness d(cm).

θ_p and θ_s are the angles to the surface-plane of the sample made by the incident and emergent beams respectively.[4]

Pellet thinner than critical thickness

It has also been shown[5] that under constant conditions of excitation, the characteristic radiation excited in a pellet d cm thick will have an intensity I_d whose value can be calculated from the consideration that the contribution dI to I_d of an element of volume of constant area A sq.cm and of thickness dx, located at a depth x, is:

$$dI = K \exp\left[(-\mu_p \csc \theta_p + \mu_s \csc \theta_s)\frac{W}{Ad}x\right] dx \tag{2}$$

The integrated equation may be written:

$$I_d = K \int_0^d \exp\left(-a\frac{W}{Ad}x\right) dx = \frac{K}{a}[1 - \exp(-ad)] \tag{3}$$

where

$$a = (\mu_p \csc \theta_p + \mu_s \csc \theta_s)\frac{W}{Ad} \tag{3a}$$

At infinite thickness ($d = \infty$) this reduces to expression (1). Eq. (1) restated is:

$$I\infty = K/a \tag{4}$$

and the ratio of the intensity from a thin pellet I_d to the intensity from an "infinitely" thick pellet $I\infty$ is

$$\frac{I_d}{I\infty} = 1 - \exp(-ad) \tag{5}$$

Pellet mounted on disc

It has been further shown[6] that the intensity I_1 of the characteristic X-radiation from a substrate covered by a thin film *not* containing elements present in the substrate obeys the exponential absorption law:

$$\ln[I_0/I_1] = ad \tag{6}$$

where I_0 is the intensity from the bare substrate (metal-filled disc alone).

In our experiments, however, the pellet does contain the same element as the substrate. Kaelble and McEwan[7, 8] have demonstrated that where the substrate disc and the thin pellet contain the same elements, the intensity I consists of two components, namely I_1, the intensity from the substrate as modified by the absorption of the pellet, and I_2, the intensity from the pellet alone:

$$I = I_1 + I_2 \tag{7}$$

From this relationship I_1, which would otherwise by unknown, can be calculated as follows:

$$\text{From (6): } I_1 = I_0 \exp(-ad) \tag{8}$$

$$\text{From (5): } I_2 = I\infty - I\infty \exp(-ad) \tag{9}$$

where I_2 is identical with I_d of equation (3).

Therefore:

$$I = I_0 \exp(-ad) - I\infty \exp(-ad) + I\infty$$
$$I - I\infty = (I_0 - I\infty) \exp(-ad)$$

and

$$ad = \ln[I_0 - I\infty)/(I - I\infty)] \tag{10}$$

From eq. (5) it is apparent that the intensity, $I\infty$, that would be observed from an infinitely thick sample can be calculated from the intensity, I_d, observed on a thin film of the same composition, provided that the absorption characteristics, a, of the film are known from eq. (9).

$$I\infty = I_2/[1 - \exp(-ad)]$$

from eq. (8):

$$\exp(-ad) = I_1/I_0$$

therefore

$$I\infty = I_2/[1 - (I_1/I_0)] = I_2 I_0/(I_0 - I_1) \tag{11}$$

The value of $I\infty$ calculated by eq. (11) can be used in eq. (10) to calculate ad, from measurements of I_0, I, and I_2.

$$ad = (\mu_p \csc \theta_p + \mu_s \csc \theta_s)\frac{W}{Ad}d \tag{12}$$

If we let

$$M = \frac{1}{A}(\mu_p \csc \theta_p + \mu_s \csc \theta_s)$$

then

$$ad = MW \tag{13}$$

and

$$M = ad/W$$

from eq. (10)

$$M = \frac{1}{W} \ln \left[(I_0 - I\infty) / (I - I\infty) \right] \tag{14}$$

$$M = \frac{1}{W} \ln \left[I_0^2 - I_1 I_0 - I_2 I_0 \right) / (II_0 - II_1 - I_2 I_0) \right] \tag{14 a}$$

M, therefore, is a calculable measure of the characteristic absorption of a sample weighing W (gm), of unit area, independent of the density and thickness.

Reconsidering the constant K in eq. (1), it can be separated into two components: C_i, the concentration of element i; and K', the intensity of the incident beam, the absorption of the incident (primary) radiation, and the excitation efficiency. Eq. (1) can be restated

$$I_i \infty = K' C_i / M \tag{15}$$

K' is constant for a given set of excitation conditions. By assuming a value of unity for K' we can now calculate a corrected intensity I_c which is directly proportional to the true intensity. $I_i \infty$ for element i is calculated according to eq. (11).

$$I_i \infty M = C_i \tag{16}$$

and for convenience we let

$$I_c = I_i \infty M \tag{17}$$

Methods

Preparation of standards

There are two options available for the preparation of standards. The first involves the use of solid standard reference materials. If homogeneous, well-characterized, solid reference standards are available, these can be sampled by drilling or scraping. Two to 10 mg portions of the solid standards are accurately weighed and dissolved in an appropriate reagent. The resulting solution is absorbed in a weighed portion, approximately 400 mg, of high-purity cellulose powder. The resulting moist pulp is then dried overnight at approximately 80° C. The dried powder is thoroughly mulled with a mortar and pestle made of either boron carbide or agate and pressed into a one inch die at 87,500 psi to form a thin, compact disc.

If well-characterized solid standards are not available, it is possible, and valid, to prepare standards in the liquid phase. Accurately prepared standard solutions are available for atomic absorption analysis. These standard solutions are probably the most convenient source of standard materials for the preparation of liquid phase standards for this technique. Aliquot portions of the standard solution are each diluted to give a solution with an accurately known weight of the element(s) per milliliter. Accurately measured portions of this standard solution are transferred to separate beakers and the solutions are absorbed in weighed portions of cellulose powder, and the preparation scheme follows from above.

Data collection

The conditions of excitation are selected to give adequate statistical counting rates in a convenient time period. The thick substrate discs consist of a dispersion of approximately 10 %, by weight, of finely powdered metal in a matrix of bakelite. The use of a thick sample of the pure metal, as proposed by Carr-Brion, introduces a wide disparity of counting rates between the substrate and the sample. This in turn creates problems of correcting for dead-time in the counting circuit. Empirical observations have shown that the corrected intensity, I_c, obtained through the use of a substrate made of the pure metal and a substrate made of a dilute material are indistinguishable.

The spectrograph was adjusted to the peak of the wavelength of interest and locked in position. The intensities are measured on a fixed time scheme. The appropriate intensities are measured as follows:

I_2: the intensity measured on the sample pellet alone

I : the intensity measured on the sample pellet backed by the thick substrate disc

I_0: the intensity measured on the thick substrate disc occupying the position of the sample pellet

Data reduction

The intensities are converted to counting rates, counts-per-second, and a dead-time correction is applied, if necessary. M and $I\infty$ are calculated according to eqs. (14 a) and (11) respectively, and I_c is calculated according to eq. (17).

The weight fraction, C_i, of the element of interest in the prepared standard-sample pellets is calculated. For example, 5 mg of a standard sample material containing 20 % copper is added to 495 mg of cellulose powder. The weight fraction of copper is 0.002.

A least-squares fit is made on the points I_c vs. C_i for the standards in order to obtain the coefficients α and β in the linear relationship

$$C_i = \alpha I + \beta$$

Once the slope and the y intercept, α and β respectively, of the standard curve are known it is a simple matter to apply these to values of I_c derived from unknown samples prepared and measured in the same manner. With C_i in hand it is a simple matter to calculate the percentage of element i in the original sample.

Experimental Results

A series of standard pellets was prepared from liquid standards formulated for this purpose. A second series of standard pellets was prepared from solid silver-alloy standards obtained from Smith & Underwood, Manufacturing Chemists, Royal Oak, Michigan. The liquid-phase standards were prepared by pipetting 1 ml of the standard solution onto a weighed portion of cellulose powder. The weight of the cellulose powder varied from 378 mg to 461 mg. The moist pulps were mixed and the standard preparation scheme was followed.

The solid-phase standards were prepared by dissolving a weighed portion of the standard alloys in $1:1$ HNO_3 and absorbing the resulting solution on cellulose powder. The weights of the samples taken varied between 2 mg and 9.5 mg. The weight of cellulose powder varied between 280 mg and 480 mg. The random weights of sample and diluent, cellulose powder, were used for two reasons: (1) to create a greater dispersion of absorption characteristics and (2) as a practical consideration, in that it is easier to accurately weigh a select portion of standard that it is to select an accurately weighed portion of the standard.

The liquid-phase standards were arbitrarily selected as the reference standards. The appropriate intensities for silver, copper, and zinc were measured on nine standard pellets, and I_c was calculated for each. A least-squares fit I_c vs. C_i was made by means of an orthogonal polynomial method to obtain the slope and y intercept of each calibration curve.

There were six standard samples prepared from each of six standard materials. Four samples were invalidated because of accidents during the course of sample preparation. The appropriate intensities were measured for silver, copper, and zinc on each of 32 solid-phase standard samples, and I_c was calculated for each element in each sample. I_c for each element in each solid-phase standard was fitted to the appropriate calibration curve and the corresponding concentration was calculated. These results are summarized in tables I, II, and III. Five determinations were made on each pellet, and the average is presented in the tables along with the appropriate standard deviation.

The rather monumental task of data reduction was accomplished on a time-share computer with a program written in BASIC. In practice all of the data for the standards and unknowns for a single element are read into the computer in a block. The data for the standards are reduced, and the least-squares fit is made to obtain the slope and y intercept of the standard curve. As a test of the quality of fit, the standards are then fitted to the curve, and the various terms — concentration given, concentration found, the difference, and the percentage difference — are printed out for examination. The program then passes to the unknowns and reduces the data, fits them to the

Table I

Results of silver determinations

Sample number	Standard silver, %	Silver found, %	Standard deviation	Silver found, average	Standard deviation	Coefficient variation, %	Confidence limit, 95%	Standard number
162		8.95	0.151					
163		9.90	0.261					
164		8.89	0.183					
165		10.18	0.135					
166	8.56	9.19	0.060	9.41	0.546	5.808	±1.13	TS 140
169		7.82	0.096					
170		8.05	0.113					
171		7.31	0,356					
172		7.89	0.068					
173	6.99	7.65	0.165	7.74	0.313	4.038	±0.65	TS 141
174		35.52	0.300					
175		35.77	0.262					
176		35.62	0.218					
177		35.65	0.404					
179		35.43	0.376					
180	34.34	36.22	0.457	35.70	0.429	1.201	±0.87	TS 153
181		41.39	0.262					
182		41.29	0.492					
183		41.03	0.386					
184		41.91	0.205					
185		40.63	0.195					
186	39.83	42.41	0.312	41.44	0.664	1.603	±1.36	TS 145
187		51.97	0.364					
188		50.75	0.331					
189		51.76	0.462					
190		51.98	0.377					
191		52.82	0.618					
192	49.79	51.68	0.268	51.80	0.738	1.425	±1.51	TS 148
193		56.88	0.191					
194		55.74	0.344					
196		55.40	0.222					
197	53.84	54.83	0.419	55.72	0.810	1.454	±1.70	TS 149

standard curve and prints the intensity, the weight found, and the concentration of each observation along with the sample number. When multiple observations are made on the sample it calculates the average and standard deviations and prints these also.

The results on the silver-copper-zinc samples show a significant positive bias. It was felt that this bias was due to systematic errors in the preparation of the liquid phase standards that were used as reference. To test this hypothesis and also to demonstrate the utility of the technique on samples taken from antiquities a set of previously analyzed samples

Table II

Results of copper determinations

Sample no.	Standard copper, %	Copper found, %	Standard deviation	Copper found, average	Standard deviation	Coefficient of variation, %	Confidence limit, 95%	Standard no.
162		53.98	0.204					
163		54.09	0.291					
164		52.67	0.320					
165		55.57	0.283					
166	52.8	53.13	0.455	53.89	1.042	1.933	±2.15	TS140
169		86.48	0.368					
170		89.08	0.421					
171		87.19	0.555					
172		89.17	0.485					
173	84.8	85.65	0.413	87.52	1.475	1.685	±3.05	TS141
174		26.96	0.353					
175		27.13	0.191					
176		26.47	0.146					
177		25.99	0.233					
179		26.67	0.214					
180	25.7	26.61	0.272	26.64	0.439	1.646	±0.90	Tn153
181		31.23	0.191					
182		30.91	0.116					
183		30.88	0.167					
184		31.62	0.128					
185		30.89	0.269					
186	30.4	30.83	0.194	31.04	0.375	1.207	±0.77	TS145
187		17.34	0.149					
188		16.93	0.068					
189		17.12	0.204					
190		16.61	0.130					
191		17.36	0.091					
192	15.8	17.10	0.083	17.08	0.286	1.673	±0.58	TS148
193		42.03	0.097					
194		40.95	0.248					
196		40.75	0.387					
197	40.0	40.75	0.328	41.119	0.603	1.466	±1.26	TS149

Table III

Results of zinc determinations

Sample no.	Standard zinc, %	Zinc found, %	Standard deviation	Zinc found, average	Standard deviation	Coefficient of variation, %	Confidence limit, 95%	Standard no.
162		39.08	0.240					
163		39.44	0.247					
164		38.91	0.077					
165		40.13	0.224					
166	38.9	38.81	0.299	39.27	0.523	1.331	±1.07	TS140
174		21.16	0.145					
176		20.71	0.087					
177		21.24	0.175					
179		21.04	0.204					
180	21.0	21.09	0.142	21.05	0.231	1.098	±0.47	TS153
181		24.69	0.202					
182		24.44	0.247					
183		24.24	0.231					
184		24.71	0.193					
185		24.20	0.230					
186	24.2	24.73	0.214	24.50	0.302	1.233	±0.61	TS145
187		15.94	0.138					
188		15.31	0.040					
189		15.82	0.068					
190		15.46	0.048					
191		15.74	0.161					
192	15.6	15.84	0.086	15.69	0.242	1.540	±0.49	TS148
193		4.80	0.024					
194		4.78	0.053					
196		4.83	0.074					
197	4.6	4.74	0.077	4.79	0.070	1.458	±0.21	TS149

was sought. No adequately analyzed samples of silver alloys could be found. However, Mr. John Gettens at the Freer Gallery of Art kindly agreed to let us use some of the excess of the samples taken from the Chinese Ceremonial Bronzes. The samples have been analyzed and the results are reported in the Freer Bronze Book, volume II.[9]

Reference pellets were prepared from solid reference standards obtained from the National Bureau of Standards. The standard and unknown sample pellets were prepared by the same method as the silver pellets. Three pellets were prepared from each of 13 samples of bronze. The appropriate intensities were measured for copper, tin, and lead and the data reduction was carried out according to the scheme described above. The results are presented in tables IV, V, and VI. It can be readily seen that there is a significant improvement in the agreement between the results of wet chemical and X-ray fluorescence both sample and analysis when reference pellets are prepared similarly.

Table IV

Results of Copper Determinations

Sample no.	Wet. chemical, %	Copper found, %	Copper found, avg.	Standard deviation	Confidence limit, 95%	Coefficient of variation, %	Freer no.
284		80.6					
285		79.5					
286	76.4	83.4	81.2	1.91	±4.33	2.4	48.1
287		73.9					
288		76.9					
289	74.4	76.1	75.7	1.44	±3.25	1.9	42.14
290		72.9					
291		77.3					
292	74.9	75.3	75.4	2.06	±4.65	2.7	41.8
293		73.4					
294		74.7					
295	70.3	71.7	73.3	1.46	±3.30	2.0	31.10
296		73.6					
297		72.4					
298	67.4	70.5	72.2	1.55	±3.51	2.1	30.26
299		76.4					
300		73.9					
301	74.5	72.8	74.3	1.68	±3.79	2.3	11.37
302		84.9					
303		86.0					
304	85.9	89.3	86.7	2.10	±4.75	2.4	24.13
305		93.1					
306		90.2					
307	81.9	93.3	92.2	1.72	±3.89	1.9	13.30
308		76.0					
309		78.2					
310	73.4	75.5	76.6	1.36	±3.07	1.8	12.72
311		72.9					
312		74.7					
313	70.4	73.0	73.6	1.08	±2.45	1.5	11.82
314		70.2					
315		68.9					
316	69.2	72.7	70.6	1.71	±3.87	2.4	11.81
317		83.9					
318		87.7					
319	84.6	92.1	87.9	3.63	±8.21	4.1	09.333
320		67.4					
321		70.5					
322	68.9	69.4	69.1	1.51	±3.41	2.2	09.254

Table V

Results of Tin Determinations

Sample no.	Wet. chemical, %	Tin found, %	Tin found, avg.	Standard deviation	Confidence limit, 95%	Coefficient of variation, %	Freer no.
284		19.01					
285		18.74					
286	18.1	19.20	18.98	0.211	±0.477	1.1	48.1
287		16.51					
288		16.33					
289	15.7	16.90	16.58	0.255	±0.577	1.5	42.14
290		14.59					
291		15.14					
292	14.3	15.16	14.96	0.287	±0.649	1.9	41.8
293		10.99					
294		11.06					
295	10.9	10.83	10.96	0.123	±0.278	1.1	31.10
296		14.61					
297		14.66					
298	14.0	14.43	14.57	0.112	±0.253	0.8	30.26
299		13.02					
300		12.63					
301	12.4	12.42	12.69	0.267	±0.604	2.1	11.37
302		4.90					
303		4.75					
304	4.1	5.00	4.88	0.122	±0.276	2.5	24.13
305		11.73					
306		12.75					
307	17.8	10.12	11.53	1.151	±2.604	10.0	13.30
308		7.88					
309		8.55					
310	7.7	8.24	8.23	0.297	±0.672	3.6	12.72
311		4.48					
312		4.86					
313	4.9	4.75	4.70	0.175	±0.396	3.7	11.82
314		6.50					
315		6.34					
316	5.6	6.70	6.52	0.174	±0.394	2.7	11.81
317		2.85					
318		2.80					
319	3.5	3.05	2.90	0.122	±0.276	4.2	09.333
320		5.22					
321		5.18					
322	3.8	5.13	5.18	0.064	±0.145	1.2	09.254

Table VI

Results of Lead Determinations

Sample no.	Wet. chemical, %	Lead found, %	Lead found, avg.	Standard deviation	Confidence limit, 95%	Coefficient of variation, %	Freer no.
284		3.09					
285		3.09					
286	3.0	3.28	3.15	0.106	±0.240	3.4	48.1
287		6.85					
288		7.31					
289	7.8	6.42	6.86	0.394	±0.891	5.7	42.14
290		8.94					
291		9.76					
292	10.0	8.78	9.16	0.476	±1.077	5.2	41.8
293		12.52					
294		11.82					
295	14.7	11.79	12.04	0.408	±0.924	3.4	31.10
296		13.15					
297		12.39					
298	13.4	12.81	12.78	0.352	±0.796	2.8	30.26
299		8.97					
300		9.42					
301	10.4	10.02	9.47	0.464	±1.050	4.9	11.37
302		6.81					
303		7.37					
304	7.1	7.20	7.13	0.262	±0.592	3.7	24.13
305		1.03					
306		1.02					
307	0.3*	0.92	0.99	0.056	±0.126	5.6	13.30
308		14.11					
309		14.53					
310	15.8	13.67	14.10	0.422	±0.956	3.0	12.72
311		18.28					
312		14.64					
313	14 1	17.14	16.69	1.636	±3.700	9.8	11.82
314		18.63					
315		20.59					
316	21.5	21.04	20.09	1.144	±2.581	5.7	11.81
317		8.61					
318		9.87					
319	7.9	9.01	9.16	0.680	±1.538	7.4	09.333
320		21.31					
321		23.96					
322	21.8	21.49	22.25	1.312	±2.967	5.9	09.254

* 0.3% lead is estimated by emission spectrometry.

Conclusions

This method of analysis is adaptable, sensitive, and suitable for the routine analysis of very small samples removed from antiquities. The method is applicable to samples of any material, not necessarily metallic, which can be dissolved, absorbed onto a suitable carrier, and formed into a pellet of less than critical thickness to the X-ray beam, for the element being analyzed.

Reference standard samples are easily prepared from available solid standard materials. Liquid standards can be synthesized and used in the absence of well-characterized solid materials. It is, however, recommended that standard samples be prepared from well-characterized solid materials. The solid standards need not have a composition similar to the samples to be analyzed. In fact, NBS standard brasses could be used, for instance, as a source of copper for the preparation of standard samples for the analysis of silver-copper alloys.

This method is economical in the amount of sample required for reliable results. By taking a number of small samples, instead of one large sample, it is possible to obtain a reliable statistical estimate of the bulk composition of the object. This will also allow the worker to make a reliable estimate of the accuracy and precision of the analytical results as recommended by the Conservation Committee of the International Council of Museums in September 1969.

References

1. Rose, J. J., Cuttitta, F., and Larson, R. R. "Use of X-ray Fluorescence in Determination of Selected Major Constituents in Silicates," U.S. Geological Survey Professional Paper 525B, 1965, p. B155.

2. Glocker, R., and Schreiber, H. *Ann. Physik,* 65 (1928) 1089.

3. Carr-Brion, K. G. "The X-ray Fluorescence Determination of Zinc in Samples of Unknown Composition," *Analyst,* 89 (1964) 346.

4. Liebhafsky, H. A., Pfeiffer, H. G., Winslow, E. H., and Zemany, P. D. *X-ray Absorption and Emission in Analytical Chemistry,* New York, John Wiley, 1960, p.168.

5. Ibid., p.154.

6 Ibid., p. 150.

7. Kaelble, E. F., and McEwan, G. J. "X-ray Spectrographic Measurement of Wax Film Thickness," presented at the 11th Annual Symposium on Spectroscopy, Society for Applied Spectroscopy, Chicago, 1960.

8. Johns, W. D. "Measurement of Film Thickness." In E. F. Kaelble, *Handbook of X-rays.* New York, McGraw-Hill, 1967, p. 44-1 ff.

9. Gettens, R. J. The Freer Chinese Bronzes, Volume II, Technical Studies, Washington, D.C., Smithsonian Institution, 1969.

HEATHER LECHTMAN

The Gilding of Metals in Pre-Columbian Peru

The gilding of metals and alloys was an important technique widely adopted by the metalworkers of pre-Columbian South America, particularly in Peru, Ecuador, and Colombia. A wide variety of gilding practices was employed by these craftsmen, ranging from the simple mechanical attachment of gold leaf through the "mise-en-couleur" process — perhaps the best known because of its consummate use by the Indians of Colombia to gild objects they made from tumbaga — to the much more difficult method of "fusion gilding" employed by the Esmeraldas peoples of Ecuador.[1] In fact, some of the most sophisticated and inventive metallurgy in all of these countries — or, indeed, anywhere — was developed in association with the problem of producing a golden surface on a base metal or alloy. One often thinks of gilding as simply the final step in finishing an object, as a process almost incidental to the primary techniques of its fabrication. But the ingenuity that characterizes many of the gilding methods we observe on these early objects demonstrates the importance attributed to a golden surface as well as the marvelous variety of methods devised to achieve it.

In Peru, one of the most intensive periods of metal production and of prolific manufacture of metal objects occurred during the ascendancy of the Chimu culture (ca. A.D.1000–1470), reaching its peak with the establishment of the Chimu Empire, whose capital was Chan Chan. At its height, this empire may have extended from the Guayaquil Gulf of Ecuador to the Chillon valley near Lima (fig.1). Although the view is often expressed that the quality of Chimu metalwork is far inferior to that of the Mochica, who preceded the Chimu in the Moche valley, since much of the earlier culture's finesse had been sacrificed for the sake of quantity production, nevertheless virtually all of the metals and metalworking techniques that were developed in pre-Conquest Peru were frequently and successfully utilized by the Chimu smiths.[2]

Since metal gilding and silvering by various processes were already well established by the Mochica, it is not surprising to find them as common techniques of the Chimu craftsmen. The feature of particular interest during the later period, however, is the large size of many of the sheet metal objects whose surfaces were made golden. There has been a great deal of speculation about the Indians' methods of gilding such broad areas of sheet, including, for lack of a better explanation and, indeed, as a last resort, the use of mercury or amalgam gilding. There is absolutely no evidence, however, that mercury was employed. In fact, none of the published analyses of Peruvian gilt objects gives any indication of the presence of mercury. In my own studies, though I systematically analyze for mercury in the objects I examine, I have never detected it.[3] On the contrary, it now appears that the Chimu used a process which I have elsewhere termed "depletion gilding" — some may prefer to think

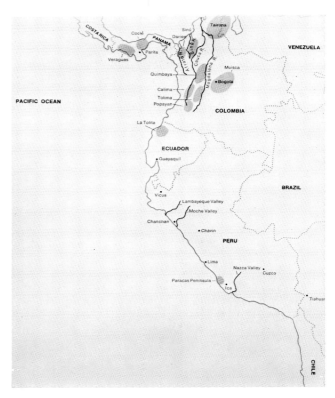

1. Map of major gold producing cultures and sites in pre-Columbian South America (from catalogue of the exhibition "The Gold of Ancient America," Boston, Museum of Fine Arts, 1968).

of it as enrichment gilding — which was based upon the use of alloys in which gold was deliberately incorporated as one component and the subsequent depletion of the less noble metals from the surfaces of those alloys, leaving the gold in situ. It was a process well suited to the gilding of large areas of metal during a period when gold was plentiful and could be used with little regard to economic efficiency.

Many of the gilt objects characteristic of the Chimu seem, at first sight, to be gilded silver.[4] In an earlier study, I discussed in some detail the manufacture of two small, decorative discs reproduced here in figs. 2 and 3.[5] Both have an extremely thin and uniform surface coating of gold above a substrate that appears at first glance to be of silver. The silver shows through in many areas where the gold has been worn away and, in the case of the pierced disc, fig. 3, the gilding itself has a pale greenish hue, characteristic of gold alloyed with a high percentage of silver. Examination of the surfaces gave no indication of the method of gilding employed, however. There were no signs of gold leaf or foil nor of any gold layer externally applied. All of the depressions in the traced design motifs on the disc with central boss were uniformly gilt with no accumulation of gold within these very narrow lines.

The chemical analyses of metal samples removed from the discs and reported in table I show that the objects are not of silver but are of an alloy of silver and copper with considerable spread in the concentration ranges of these two elements. Electron microbeam probe analyses of metal cross-sections from both discs further revealed that the gold not only appears at their surfaces but occurs throughout the metal, with an increased concentration at the surface. The discs are, therefore, made of ternary alloys of copper, silver, and gold, with the gold present in low proportion throughout except at the external surfaces, where it is more concentrated.

Another object, almost identical in fabrication to the discs, which illustrates well the various metallurgical phenomena common to all three artifacts, appears in fig. 4. Like the pierced disc, this small plaque is uniformly covered with a very thin, pale, and slightly greenish layer of gold. Where the gold has been abraded, the silver beneath it shows through to the surface. Again, surface examination revealed no clues about the possible method of gilding employed.

An unetched metallographic cross-section of a fragment of the plaque removed from the broken corner is reproduced in fig. 5, while a more highly magnified detail of one surface of this same metal section is given in fig. 6. The alloy consists of bands of two phases, a copper-rich one and a silver-rich one (present in the original casting from which this sheet was fabricated as dendrites surrounded by eutectic), heavily extended during the manufacture of the sheet. Near the surface, the copper-rich phase has been replaced by cuprite (Cu_2O), while the lighter silver-rich bands have resisted the corrosion due to burial to a much larger extent. Furthermore, both surfaces of the sheet have thickened, silver-enriched zones which are virtually copper free. The copper was depleted from the surfaces by oxidation during the numerous annealing operations to which the metal was subject in its formation into sheet. The copper oxide scale that formed was presumably removed with a mild acid pickle before further working and annealing ensued.[6] With the removal of sufficient copper, the silver-enriched zones formed at the surfaces would give the impression that such objects are made of silver.[7] This is the silver that shows through beneath the worn areas of gilding. Actually, the enriched layers are alloys of silver and gold, but the gold content is so low that the color of the alloy remains white. No distinct layer of gold can be seen, however, even at a magnification of 500 (fig. 6).

A plot of the relative concentrations of copper, silver, and gold as they vary across the metal section of the plaque is

Table I

Chemical analyses of objects gilt by a depletion method*

Figure	M.I.T. no.	Object	Provenance	Culture	Composition of Alloy, % by weight		
					Cu	Ag	Au
2	217	Disc, with central boss (collection D.T. Easby, Jr.)	Probably Lambayeque	Chimu	60.8	29.2	10.1
3	218	Disc, with pierced design (A.M.N.H. no. 41.2/5876)	Trujillo area	Chimu	39.0	51.0	7.5
4	335	Square ornament, repoussé (collection J. B. Bird)	?	Chimu	47.5	42.4	6.0
	221	Fragments of wall plaques (A.M.N.H.)	?	Probably Chimu	65.1	12.5	15.0
8	352	Mummy mask (Museum of Primitive Art no. 57.161)	Lambayeque	Chimu	11.8	48.7	39.6
	351	Nose of mummy mask, no. 352			10.2	45.7	41.6
12	356	Mummy mask	Lambayeque	Chimu	35.1	27.1	35.5
20	366, 367	Bangles (A.M.N.H. no. 41.2/6447)	Viru	Mochica (?)	45.3 46.6	43.7 42.6	7.5 7.2

* All analyses are wet chemical. The gold and silver were determined gravimetrically, the copper colorimetrically by iodometric titration.

2. Gilt disc with central boss, probably Lambayeque, M.I.T. no. 217 (lent for study by Mr. and Mrs. Dudley T. Easby, Jr.).

3. Gilt disc with pierced design, Trujillo region. M.I.T. no. 218 (American Museum of Natural History no. 41.2/5876).

4. Gilt square ornament with raised figure, provenance unknown. M.I.T. no. 335 (lent for study by Junius B. Bird).

given in fig. 7. It is very close to similar plots made of the two Chimu discs. The analysis was performed with an electron microbeam probe, and the trace for each element indicates the change in concentration as the beam traversed from the surface of the metal to a depth well beyond the zones of surface enrichment. In the body of the metal, the copper and silver traces alternate in opposition, as would be expected, as the two phases are encountered. The gold concentration is almost constant throughout the alloy, however, changing dramatically only near the surface.

Marked changes in the concentration levels of the three elements occur within approximately 10 microns of the surface. The copper decreases rapidly and is totally depleted within the last 5 microns. The full width of the enriched-silver layer is about 10 microns, and the concentration of silver within this zone has risen. Most important, however, is the abrupt increase in the amount of gold present at or near the surface. The gold concentration begins to rise above its normal level inside the enriched-silver zone and reaches a steep peak within about 2 or 3 microns of the surface. The silver concentration remains high here, and both silver and gold are alloyed at the surface itself, accounting for the pale, somewhat greenish color of the gilding. The fact that the gold concentration rises as abruptly and as steeply as it does eliminates the possibility that the gold had been applied externally, in the form of leaf, and the object heated to form a permanent diffusion bond. Experiments designed to test this procedure showed that, when the two metals alloyed, a broad zone of interdiffusion was produced with a gradual decrease in gold concentration with depth inside the alloy, a picture quite different from that presented in fig. 7. Even when little alloying occurred and an appreciable thickness of pure gold remained outside the silver zone, there was still a much more gradual decrease in gold concentration with depth than that characterized by the trace in fig. 7.[8]

Given the thinness and uniformity of the gold, its evenness in coating depressed areas, its ability to coat such depressions no matter how narrow without accumulating or clumping inside them, the lack of any visual evidence for the presence of an externally applied layer of gold, the deliberate addition of gold, albeit in low concentration, to the alloy itself, and the characteristic abrupt change in gold concentration at the surface shown by the probe traces, I have suggested that the gilding on these objects and others like them was produced by the selec-

5. Gilt square ornament, no. 335. Cross-section showing striations of alpha (light) and beta (dark) phases elongated in the direction of working of the metal. Note the thickened enriched-silver layers at both surfaces. x 200, As polished.

6. Gilt square ornament, no. 335. Detail of one surface showing the thickened enriched-silver zone with massive corrosion of the copper-rich phase beneath it. x 500, As polished.

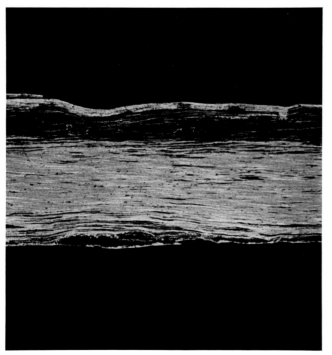

7. Gilt square ornament, no. 335. Electron microbeam probe traces of Au, Ag, and Cu concentrations across the gilded surface of a cross-section of the metal.

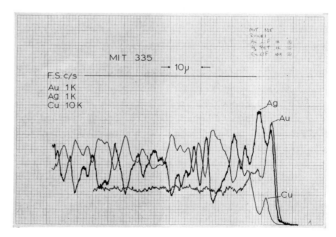

tive removal of some of the silver in the enriched zone, thereby depleting the surface of silver and leaving the gold in situ. It is this process that I have chosen to call "depletion gilding."

The point was made earlier that one of the more interesting aspects of Chimu gilt metalwork is the size of object which these craftsmen often undertook to gild. Thus far I have discussed only artifacts of minor importance, small in size and decorative in purpose. At the other extreme is one of the largest (28 3/4 inches wide x 16 1/4 inches high) and most impressive mummy masks of Chimu origin from Batan Grande in the Lambayeque Valley, reproduced in fig. 8. It is now in the collection of the Museum of Primitive Art, New York City. The nose and the two dangles beneath it were made separately and attached mechanically to the mask with "staples" made of thin strips of sheet metal. Until the present laboratory study of this object it was thought to be made entirely of gold.[9] The analyses given in table I show that, to the contrary, it is a ternary alloy of copper, silver, and gold similar to those discussed above but with a considerably higher gold content, of about 40 weight percent. The sheet metal of which the nose was made is identical in composition to that of the mask proper, as indicated in the table. An alloy of this composition is white when cast, yet the mask has a rich yellow appearance, characteristic of gold with a high silver content. Occasionally one sees on the surface small areas where the gold has worn through, and white metal shows from beneath. The surfaces of the mask are gilt, smoothly and uniformly covered with gold.

The Museum of Primitive Art most generously allowed a small fragment of metal to be removed from a broken edge in the proper upper right corner of the mask as well as a small sliver from the reverse side of the nose. Portions of these samples were used for wet microchemical analyses, while the remainder underwent metallographic examination. An etched cross-section of the mask fragment is given in fig. 9. The striated appearance is characteristic, as we have seen, of heavily worked sheet metal, the thin bands elongated in the direction of working. The very small grains, though fully recrystallized, are evidence of fairly extensive deformation and a final annealing at a temperature not much higher than needed to soften the alloy. The depletion of copper along both surfaces leaving zones of a lighter etching Ag-Au alloy suggests, however, that earlier processing anneals were more drastic. Fig.10, a more highly magnified detail of one of these surfaces, shows more clearly the enriched zone and the difference in size and etching properties of the crystals within it as compared with those in the body proper of the sheet. No discreet gold layer can be observed on the section at this magnification (x 500).

More interesting than the photomicrographs is the set of electron microbeam probe Ag-Cu-Au concentration traces obtained from this section (fig. 11). The almost complete removal

8. Gilt mummy mask, Batan Grande, Lambayeque. M.I.T. no. 352 (Museum of Primitive Art no. 57.161).

of copper from the surface is quite apparent, as is the rise in gold concentration to a peak value of approximately 52 %.[10] Although some silver has definitely been removed from the last two or more microns of the enriched alloy zone, the gold is nowhere entirely free of silver, which accounts for its decidedly yellow, as distinct from richly golden appearance. By contrast, the alloy itself is white and appears so beneath the thin gilt surface. Comparing this set of traces with that of the low-content gold alloy (fig. 7), one notices that the depth of metal affected by the depletion gilding process, that is, by the removal of surface silver, is considerably greater in the case of the mask, and the rise in gold concentration is accordingly less abrupt and less steep.

A second mummy mask, not as imposing as the first but still large (19 inches wide x 11 3/8 inches high) is reproduced in fig.12. Two photomicrographs (figs.13 and 14) taken of a small, sectioned fragment removed from the mask, show a structure similar to that of its larger counterpart in terms of the overall deformation of the metal, but this alloy is two-phase as the alternating light- and dark-etching bands indicate. The electron microbeam probe traces reproduced in fig.15 are also very close to those of fig. 11, given the differences in composition of the two alloys. In the case of the smaller mask, the removal of silver from the surface is even more apparent in the concentration profiles, while the gold peak is slightly higher than the maximum achieved with the larger mask, reaching a concentration of approximately 56 %. The interpretation of the two sets of data must be the same, however, and whatever process was used to gild the one was undoubtedly used on the other as well.

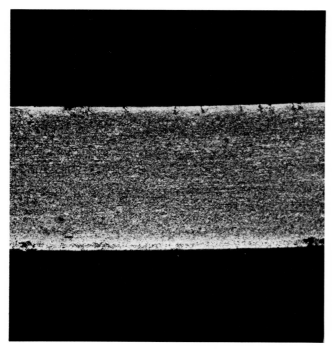

9. Gilt mummy mask, no. 352. Cross-section showing the severely worked metal with tiny grains and enriched Ag-Au alloy surfaces. x 200. Etch: $KCN + (NH_4)_2 S_2O_8$.

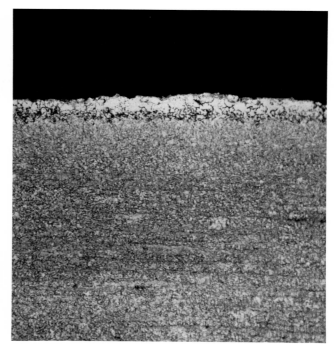

10. Gilt mummy mask, no. 352. Detail of one surface showing the enriched Ag-Au layer. x 500. Etch: $KCN + (NH_4)_2 S_2O_8$.

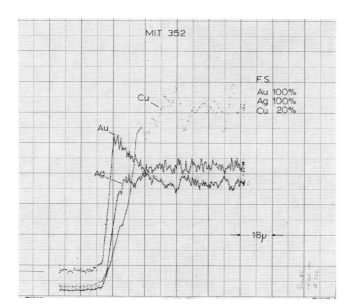

11. Gilt mummy mask, no. 352. Electron microbeam probe traces of Au, Ag, and Cu concentrations across the gilt surface of a cross-section of the metal.

There are various chemical processes that must be considered as possibly having been employed in these depletion gilding techniques. The well-known parting operation that uses nitric acid will remove copper and silver from a gold alloy (provided the gold concentration is not too high), leaving behind nearly pure gold. It seems most unlikely that a distilled acid of this kind could have been available in the culture under consideration, but there are a number of naturally occurring corrosive minerals based on ferric sulphate which are readily available (particularly in arid areas such as the coast of Peru), and it is highly probable that these minerals were used to produce similar results.

For a long time I thought that the South American smiths used a cementation process of the kind that has long been employed in the refining of gold-silver alloys and that such a process might, by suitable modification, serve to give an enriched gold layer on fabricated objects of low gold content. Many medieval and 16th-century metallurgical recipe books refer to the coloring of gold by applying a layer of some reactant mixture and then heating. These mixtures usually contain iron oxide or iron sulphate and salt, and often other ingredients are added. In 16th-century Japan, for example, gold coinage was actually made of an alloy containing from 25 to 50 % silver which was enriched by painting a mixture of iron sulphate, copper sulphate, potassium nitrate, sodium chloride, and resin on the surfaces and gently heating.[11] All of these processes, however, deal with alloys of relatively high gold content, and their application to the gilding by surface depletion of low gold alloys has not been reported in the literature.

In an earlier paper I outlined the essence of the cementation process.

In all cementation recipes, the gold or gold-containing alloy is packed in a reactive powder (the cement) which, when heated, combines chemically with the impurities on the surface and, eventually, by diffusion, with the impurities throughout the entire body. The cement, which invariably contains salt, reacts to form chlorides of silver, copper, and other impurity metals, leaving the gold unattacked. Both the reagent and the reaction products are absorbed in the largely inert matrix of brick dust or some similar material. Additional ingredients may be ammonium chloride, potassium nitrate, copper sulphate, iron sulphate, vinegar, or urine. The most direct

12. Gilt mummy mask, Lambayeque. M.I.T. no. 356 (lent for study by Brigitte Lapiner).

13. Gilt mummy mask, no. 356. Cross-section showing the striated, worked structure and the enriched Ag-Au surface zones. x 200. Etch: $KCN + (NH_4)_2 S_2O_8$.

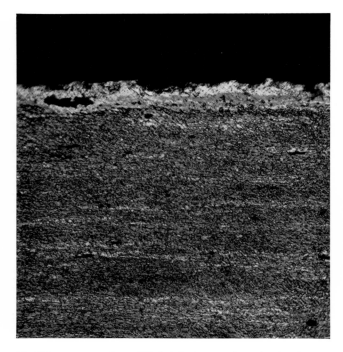

14. Gilt mummy mask, no. 356. Detail of one surface showing the enriched Ag-Au layer. x 1000. Etch: $KCN + (NH_4)_2 S_2O_8$.

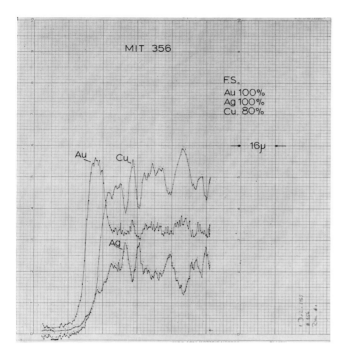

15. Gilt mummy mask, no. 356. Electron microbeam probe traces of Au, Ag, and Cu concentrations across the gilt surface of a cross-section of the metal.

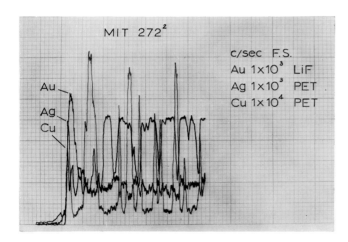

16. Electron microbeam probe traces across the surface of a section of cemented sheet metal prepared in the laboratory (60/30/10 Cu-Ag-Au alloy).

method is simply to place the salt-clay mixture in an earthenware crucible, add a layer of gold in some form with a high surface area such as granules or thin sheet, then another of cement, *stratum super stratum* until the crucible is filled. It is then luted and placed in a furnace at a temperature well below the melting point of the alloy, generally for from 12—24 hours. The copper and silver in the gold are attacked by the chlorine generated and react to form copper and silver chlorides. Depending upon the furnace temperature, these salts will either melt and be taken up by the clay matrix or by the walls of the crucible itself, or will remain solid and can be dissolved later from the surface of the gold. The process may be repeated as many times as necessary and is a drastic and thorough procedure for the removal of all the impurities.[12]

Clearly, if such a method were used to gild low-gold-content alloys, the cement would have to be strong enough and the rate of chemical reaction fast enough to allow for the controlled removal of enough silver to give the surface a golden color without diffusion of the underlying silver to the surface. As we have seen, the surface need not be pure gold for the metal to appear golden, and the thickness of the gold-silver alloy need be only a few microns at most.

To test the feasibility of the method, a ternary alloy containing 60% copper, 30% silver, and 10% gold was cast and a slice approximately 5 mm thick was subsequently put through numerous sequences of hammering, annealing (in a gas flame at a dull red heat), and pickling (in 10% sulphuric acid) until a sheet 0.7 mm thick was formed. The sheet looked quite like silver when it was completed. Small pieces of the sheet, packed around with a cement mixture made up of two parts of ground (approximately 50 mesh) common brick dust and one part of ground (100 mesh) rock salt, were placed in fire clay crucibles. The cement was very slightly dampened with urine immediately prior to use, and the crucibles were luted before placement in a furnace. After some trial and error, it was found that exposure to a temperature of 350° C for a period of ten minutes produced a continuous, compact, and smooth layer of gold on all surfaces of the metal sheet. Several pieces of sheet were "decorated" with simple surface designs made with a tracing tool before they were cemented. The gold layer formed evenly within these depressions showing that gilding can be produced by this method on an object whose surfaces have already received decorative tooling. Fig.16 reproduces the electron microbeam probe traces for copper, silver, and gold taken across a section of one of these sheets successfully gilt in the laboratory. Its concentration profiles are not dissimilar to those of the Chimu plaque except that the high, narrow gold peak at the surface contains virtually no silver or copper. (The very narrow silver and copper peaks at the extreme surface of the gold are undoubtedly due to the presence of small particles of silver and copper corrosion products still adhering to the metal.) The concentration gradient of the gold rises abruptly at the surface, however, just as it does in the trace of the Chimu plaque (fig. 7). The gold surface layer is only about 2 microns thick, yet the sheet has a distinctly golden though matte appearance. Burnishing produced the highly reflective surface characteristic of the Chimu objects themselves.

The thickness of the gold layer formed depends upon the temperature and duration of the treatment as well as upon the strength of the cementing material. These, in turn, must be chosen according to the composition of the alloy and the size (surface area) and thickness of the object being treated. For the moment it is apparent that such coatings can be produced relatively simply on alloys of very low gold content.

Anticipating that cementation would be as effective in gilding the alloys of higher gold content as it proved to be with the low gold alloys, a series of experiments was carried out with sheet metal made from an alloy containing 48 % silver, 40 % gold, and 12 % copper. The ingot, originally 6.4 mm thick, was reduced to a thickness of approximately 0.9 mm either by hammering or by passing the metal through a hand-operated rolling mill. The annealing and pickling operations that followed cold working gave rise to the pronounced silver-gold surface enrichment layers one sees in the photomicrograph of fig.17.

Three different reactant mixtures were used: one was identical with that described above; another contained potassium nitrate (saltpeter) as an added source of oxygen, and the last contained additional iron oxide (Fe_2O_3) to perform the same function.[13] Small pieces of the sheet were placed in luted fire clay crucibles and underwent cementation for periods of from 10 minutes to 16 hours at temperatures ranging from about 400° C to 800° C. There was an appreciable reaction at all temperatures between each cement and the metal, producing a layer of crystalline, black corrosion product (presumably a mixture of copper and silver chlorides but not yet analyzed) which adhered to the metal but was easily chipped away. But it was only at the highest temperature (800° C), with the simple salt and clay mixture, that a surface layer of gold formed which could be seen without the aid of a microscope. Electron microbeam probe traces across sections of such "gilt" sheet alloy revealed, however, that the metal had become enriched in gold not only at its surface but quite uniformly throughout its depth. This situation gave rise to sets of traces such as those reproduced in fig.18. There the probe concentration profiles for silver and gold in an untreated piece of metal (no. 383) are compared with the profiles for an identical piece of metal (no. 384) after cementation for two hours at 800° C. The overall gold concentration has risen, the silver level has dropped, but

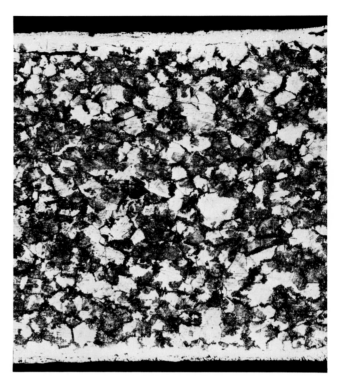

17. Cross-section of experimental sheet produced in the laboratory from a 48 : 40 : 12/Ag-Au-Cu casting. Note the thick enriched Ag-Au surface layers. x 100. Etch: $KCN + (NH_4)_2 S_2O_8$ over silver etch ($K_2Cr_2O_7 + NaCl + H_2SO_4$).

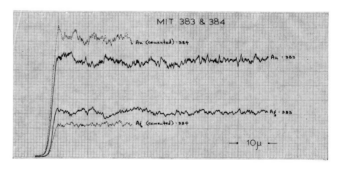

18. Electron microbeam probe traces showing Ag and Au concentrations in a cemented and an uncemented piece of laboratory-prepared sheet metal alloy (48 : 40 : 12/Ag-Au-Cu).

both changes have occurred uniformly throughout the sample. At these high temperatures the rate of chemical reaction at the surface of the metal, which removes copper and silver from the surface, is balanced by the high rate of diffusion of these metals through the body of the sample. This results in depletion of copper and silver from the body at least as rapidly as from the surface so that a preferential concentration of gold at the surface never occurs. Thus the enrichment of gold is a volume or bulk enrichment rather than a true surface gilding. At the lower temperatures, on the other hand, the reactions occur too slowly for any surface build up of gold within "reasonable" periods of time. It would seem, then, that cementation can effect surface gilding, but the conditions under which the process can be controlled so that the gilding is confined to the surface alone are not always easily achieved.

Earlier in this discussion I pointed out that the Chimu were almost certainly not distilling nitric acid nor are they likely to have had available sulphuric acid, which is also a parting agent for silver and gold. Nevertheless, they probably did have abundant supplies of at least some of the naturally occurring corrosive minerals such as ferric sulphate or cupric sulphate, which, in aqueous solution, are acidic and are capable, under certain conditions, of removing silver and copper alloyed with gold.[14] These conditions generally involve the addition of salt and/or alum and vinegar to the solution.

Recipes for such "coloring" procedures, the purposes of which were to improve the color of gold containing impurities, are found in some of the earliest technical treatises we have, such as the Greek papyrus from Thebes, known as Papyrus X, now in Leyden.[15] In recipe no.15, the Leyden Papyrus directs one in how

"To color gold to render it fit for usage. Misy, salt, and vinegar accruing from the purification of gold; mix it all and throw in the vessel (which contains it) the gold described in the preceding preparation; let it remain some time, (and then) having drawn (the gold) from the vessel, heat it upon the coals; then again throw it in the vessel which contains the above-mentioned preparation; do this several times until it becomes fit for use."[16]

For our purposes, however, it is not necessary to look to the ancient Near East for documentation of such techniques. In the sixteenth century manuscript entitled "Historia general de las cosas de la Nueva España," recorded and compiled by Fray Bernardino de Sahagún, a Spanish priest living among the Aztecs of pre-conquest Mexico, there is a section devoted to Indian metalworking techniques which includes a passage describing the final operations for finishing the surface of a cast gold (i.e., tumbaga) object. The Indian craftsman whom Sahagún quotes reports:

"And when it was cast, whatsoever kind of necklace it was which had been made — the various things here mentioned — then it was bur-

nished with a pebble. And when it had been burnished, it was in addition treated with alum; the alum with which the gold was washed [and] rubbed was ground. A second time [the piece] entered the fire; it was heated over it. And when it came forth, once more, for the second time, it was at once washed, rubbed, with what was called 'gold medicine.' It was just like yellow earth mixed with a little salt; with this the gold was perfected; with this it became very yellow. And later it was polished; it was made like flint, to finish it off, so that at last it glistened, it shone, it sent forth rays."[17]

Though the identification of mineral substances in early literature, especially when twice translated, is notoriously difficult, it is reasonable to think that the alum used by the Indians was actually potassium alum, while the yellowish earth could have been any one of the corrosive ferric sulphates or basic ferric sulphates, the mineralogy of which is so confused. In European literature they were commonly called *misy,* though the most conspicuous of all the basic sulphates is actually the mineral copiapite which occurs as a yellowish or yellowish-brown efflorescence on rocks and takes its name from Copiapo, a city near the coast of Chile where large amounts are found and where it was first identified. Butlerite, Botryogen, and Hohmannite (which are chemically similar except for hydration) are also common in the area. Copiapite and Coquimbite, another of the ferric sulphates, occur in Peru also, however,[18] and Muelle and Wells reported finding ferric sulphate among the pigments and other materials prepared for use in the wall paintings at Pachacámac. They considered its presence there as a possible indication of trade with Chile, but it might have come from a source in Peru.[19]

At first we interpreted this statement in Sahagún as a reference to a cementation process (assuming that the neccessary heating operation had been overlooked or subsumed under the heating that followed the alum treatment, supposedly for cleaning), but now it seems more likely that the whole passage is to be interpreted literally, with the "yellow earth" being nothing more than one of the many hydrated ferric sulphate minerals and the "salt" nothing more than sodium chloride. Several experiments were, therefore, undertaken to see if such a mixture would gild the high-gold alloy sheet metal by selectively removing the copper and silver. Pieces of such sheet, made in the laboratory, were immersed in aqueous pastes of ferric sulphate and salt or ferric sulphate, salt, and iron oxide.[20] These were allowed to remain at room temperature for two days, when they were removed and washed. The thin, black scale that had formed on all the surfaces was dissolved away with a hot and strong solution of sodium chloride.[21] The resulting sheet had a characteristic reddish-brown color, the color of parted gold in finely particulate form, but, when burnished, it immediately became a rich, smooth, and shiny yellow. Or, when the sheet was subjected to moderate heating ($270°$ C for 30 minutes), the gold consolidated, forming a coherent, smooth layer on all surfaces.[22] Nothing could be more simple!

Ferric sulphate is a highly corrosive substance, acting in solution almost as a mixture of ferrous sulphate and sulphuric acid. Both copper and silver are dissolved by it, the reaction (ignoring the detailed electrochemistry of the ions) being:

$$Cu + Fe_2^{+++}(SO_4^{--})_3 \rightarrow Cu^{++}SO_4^{--} + 2Fe^{++}SO_4^{--}$$

A similar reaction occurs with silver. The presence of Cl^- ions from the salt addition would accelerate the reaction and perhaps externally precipitate relatively insoluble $AgCl$. The action ceases when all the Fe^{+++} ions have been reduced, but it would continue through atmospheric oxidation. But more than electrochemistry is involved: physically the residual gold is left in situ in a submicroscopically porous state that is easily made coherent by burnishing or heating.[23]

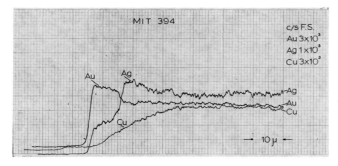

19. Electron microbeam probe traces across the surface of a section of sheet metal, prepared in the laboratory, and treated with an aqueous paste of ferric sulphate and salt (48:40:12/Ag-Au-Cu alloy).

Fig.19 reproduces a set of concentration traces for copper, silver, and gold taken with an electron microanalyzer across a section of high-gold alloy sheet which was treated by this parting depletion method. The depth of metal from which copper was originally removed during annealing is particularly great in this sample (approximately 30 microns) because it was given three anneals of one hour each at 750° C during fabrication of the sheet from the cast ingot. Indeed, the silver curve still shows an elevated silver concentration at a depth of between 12 and 30 microns from the surface. The parting action of the acid paste has effectively removed most of the silver to a depth of 12 microns below the surface, however, and the once broad silver peak falls off rapidly in this zone. The gold concentration rises abruptly as the silver decreases, reaching a peak value of approximately 59 %. The gold peak is quite broad, almost 8 microns in width.[24] A sharper, narrower peak could probably have been achieved with quite as satisfactory a visual effect in terms of the covering power of the gold had the reaction time been briefer. Nevertheless, this relatively uncomplicated technique which utilizes commonly occurring

materials and is effective even without the use of heat, has produced a gilt surface which is very close in color to the gold of the two mummy masks described above. The process accounts well for the many aspects of this type of gilding one associates with Chimu work: its thinness and evenness, its ability to coat depressed areas and edges of sheet metal, its rather high silver content, and the shape of the microbeam probe traces characteristic of the gilt metal. Certainly one can expect that it would be fully as effective in gilding the low-gold content alloys as it obviously is in producing a gold surface on the alloys richer in that precious metal. It forms a gold layer on an alloy which certainly cannot be considered gold and which is, on the contrary, white in its normal aspect. Again, as in the case of cementation, this use of the technique is unique, as far as I am aware.

Regardless of the precise method or methods used by the Chimu for their "depletion gilding," the very fact that the process relies upon the removal of the less noble elements from a gold-containing alloy is of prime importance. This approach to gilding metal is one we are quite used to associating with the pre-Columbian peoples of Colombia, Ecuador, and later of the Isthmian cultures in their development and use of the alloy tumbaga. Tumbaga is a binary alloy of copper and gold whose composition has been found to vary anywhere from 5 % copper, 95 % gold to 90 % copper, 10 % gold, usually falling between 30 and 65 % copper.[25] By removing copper from the surface of the alloy either by oxidation followed by acid pickling or by acid pickling alone, the surface becomes enriched in gold, and an object made from tumbaga is thus quite easily gilt.[26] This gilding or coloring process is usually referred to as "mise-en-couleur." I strongly suspect, however, that one of the principal methods used for gilding tumbaga was, in fact, the ferric sulphate depletion method or a similar technique based upon selective corrosion of copper and simultaneous redeposition of the gold. Gilding occurs considerably more rapidly with this technique than with either of the others,[27] although as in the case of gold-silver alloys, there is an upper limit to the concentration of gold within the alloy above which the corrosive activity of the acid is confined entirely to the surface. Thus objects made of high-gold tumbaga can truly be "colored" by this method, but the enrichment of gold will be extremely superficial.[28] Tumbagas higher in copper will corrode much more deeply, however, forming a substantial coating of gold resistant to normal conditions of wear.

It should also be noted that, whereas the ferric sulphate method will work equally well on the ternary alloys (high silver content) and on tumbaga, the various organic reagents that will gild tumbaga are not effective in creating a gold surface on the copper-silver-gold alloys. The question of which of all these methods was used on any individual tumbaga object can be

20. Two gilt bangles, Viru. M.I.T. nos. 366 and 367. x 3 (American Museum of Natural History).

resolved by examining cross-sections of the gilt castings. The structure of the metal at the surface will indicate whether a corrosion-redeposition technique or an oxidation-pickling sequence was employed. Several tumbaga samples already studied strongly suggest that the gilding was produced by the former process.

Copper-rich tumbaga was introduced into the repertoire of the Colombian goldsmith as early as A.D. 500, but the gold-rich variety was in use several centuries earlier. By the time the Chimu were dominant along the coast of Peru, the use of tumbaga and its associated depletion gilding techniques was widespread throughout Colombia and had moved North to Panama and Costa Rica. Although the Peruvians rarely used this particular alloy, and despite the fact that theirs was a metallurgy

which concentrated on the manufacture and use of sheet metal in contrast to the extensive use of casting by the Colombians and their neighbors to the north, nevertheless it would be unreasonable, I believe, to think of the various forms of depletion gilding in these two geographic areas as anything but a diversity of techniques stemming from a common approach or tradition of metallurgical practice. We are witness to the development of a shared concept, that of depletion or enrichment, by different peoples using different metal alloys and arriving at technical solutions adequate to their individual situations. There is as yet insufficient evidence for the source of this shared concept. It may be that, by the Chimu period in Peru, there was abundant contact between the metalworkers of Peru and Colombia so that the idea disseminated among craftsmen of both peoples, the impetus coming largely from Colombia. On the other hand, it is equally possible that depletion gilding was practiced much earlier in Peru and that the idea spread through Peru on to Colombia or, finally, that it originated from a single source which then influenced them both.

We still do not know the origin of the technique of tumbaga casting and gilding as it was practiced in South America. Some believe that the process originated in Guiana and later traveled west to Colombia.[29] In any case, that it should have been so widely used in Colombia is not extraordinary in view of the rich sources of gold in that country, whereas silver, by contrast, is quite scarce. It is also not difficult to understand the impetus to the development of depletion gilding during the period of the Chimu Empire. Gold was mined in great quantity and was used, apparently, without much concern for economizing. Gilding by depletion, for example, is not a technique which would have been amenable to craftsmen who were trying to "save" gold, for the major portion of the gold in the alloy is never utilized. At the same time, the fact that objects were often gilt rather than made of gold shows that some economic pressures were felt, and the metal was certainly highly prized. On the other hand, depletion gilding is an excellent technique for producing a gold surface on large expanses of sheet metal. Not only were mummy masks gilt in this fashion, but sheets of metal used as plaques to adorn the walls of imperial buildings or of temples were also gilt by depletion. Several broken fragments from such gilt plaques were analyzed (see table I) and proved to have been made from the low-gold-bearing alloy.[30] Silvered plaques were also in use at this time, made of sheet metal hammered from the same alloys of silver and copper as those used for the Chimu effigy beakers, mentioned earlier.[31] Is it unreasonable to postulate that craftsmen already skilled at fashioning silvered sheet in large quantity by depletion methods would be "ripe" for devising — certainly for accepting — techniques which would gild alloys in a conceptually related way?

At this point it becomes important to look much more closely and systematically at gilt metals from the Mochica culture. The quality and sophistication of Mochica metalwork is unsurpassed in Peru, and there is no doubt that the Chimu inherited a good portion of their metalworking tradition from their predecessors in the Moche valley and undoubtedly from the valleys farther north as well.[32] Was depletion gilding one of the processes already part of this heritage? Fig. 20 reproduces two tiny bangles, fabric ornaments, from the Viru valley, made of the low gold-bearing ternary alloy and gilt by depletion. They are probably of Mochica origin.[33] What further evidence, if any, is there of the early use of these techniques in Peru? Perhaps, when we have a clearer picture of the temporal development of gilding in Peru, we will also arrive at a fuller understanding of the extent to which certain traditions of metalworking in the Northwest portion of South America were cross-culturally rather than individually determined.

Acknowledgments

I should like to thank those individuals who so kindly let me borrow, for purposes of study, the objects which form the basis of this research report: Junius B. Bird, Mr. and Mrs. Dudley T. Easby, Jr., Julie Jones, and Brigitte Lapiner. The wet microchemical analyses were performed by Stephen M. Nagy of the Central Analytical Laboratory, Department of Metallurgy and Materials Science at the Massachusetts Institute of Technology. Many hours of patient data collection with the electron microbeam probe, so essential to interpreting the techniques of fabrication of the artifacts, were generously provided by Stephen L. Bender and John K. Hill of the Ledgemont Laboratory, Kennecott Copper Corporation, and by Joseph A. Adario of the X-ray and Electron Optics Group at M.I.T. Cyril Stanley Smith will accept my thanks only in part for his stimulating insights into the ancient processes we believe the Chimu used for depletion gilding. The rest, he says, are due to Sahagún. I am grateful, too, for the support this research has received in grants from the National Endowment for the Humanities; the Sloan Fund at M.I.T.; and Dominique de Menil.

Notes

1. Bergsøe, Paul. "The Gilding Process and the Metallurgy of Copper and Lead among the Pre-Columbian Indians," *Ingeniørvidenskabelige Skrifter,* no. A46 (1938), 29–37.
2. Two exceptions are the manufacture and use of Cu-Sn bronze and the technique of metal-in-metal inlay, both used extensively by the Inca.
3. Mercury is an element quite sensitive to spectrographic analysis and is usually detectable to 100 ppm or better. Contrary to the widely held view that mercury "evaporates" from a metal surface while the object is buried and that therefore it may not be detected after considerable time has elapsed, the mercury applied in amalgam gilding forms a series of intermetallic compounds with the amalgamated surface and ceases to exist in its free form. These compounds have totally different properties from mercury and are extremely persistent. For example, mercury has often been detected on amalgam gilded objects from the Near East that date to the 6th century A.D., much earlier than the Chimu era. See H. Lechtman, "Ancient Methods of Gilding Silver—Examples from the Old and the New Worlds," in *Science and Archaeology,* Cambridge, Mass., M.I.T. Press, 1971, 2–30; Paul Bergsøe, note 1 above; William C. Root, "Metallurgy," *Handbook of South American Indians,* bulletin 143, vol. 5 (1949), 205–225.
4. This paper is concerned only with those objects that appear to have been made of silver over which there is a gold coating. I have not yet begun examination of gilt copper objects from this period.
5. See "Ancient Methods of Gilding Silver," note 3, above.
6. A much more detailed account of the formation of these layers is given in Lechtman, "Ancient Methods of Gilding Silver"; and in P. Rivet and H. Arsandaux, "La métallurgie en Amérique précolombienne," *Travaux et Mémoires de l'Institut d'Ethnologie,* 39 (Paris, 1946), 94–100.
7. The Chimu took advantage of this "silvering" effect by making many of their objects, especially the well-known effigy beakers, from a binary silver-copper alloy. The sheet metal automatically became "silvered" as it was worked and annealed, and many of the objects from this period thought to be of silver are actually made from this alloy.
8. The results of these experiments are given in Lechtman, "Ancient Methods of Gilding Silver," where the microbeam probe traces of concentration vs. depth are found in fig. 1.36.
9. Originally such mummy masks were adorned with paint (usually red cinnabar), other metals such as copper, textiles, and feathers. Some traces of red paint remain on this example, but the only vestiges of the other decorative appendages are the holes through which they were secured to the mask. As recently as 1969, in the catalogue of the exhibition "The Gold of Ancient America" sponsored jointly by the Museum of Fine Arts, Boston, the Art Institute of Chicago, and the Virginia Museum, the entry for this object describes it as "hammered and repoussé gold" (see Allen Wardwell, *The Gold of Ancient America,* Boston, Museum of Fine Arts, 1968, pp. 34–35).
10. Because the probe averaged the composition over a depth of about 4 microns, the actual surface must have been much richer in gold than this. Porosity in a pure gold layer will also account for low probe readings.
11. Gowland, W. "Metals and Metal-working in Old Japan," *Trans. Japan Society,* 13 (1915), 30–32; and W. Gowland, "Japanese Metallurgy, Part 1, Gold and Silver and Their Alloys," *J. Soc. Chem. Ind.,* 15 (1896), 404–413.

12. See Lechtman, "Ancient Methods of Gilding Silver."

13. The two additional cement mixtures were made up as (a) 1 part brick dust: 1/3 part $NaCl$: 1/10 part KNO_3; (b) 1 part brick dust: 1/3 part $NaCl$: 1/3 part Fe_2O_3. The simple salt-brick dust mixture proved most effective of all three. Even the addition of Fe_2O_3 did not increase the reaction rate noticeably.

14. In my original presentation of this material, I commented upon the possibility of the use of acid solutions such as aqueous ferric sulphate or ferric sulphate and salt as the parting agents for copper-silver-gold alloys. At that time, however, I had not yet tested this supposition in the laboratory. See Lechtman, "Ancient Methods of Gilding Silver."

15. The existence of these recipes was brought to my attention by Shirley Alexander in May 1968. She has made a special study of ancient and medieval manuscripts that treat the gilding or coloring of metals, and wrote her doctoral dissertation on the subject of "Problems of Metal Usage in Some Late Antique and Early Christian Manuscripts" in 1968. She is presently teaching in the Department of Art, University of Texas, Austin.

16. *Misy* is usually interpreted as meaning copper or iron sulphate. Recipes 25 and 69 of this manuscript also deal with the coloring of gold and include other materials as alum and urine in the preparations. The translation used here is from Earle R. Caley, "The Leyden Papyrus X: An English Translation with Brief Notes," *J. Chemical Education,* 3 (1926), 1149–1166.

17. This manuscript is known as the *Florentine Codex* and was written originally by Sahagún in his transcription of Náhuatl, the language of the Aztec. It has recently been translated into English. Bernardino de Sahagún, *General History of the Things of New Spain,* trans. and ed., Charles E. Dibble and Arthur J. O. Anderson, Monographs of the School of American Research and the Museum of New Mexico, no. 14, Santa Fe, 1959, part X, book 9, p. 75.

18. Dr. Georg Petersen, who has made a careful study of the mineral resources available to the early cultures of Peru, told me that he has found Copiapite at Mirador (Ancash) and Cerro de Pasco and Coquimbite at Provincia de Castillo (Arequipa), Carahuacra, Yauli, Canta, Salpo, and Otuzco. There are undoubtedly many other sites where these minerals occur at or near the surface (personal communication, Lima, Peru, July 1970).

19. Muelle, Jorge C., and Wells, Robert. "Las Pinturas del Templo de Pachacámac," *Revista del Museo Nacional,* 8 (1939), 265–282.

20. The actual mixture used was 1 part $Fe_2(SO_4)_3 \cdot n\ H_2O$: 1 part $NaCl$: ~ 1/2 part Fe_2O_3. The addition of iron oxide increased the rate of reaction because of the presence of added oxygen. Mixtures of KNO_3, $NaCl$, and Fe_2O_3 were also used successfully, but the rate of reaction was considerably slower than with the ferric sulphate paste.

21. Moderate heating of the pasty mixtures would undoubtedly reduce the length of time necessary to produce good gold surfaces. Reaction times of less than an hour are probably feasible. It is interesting to note that the goldsmiths who produce fine filigree jewelry of gold (usually ranging from 14 k to 20 k) in such north Peruvian coastal towns as Monsefu and Catacaos, use a water solution of salitre (KNO_3)/sal commun ($NaCl$)/alumbre [$KAl\ (SO_4)_2 \cdot 12H_2O$] in the proportions 2/1/1 to give the jewelry a bright, rich golden surface after all soldering and other operations are completed. The pieces are a pale yellow to white color before treatment with this preparation. They are placed in an earthenware dish, immersed in the solution, and heated until the solution thickens, becoming pasty and

yellow. They are removed when they have developed a bright golden surface, usually within 2 to 5 minutes.

22. Similar experiments were originally carried out by Bergsøe in 1938. In discussing whether the Indians of Ecuador had developed a process for refining gold, he refers to the passage in Sahagún, the Japanese method of cementing gold for coinage, and his own experiments in removing silver from a powdered alloy of 85 % gold, 15 % silver by the hot salt-clay cementation process. His experiments were entirely successful in purifying the gold. He does not, however, expand his discussion to include gilding of low-gold alloys. Bergsøe, P. "The Gilding Process among the Pre-Columbian Indians," pp. 48–49.

23. The gold is continually redeposited and continues to serve as cathode in a self-perpetuating electrolytic cell, of which the alloy, forming the anode, is perpetually dissolved. The deposited gold, however, remains in such a geometry that there is always maintained a series of open connected channels through which the Cu^{++} and Fe^{++} ions can diffuse out and new Fe^{+++} diffuse in. The net effect is precisely like that in the nitric acid parting operation used by assayers, which will not occur if the alloy is richer than about 50 atomic percent in gold (64.6 weight percent), for the open channels cannot then be maintained. The analogy of this process to the form of corrosion of brass known as dezincification will be noted. Actually, the first hints of the nature of the pre-Columbian gilding process occurred in our laboratory when Professor Cyril Stanley Smith noted that the microstructure of a gilded tumbaga casting was identical with that of brass so corroded. For a general discussion of parting limits, see Ulick R. Evans, *The Corrosion and Oxidation of Metals* (London, 1960), pp. 350–351; a more detailed investigation of the parting limits for gold-silver alloys is given in Georg Masing and Hildegard Gaubatz, "Über Resistenzgrenzen der Gold-Silber-Legierungen," *Z. für Metallkunde,* 34 (1942) 109–113.

24. The sample of sheet metal used in this experiment was sawn from a larger piece of sheet that had undergone the 3 hour annealing time and had developed a broad enriched silver-gold zone. Accordingly, the two flat surfaces of the sample also had the enriched zone, whereas the two sawn edges did not. Interestingly, the rate of parting was much more rapid below the two sawn edges than it was below the flat surfaces. For example, the gold layer formed was approximately 47 microns deep below one sawn edge as compared with 8 microns below the flat surface. This indicates that the presence of copper at the surface accelerates the action and that silver is removed more rapidly when copper is available as well.

25. Root, William C. "Gold-Copper Alloys in Ancient America," *J. Chemical Education,* 28 (1951), 76–78.

26. A full description of the two methods by which tumbaga is generally considered to have been gilt by the Indians as well as the range of alloys most suitable for treatment by each is given in William C. Root, "Pre-Columbian Metalwork of Colombia and Its Neighbors," in *Essays in Pre-Columbian Art and Archaeology,* by S. K. Lothrop and others (Cambridge, 1961), pp. 242–257. Here Root explains the use of the clay-salt treatment as a process for removing silver from the surface of tumbaga, to make the gold more yellow.

27. As early as 1910, Oswald H. Evans described his successful experiments in gilding tumbaga with urine, which caused a coating of hydrated copper salt to form on the metal. This was readily soluble in acid plant juice, although he points out that gilding with such natural organic reagents is a very slow and tedious process. Stone and Balser found it took three weeks to form a yellowish-green layer

on the surface of a piece of tumbaga from Costa Rica when it was treated with the juice of the oxalis plant. See Oswald H. Evans, "A Note on the Gilded Metal-work of Chiriqui, Central America," *Nature* 82 (1910), 457; Doris Stone and Carlos Balser, *The Aboriginal Metalwork in the Isthmian Region of America.* San José, Costa Rica, Museo Nacional (1958), 20–21.

28. Contemporary goldsmiths still use such processes to heighten the gold color of pieces made of commercial gold, usually 18–22 karat. Herbert Maryon lists several of these methods in his book *Metalwork and Enamelling,* London, 1959, pp. 260–262.

29. See Rivet and Arsandaux, pp. 60–66 and p. 80, note 6 above.

30. The practice of sheathing walls of buildings with sheets of silver or gold was particularly characteristic of the Inca but apparently was favored by the Chimu as well. An interesting reference in the chronicle (1571) of the Spaniard Pedro Pizarro gives some indication of the covering of a temple gateway at Chan Chan with silver: "while going down from Curamba to a plain where there was a village of mamaconas . . . I entered . . . a hut where I found these slabs of silver . . . which were as many as ten in number, and had a length of twenty feet and a width of one foot, and a thickness of three fingers . . . These slabs, Indians told [us], were [being] carried to Trugillo in order to build there a house for their idol who was called Chimo. The gateway of this [idol's house] was found later, and it was worth ninety thousand castellanos." Pedro Pizarro, *Relation of the Discovery and Conquest of the Kingdoms of Peru,* trans. Philip Ainsworth Means, the Cortes Society, New York, 1921, pp. 240–241.

31. Two Chimu wall plaques from the N. Coast of Peru, made of silver-copper alloy, are illustrated in André Emmerich, *Sweat of the Sun and Tears of the Moon* (Seattle, 1965), p. 30 and fig. 45.

32. Disselhoff and Linné claim that the Mochica used copper-gold alloys and illustrate, as an example of such use, the large death mask from the Huaca de la Luna in the Moche Valley, now in the Lindenmuseum, Stuttgart. The mask is described as made of a gold and copper alloy with silver plate over portions of the surface. No details are given of the composition of the metal, but the surfaces of the mask are golden. See H. D. Disselhoff and S. Linné, *The Art of Ancient America,* New York, 1960, pp. 175 and 179.

33. These bangles were found by William D. Strong and may be associated with a particular tomb at Huaca de la Cruz. If so, they are Mochica period (Mochica IV). Junius B. Bird, personal communication, December 1969.

EARLE R. CALEY

Chemical Composition of Ancient Copper Objects of South America

Since some 575 analyses of ancient copper and bronze objects of South America have been published, it might be supposed that our knowledge of the composition of such objects would now be adequate, but this is far from true, especially for copper objects. The reason is that the great majority of these published analyses are unsatisfactory in various respects. About 42 % are mere qualitative analyses, either chemical or spectroscopic, usually made for the specific purpose of determining whether the objects examined were composed of copper or of bronze. About 11% are quantitative analyses in which only a single element, either copper or tin, was determined, often for the same purpose. In about 20 % of the analyses only two elements, usually copper and tin, were determined. In most of the remaining analyses either three or four elements were determined, so that only a small fraction of the quantitative analyses are reasonably complete. Moreover, the results of many of these better analyses are inconsistent or contradictory. Apart from lack of completeness, there are other defects in nearly all the published analyses. In general no information is given about sampling, so that doubt exists as to whether the samples taken for analysis were truly representative of the composition of the original metal of the objects. The very low summations of some of the analyses indicate that oxidation products were sometimes included in samples. Very little is said about the analytical methods employed, but very probably some of them were lacking in accuracy. In addition to these defects from the standpoint of analysis, a considerable proportion of the published analyses are of little significance from the standpoint of archaeology because they were made on samples taken from objects of uncertain provenance, especially with respect to date.

The purpose of this paper is to examine critically the better previous analyses, to publish some new analyses, and to draw some tentative general conclusions about the chemical composition of the ancient copper objects of South America. Analyses of South American bronze objects will be considered only from the standpoint of the composition of the copper in the alloys of these objects.

Previous Analyses of Copper Objects

Listed in table I are the results of all the better analyses of copper objects from Argentina published prior to 1922. The negative signs in this table and in the four succeeding tables indicate that the presence of a given element was not reported. It is uncertain whether the element was found to be absent or whether no attempt at a determination was made. On the assumption that the determinations are correct as reported, the summations of the first five analyses and the last analysis leave little room for the presence of additional elements in significant proportions. The summations of the other four indicate that some element or elements were undetermined.

Because of the high summation of the analysis and the presence of iron as the only impurity, it is not unreasonable to conclude that Object 1 was formed from native copper. The presence of tin, lead, or both, in Objects 2 to 9 inclusive, and the presence of arsenic and sulfur in Object 10 show that the metal of these objects was produced by smelting. When the analyses of table I were the only ones available, it would have been logical to conclude that Object 10 had a decidedly atypical composition because of its arsenic content. That the contrary may be true for Argentine copper objects as a whole is indicated by recent analyses.

The only recent analyses of copper objects from Argentina are those reported by a single investigator. Of the 32 analyses that were made, 8 are listed in table II. These particular analyses were selected because they are the only ones in which tin and antimony were separately determined. The proportions of the other elements listed in the tables are generally typical of those reported in all 32 analyses. Fester found that zinc was present in 18 of the 32 objects in proportions ranging from 0.20 % to 1.22 %. These he designated as Series A. The others, designated as Series B, contained no zinc, but usually contained small proportions of silver.

Although these recent analyses are generally much superior to the early analyses, particularly in respect to the number of elements determined, the correctness of the data reported for certain elements is open to question. At least 0.01% iron is almost invariably present in ancient copper generally, but in these analyses only traces are reported in four of the objects and none in the others. Nickel in similar low proportion is almost as common an impurity as iron, yet only traces are reported in two of the objects and none in the rest. In 24 of the analyses tin and antimony are reported as the sum of the percentages of the two, presumably from the weights of the residues obtained by treating the samples with nitric acid, but no proof is given that both metals were present in all the residues. Since antimony was certainly present in some of the samples, it might be expected that bismuth might also be present in a few, but apparently no attempt was made to determine this element. Sulfur was determined in only two objects and may have been present in others. Lack of sufficient sample is given as the reason for not attempting other sulfur determinations.

The most striking feature of these analyses is the reported presence of arsenic in all the objects. Moreover, it is the chief impurity. In Series A the proportions range from a low of 1.17 % to a high of 7.11%, the average being 3.60 %. In Series B the proportions range from 1.17 % to 6.68 %, the average being 2.39 %. The average arsenic content of all 32 objects is 3.07 %.

As will be seen by comparing table I with table II the lack of

Table I

Percentages of various elements from early analyses of copper objects from Argentina

No.	Site	Description	Cu	Ag	Sn	Pb	As	Fe	S	Total
1	La Toma, Catamarca	Axe	99.84	–	–	–	–	0.07	–	99.91
2	Tastil	Chisel	99.70	–	–	0.08	–	0.17	–	99.95
3	Huasayaco, Catamarca	Bracelet fragment	99.66	–	0.24	–	–	–	–	99.90
4	Calchaqui Region	Axe	99.10	–	–	0.30	–	0.46	–	99.86
5	Belén, Catamarca	Ceremonial axe	98.62	1.02	0.20	–	–	trace	–	99.84
6	Belén, Catamarca	Axe	98.43	–	0.72	0.42	–	–	–	99.57
7	Musquin, Catamarca	Spatula	97.32	1.83	0.17	–	–	–	–	99.32
8	Fuerte Quemado, Catamarca	Chisel	96.97	–	0.39	–	–	1.71	–	99.07
9	Casabindo, Jujuy	Bell	96.36	–	0.64	–	–	–	–	97.00
10	La Paya, Salta	Sheet fragment	90.75	–	–	–	5.20	2.51	1.46	99.92

Sources:
No. 1. E. Nordenskiöld, *The copper and bronze ages in South America*, Göteborg, 1921, p. 170.
Nos. 2, 4, and 10. (a) A. De Mortillet, *Annual Report of the Smithsonian Institution*, Washington, D.C., 1908, p. 263.

(b) E. Boman, *Antiquités de la région andine de la République Argentine et du désert d'Atacama*, Paris, 1908, vol. 2, p. 868.
Nos. 3, 5, 6, 7, and 8. P. A. Sanchez Diaz, *El bronce calchaqui*, Buenos Aires, 1900, p. 99.
No. 9. E. von Rosen, *En förgängen värld*, Stockholm, 1919, p. 365.

Table II

Percentages of various elements from recent analyses of copper objects from Argentina

Series and no.	Description	Cu	Ag	Sn	Pb	As	Sb	Fe	Ni	Zn	S	Total
A 1	Awl	94.75	–	None	1.02	2.12	None	None	None	0.37	–	98.26
2	Axe	97.28	–	None	0.12	2.65	None	Trace	–	0.20	–	100.25
3	Ceremonial axe	95.07	–	None	1.30	3.37	Trace	–	None	0.78	–	100.52
4	Headband part	92.33	–	2.05	None	3.40	0.42	Trace	–	1.22	–	99.42
5	Headband fragment	90.73	–	1.57	None	3.81	2.94	None	None	0.30	–	99.35
B 1	Breastplate	96.87	None	1.56	None	1.17	0.47	None	None	None	–	100.07
2	Wedge fragment	97.09	0.07	1.02	None	1.30	0.38	None	None	None	–	99.86
3	Axe fragment	91.56	None	0.91	None	6.88	0.32	None	None	None	0.25	99.92

Source:
G. A. Fester, *Chymia* 8 (1962), 21—31.

Table III

Percentages of various elements from analyses of copper objects from Bolivia

No.	Site	Description	Cu	Pb	As	Fe	S	Other	Total
1	La Toma	Axe	99.84	–	–	0.07	–	Co-trace	99.91
2	Tiahuanaco	Clamp	98.64	–	–	0.43	0.87	–	99.94
3	Copacabana	Axe	96.36	–	0.51	0.07	–	–	96.94
4	Tiahuanaco	Clamp	95.65	0.12	–	1.63	2.55	Sb-trace	99.95

Sources:
Nos. 1 and 3. E. Nordenskiöld, *The Copper and Bronze Ages in South America*, Göteborg, 1921, p. 170.

Nos. 2 and 4. A. De Mortillet, *Annual Report of the Smithsonian Institution*, Washington, D.C., 1908, p. 263.
E. Boman, *Antiquités de la région andine de la République Argentine et du désert d'Atacama*, Paris, 1908, vol. 2, p. 868.

Table IV

Percentages of various elements from early analyses of copper objects from Peru

No.	Site	Description	Cu	Sn	Pb	As	Sb	Bi	Fe	Zn	Other	Total
1	Chepen	Implement	99.62	0.02	–	–	–	–	–	–	S-0.27	99.91
2	Chepen	Knife	98.61	None	None	–	–	–	–	–	–	98.61
3	Pacasmayo	Adze	98.41	–	–	1.55	–	–	0.03	–	–	99.99
4	Chepen	Knife	98.25	Trace	None	–	–	–	–	–	–	98.25
5	Chancay	Hoe	98.2	None	–	None	0.7	None	–	None	–	99.5
6	Chancay	Knife	97.7	None	–	–	–	–	Trace	None	–	97.7
7	Chanchan	Lance head	97.43	–	–	2.14	–	–	Trace	–	S-trace	99.57
8	Chepen	Knife	96.68	None	None	–	–	–	–	–	–	96.68
9	Trujillo	Implement	95.95	–	–	4.03	–	–	0.05	–	–	100.03
10	Chancay	Hoe blade	95.62	None	None	4.27	0.08	None	–	None	Ag-none	99.97
11	Lima	Adze	95.22	–	–	4.43	–	–	0.21	–	–	99.86

Sources:

Nos. 1, 2, 4, and 8. C. W. Mead, *Prehistoric Bronze in South America,* New York, 1915, pp. 22–23.
Nos. 3, 9, and 11. A. Baessler, *Altperuanische Metallgeräte,* Berlin, 1906, p. 8.

Nos. 5, 6, and 10. E. Nordenskiöld, *The Copper and Bronze Ages in South America,* Göteborg, 1921, pp.168–169.
No. 7. M. Loeb and S. R. Morey, *J. Am. Chem. Soc.,* 32 (1910) 652–653.

Table V

Percentages of various elements from analyses of copper ingots from Peru

No.	Site	Cu	Ag	Au	Sn	Pb	Fe	Ni	S	Other	Total
1	Mochica	99.57	Trace	0.20	0.20	–	–	–	–	–	99.97
2	Mochica	98.90	0.42	–	–	–	–	–	–	As-0.10	99.42
3	Mochica	98.53	0.04	–	–	–	–	–	–	–	98.57
4	Mochica	98.04	Trace	–	–	–	–	–	–	–	98.04
5	Ica	97.77	Trace	None	None	None	1.44	0.01	0.18	Sb-trace	99.40

Sources:

Nos. 1–4. A. L. Kroeber, *American Antiquity,* 20 (1954), 160–162.

No. 5. E. R. Caley, and D. T. Easby, *American Antiquity,* 25 (1959), 59–65.

agreement or correlation between the early analyses and the recent analyses of copper objects from Argentina is almost total. One marked discrepancy is that arsenic was found in only one object of the earlier series but is reported to be present in all objects of the later series. Possibly it was present in more objects of the earlier series but was not determined. Some of the reported percentages of copper in this series may be too high because they include arsenic. When copper is determited in the usual way by electrolysis, most of any arsenic in solution plates out with the copper, and if the resulting dark color of the mixed deposit is ignored the calculated percentage of copper will include most of the percentage of arsenic. Certain other discrepancies between the two sets of data may be ascribed to deficiencies in the earlier analytical procedures, but this can only be a partial explanation. Since all the objects recently analyzed came from a single small area near

Belén in Catamarca Province, there is some possibility that their composition is peculiar to objects produced in that area. However, Objects 5 and 6 of table I came from Belén or vicinity, and most of the objects analyzed earlier came from this province. The most likely explanation of the lack of agreement is that most of the objects analyzed earlier are of an entirely different period than those analyzed later.

Analyses of the few Bolivian objects in which at least three elements were determined are listed in table III. The high proportion of copper and the apparent lack of impurities in Object 1 indicate that it may have been formed from native copper, but the metal of the other three was certainly produced by smelting. The low summation of the third analysis indicates the presence of an undetermined element or elements. No recent analyses of Bolivian copper objects have been published.

Listed in table IV are all the better analyses of Peruvian copper objects published prior to 1922. The deficient summations of the second, fourth, sixth, and eighth analyses indicate that some element or elements were undetermined. That any of the objects were formed from native copper is not indicated with certainty by any of the analyses. Arsenic was found to be a principal impurity in nearly half the objects, and some of the rest may have contained this element. More recent quantitative analyses of copper objects from Peru, all of them in the form of ingots, are listed in table V. The deficient summations of the third and fourth indicate that some element or elements were undetermined. On comparing table III with table IV it will be seen that agreement or correlation between the early analyses and the recent analyses is generally lacking. This may be explained in much the same way as the lack of agreement between the early and recent analyses of copper objects from Argentina.

Because of all this lack of agreement among the analyses so far published, few specific conclusions and no generalizations can be derived from them about the composition of the copper objects of any particular region, or of South America as a whole. Until a sufficient number of complete and exact quantitative analyses of definite provenance become available, adequate knowledge of the chemical composition of these objects is not possible. Moreover, the objects selected for analysis should be representative of all the varieties found at all the principal sites and should range in date from the earliest to the latest. The new analyses here published will serve as an example of what needs to be done, but they represent no more than a start toward a sufficient body of analytical data.

New Analyses of Copper Objects from Peru

The objects selected and sampled for analysis are listed in table VI with the sites from which they came and their date periods in centuries A.D. These are approximate periods based solely on archaeological evidence. Unfortunately, no method for the closer dating of objects of this sort is available at present. All these objects are in the collections of the National Museum of Anthropology and Archaeology of Lima, Peru. I am indebted to Jorge O. Muelle, Director, and to Toribio M. Xesspe, Assistant Director, of that museum for their willingness to allow the destructive sampling of these objects for analysis, and to Arturi Alcalde Mongrut, a chemist of Lima, for making all the necessary arrangements for obtaining the samples and sending them to me for analysis. Three of the samples, nos. 2, 11, and 14, were in the form of clean drillings taken from the original metal. The remainder were in the form of severed sections. All external corrosion products were removed from these sections, and pieces of suitable weight for analysis were cut from the clean metal.

Table VI

Peruvian copper objects analyzed

No.	Site	Description	Period
1	Vicús, Piura	Barbed spear	IV–VIII cent.
2	San Pablo, Cajamarca	Ornament	IV–VIII cent.
3	Lambayeque	Needle or punch	IV–VIII cent.
4	Tantamayo	Tumi	IV–VIII cent.
5	Batán Grande, Lambayeque	Rectangular sheet	IV–VIII cent.
6	Batán Grande, Lambayeque	Lance head	VIII–XII cent.
7	Batán Grande, Lambayeque	Rattle	VIII–XII cent.
8	Chimbote	Flat fragment	VIII–XII cent.
9	Chimbote	Fragment (fused ?)	VIII–XII cent.
10	Litoral Norte (Chanchán ?)	Bell without clapper	VIII–XII cent.
11	Gotush, Chavín	Axe	X–XII cent.
12	Jauja	Tumi	X–XII cent.
13	Tablada de Lurín	Tupo	X–XII cent.
14	Pargo, Ayacucho	Club head	XII–XV cent.

The results obtained on the analysis of the samples are listed in table VII. Some of these results were obtained by gravimetric analysis, some by spectrographic analysis, and some by both methods. The gravimetric determinations were made by me and the spectrographic ones by Professor Lowell W. Shank of the department of chemistry of Western Kentucky University. Details of the analytical procedures have been published elsewhere.[1] Copper, silver, and sulfur were determined solely by gravimetric methods, antimony and bismuth solely by spectrographic methods, and the other elements by both methods. In general, the percentage figures obtained by the two methods agreed well and were averaged to obtain the figures shown in the table. However, there were a few exceptions. For example, the figures shown for nickel in nos. 7 and 8 are only the gravimetric results because the spectrographic method did not yield consistent and reliable results for such high percentages. The word none in the table indicates that nothing was found by the procedures used. Some may have been present where an absence is indicated, but in a percentage too low to be detected or determined by these procedures. At any rate it seems certain that no significant proportion of any given element was present where the word none appears. Zinc is not listed in the table because none was found in any of the samples by either method of analysis. The low summations obtained for nos. 4, 6, 7, 11, and 14 may be attributed to undetermined oxygen present in the mass of the metal in the form of oxides. These may have been formed when the metal was smelted or worked, by internal corrosion during burial in the ground, or by a combination of both causes.

The high copper content, the particular impurities present in low enough proportions, and the high summation of the analysis indicate with some certainty that the metal of Object 1 is

Table VII

Percentages of various elements from new analyses of copper objects from Peru

No.	Cu	Ag	Au	Sn	Pb	As	Sb	Bi	Fe	Ni	Co	S	Total
1	99.86	0.04	0.01	None	None	None	None	None	0.04	None	None	None	99.95
2	98.17	0.09	0.04	None	0.07	1.18	None	0.06	0.04	0.03	None	None	99.68
3	99.54	None	None	None	0.02	0.21	None	None	0.06	0.05	None	0.15	100.03
4	96.75	0.62	0.03	0.19	None	1.21	0.30	0.18	0.02	0.03	None	0.08	99.41
5	96.36	None	None	0.01	0.07	2.91	0.05	0.18	0.06	0.16	0.01	None	99.81
6	94.35	0.03	None	None	None	2.67	None	0.15	0.02	0.02	None	None	97.24
7	92.75	0.07	0.02	None	0.06	3.07	0.26	0.25	0.04	2.68	0.01	None	99.21
8	98.19	0.02	None	None	0.06	0.77	0.24	0.13	0.02	0.62	None	None	100.04
9	98.25	0.83	0.01	None	0.01	0.53	None	0.17	0.01	0.02	None	None	99.83
10	97.23	0.01	None	0.05	0.29	1.67	0.23	0.14	0.01	0.07	None	0.04	99.74
11	97.25	0.05	1.21	None	0.18	0.48	None	0.09	0.01	0.02	None	0.02	99.31
12	98.35	None	None	1.26	None	0.45	None	None	0.07	None	None	0.04	100.17
13	99.73	None	0.01	None	None	None	None	None	0.03	None	None	None	99.77
14	97.57	0.05	None	None	0.07	1.35	None	0.03	0.08	0.05	0.01	None	99.21

native copper. The metal of Object 13 was probably also native copper originally in spite of the lower percentages of copper and the lower summation. The sample was found to contain cuprous oxide, which fully accounts for these lower figures. Against its identification as native copper is the apparent absence of silver, a normal impurity. However, silver is sometimes present in very low proportion, and it may have escaped detection. On the whole it seems very probable that the metal of Object 13 is native copper modified by some internal oxidation such as could have been produced by heating and working the native metal. The metal of all the other objects obviously consists of manufactured copper of widely different degrees of purity. The metal of Object 3 has the highest purity, with a total of less than 0.5 % of elements other than copper, whereas that of Object 7 has the lowest purity, with a total of 6.5 % of such elements, not counting the oxygen that was apparently also present. This wide range of difference in purity indicates the use of ore charges of widely different composition, wide variations in smelting technique, or both. That sulfide ores were smelted is indicated both directly and indirectly by the analytical data. The presence of small proportions of residual sulfur in four of the samples is a direct indication, and the presence of considerable arsenic in all the samples, along with antimony, bismuth, or both, in most of them is an indirect indication. More extensive direct evidence for the use of sulfide ores for the production of copper in ancient Peru has been presented elsewhere.[2] Although sulfide ores were certainly used, they may not have been used exclusively, for partly oxidized sulfide ores, or even completely oxidized minerals, such as cuprite or malachite, may have been included in the charges that were smelted. There is even the possibility that scrap copper in the form of broken or worn tools was included.

The frequency of occurrence and certain significant proportions of the various impurities in the metal of the smelted copper objects are shown in table VIII. It will be seen from tables VII and VIII that the percentages of nickel, gold, or tin in certain single samples were found to be abnormally high as compared to the percentages of these metals in the other samples. If these atypical percentages are excluded, the average percentages of these three metals would be those in the last column of table VIII. These averages are probably more nearly representative of the average proportions in smelted Peruvian copper than those obtained by simply averaging all the results. If the next highest percentage of nickel, which also seems

Table VIII

Frequency of occurrence and proportions of impurities in smelted coppers

Element	Frequency of occurrence, %	Highest proportion, %	Next highest proportion, %	Overall average proportion, %	Weighted average proportion, %
As	100	3.07	2.91	1.38	
Fe	100	0.08	0.07	0.04	
Ni	92	2.68	0.62	0.31	0.10
Bi	83	0.25	0.18	0.12	
Ag	75	0.83	0.62	0.15	0.03
Pb	75	0.29	0.18	0.07	
Sb	42	0.30	0.26	0.09	
Au	42	1.21	0.04	0.11	0.01
S	42	0.15	0.08	0.03	
Sn	33	1.26	0.19	0.13	0.02
Co	25	0.01	0.00	0.003	

atypical, is also excluded, the average for nickel would be 0.05 %, which is about the average proportion found in much ancient copper from other regions of the world. It is evident that nickel is a usual impurity in ancient Peruvian smelted copper, a fact that has not been disclosed by previous analyses of such metal, apparently because the analysts failed to examine their samples for this particular impurity. The relatively high proportion of gold in Object 11 might conceivably be the result of the accidental inclusion of gold ore in the mixture that was smelted, but a more likely explanation is the inclusion of gilded scrap copper or some copper-gold alloy, particularly the base alloy known as tumbaga, which was widely used in South America. The proportion of tin (1.26 %) in Object 12 is not high enough to classify the metal as a bronze, since a tin content of at least 2 %, or even 3 %, is usually considered the lower limit for this alloy. However, it is very high for an accidental impurity resulting from the smelting of ordinary copper ores, for these usually contain little or no tin. That it was probably introduced by the smelting of an unusual ore seems to be indicated by the results of some analyses of ancient copper objects found in northwest Argentina (table II). It is also possible that tin ore was accidentally added to the charge that was smelted, but this explanation seems less likely. That the tin in Object 12 was introduced by the inclusion of scrap bronze in the charge is even less likely, because the date of the object is probably earlier than the first manufacture of bronze in ancient Peru. The two highest percentages of silver seem atypical both for this series of new analyses and for the older ones listed in tables IV and V. If these two high percentages of silver are excluded, the average proportion of this impurity would be that shown in the last column of table VIII. However, similar high proportions of silver are reported in some analyses of Peruvian bronzes, as is shown by the data of table IX. The occasional presence of these high

proportions of silver is not surprising, since copper ores and silver ores frequently occur in close association in Peru.[3]

Arsenic is clearly the chief impurity or principal minor component of the metal in the series of table VIII. Although the two highest percentages of arsenic fall below three of the percentages reported in the previous analyses listed in table IV, the frequent occurrence of high proportions of arsenic in Peruvian copper is essentially confirmed. Whether arsenic in such high proportions should be classed as an impurity is a matter of definition or convention. When the proportion of tin in copper amounts to 2 %, or according to some 3 %, the tin is no longer regarded as an impurity but is then considered to be the minor component of a tin bronze. The same distinction may be based on the proportions of arsenic in copper, since the two elements have a similar effect on modifying the physical properties of copper. Copper containing as much as 2 % arsenic could be called an arsenic bronze, although the usual term is arsenical copper. However, this particular term is often applied to copper that contains lower proportions, even to copper that contains as little as a few tenths of a percent of arsenic when this is the main impurity.

Absence of Arsenic in Tin Bronzes

In view of the frequent presence of arsenic in the copper it seems reasonable to expect that this element would also be present in the tin bronzes. However, except for one analysis in which the proportion of arsenic is reported as 0.10 % and another in which a trace is reported, this element is not listed in any published analysis of South American bronze objects, as is illustrated by the better analyses of Peruvian bronze objects listed in table IX. Although there is no certainty that these bronzes were examined for arsenic, the summations leave little or no room for its presence, certainly not in the high proportions frequent in Peruvian copper. In a complete analysis

Table IX

Percentages of various elements from selected analyses of bronze objects from Peru

No.	Site	Description	Cu	Ag	Sn	Sb	Fe	S	Other	Total
1	Eastern Peru	Axe	96.44	None	3.36	—	Trace	0.23	Pb-none	100.03
2	Machu Picchu	Axe	95.63	0.37	3.99	—	—	0.40	—	100.39
3	Machu Picchu	Knife	94.26	—	4.82	—	0.32	0.23	—	99.63
4	Eastern Peru	Axe	93.94	0.65	5.58	—	None	0.08	Pb-trace	100.25
5	Machu Picchu	Chisel	93.90	—	5.53	—	0.06	0.15	—	99.64
6	Machu Picchu	Axe	93.70	—	5.01	—	0.87	0.44	—	100.02
7	Uncertain	Axe	93.25	0.88	5.10	0.60	—	—	Au-0.15	99.98
8	Machu Picchu	Knife	90.09	0.68	8.99	—	—	0.13	—	99.89

Sources:

Nos. 1 and 4. H. W. Foote and W. H. Buell, *The American Journal of Science* [4] (1912), 34, 128–132.

Nos. 2, 3, 5, 6, and 8. C. H. Mathewson, *The American Journal of Science* [4] (1915), 40, 531.

No. 7. A. L. Kroeber, *American Antiquity* 20 (1954), 160–162.

of a sample of clean metal taken from a typical Peruvian bronze object, Professor Lowell W. Shank and I found direct evidence for the absence of arsenic in Peruvian bronze. This object is in the collections of the National Museum of Anthropology and Archaeology of Lima, and its date is probably about fifteenth century. The results of the analysis are shown in table X. Not only arsenic was found to be absent but also many of the other impurities frequently present in Peruvian copper.

Since few impurities in appreciable proportions are associated with the tin in ancient bronzes it is possible to calculate the approximate composition of the copper component of the alloys by prorating the percentages of all components except tin over a range of 100 %. The calculated compositions of the copper in the bronzes of tables IX and X are shown in table XI.

Table X

Complete analysis of a bronze axe from Cuzco

Element	%
Cu	95.45
Ag	0.04
Sn	3.64
Fe	0.09
S	0.48
Au, Pb, As, Sb, Bi, Ni, Co	None
Total	99.70

Table XI

Calculated compositions of the copper component of Peruvian bronzes

Bronze listed Table	No.	Cu %	Ag %	Au %	Pb %	Sb %	Fe %	S %
IX	5	99.78	–	–	–	–	0.06	0.16
IX	1	99.76	None	–	None	–	Trace	0.24
IX	3	99.42	–	–	–	–	0.34	0.24
X		99.37	0.04	None	None	None	0.09	0.50
IX	4	99.23	0.69	–	Trace	–	None	0.08
IX	2	99.20	0.38	–	–	–	–	0.42
IX	8	99.11	0.75	–	–	–	–	0.14
IX	6	98.62	–	–	–	–	0.92	0.46
IX	7	98.28	0.93	0.16	–	0.63	–	–

Comparison of the data in table XI with those in tables IV, V, and VII is difficult because of the differences in the numbers of elements determined or undetermined. However, the presence of relatively high proportions of silver in nearly half the analyses of table XI and of relatively high proportions of sulfur in all but one, as well as the absence of arsenic, appears to indicate that the copper in the bronzes came from different ores, was made by a different process, or both. That sulfide ores

were smelted is obvious from the proportions of residual sulfur. The composition of the copper that entered into the bronzes may also have been influenced by the way these were manufactured. In view of the kind of ore that was used, the production of a satisfactory bronze by the direct reduction of a mixture of copper ore and tin ore (cassiterite) with charcoal seems very unlikely. If this type of process was used at all, the copper ore was in all likelihood first roasted to burn off nearly all the sulfur before mixing it with the cassiterite and charcoal. In view of the long tradition of copper manufacture in South America it is much more probable that in bronze manufacture the sulfide ore was not only roasted but was afterward smelted with charcoal to produce copper. This copper was then either smelted with a mixture of cassiterite and charcoal to produce the bronze or, more probably, melted with metallic tin separately smelted from cassiterite to form the alloy directly. Either way, the copper had to be melted a second time at a high temperature, which would tend to volatilize any residual arsenic in the smelted copper. This may in part account for its observed absence from the bronzes.

Extent of Use of Arsenical Copper

The analyses at present available indicate that most of the copper manufactured in ancient South America contained arsenic as the chief impurity or as the minor component of a copper-arsenic alloy. For the tabulation in table XII all the analyses published by Fester[4] are included but not the calculated compositions of table XI. Since there is considerable likelihood that arsenic was present but not determined in some of the objects that were analyzed the total number and the total percentage given in this table are probably low. This is indicated by the representative series of Peruvian objects listed in table VII, where arsenic was found in 12 of the 14 objects analyzed, about 86 %. These percentages are merely tentative and very probably will be modified in one direction or

Table XII

Proportions of arsenic reported in 76 analyses

Arsenic content %	Number of analyses	Percentage of analyses
Below 1	7	9.2
1–2	14	18.4
2–3	11	14.5
3–4	10	13.2
4–5	4	5.3
5–6	3	3.9
6–7	2	2.6
Over 7	1	1.3
Totals	52	68.4

the other when additional analyses are made. The same applies to the distribution of ranges of arsenic content shown in table XII. Only when much more data are available will a statistical study of such distribution be worthwhile.

The analyses also indicate that objects from some localities are composed of arsenical copper but not those from others. All the copper objects from a particular site near Belén in northwest Argentina contained arsenic.[4] The same is true of the objects from Batán Grande, Lambayeque in Peru (tables VI and VII). On the other hand, arsenic was absent from objects from two of the sites listed in these tables, from objects from Chepen (table IV), and from objects from two other sites in Peru (table V).

The data of tables VI and VII indicate a minimum time period of five centuries for the use of arsenical copper in ancient Peru and a maximum period of twelve centuries, with some likelihood that the actual period of use was some intermediate number of centuries between these two extremes. A considerable number of more closely dated Peruvian copper objects must be made before the exact period can be determined. These analyses may also show that arsenical copper was used for different lengths of time in different parts of the general region of ancient Peru. Not even a rough time estimate is at present possible for any other region of South America.

Probable Intentional Manufacture of Arsenical Copper

The recent paper by Charles[5] on the intentional manufacture of arsenical copper in the ancient Aegean region is very pertinent for any consideration of the question as to whether the widespread manufacture of arsenical copper in ancient South America was entirely accidental or was more or less deliberate. The arsenic present in such copper must come either from copper ores that contain it or from arsenic minerals. Arsenic in the form of various compounds is usually present in various proportions in complex copper ores. When such ores are smelted the copper that is produced may also contain this element, especially when primitive methods are used. However, because of the low vaporization points of arsenic and especially of arsenious oxide, its usual oxidation product, and because of the high temperature necessary for smelting, most of the arsenic is volatilized and does not enter the copper. Only when the ore contains an exceptionally high proportion of arsenic will the resulting metal contain as much as a few percentage points of this element. The invariable presence of arsenic in excess of 1 % in all the copper objects from the site near Belén in northwest Argentina can thus be explained, for the only copper deposits within a reasonable distance from this site contain unusually high proportions of arsenic. These deposits are at Capillitas about 50 kilometers away, where remains of primitive furnaces have been found. The copper is

largely in the form of copper sulfarsenites (enargite and tennantite). In the opinion of Fester[4] the ancient workers smelted only the oxidized outcrops of these minerals in the form of arsenates, but these also must have contained high proportions of arsenic. The ancient production of arsenical copper at the Capillitas mines cannot be regarded as deliberate, since this was the only kind of copper that could be produced there. That arsenical copper was sometimes also unavoidably produced in ancient Peru seems probable, since deposits of copper ores composed of complex sulfides containing arsenic occur at various places in the eastern Andes of that country.[3] However, the arsenic content of these ores is variable and sometimes so low that the smelting of them would have produced copper containing very little arsenic. Since the many deposits of copper ores in the coastal range of Peru are composed mostly of oxidized copper minerals free from arsenic,[3] metal produced from them would not usually have contained any of this element. If the smelting of copper ores in ancient Peru was done on a purely random basis it would therefore follow that the majority of surviving objects should not be composed of arsenical copper. But the evidence of the analyses shows the opposite. This evidence is indicative not only of a preference for arsenical copper but also of its intentional production.

The reason for the ancient preference for arsenical copper is by no means obscure. Such copper is superior to the pure metal because it is easier to cast and to work. This superiority is so marked that it could not have escaped for long the attention of ancient metallurgists with experience in handling both kinds of copper. That they were ever aware that the difference was due to the presence of some distinct substance in the metal is very improbable. What is probable is that they came to realize through trial and error that a superior metal was produced only when some particular mining or smelting procedure was followed. For example, the discovery of a deposit of highly arsenical copper ore and the smelting of some of it would lead naturally to the repeated smelting of ore from this deposit, and, on exhaustion of the ore, to a deliberate search for another deposit of similar ore. Charles[5] suggested that the procedure generally used in the Aegean world was the deliberate addition of arsenic minerals to ordinary copper ores before smelting. His argument is that the smelting of the usual run of copper ores of that region could not have led to the regular production of arsenical copper, and that therefore the arsenic must have been added in some form. The same argument may be applied to Peru. He pointed out that most of the minerals containing arsenic are easy to recognize, including those that contain both arsenic and copper, such as the enargite and the tennantite often associated with deposits of the common sulfide ores of copper. He also suggested that the operation of hand sorting, which was necessary to separate the ore from the excess of gangue before smelting, may have included the deliberate selective enrichment of it with these arsenic minerals. Another possibility is the addition of arsenic minerals to molten copper obtained by smelting ordinary copper ores. The addition of one of the copper arsenides, such as domeykite, to the molten metal is a simple way to produce arsenical copper. This process would have been quite feasible in South America, for domeykite is a fairly common mineral in the Andes region, especially in Bolivia.[3]

The apparent absence of arsenic from South American bronze and from the copper used in making it (tables IX, X, and XI), or at least the absence of any proportions approaching those in the arsenical copper, would seem to be an indirect indication that arsenical copper was intentionally produced. Although, as discussed before, the process of making bronze would have tended to reduce the arsenic content of the alloy below that of the copper used in its manufacture, this copper could not have had a high arsenic content initially without leaving some arsenic in the bronze. In other words, the copper used for its manufacture probably contained little or no arsenic, which raises the possibility that in Peru, at least, this very often is true of the smelted copper, whether it was used directly for making objects or to produce either arsenical copper or tin bronze.

General Conclusions

The analytical data now available make possible the following general conclusions about the chemical composition of the ancient copper objects of South America:

1. Only a small proportion of these objects was fashioned from native copper.

2. The number and variety of the impurities in the copper generally used in their manufacture show that it was smelted from a variety of ores, including complex sulfide ores.

3. Most of the objects are composed of arsenical copper, some of which was probably manufactured intentionally.

4. An adequate body of detailed information about their composition will require many more careful analyses of widely selected objects of known provenance.

References

1. Caley, E. R., *Analysis of ancient metals,* New York, 1964.

2. Caley, E. R., and Easby, D. T., *American Antiquity,* 25 (1959), 59–65.

3. Weed, W. H., *The copper mines of the world,* London, 1908, 173–195.

4. Fester, G. A., *Chymia,* 8 (1962), 21–31.

5. Charles, J. A., *American Journal of Archaeology,* 71 (1967), 21–26.

SEYMOUR Z. LEWIN

A New Approach to Establishing the Authenticity of Patinas on Copper-base Artifacts

Despite a considerable number of investigations into, and speculations on, the chemical nature and physical state of corrosion patinas, very few objective criteria have until now been adumbrated which can be stated with even a moderate degree of confidence for distinguishing between a patina formed by natural corrosion processes occurring during prolonged burial and those that have been artificially induced. The pertinent literature for copper and copper-base artifacts has been gathered and critically reviewed (see S. Z. Lewin and S. M. Alexander, *Art and Archeology Technical Abstracts,* 6, no. 4 [1967], 201–283, and vol. 7, no. 1, 279–370 [1968]), and this analysis has shown that "the rather limited present-day understanding of the nature and structure of patinas on metal is the consequence of the availability of only a small body of suitable study material, coupled with considerable complexity of the chemical systems involved, necessitating X-ray diffraction and similarly sophisticated investigational techniques."

Criteria of Authenticity

At best, only tentative guidelines can be developed from the earlier literature in this field. It appears that the following propositions may be valid, but the available data are not adequate to establish their limits of reliability.

1. The presence of a substantial thickness of massive cuprite immediately contiguous with the core of residual metal indicates that the patina is probably natural (fig. 1). However, the converse of this proposition is not true. That is, the absence of a substantial layer of cuprite next to the residual metal does not necessarily imply that the patina is artificial (fig. 2).

2. The presence of very pronounced intergranular corrosion, i.e., of penetration of the corrosion into the residual metal core along the boundaries and interfaces between the metal grains (i.e., crystals), indicates that the patina is probably natural (fig. 3). Again, the converse of this proposition is not true; i.e., the absence of evidences of extensive intergranular corrosion cannot be taken as proof that the patina was artificially produced (fig. 4).

3. The presence of a layered, banded, or periodic structure (sometimes referred to as Liesegang phenomena) in the crust of corrosion products indicates that the patina is probably natural (fig. 5). However, the absence of such a feature does not imply that the patina is artificial (fig. 6).

One of the ambiguities in the above propositions is the fact that special (secret) techniques could be known to some individuals by means of which the growth of massive cuprite, intergranular corrosion, or banded structures can be induced in the course of artificially patinating an object. Such ambiguities will only be resolved through the publication of fundamental studies of the mechanisms and rates of the oxidation, crystal growth, and mass transport phenomena involved in the formation of the corrosion crust.

An aspect of corrosion patinas that has heretofore been almost entirely ignored is the fact that certain of the corrosion products occur in two or more polymorphic forms. It seemed to us possible that in some cases the particular polymorph which is produced during the corrosion reaction might depend very specifically upon the ambient parameters, and hence might provide a key to deducing the local conditions under which the corrosion took place.

Consequently, we have undertaken in our laboratories at the Washington Square center of New York University a program of fundamental research into the factors involved in directing the nucleation and crystal growth of the most frequently encountered corrosion products. The first of these studies to be completed has been concerned with the copper (II) trihydroxychlorides, $Cu_2(OH)_3Cl$, two polymorphs of which are very commonly found in the patinas of copper, bronze, brass, tumbaga, and other copper-base alloys which have undergone corrosion in the presence of soluble chlorides.

Atacamite Versus Paratacamite

It has indeed been found that each of the two polymorphs in question, i.e., atacamite and paratacamite, has uniquely characteristic crystallochemical properties, and that determination of the relative proportions of these phases in a corrosion patina is diagnostic of the composition of the medium in which the corrosion took place.

The design of the experiments and the detailed discussion of the resulting observations and data have been published elsewhere (J. B. Sharkey and S. Z. Lewin, *Amer. Mineral.* 56, 179–192, 1971; J. B. Sharkey, Ph. D. thesis, New York University, 1970); it will suffice here to summarize those aspects which bear on the problem of determining patina authenticity. These are as follows:

1. Atacamite and paratacamite, once formed, do not undergo phase transformations at ordinary temperatures and pressures. That is, it is not possible at room temperature to convert one of these phases into the other. From this fact, the very important conclusion follows that the relative proportion of atacamite to paratacamite now found to be present in the patina on an artifact *is the same as the proportion in which these two phases were originally formed* by the corrosion process.

2. The relative proportion of atacamite to paratacamite is sensitive to the (*a*) pH in the immediate vicinity of the nucleation sites, (*b*) concentration there of copper salts, (*c*) concentration of chloride ions, and (*d*) temperature. However, it is not affected by the rate of formation of the corrosion products.

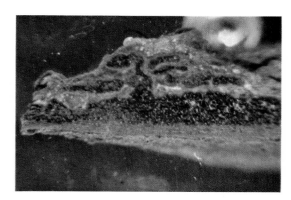

1. Natural patina on a fragment from an Egyptian bronze, showing a substantial thickness of massive cuprite (red) immediately bordering on the core of residual metal.

4. Cross-section of Roman bronze coin. Even at the border of the residual metal, there is negligible evidence of intergranular corrosion. Removal of the corrosion crust leaves a metal surface that is rough and etched in appearance, but solid and nonporous even when examined metallorgraphically at high magnification.

2. Cross-section of a copper tool from the Royal Cemetery at Ur, showing several extensive regions where there is an absence of cuprite as the corrosion product that is in direct contact with the cores of residual metal.

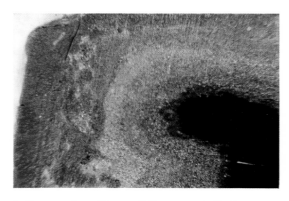

5. Cross-section of Roman 90 % copper—10 % silver coin, showing layered structure of the corrosion products. The core of residual metal is shown in black and gray, and it is covered by successive bands of cuprite, malachite, nantokite, cuprite, malachite, cuprite, and malachite, in that order.

3. Detail of the cross-section of a Roman 90 % copper—10 % silver coin; inner core of residual metal shows intergranular corrosion invading the duplex structure of the metal. Dark masses are corrosion product; pink areas are copper-rich grains; silvery areas are the copper-silver eutectic.

6. Corrosion crust of a copper object from Ur. The entire corrosion crust consists of a thick matrix of cuprite. Scattered randomly within this matrix there occur occasional pockets of malachite, but the latter is not present as a distinct band or layer.

The first four factors given in the preceding paragraph are intimately related to each other, for the pH determines the degree of hydrolysis of the copper salts, the copper (II) ion interacts with chloride ions to form a series of complex ions, and all of these equilibria are sensitive to the temperature of the medium.

If the polymorph composition of the corrosion product is plotted as a function of the copper (II) chloride and/or sodium chloride concentration, characteristic curves are obtained, as shown in figs. 7 and 8. Theoretical analysis of these data establishes that it is the concentration of the monochloro complex ion $CuCl(H_2O)_5{}^+$, that determines the extent of formation of atacamite, whereas the uncomplexed copper (II) ion, as well as the higher chloro copper complexes, promote the formation of the paratacamite polymorph.

From these results, the important conclusion follows that the order of magnitude of the *concentration of the (dissolved) copper chloride complex ions in the corroding medium can be inferred* from the polymorph composition of the copper (II) trihydroxychloride in the patina.

Thus, if the copper salt concentration in the corroding medium is very low, as would be the case for the progressive, centuries-long corrosion of buried artifacts, then only paratacamite will be found in the patina.

On the other hand, if the patina contains atacamite, or a mixture of atacamite and paratacamite, the concentration of copper salts in the immediate vicinity of the artifact must have been at least 0.01 M if the soil in contact with the object was rich in chalk or powdered limestone, and at least about 0.05 M if not.

Unless there is some reason to believe that there were present unusual natural agencies (such as the existence of sulfide ore mine tailings in the immediate vicinity of the artifact), or special burial conditions (such as a more noble metal in electrochemical contact with a copper-base artifact, causing the latter to corrode rapidly and extensively, and thus to generate high local copper salt concentrations), all of which would result in a very deeply corroded object, the detection of a mixture of atacamite and paratacamite in a patina on a fairly well-preserved object implies that the corrosion was induced artificially either by a solution containing a moderate to large concentration of a copper salt or by acid which would attack the metal surface and generate such concentrations of copper salts.

Hence, a new criterion is now available for establishing the history of a patina; if the bulk of the patina contains detectable proportions of atacamite (with or without paratacamite), and if the object is not extensively and deeply corroded, then the probability is great that the patina is false, i.e., that it has been produced by other than natural agencies.

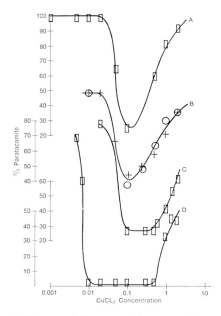

7. The crystal character of the copper (II) trihydroxychloride formed in aqueous $CuCl_2$ solutions by five different reaction schemes; *A*, corrosion of copper metal; *B*, oxidation of $Cu_2O(+)$ and $CuCl(O)$; *C*, replacement of $Cu_2(OH)_2Co_3$ (malachite); *D*, indirect precipitation product of $CaCo_3$.

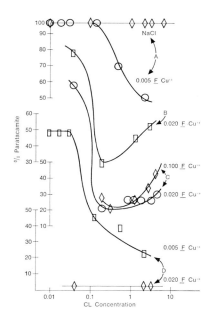

8. The crystal character of the $Cu_2(OH)_3Cl$ formed in a given $CuCl_2$ solution as a function of added NaCl. *A*, corrosion of copper metal; *B*, oxidation of CuCl; *C*, replacement of $Cu_2(OH)_2CO_3$ (malachite); *D*, indirect precipitation product of $CaCO_3$.

The details of the X-ray diffraction method of determining the atacamite/paratacamite composition of a sample are given in the paper by Sharkey and Lewin cited earlier. It has been successfully employed on specimens of patina as small as 0.1 mg.

Finally, it should be explicitly noted that the detection of only the paratacamite polymorph in the patina of an artifact is consistent with, but does not necessarily establish, its authenticity. A thin coating of pure paratacamite forms on copper-base objects which have been left in an aqueous chloride solution for moderate periods of time, e.g., several months to several years.

Any consideration of patina compositions must, of course, start from the premise that the corrosion products under study have indeed come from the underlying metal, and are not mineral powders which stem from other sources and have been affixed to the artifact in order to simulate the appearance of a natural patina. Accordingly, the first step in the chemical investigation of any patina should consist in testing for the presence of glues, resins, or other fixatives.

Malachite and Azurite

The two different copper (II) hydroxycarbonates, i.e., malachite, $Cu_2(OH)_2CO_3$, and azurite, $Cu_3(OH)_2(CO_3)_2$, are also commonly encountered in the patinas of copper-base artifacts, and we have undertaken to investigate the conditions of their formation and stability. These studies (A. Koplewicz, M. S. thesis, New York University, 1970) have shown that malachite is formed on a copper-base metal surface in the presence of condensed water over a wide range of copper salt and bicarbonate ion concentrations (fig. 9), and over a restricted range of copper salt and carbonate ion concentrations (fig.10). Under no conditions, in the absence of added gaseous carbon dioxide, was azurite formed.

Thermodynamic reasoning indicates that for the assumed interconversion reaction between malachite and azurite:

$$3\,Cu_2(OH)_2CO_3 + CO_2(g) \rightleftarrows 2\,Cu_3(OH)_2(CO_3)_2 + H_2O(l)$$

the equilibrium constant, K, is equal to the reciprocal of the partial pressure of carbon dioxide, i.e., $1/pCO_2$. Free energy calculations show that if equilibrium were established at 25° C and one atmosphere total pressure, malachite should be the principal phase present when pCO_2 is less than $10^{-2.5}$ atm. (= 0.003 atm. = 2.4 mmHg), and azurite should predominate at CO_2 partial pressures greater than this value (R. M. Garrels, and C. L. Christ, "Solutions, Minerals, and Equilibria," New York, Harper and Row, 1965, p. 155). The situation is shown graphically in fig.11. Since the partial pressure of CO_2 in normal air at the surface of the earth is about $10^{-3.5}$ atm. (= about 0.24 mmHg), it is evident that under ordinary conditions azurite should tend, in the presence of moisture, to lose CO_2 and change into malachite.

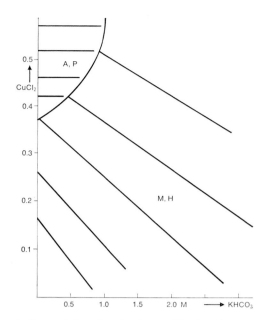

9. Concentration domains for precipitation of various solid phases by mixing equimolar quantities of solutions of $KHCO_3$ and $CuCl_2$. Horizontal axis shows initial concentration of the $KHCO_3$ solution; vertical axis that of the $CuCl_2$ solution. A = atacamite; P = paratacamite; M = malachite; H = copper (II) hydroxide.

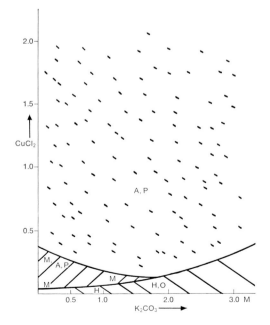

10. Nature of precipitated phases when equimolar quantities of $CuCl_2$ and K_2CO_3 solutions are mixed. Symbols are as in fig. 9; O = copper (II) oxide.

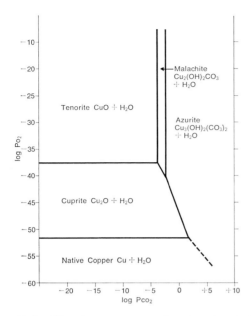

11. Stability of copper compounds as function of pO_2 and pCO_2 at 25° C and 1 atmosphere, or slightly greater than 1 atmosphere, total pressure. Pure liquid water is assumed present in all cases. From Garrels and Christ, "Solutions, Minerals, and Equlibria."

Our experiments have shown that this does in fact occur readily when azurite is immersed in water; the transformation is promoted by increase in temperature, and is base-catalyzed, i.e., is accelerated by the presence of alkali. We have also found that malachite converts to azurite if a high partial pressure of carbon dioxide is maintained in the system. However, the interconversion of one of these minerals to the other does not take place, regardless of pCO_2, if the solid phase is kept dry.

From these data it follows that the relative proportions of malachite and azurite in a patina may provide some insight into the CO_2 content of the surroundings of the artifact when it was last in a humid or wet state for an extended period of time. Most immersion treatments of patinated objects, for the purposes either of cleaning or of combatting "bronze disease," will tend to destroy any azurite originally present. It is clear from the foregoing that in terms of our present knowledge the detection and determination of the proportions of malachite and azurite in a patina provide no reliable clues as to its authenticity.

MADELEINE HOURS and F. MICHEL

Scientific Methods in the Study of the Metallurgy of Antiquity at the Louvre

The development of scientific research in recent years is such that it tends to enter realms that until just recently were unknown. Thus we have seen the methods of analysis of art criticism transformed under the influence of photography — the work of André Malraux, for example — of radiology, and of optics. Studies of the materials of a picture are clarified by the methods of infrared spectrography or of chromatography. It is the same in the realm of archaeology. The archaeologist in the field has for some time used the scientific methods of magnetic prospecting, the dating methods of carbon 14, thermoremanence, the methods of dendrochronology, and thermoluminescence. In the history of the study and analysis of museum objects, the use of scientific methods is clearly only in its beginnings. Nevertheless, art historians and curators of museums believe that a worthy publication can no longer be content with giving a historical and aesthetic description but ought also to analyze the structure of the object and situate it in the evolution of technological development.

The inventory of the collections of a large museum such as Boston's, or the Louvre, ought henceforth to furnish precise data. Thus objects in the Egyptian department of the Louvre listed as being made of gold were, in the inventory of the 19th century, proved to be made of electrum, a gold alloy containing a large quantity of silver. Objects entitled "bronze" in old catalogues were often dependent on their appearance, corrosion, and patina. In fact, systematic analyses have pointed out the variety of metals and alloys used in antiquity and the necessity of giving an object a precise description leads the historian and archaeologist to obtain assistance through laboratary analysis. These analyses enable us: (1) to determine the constituents of the object; (2) to specify, by the proportion of impurities, the provenance of the minerals; (3) to characterize the metallurgical technique; and (4) to establish series of analyses following dated records to see if there is a correspondence or correlation between the results of the analyses and chronological and historical factors. In other words, the archaeologist must collaborate with the scientist.

It is evident that if scientific studies of museums are to give useful information, the scientist must use a standard method, and the interpretation of the results must be highly objective. However, it is equally necessary that the historian determine the choice of objects and their corresponding places of analysis.

Next serial analyses should be performed under uniform conditions. These ought, if quantitative, to furnish a great deal of information which can be used in research projects related to a particular geographic area or period. The considerable number of objects classified permits, in a museum like the Louvre (4000 metal objects in the Egyptian department), the organization of a series of examinations which, in table form, will allow us to clarify our catalogues, find the differences in origin between metals of different periods, and comprehend the technology of various peoples. (Work conducted at the laboratory tends actually to dissociate the diverse techniques of the Mediterranean peoples of the first millenium.)

But it is not only a question of the evolution of history but equally a question of authenticity that is posed. Forgers, until now, have had to put on the market objects which correspond primarily to aesthetic and historical data. The problems of technological progress have escaped them until recently, and on this basis we have a chance to reveal fakes that are so numerous and whose diffusion into collections was facilitated by the methods of casting and by ignorance of the laws of ancient metallurgy.

Standardization of the processes of analysis and care in noting the characteristics, origin, and date of objects, when possible, ought in the future to improve the scientific quality of catalogues and publications. Discerning the small differences in alloys, in techniques of manufacture, and in native impurities of minerals, all help to clarify problems of authenticity, lines of commerce in antiquity, the markets for gold and silver, and finally, the evolution of technology.

Every object that arrives in our laboratory to be examined must be accompanied by all the relevant archeological data (place and date of origin, and so on). A preliminary examination, which includes study of shape, mounting, soldering, is conducted and designed to note certain critical points and to make eventual comparisons with similar objects. Observations under magnification complete the preliminary examination, with a study of the patina, the corrosion, and the markings of the object.

Measurements are carefully taken. Sometimes, slightly corroded objects are weighed, and it is even possible to measure the densities of some of them, particularly of coins. This is a way of determining the actual gold content of gold coins. Every object is photographed, and sometimes photographs of details or macrophotographs are necessary. Sometimes infrared films will bring out certain details, and photographs made under ultraviolet fluorescent light can eventually help in restoration.

After these preliminary examinations the composition of the alloy which constitutes the object must be studied by ultraviolet spectrography. With a direct spark, the results obtained are characteristic solely of the surface.

There are two methods of analysis: to make many samplings and treat them separately, or to mix these samples. We have chosen the first procedure, for the samples are chosen according to each object and do not always represent a good statistical disposition. Moreover, we are not after a rigorous analysis, but we try to achieve results that can be reproduced and which will allow us to classify alloys in series of general characteristics, according to percentage brackets that we have already established.

The results obtained can be reproduced. However, these are spot results and representative of the surface only. We have compared the results obtained on a number of objects by direct sparking and by sparking of samples. The differences noted are variable, depending on the nature of the alloy and the way in which it has been obtained. The heterogeneity of the alloy is the most important factor in the variations of superficial and internal composition. But on the whole, the combination of the two types of results allows us to remain within the limits we have set up.

It is preferable to complete the study of the composition by a study of the structure and technique. In certain favorable cases, it is possible to remove a small fragment of metal and to make a metallurgical cross-section, and the microscopic examination is advanced enough to study the metal corrosion. For bronzes, for example, different layers of copper salts can be distinguished: malachite or green carbonate on the surface, and the red oxide between the metal which is still healthy and the carbonate. It is also possible to note the intercrystalline corrosion.

The analysis of the arrangement of the various strata is very interesting in the case of false patinas, or when the object has been treated for restoration. It is also possible to expose a false patina in a bronze statue, even if the patina was produced from crushed malachite. This phenomenon is traced through the discontinuity of the strata, and also by the absence of intercrystalline penetration.

Once the analysis of the corrosion is finished, one can move on to attack the metal microchemically to dissolve certain regions in the metal and thus to lay bare the metallurgical phases of the alloy.

These analyses allow us to reveal restorations: false patinas and metallic parts which have been added to complete an object. A Tibetan Krishnayamari belonging to the Guimet Museum is an example. The central foot of this figure is attached with little bolts by a mortise process. The composition of the foot is totally different. The statue is a bronze lead statue, containing mainly copper, tin (about 6%), lead (12%), arsenic, antimony, and iron impurities (0.30%), and very slight traces (less than 0.01%) of nickel, aluminum, and manganese. Microscopic analysis of the surface reveals a greenish-white layer, composed primarily of copper carbonate mixed with an organic substance, poorly adhesive to the metal. The copper carbonate is the same on the detached foot and the rest of the object. The analysis has thus revealed a heterogeneous part of the object, that is, the foot, which had been added, fixed by mechanical means and made out of an alloy com-

pletely different from the alloy of the rest of the body. It must certainly be a restoration, and this hypothesis seems confirmed by the nature of the patina.

Laboratory study is useful, too, in making a choice from a series of objects. It is from this point of view that we examined fragments of a Roman chariot, originating from the sale of the Alessandro Castellani collection in Rome, in 1884. These fragments were acquired by Henry of Germany, who reconstituted the chariot on a wooden frame and wheels. This reconstituted chariot was part of the International Exhibition of 1889, and in 1927 was given to the National Museum of Cars and Tourism in Compiegne. The interpretation and arbitrariness which inevitably follow every reconstitution can only have become more apparent after eighty-five years, and it was thought useful to perform a scientific analysis of these elements in order to perhaps obtain a better interpretation. The intrusive character of some fragments has thus been confirmed after scientific examination.

The study of corrosion and its evolution is necessary to the good conservation of art objects. The nature and importance of this corrosion, the composition of the alloy, the technology of the object, all can help determine the nature of the treatment for conservation and the methods of restoration.

While dealing with the various needs of those responsible for museums and departments, we must not forget the goal we have set for ourselves: to make a systematic study of ancient metallurgy, by regions and epochs, where sporadic results come to augment the basic work and the stock of information already available. The information pertaining to a single object is ample: results of analyses, information of a chronological or historical nature, technique. This information has already become unmanageable. Therefore, we are planning a card catalogue with punched cards, which can be sorted by a computer. For every object, there will be an "identification" card which will contain all archeological and historical information, and one or more "result" cards, depending on the different metallic compositions of the object or a too great heterogeneity of the alloy. When a great number of objects have been thus catalogued, we expect to undertake a serial classification, based on objects of known origin. It will then be possible, using the greatest number of criteria, to integrate into this series objects with little indication as to origin, or, on the other hand, to eliminate some which will prove to be fakes.

At the same time, along with the problems which various museum departments give us, we have undertaken an in-depth study of Egyptian metallurgy. These metal objects, numbering around 4000, belong to the Egyptian Antiquities section of the Louvre. It will be a work requiring time and labor, which will no doubt bring precious information to the history of ancient metallurgy. Following is an account of the analysis of a number of Egyptian arms: a small chapter in the study we have undertaken.

Spectrographic Analysis of an Egyptian Bronze Series

These bronzes belong to the Egyptian Antiquities Department of the Louvre. There are twenty-seven weapons from the ancient through new impires, including sickle swords, six daggers, four spears, and fifteen axes.

Description of the objects

The classification is according to chronological order.

No.1 E 11025-6 Axe head
Old Kingdom
Origin: Kom el Gaab
Hafting by strap passing through a perforation of the flat of the head
Medium corrosion
Measurements: 0.108 x 0.133 m

No.2 E 17283 Spear head
End of the Old Kingdom or First Intermediate
  Period
Origin: Kom Dara
Silk hafting
Quite heavily corroded
Measurements: 0.346 x 0.047 m

No.3 25219 Spear head
End of the Old Kingdom or First Intermediate
  Period
Origin: Kom Dara
Silk hafting
Quite heavily corroded
Quite strong longitudinal curvature
Measurements: 0.35 x 0.046 m

No.4 E 25220 Spear head
End of the Old Kingdom or First Intermediate
  Period
Origin: Kom Dara
Silk hafting
Well preserved
Measurements: 0.144 x 0.023 m

No.5 E 10950-C Axe
End of the Old Kingdom or First Intermediate
  Period
Transversal tab hafting
Heavily corroded
Measurements: 0.315 x 0.051 m

No.6 E 11025-I Axe
First Intermediate Period or Middle Kingdom
Origin: Kom el Gaab
Transversal tab hafting
Black surface containing organic elements
Measurements: 0.287 x 0.42 m

No.7 E 11208 Axe
First Intermediate Period or Middle Kingdom
Transversal tab hafting. The wooden handle

enters into the cylindrical metallic part
Leather strap on the lower part of the
  handle
Well preserved metal
Measurements: 0.718 x 0.09 m with handle

No.8 N 2166 Axe
First Intermediate Period or Middle Kingdom
Transversal tab hafting
Strong oxidation
Measurements: 0.435 x 0.065 m

No.9 E 11210 Axe
Middle Kingdom
Longitudinal tab hafting
Quite heavily corroded
Measurements: 0.099 x 0.083 m

No.10 E 12635 Axe
Middle Kingdom
Origin: Assiut
Longitudinal tab hafting — cutting edge on
  the curvilinear part of the periphery
Well preserved metal
Measurements: 0.086 x 0.086

No.11 E 12639 Axe model
Middle Kingdom
Origin: Assiut
Longitudinal tab hafting mounted on wood
Well preserved
Measurements: 0.29 x 0.052 m with handle

No.12 E 12005-B Axe model
Middle Kingdom
Origin: Assiut
Longitudinal tab hafting mounted on wood
Well preserved
Measurements: 0.296 x 0.054 m with handle

No.13 E 12005-C Axe model
Middle Kingdom
Origin: Assiut
Longitudinal tab hafting
Well preserved
Measurements: 0.044 x 0.042 m

No.14 E 12637 Axe model
Middle Kingdom
Origin: Assiut
Longitudinal tab hafting
Well preserved
Measurements: 0.045 x 0.042 m

No.15 E 10950-B Dagger blade
Middle Kingdom (?)
Trilobed shoulder with two rivets
Very strong oxidation
Length: 0.145 m

No.16 E 10928 Dagger
Middle Kingdom or Second Intermediate
  Period
Handle with wood decoration, end in curved
  bone
Medium oxidation
Length: 0.245 m

No.17 E 677 Dagger
Middle Kingdom or Second Intermediate
   Period
Same model as above number, but the
   wooden decorations have disappeared
Strong oxidation
Length: 0.287 m

No. 18 E 25689 Sickle-sword of Ramses II
New Kingdom
Well preserved
Length: 0.567 m

No.19 N 2116 Sickle-sword of Minmesout
New Kingdom
Dog or jackal on the handle
Well preserved
Length: 0.235 m

No. 20 E 11230 Axe
New Kingdom
Representing the goddess Thoueris and
   a gazelle
Well preserved
Measurements: 0.101 x 0.069

No. 21 E 5980 Axe
New Kingdom
Longitudinal tab hafting
Double-edged bevelled cutting edge
   Wooden handle
Partially corroded
Measurements: 0.597 x 0.152 m with handle

No. 22 E 3302 Axe
New Kingdom
Longitudinal tab hafting
Very heavy corrosion
Measurements: 0.136 x 0.092 m

No. 23 AF 6582 Axe
New Kingdom
Longitudinal tab hafting with large sides,
   deeply bevelled on both surfaces
Well preserved
Measurements: 0.105 x 0.072 m

No. 24 N 2163 Dagger
New Kingdom
Wooden handle with metal braces; the top of
   the handle is made of bone
Quite heavy oxidation
Length: 0.265 m

No. 25 N 2113 A Dagger
New Kingdom
Wooden handle in metal braces;
   bore in wood
Well preserved
Length: 0.297 m

No. 26 N 2113 B Dagger
New Kingdom
Wooden handle in metal braces;
   bore in wood
Well preserved
Length: 0.285 m

No. 27 AF 677 Spear head
New Kingdom
Socket hafting
Medium oxidation
Measurements: 0.279 x 0.032 m

Results

These results are set down in summary tables. These twenty-seven objects are all made of a copper-based material, which can be classified into two large series: pure copper objects and bronze objects, that is, constituted of a secondary alloy of copper and tin. It is interesting that the objects from the Old to the Middle Empire are in pure copper, with the exceptions of numbers 7, 8, and 15, but the New Empire arms are in bronze. This is logical, and these results afford extra proof for a fact already noted.

In these bronze objects, the percentage of tin varies from 3.3 to 16.8 %. Three types of alloy contain less than 5 %, five types contain from 5 to 10 %, and twelve, more than 10 %. The alloys that contain tin in large quantities are more numerous. This is a fact we have noted in a number of Egyptian objects previously analyzed, and which we are continuing to study.

The second important finding is the absence of zinc as a major element of these alloys. These alloys contain very small traces, under 0.01%, of zinc, which is just a mineral impurity. The absence of zinc from the alloy seems characteristic of ancient Egypt. This fact has been verified by other analyses done in the Research Laboratory of the Museums of France. It must be pointed out that we have found very few objects containing up to 5 % zinc, and these objects are all dated from the Low Epoch or later.

Lead enters into these alloys only in the state of an impurity, in variable amounts up to 2 %. Object no. 19 (sickle-sword of King Minmesout) contains the most: 3.2 % for the handle, 2 % for the animal (the blade contains only 0.2 %). It is possible that this lead was added on purpose, in order to facilitate the casting of these two parts. Lead added in quantities up to 30 % is an aid in making alloys. The lead bronzes were classical in ancient Egyptian metallurgy, and we have found a great amount of these in the objects examined. In general, these pieces were roughly cast and were then refined with the sculptor's chisel.

Antimony is also an impurity common to minerals. The amount varies from 0.1% to 1.7 %. All the objects analyzed up to now contain antimony. Arsenic is also an impurity, but it seems to be a characteristic element of Egyptian bronzes and will certainly prove to be an important criterion in the classification we are undertaking. The amount of arsenic varies greatly, from 0.1% to more than 2 %. The standards we possess do not allow us at present to gauge arsenic in quantities greater than 2 %.

Table I

Elements found in analysis of the bronze series

Object no.	Cu	Sn	Pb	Sb	As	Fe	Ni	Mn	Zn	Al	Ag	Au	Mg
1	X	t	t	0.9	0.8	0.1	t	–	t	t	p	p	p
2	X	t	0.6	0.6	0.2	0.2	t	t	t	t	p	p	p
3	X	t	0.1	0.1	ps	0.1	0.1	–	t	t	p	p	p
4	X	t	0.1	0.9	1.9	0.2	t	t	t	t	p	p	p
5	X	0.1	0.1	1.7	0.5	0.3	t	–	t	t	p	–	p
6	X	t	0.5	1.2	0.5	0.2	t	–	t	t	p	–	p
7 blade + sheath	X	4.7	0.8	1.1	0.5	0.1	t	–	t	t	p	–	p
8	X	12.3	1.2	0.9	0.6	0.2	t	–	t	t	p	p	p
9	X	t	t	0.3	ps	0.2	t	–	t	t	p	p	p
10	X	0.2	0.1	1.0	0.1	0.3	t	t	t	t	p	p	p
11	X	t	t	0.6	1.0	0.7	t	t	t	t	p	–	p
12	X	t	t	0.5	0.8	0.4	t	t	t	t	p	–	p
13	X	t	t	0.9	0.8	0.3	t	t	t	t	p	–	p
14	X	t	t	0.5	0.3	0.3	t	t	t	t	p	–	p
15	X	10.7	2.3	0.4	0.5	0.1	0.2	–	t	t	p	–	p
16 sheath	X	5.0	1.7	1.0	ps	0.3	t	t	t	t	p	p	p
16 blade	X	6.6	0.8	1.0	0.1	0.2	–	t	t	t	p	–	p
17 sheath	X	t	t	0.4	0.5	0.1	0.1	t	t	t	p	–	p
17 blade	X	0.6	0.1	0.4	1.8	0.1	0.1	t	t	t	p	p	p
18 blade + sheath	X	7.0	0.1	0.1	0.9	0.3	0.2	t	t	t	–	–	p
19 sheath	X	10.2	3.2	1.0	0.4	0.1	t	–	t	t	p	p	p
19 blade	X	13.2	0.2	0.6	2.2	0.2	0.2	–	t	t	p	p	p
19 animal	X	8.7	2.0	0.7	0.3	0.1	t	–	t	t	p	p	p
20	X	3.3	0.5	0.5	0.6	0.2	0.3	–	t	t	p	p	p
21	X	12.8	0.2	0.5	0.4	0.2	0.2	t	t	t	p	p	p
22	X	16.8	0.1	0.5	0.1	0.1	t	–	t	t	p	–	p
23	X	9.9	t	0.8	0.1	0.1	t	t	t	t	p	–	p
24 blade + sheath	X	12.5	0.1	0.8	0.1	0.1	t	t	t	t	p	–	p
25 blade + sheath	X	10.5	t	0.6	0.2	0.1	t	–	t	t	p	–	p
26 blade + sheath	X	10.2	t	0.8	0.1	0.1	t	–	t	t	p	–	p
27	X	7.6	1.3	0.5	0.1	0.2	0.2	–	t	t	p	p	p

X: Constituent element.
p: present – not quantified.
t: small trace – less than 0.01%.
ps: strongly present – not quantified.

On first approximation, it seems that the pure copper objects contain the most arsenic. This element would therefore be an impurity native to copper.

Iron is always present in trace form, never exceeding 1%. It is a native impurity, as are also aluminum and magnesium. Nickel has been detected in all the objects, except in the dagger blade of no.16. It is in general found in traces below 0.01%, except in certain cases, and it never exceeds 0.3%. Manganese was discovered in a certain number of objects, but always less than 0.01%. This impurity could therefore be a factor in classifying. Silver is also present in very small traces. Only the sickle-sword of Ramses II (no.18) does not contain any silver. It is a native impurity of copper. The same can be said for gold, but the very small quantities make it difficult to detect. Cobalt and bismuth have not been detected in any of these 27 objects.

The normal order of classification, which goes from copper objects of the oldest periods to the bronze alloys of the New Empire, has been respected, except in three cases: the two axes, nos. 7 and 8, and the blade of a dagger, no.15. The shape of these two axes is characteristic of axes before the New Empire. It is interesting that these two objects, identical in shape, are the only two made of bronze. The bronze blade of dagger no.15 is dated Middle Empire, but without any certainty.

Of the five daggers examined, three (nos. 24, 25, 26) have the same composition of blade and handle. Number 17 is in pure copper, with clear differences in the impurities of the handle and blade. Dagger no.16 is in bronze with a low percentage of tin, the blade containing more tin than the handle.

The sickle-sword of Ramses II (no. 18) is in bronze, and the same alloy has been used for the blade and the handle. The tooth iron of King Minmesout (no. 19) is also in bronze, but the handle, the blade, and the dog or jackal lying on the handle, are made of three different alloys.

No sampling of these objects was possible in order to make metallurgical sections. It will be interesting to study these objects at a later date, and particularly to study the daggers by X- or gamma rays, in order to determine how they have been mounted.

Conclusion

The conclusions that can be drawn from these results, and from those already obtained at the Research Laboratory of the Museums of France, cannot be considered definitive until a great number of Egyptian objects have been analyzed in a systematic fashion. But we can already predict the orientation of these results: (1) the oldest objects seem to be, for the greatest part, made of pure copper; (2) the objects of the New Empire are in most cases in bronze, the quantity of tin being quite important (10 % and more); (3) the absence of zinc is the principal characteristic of Egyptian metallurgy, and zinc seems to appear in alloys only after the Low Epoch; and (4) arsenic will certainly be an important factor in classification. The presence of other elements, such as cobalt, manganese, and bismuth, will bring more precise details.

From now on, however, it will be necessary to deal with all this information by computer, and we are going to set up a card catalogue with punched cards. This will allow for the automated management of the archeological information and scientific results. We also hope, in the light of a great number of analyses, to build a classification based on numerous criteria, which will allow, without doubt, better knowledge of the metallurgy of ancient Egypt, and of ancient metallurgy in general.

ROBERT H. BRILL, WILLIAM R. SHIELDS, and J. M. WAMPLER

New Directions in Lead Isotope Research

At the 1965 seminar on the Application of Science in Examination of Works of Art held at the Museum of Fine Arts, Boston, we presented a paper dealing with isotope ratios of lead extracted from ancient objects.[1,2] It was demonstrated there that isotopic ratios can reveal information about the possible geographical origins of the leads studied and, consequently, about possible provenances of the objects from which the leads came. Since then research in this field has advanced considerably through the use of much more accurate and precise experimental methods and by the application of the technique to additional types of lead-containing materials.[3-5]

The usefulness of this technique centers around the fact that deposits of galena ore (lead sulfide) laid down at different geological times or under different geochemical circumstances may often vary considerably in isotopic composition. That is to say, lead deposits occurring in different mining regions may contain different relative proportions of the four stable isotopes of lead, Pb^{204}, Pb^{206}, Pb^{207}, and Pb^{208}. By determining the isotopic composition of lead extracted from ancient objects it becomes possible in some instances to match these compositions with those of ores from known mining regions. Even when direct connections cannot be made with specific mining regions, as is often the case, these data are nonetheless very valuable, for they serve to classify ancient objects into groups which contain the same kinds of lead and which, therefore, could have had a common origin.

Briefly, the advantages of this technique are that it requires only very small sample sizes, that isotopic compositions are quite insensitive to the chemical history of the objects studied, and that it is applicable to a wide variety of materials. It is this latter point, the versatility of this technique, which is to be emphasized in this paper.

There are two limitations which must always be borne in mind when interpreting lead isotope data. The first is that although a given lead deposit will have its characteristic isotope ratios, these ratios will not, in general, be unique to that deposit. Leads from different geographical sources — sometimes far removed from one another — may often be indistinguishable on the basis of isotope data if they result from geologically similar events. Therefore, although it is possible to assert that a particular lead definitely could not have come from some particular mining region, it is not usually possible to assert that a given lead must have come from some particular region, because there may be other regions which have leads of similar isotopic composition. The other limitation stems from the fact that in ancient times — as at present — lead and other metals were often salvaged and remelted to be used again. If leads from different sources are melted down together, the isotope ratio of the resulting mixture is somewhere

intermediate between the ratios of the starting metals.

At present, we know both of these problems exist, but we do not know just how serious either one will be as work progresses. Until a more comprehensive catalogue has been assembled of data on ores from mines actually suspected to have been exploited in early times, it will not be possible to assess the extent of ambiguity arising from different ores having similar ratios. Concerning the mixing problem, there is evidence that mixing occurred and sometimes that evidence comes in dramatic forms, such as the ingots and bronze statues recovered from ancient shipwrecks excavated off the coast of Turkey and in the Straits of Messina.[6] It is believed by the excavators that these metals were partial cargoes of scrap metal in transit from one port to another. On the other hand, our most recent data on lead extracted from Greek and Roman bronze coins provide good reason for encouragement that mixing might be less of a problem than we thought previously.[7] Of 54 coins studied, only 4 did not fall within the isotopic groups that one would expect according to their mint marks; and one of those turned out to be an ancient forgery. This implies that even with coins — a well-traveled form of metal — a consistent correlation persists between isotopic composition and geographical origin.

Because other aspects of this research are being reported elsewhere, it was decided to concentrate here on a group of objects selected to illustrate the versatility of lead isotope studies. These objects represent several very diverse types of historical materials, including metallic leads, bronzes, white-lead pigments, glasses, and silver and gold objects. Detailed descriptions of all the objects, along with pertinent references, are compiled in the catalogue at the end of the paper. The data are plotted in fig. 1.

We are now in the process of analyzing all of our samples of ores from ancient mining regions. Therefore, rather than attempt to draw definitive conclusions concerning the geographical origin of the leads dscussed here, we shall for the present limit our interpretations to a few general comments.

Three Early Bronzes

Ancient bronzes often contain substantial and deliberately added proportions of lead. Professor Caley, for example, has reported analyses of Greek bronze coins dating from about 330 to 307 B.C. which contain between 3 and 5 % lead; and mid-second century B.C. bronze coins often contain as much as 10—30 % lead.[8] But high lead contents are by no means restricted to bronzes used for coinage. By at least the third century B.C., and on into Roman times, bronzes used for making statues and other objects were often heavily leaded.

By extracting lead chemically from small samples of leaded bronzes, it becomes possible to study them by the same

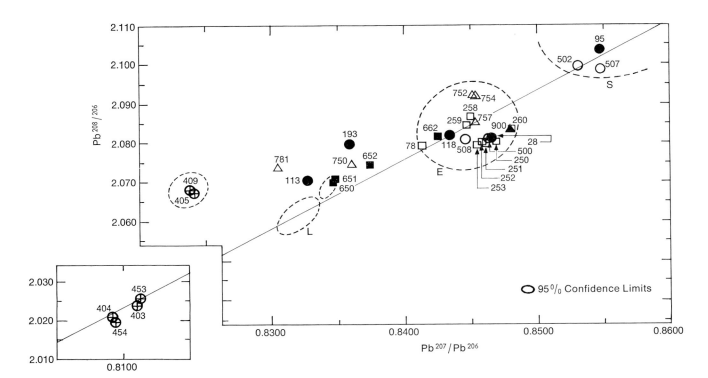

1. Isotope ratios for lead extracted from various types of early materials. ● galena ores; ■ bronzes; ○ white leads; □ caming; ⊕ glasses; △ silvers; ▲ golds. The loops labeled L, E, and S are groups described in earlier publications. The loop to the far left encloses several Mesopotamian and Iranian glasses and that to the right of L contains leads from a few specimens from Asia Minor. The diagonal line indicates the general trend of all data on ancient objects. Offset portion shows Egyptian glasses.

scheme as is applied to metallic lead objects. Our major effort with bronzes to date has been the study of Greek and Roman coins mentioned above. This study has proved valuable not only from a numismatic point of view but also because it provides an excellent background against which data on other bronze objects can be compared. At present we have studied the lead in about a dozen bronze statues and other objects but have selected only three of them for mention here.

The first object is a large fragment from an over-lifesize draped male statue found at Casanuovo (near Reggio), and now in the Museum of Fine Arts in Boston. It dates from about the second century A.D. Chemical analyses of two samples removed from this object were carried out by Miss Heather Lechtman, who later provided us with some of the sample which remained after her analyses. The samples were found to contain 19.9 % and 23.8 % lead. The second bronze is of Etruscan origin. This is a thymiaterion of the third century B.C.

in the collection of the R. H. Lowie Museum in Berkeley. Miss Lechtman's analysis of this object showed that it contains 27.8 % lead. The third bronze is a head of Julia Domna at the Fogg Art Museum. This object, found in Syria, was recently published by Ulrich Hiesinger,[9] and is thought to date from a few years prior to A.D. 200. It contains 21.2 % lead, according to Miss Lechtman's analysis. The three bronze objects are illustrated in figs. 2 through 4.

Previously we have found several leads from objects excavated both in Italy and in the Near East which are within one diffuse and rather broad range of isotopic compositions. This range was designated in previous publications as "Group X," which isotopically falls between Groups L and E.[10] (The latter correspond, respectively, to leads of the "Laurion" and "English" types, both of which differ from the leads in "Group X.") This overlapping of leads from Italy and the Near East is perhaps the most vexing example that has arisen of the ambiguity

2. Large fragment of bronze statue, ca. 2nd cent. A.D. Museum of Fine Arts, Boston. 01.7524. (*Master Bronzes from the Classical World,* no. 237, p. 248.)

brought about by leads from different regions having similar isotopic makeups, but it is hoped that the picture will be straightened out to some extent when additional data on ores have been obtained.

The lead in the large statue fragment (Pb-650) is very much like that contained in a small group of leads extracted from bronze coins minted in Asia Minor.[11] We have also analyzed an ore from Balya in northeastern Turkey (Pb-113) which is quite close to those leads in its composition. Our suspicion is that this lead, despite the statue's having been found in southern Italy, could be of more easterly origin, namely, Asia Minor; but this must remain only a suspicion until more ores from Italy and other large bronzes have been studied.

The thymiaterion lead (Pb-652) seems to be related to three or four leads of undisputed Italian origin (not plotted here), which is to be expected. Not far from this sample on the graph (but deviating from the general trend) is an ore sample from the Populonia region (Pb-193). These two leads are not identical, but they are near enough alike to support the hypothesis that at least some Etruscan bronzes contain leads from this region. This comes as no surprise because of the long-standing history of mining in the region, but the inference drawn is not a trivial one, for we know that ores occurring in some nearby mining regions — Sardinia and Bottino — are of quite different isotopic compositions. We shall be very interested to have the results of experiments planned on two further groups of Etruscan and Roman bronzes provided by Mr. Arthur Beale and Dr. Arthur Steinberg.

The lead from the Julia Domna portrait (Pb-662) differs from those in the other two bronzes, even though it is not far displaced from them on the graph. It is surrounded by a dozen or more other leads from various materials which are associated either with the area around Istanbul or with sites which we might best describe as being located in the Levant. Some of the sites represented by these objects are Constantinople, Heraclea, Soloi in Cilicia, Antioch, Shavei Zion, Beth Shean, Jelemie (not far from present-day Haifa), and Alexandria. Lead of the sort found in these objects, and in the rest of the "Group X" specimens, seems to have circulated freely around the coast of the eastern Mediterranean in a sort of plumbeous crescent. The lead in the Julia Domna head is almost identical to an ore (Pb-118) coming from near the Black Sea Coast not far from Trabzon; but there may be other ores of this type located closer to the general region described. For example, Forbes[12] mentions lead deposits at Gebel Akra (near Antioch) — although he seems to doubt that they were worked in ancient times.

Our findings on the Julia Domna are consistent with Hiesinger's "eastern" attribution of the object, which is based not only on the fact that the object was found at Selimiyeh in Syria

3. Bronze thymiaterion, 3rd cent. B.C. R. H. Lowie Museum, Berkeley. (Sample Pb-652.) Photo courtesy of Lowie Museum of Anthropology, University of California, Berkeley.

4. Bronze portrait of Julia Domna, ca. A.D. 200. Fogg Art Museum. (Sample Pb-662.) Photo courtesy of the Fogg Art Museum.

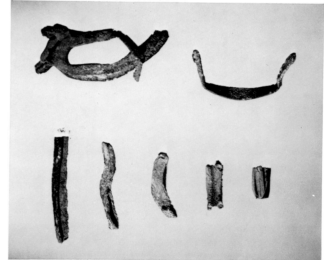

5. Strips of lead caming from medieval stained glass windows. Top: Coventry (Pb-250 and 251). Bottom: Canterbury (Pb-252 and 253); Zerek Camii (Pb-258 and 259); Heiligenkreuz (Pb-260).

but on stylistic and historical considerations as well. There is some question as to whether the bronze was cast nearby — at Julia Domna's native city of Emesa possibly — or in some more distant locality. While isotope data cannot be expected to tell us where the bronze was actually cast, it is true that once we learn the geographical source of the rest of this "Levantine" lead we shall also know the source of the lead contained in this particular object. But perhaps this case illustrates another point. It may sometimes be that the association of the lead from some specific object with some specific ore deposit is not really as important as being able to associate it with the lead found in other objects.

White Lead Pigments in Paintings

One of the most ubiquitous pigments in the history of art materials is white lead. It has been found in a Fayoum painting;[13] its preparation was discussed by early authors (Pliny, Theophilus, and Vitruvius, for example); and it seems to have been in more or less continuous use, throughout the Western world from Roman times to the present. There are probably few painters of note or otherwise who did not at one time or another in their careers make some use of this pigment. Therefore, in the study of the history of paintings, which is so fraught with questions of who, when, or where — not to mention questions of authenticity — isotope investigations of lead-containing pigments might prove very fruitful.

Since these prospects were originally raised at the 1965 seminar, a suite of samples of white lead and of lead-tin and lead-antimony yellow pigments has been assembled, but experimental work has only recently been begun on them. Our experience with other lead-containing materials has indicated that high-accuracy and high-precision data are indispensable if real benefit is to be obtained from lead isotope studies.[14] Because pigment samples are often notoriously small and likely to consist more of vehicle or varnish than pigment itself, the initial surveying experiments were delayed until instrumental techniques were developed which would yield acceptably high accuracy on what seem to be diminishingly small samples. Now that these methods have been developed,[15] the survey in underway.

It is difficult to say what the greatest potential of this research is until more data are in hand. The questions directly related to lead isotope information are those involving "where," but it could be that questions of the "who" and "when" types might also someday be resolvable indirectly. We hope that patterns will be found circumscribing the works of individual painters, or schools of painters and localities, or of different periods within the works of an individual artist. It is reasonable to expect that the earlier the period the more likely the data are to make sense in a straightforward way, because there

probably was less commerce — or at least fewer production centers — in earlier periods. While awaiting the outcome of a full body of data there are presented here a few examples of initial results for the purpose of informing curators that this method has something of value to offer.

One important favorable factor concerning the sampling of white leads is that it was often used as a ground, and there are fewer objections to removing a sample of white ground smeared over the edge of a support, or seeping through the back of a canvas, than to removing paint from central figures or highlights. Unfortunately, in earlier times the lead-containing yellow pigments were often used primarily for highlights and are consequently more difficult to sample. The samples discussed here are all of white lead and were collected by Dr. Robert Feller of the Mellon Institute, who is a principal participant in this research.

Sample Pb-500 is of white lead from a painting with a Dutch attribution, painted in 1651. The lead is virtually identical to a Derbyshire ore (Pb-28) and a group of metallic leads known to have come from that region. While one is faced here with the customary, troublesome ambiguity about ores from different regions having the same isotope ratios, we feel this is reasonably convincing evidence that the lead in this pigment is of English origin. This gains credence through some extremely useful information passed on to one of the authors by Mr. Trevor Brighton. Mr. Brighton pointed out that there was a well-established trade connection which brought Derbyshire lead, via the port of Hull, to the Low Countries during the 17th and 18th centuries. The pigment, of course, need not have been manufactured in England, but could just as well have been prepared in the Low Countries from English lead that found its way into a local workshop.

A second painting from the Low Countries, sample Pb-508, a Flemish panel painting of ca. 1520, was found to contain lead similar to that from the Dutch painting. But this determination had to be made on a very small sample, and the technique used did not yield as accurate and precise a value. Therefore, it is possible either that this lead might actually be identical to the Derbyshire lead, or it might be slightly different, resembling, for instance, some leads known to occur in Yorkshire.[16] In any event, it looks like an English lead.

In contrast to the first two white leads mentioned, two samples coming from Italian paintings are entirely different from the "English" leads. These samples are from a painting attributed to the school of Titian, which was done in the 16th century (Pb-502), and a Tuscan panel painting of ca. 1300 (Pb-507). Both of these are in a range of isotopic composition which includes leads from other types of objects (mosaic tesserae and bronzes) associated with northern and central Italy. Ores with this type of lead are known to occur in Italy, but we have also analyzed metallic leads of Roman dates excavated in Spain and on Majorca which have similar compositions.[17]

An important association arises here, however, because one of the few lead ores we have yet been able to analyze from Italy is very much like that in the two Italian white leads. This ore (Pb-95) came from galena deposits at Bottino, a mining region which has a well-documented history of having been worked in the Middle Ages and later under Cosimo I in the 16th century. The galena ores there apparently are unusually rich in silver, which explains why they were being worked extensively. In order for the lead to be cupeled for silver, however, very great quantities of lead had to be produced first. Therefore, lead from the Bottino mines must have been used in considerable quantities throughout central Italy and could well have been employed for making the white lead pigments being used by some Tuscan painters.

A survey — even a cursory one — of ores from other deposits known to have been worked from the Middle Ages and later in Italy (for example, those in the Montieri region near Sienna) would be extremely valuable for the interpretation of data on Italian pigments.

As a matter of incidental interest, the lead in a specimen of white lead of fairly recent date (Pb-501) collected in Kansu Province in China in 1925 by E. W. Forbes has an isotopic composition which is entirely different from those discussed here. In fact, in order to plot it on the same graph as these data, the coordinates would have to be extended about sixfold to the right beyond the scale used here. This indicates that the lead is very old, geologically, which is consistent with a Chinese origin. The only other leads anything like this which we have so far found among our objects are those extracted from a Chou Chinese bronze ceremonial vessel, a piece of metallic lead from Ur, and a galena ore and lead coin from India.[18] Undoubtedly, however, the investigation of other East Asiatic lead-containing artifacts and materials will uncover many more similar specimens. We have on hand some useful samples of this sort provided by Professor Kazuo Yamasaki and Mr. W. T. Chase. It is clear that the findings presented here, as promising as they are, must be regarded as only preliminary. Considering how complicated the situation may be concerning lead in pigments, it will undoubtedly require a good deal of further research to develop any firm working rules.

Caming in Medieval Stained Glass Windows

There are many questions still to be answered concerning the provenance of medieval stained glasses and the relationships between different manufacturing centers and cathedral sites. In order to help answer some of these questions, various approaches, including chemical analyses of the glasses, oxygen isotope determinations, and other means of scientific investigations have been undertaken.[19] In this connection it seemed worthwhile to make a few trial experiments to see if isotope determinations on the lead camings holding the glasses in place might also be of help. We have, therefore, surveyed a few specimens of caming from Coventry, Canterbury, Heiligenkreuz, and the Zerek Camii in Istanbul (see fig. 5).

The results on these samples were as expected, that is, the use of locally available lead seemed to be verified. The Coventry and Canterbury specimens (Pb-250, 251, and Pb-252, 253, respectively) closely match a type of lead occurring in Derbyshire (Pb-28) — and perhaps in other parts of England as well. The Heiligenkreuz sample (Pb-260) is not very different from certain English ores, and if there were any a priori reason to connect them historically, the case could perhaps be argued further. It is far more likely, however, that this is another example of the "overlapping" problem; that is, that the Heiligenkreuz lead came from a deposit somewhere in Central Europe which is similar geologically to the English formations and therefore has a similar isotopic composition. It is interesting, however, that the lead in an actual piece of glass from a stained glass window from St. Michael's on Wachau (Pb-480) is entirely different from the lead in the Heiligenkreuz caming, even though it dates from only a few years later. (The St. Michael's glass dates from 1300—1310, and the window from which the Heiligenkreuz caming was removed dates from ca. 1295.) The lead in the glass is, in fact, different from all the other leads we have seen in our studies. It will be interesting to have the outcome on a suite of about 20 additional lead caming samples from windows in various other medieval settings, which are now being studied.

The specimens from the Zerek Camii (Pb-78, 258, and 259) are perhaps the most intriguing of this set, since there is some controversy over the place that these windows play in the history of stained glass. We already have chemical evidence on the glasses themselves[20] establishing that they are the production of an entirely different glassmaking tradition than windows in western Europe. This is in accord with Professor Megaw's views on the subject.[21] He has suggested that these windows are an example of stained glass of eastern manufacture which might predate their western counterparts.

The isotopic compositions of two of the caming samples are very close to one another, while the third sample differs somewhat. However, all three fall within the range containing the leads described above as coming from the Levant. They especially resemble leads from a few Roman bronze coins minted in Constantinople and Heraclea, and one of them (Pb-78) is a close match for lead extracted from a red opaque glass tessera from a 9th—10th century mosaic in Hagia Sophia. We believe, therefore, that the leads in the caming from the Zerek Camii windows have a general association with leads from eastern sources and that the evidence at hand so far indicates that those types of lead were used locally (in Constantinople) for other purposes, implying a local manufacture of the caming.

It may seem inconsequential to prove that local lead was used for the caming, because that might have been the case even if the glass itself had been transported from some distance, but it nevertheless strikes us as being one additional bit of evidence in a growing scientific case supporting Professor Megaw's viewpoint, that is, to the extent that the windows are of local manufacture.

Some Glass Cored Vessels

Ancient red, yellow, and green opaque glasses often contain from 3 to 30 % lead oxide. In the yellow and green opaques the lead is present in the form of $Pb_2Sb_2O_7$ or $PbSnO_3$, two yellow pigments; and in the reds, it had been added because it helped in the precipitation of cuprous oxide, which gives the glasses their red color.[22] Isotope determinations have been made on lead extracted from about 75 early glasses ranging in date from ca. 1500 B.C. until the 16th century A.D. The isotopic variation is considerable, spanning (with one important exception) approximately the same range as leads from most of the other ancient materials studied. Among the earlier glasses the data group the objects in some very interesting ways,[23] but in glasses of the late centuries B.C. and early centuries A.D. the data tend to spread out somewhat, indicating a multiplicity of sources and probably a certain degree of mixing. Both of these effects are quite reasonable if one considers glasses attributed to a site like Alexandria. The area had no ready supply of local lead and was also a very active trade center, through which goods from many far-flung places in the ancient world would have passed.[24]

One of the most significant results established so far is that the lead in the yellow opaque threading of at least some 18th dynasty cored vessels from Egypt is of local origin, and probably came from ore deposits in the Eastern Desert. Moreover, this lead is markedly different from that found in similar yellow threadings of two contemporaneous cored vessels studied from Nuzi and Tell al Rimah in Mesopotamia (Pb-408 and 409) (see fig. 6). The latter are part of a group also containing some later glasses from Nimrud (8th to 7th century B.C.) and some glasses and faience beads from Hasanlu (1000—800 B.C.). This group contains a type of lead which is distinctly different from other leads we have seen as yet, although it also includes some of the metallic lead finds from Nimrud. The two cored vessel leads are plotted on the graph within the small loop marking off this characteristic type of lead. The results imply that a lead of some recognizable type, probably coming from a highly localized source, was in use for many centuries for glass-making and related activities.[25] We hope, of course, that some-

6. Fragments of Mesopotamian glass cored vessels. Left: Nuzi, 1450—1375 B.C. (Pb-408). Right: Tell al Rimah, *ca.* 1500 B.C. (Pb-409).

7. Gold coin of John II Comnenus, 1118—1143 (Pb-900). Sample was taken by light filing on edge of coin. (Pierced hole was already in coin when received.)

day the actual location of the deposit will be identified.

The data on the Egyptian glasses (Pb-404, 405, 453, and 454) fall off the graph in the direction indicated by the offset portion. The association with ore deposits in the Eastern Desert is based on an ore sample from Um Gheig (Pb-137), and is well substantiated by determinations made on several samples of kohl removed from Egyptian alabaster cosmetic pots of various early dates.

Silver and Gold Coins and Other Objects

In ancient times most of the silver used for coins and works of art was probably obtained through cupellation, a process by which naturally occurring silver was extracted from lead. It is believed, therefore, that most ancient silvers should contain some traces of the parent leads from which they were obtained.

By extracting these traces of lead from silver coins or other objects, and using them for isotopic determinations, it thus becomes possible to apply the same scheme to silvers as has been applied to leads themselves.

Two special complications arise in the silver studies. Because of the inherent value of the metal itself, damaged objects or booty and worn or obsolete coins would never have been deliberately discarded but instead were saved to be melted down and used again. Compared with most other lead-containing materials then, there may be a greater probability that silvers might be mixtures of metal from different sources. In addition, there is (either rightly or wrongly) a mystique associated with precious metals from the ancient world, and curators are understandably more reluctant to have samples removed from these objects than they are from objects of more mundane metals. With recent improvements in techniques, however, sample size requirements have become so small that the quantities of metal sacrificed will in many instances be of much less value than the information gained from them.[26]

Fortunately, there was made available to us by the generosity of Professor A. A. Gordus a group of Sasanian coins[27] ideally suited for the initial exploration of silver objects. These coins had all previously been sampled for chemical analysis, so that the removal of small additional quantities of metal raised no objections. Secondly, the coins were well dated and came from known mints; but most importantly they also provide a basis for approaching some other most significant art historical problems, such as that of the origin and dating of Sasanian silver objects.

We have so far determined ratios for only eight silver coins and three samples removed from silver objects, two of which are of alleged Sasanian origins. At this early stage it is difficult to appraise the overall prospects, but we shall report some of the initial findings.[28] The data indicate that there is a spread in the samples. They generally cover the same range as the Groups E and S. This spread is probably the result of both mixing effects and the natural variability among the galena ores drawn upon.

Actually the samples do pair off somewhat rather than fill in the range involved. Two of the coins studied (Pb-752 and Pb-754) are of Shapur II and Khousrou I. These fall roughly at the central tendency of this small group of silvers. Two very interesting samples are Pb-750 and Pb-781. The first is a Parthian coin, the other a bit of metal, perhaps scrap from a silver-smithing shop, excavated at Nushijan. The latter dates from either the Achaemenid or the Parthian period. These samples both vary from the Sasanian coins and fall more or less in the old "Group X." However, they have unusual Pb^{204} contents, which may become a means of identifying some specific ore deposit.[29]

Interestingly, an Umayyad silver dirhem minted in Damascus (Pb-757) corresponds closely to a group of leads extracted from bronze coins in use in the same region several centuries earlier. These leads fall just at the limit of the range of "Levantine" leads referred to earlier. This probably indicates a long-standing exploitation of one special lead deposit by metallurgists of the region. We also have under study now some additional Parthian, Greek, and Roman silver coins provided by Professor Caley and expect that the results on these specimens may help in the interpretation of the silver specimens reported here.

Similar possibilities suggest themselves for the study of early gold objects, but the picture is a little different from that involving the silvers. Chemical analyses of ancient golds are not very common, but at least some specimens contain appreciable proportions of lead. It is not quite as clear, however, as it is with the silvers, how that lead has come to be in the gold. The lead may be a natural accompanying trace occurrence or it may have been introduced by metallurgical processing, or both. One might anticipate, too, that the mixing problem could be serious with gold, because of its great value. On the other hand, it is possible that the sources of gold, particularly in earliest times, were more limited and there may be fewer isotopic types of lead to be dealt with. Despite these signs of caution, it nevertheless seems very worthwhile to explore the possibilities. Even if the applications were ultimately limited to only a few early sources, distinctions among, for example, Egyptian, Mesopotamian, and Aegean gold objects would be very valuable to archaeologists. Such studies should ultimately be expanded to include determinations on geological samples from gold-mining regions.

At present only one gold has been analyzed, and that has produced a very interesting result. The sample was from a Byzantine coin (Pb-900), a nomisma of John II Comnenus (1118—43). The coin is illustrated in fig. 7. The lead in this gold is an almost perfect match for that in the lead caming from the Heiligenkreuz window (Pb-260) discussed above. This match may be only coincidental, because gold from many sources was undoubtedly in circulation in the Byzantine world, and it probably contained lead of various isotopic compositions. But the match is so close that one cannot dismiss it without some speculation as to whether these two metals could have had a common origin. There are several lead-producing regions located not far from Heiligenkreuz, and at least one of these, the Tauern range, was also a gold field in early times. It is entirely possible that gold from one of these regions could have reached Constantinople (either during the Middle Ages or earlier) by way of trade with Central Europe along the Danube, or through Venice. Therefore, these two objects, which are of such incongruous types, could contain metals having a common origin. This possibility leads to a familiar situation. Once again, the results on a single historical object leave us wishing for further data on ores; in this instance, ores from silver- and gold-producing regions which might have had connections with the Byzantine world.

Acknowledgment

The analyses reported here were performed at the National Bureau of Standards by I. L. Barnes, T. J. Murphy, and their co-workers of the Analytical Mass Spectrometry Section, and by one of the authors (J. M. W.) while he was a guest worker at the bureau.

Catalogue of Samples

(Where references are cited only as numbers, these refer to references and notes in the main text.)

Galena Ores

Pb-28 Great Rutland Cavern (Roman Steps), Matlock, Derbyshire, England. Collected by R. H. Brill and Archie Sprinthall, Matlock. (0.001% Ag). Ref. 1, 2, 4, 5.

Pb-95 Bottino, Tuscany, Italy. From Brian H. Mason; American Museum of Natural History, no. 917. (0.18% Ag).

Pb-113 Balya (near Balikesir), Turkey. From Myles Walsh, courtesy Rasih ve Ihsan, mine owners. (0.08—0.15% Ag). Ref. 5.

Pb-118 Yukari Maden Köyü (near Artvin), Turkey. From Myles Walsh, courtesy Mining Assistance Commission. (0.05% Ag). Ref. 5.

Pb-137 Um Gheig (25° 30′ N—34° 30′ E), Eastern Desert, Egypt; from Middle Miocene limestone, gypsum and evaporite series. From A. M. Abdel-Gawad then with the Atomic Energy Establishment, Inchess, U.A.R., Ref. 1, 2, 4.

Pb-193 Campiglia Marittima, Italy. From Gabor Dessau, University of Pisa. (0.02% Ag). Ref. 1, 2, 5.

Bronzes

Pb-650 Large fragment of draped male statue in bronze. Found at Casanuovo near Reggio; *ca.* second century A.D. Sample is from welding metal joining two large portions of cast drapery. Museum of Fine Arts, Boston; no. 01.7524. M.I.T. sample 177-2. Bronze contains 67.7% Cu, 3.1% Sn, 19.9% Pb. (Analysis by Heather Lechtman.) Ref. D. G. Mitten and S. F. Doeringer, *Master Bronzes from The Classical World,* Fogg Art Museum, 1967, no. 237, p. 248. Sample from Miss Lechtman.

Pb-651 From same object as Pb-650. Sample from protuberance of metal on inside of drapery. M.I.T. sample 177-4. Bronze contains 65.7% Cu, 6.6% Sn, 23.8% Pb. (Analysis by Heather Lechtman.) Sample from Miss Lechtman. Lead isotope ratios identical to Pb-650.

Pb-652 Thymiaterion of bronze. Etruscan; 3rd century B.C. R. H. Lowie Museum of Anthropology, Berkeley; no. 8-3406. Bronze contains 69.88% Cu, 6.46% Sn, 22.79% Pb. (Analysis by Heather Lechtman.) Ref. Mitten and Doeringer, *op. cit.,* no. 221, p. 218. See also sale catalogue of the Bourguignon Collection, *Vente Hôtel Drouot,* 18—20 Mars 1901, p. 51 (no. 224) and p. 58. Sample from Miss Lechtman.

Pb-662 Portrait head of Julia Domna in bronze, found at Selimiyeh in Syria; a few years prior to A.D. 200. Fogg Art Museum no.1956.19; M.I.T. sample 284. Bronze contains 66.4% Cu, 6.8% Sn, 21.1% Pb. (Analysis by Heather Lechtman.) Ref. Ulrich W. Hiesinger, *American Journal of Archaeology,* vol. 73, 1969, pp. 39—44, and plates 15 und 16. Sample from Miss Lechtman.

White Leads

Pb-500 White lead pigment from painting, "Girl in Red with Whistle." Dutch (?), 1651. Sample from Robert Feller, courtesy of Eric C. Hulmer.

Pb-501 White lead pigment from Lan-Chou-Pu, Kansu Province, China. Collected by E. W. Forbes in 1925. E. W. Forbes collection, Fogg Art Museum. Sample from Robert Feller.

Pb-502 White lead pigment from painting, "Portrait of a Lady." Italian, School of Titian, 16th century. Sample from Robert Feller, courtesy of Eric C. Hulmer.

Pb-507 White lead pigment from panel painting, "Madonna and Child." Italian, Tuscan, *ca.* 1300. Sample from Robert Feller courtesy of Eric C. Hulmer.

Pb-508 White lead pigment from panel painting, "St. Jerome and Lion." Flemish (?), *ca.* 1520. Sample from Robert Feller courtesy of Eric C. Hulmer.

Lead Caming

Pb-78 Caming from the Zerek Camii, Istanbul, *ca.* 1125. Found with fragments of stained glass windows in vaults beneath bema. From A. H. S. Megaw. Ref. 21.

Pb-250 Caming from Coventry Cathedral, 13th-14th century. Chapter House Trench I, found with glass fragments, December 1965. From Brian Hobley, Herbert Art Gallery and Museum.

Pb-251 Same source as Pb-250.

Pb-252 Caming from Canterbury Cathedral, *ca.* 1200—1220. From Jesse Tree Panels, thought to be original caming. From Madeline Caviness, courtesy of the Dean and Chapter of Canterbury Cathedral.

Pb-253 Same source as Pb-252.

Pb-258 Same source as Pb-78.

Pb-259 Same source as Pb-78.

Pb-260 Caming from Heiligenkreuz Stiftskirche, *ca.* 1295. From apse window. Sample from Eva Frodl-Kraft.

Glasses

Pb-404 Cane of yellow opaque glass. El Amarna, 18th Dynasty. Contains 6—10% lead in form of $Pb_2Sb_2O_7$ colorant-opacifier. University College, London. Ref. 4. From Harry Smith.

Pb-405 Same as 404, but color is slightly different.

Pb-408 Yellow opaque glass threading from cored vessel. Nuzi, 1450—1375 B.C. Glass is somewhat weathered but intact, and $Pb_2Sb_2O_7$ colorant-opacifier remains. Semitic Museum, Harvard University; Nuzi no. M 100/1. Ref. 4 and D. Barag in Oppenheim et al., *Glass and Glassmaking in Ancient Mesopotamia,* Corning, 1971; Nuzi no. 5 and note 29.

Pb-409 Weathered remains of yellow opaque threading from cored vessel. Tell al Rimah, *ca.*1500 B.C. Glass is completely weathered but traces of $Pb_2Sb_2O_7$ colorant-opacifier remain.

Institute of Archaeology, London; no. TR 3623. Ref. 4 and D. Oates, *Iraq,* XXIX, pt. 2, (1967), p. 93 and plate XXXVII. (Shows a similar object.) From David and Joan Oates.

Pb-453 Yellow opaque glass threading from cored vessel. El Amarna, 18th dynasty. University College, London; Box no. UC 22938. Ref. 4. From Barbara Adams.

Pb-454 Similar to Pb-453. From Box no. UC 22937.

Pb-480 Fragment of green transparent glass from stained glass window. St. Michael's i.d. Wachau, Austria, 1300–1310. Probably contains between 20 and 30 % PbO. Sample from Eva Frodl-Kraft.

Silver and Gold Objects

Pb-750 Silver coin, Parthian, *ca.* A.D. 100. University of Michigan no. 4066. Ref. 27. From Adon A. Gordus.

Pb-752 Silver coin, Sasanian, Shapur II, *ca.* A.D. 350. University of Michigan no.1815. Ref. 27. From Adon A. Gordus.

Pb-754 Silver coin, Sasanian, Khousrau I (regnal year 45), *ca.* A.D. 575. Minted at Zarang (?). University of Michigan no. 3977. Ref. 27. From Adon A. Gordus.

Pb-757 Silver coin. Umayyad, *ca.* A.D. 720. Minted in Damascus. University of Michigan no. 4024. Ref. 27. From Adon A. Gordus.

Pb-781 Small fragment of metallic silver, possibly scrap from silver-smithing shop. Nushijan, excavated fragment; Parthian or Achaemenid Period. University of Michigan no. H-2000. Ref. *Journal of the British Institute for Persian Studies,* vol. III, 1969. From Adon A. Gordus, courtesy of the British Institute of Persian Studies.

Pb-900 Gold coin. Nomisma of John II Comnenus 1118–1143. Minted in Constantinople. Ref. thought to be the same as no. 8, plate LXVI in *Imperial Byzantine Coins in the British Museum,* 1908; and no.11, plate LIII in J. Sabatier, *Monnaies Byzantines,* p.196 and plate LIII. This coin was sampled by a very light filing on its perimeter. The hole in the coin (fig. 7) was present *before* it was received for analysis. From Mr. Timothy Boatswain.

Notes

1. Brill, R. H., and Wampler, J. M. "Isotope Ratios in Archaeological Objects of Lead," in *Application of Science in Examination of Works of Art,* Boston, Museum of Fine Arts, 1965, pp.155–66.

2. For a somewhat earlier account see: Brill, R. H., and Wampler, J. M. "Isotope Studies of Ancient Lead," *American Journal of Archaeology,* 71 (1962) 63–77.

3. Brill, R. H. "Lead Isotopes in Ancient Glass," *Annales du 4e Congrès des Journées Internationales du Verre (1967),* Liège, 1969, pp. 255–61.

4. Brill, R. H. "Lead and Oxygen Isotopes in Ancient Objects," *Philosophical Transactions of the Royal Society London* A. 269, pp.143–164 (1970) [143]. This paper also appears in *The Impact of the Natural Sciences on Archaeology,* T. E. Allibone, ed. London, Oxford University Press, 1971.

5. Brill, R. H., and Shields, W. R. "Lead Isotope Studies of Ancient Coins," in *Methods of Chemical and Metallurgical Investigations of Ancient Coinage,* E. T. Hall and D. M. Metcalf, eds., London, Royal Numismatic Society, 1972.

6. Bass, G. F. "Cape Gelidonya: A Bronze Age Shipwreck," *Transactions of the American Philosophical Society,* New Series, 57, part 8, pp. 52–122, esp.117, (1967); D. I. Owen, "Picking up the Pieces," *Expedition,* 13, no.1 (1970), 25–29. A sample of lead from the Cape Gelidonya wreck was analyzed and reported in refs.1 and 2. Samples from the other wreck will also be studied.

7. See ref. 5.

8. Caley, E. R. "The Compositions of Ancient Greek Coins," *Memoirs of the American Philosophical Society,* XI, pp. 30, 41, 97, 101, *passim,* (1939).

9. Hiesinger, U. W. "Julia Domna: Two Portraits in Bronze," *American Journal of Archaeology,* 73 (1969), pp. 39–44 and plates 15 and 16.

10. See refs.1 and 2.

11. See ref. 5.

12. Forbes, R. J. *Studies in Ancient Technology,* vol. VIII, Leiden, E. J. Brill, 1964, p. 210. The same comments appear in his *Metallurgy in Antiquity,* Leiden, E. J. Brill, 1950, p.187.

13. G. L. Stout, "The Restoration of a Fayoum Portrait," *Technical Studies in the Field of the Fine Arts,* I (1932), 86.

14. See ref. 4.

15. With new techniques of high-accuracy mass spectrometry developed at the National Bureau of Standards, it is possible to obtain acceptable results on samples containing as little as one microgram of lead, although somewhat larger samples, weighing of the order of a few milligrams, are more convenient to work with and yield more accurate results. Accuracies of 0.05 to 0.10 % in the ratios reported here are routinely obtained on the larger samples. For materials having low lead contents the samples sacrificed must be sufficient to contribute the required minimum of one microgram of lead.

16. See ref. 5, sample Pb-49.

17. Unpublished results.

18. The Chinese sample is reported in refs.1 and 2, the Indian samples in ref. 5, and the object from Ur is as yet unpublished.

19. For a preliminary account see: Brill, R. H. "Scientific Studies of Stained Glass – A Progress Report," *Journal of Glass Studies,* 12 (1970), 185–92.

20. Brill, R. H. *The Corning Museum of Glass Research Program on Medieval Stained Glasses,* April 1970.

21. Megaw, A. H. S. "Notes on Recent Work of the Byzantine Institute in Istanbul," *Dumbarton Oaks Papers,* no.17, pp.335–64, esp.362–63 (1963).

22. For general information on the scientific investigation of ancient glasses, including these two specific points, see: Brill, R. H. "The Scientific Investigation of Ancient Glasses," *Proceedings of the Eighth International Congress on Glass, 1968,* Society of Glass Technology, Sheffield, 1969, pp.47–68.

23. See refs. 1–3 and especially ref. 4.

24. The point, although a valid one, may not in fact happen to apply specifically to Alexandria, for even though much glass is traditionally attributed to Alexandria, there are those who doubt the existence of glass manufacturing there because of a lack of archaeological evidence.

25. See ref. 4.

26. See note 15 for information on sample sizes. In the case of metallic silvers and golds which contain as little as 0.1% lead, a minimum sample volume of approximately 1 mm³ is all that is required. If the lead content is greater, the minimum sample size is proportionately smaller.

27. See Dr. Gordus' contribution in this book and also those in refs. 4 and 5, as well as: A. A. Gordus, "Rapid Non-Destructive Activation Analysis of Silver in Coins," in *Science and Archaeology,* R. H. Brill, ed., Cambridge, Mass., M.I.T. Press, 1971, chapter 10.

28. A fuller account appears in ref. 5.

29. Although Pb[204] data are routinely plotted for evaluation it is not usually necessary to publish them in accounts of this sort. The Pb[204] data are most often redundant in that they rarely differentiate among samples any further than the Pb[208]/Pb[206] versus Pb[207]/Pb[206] plots as presented here.

ROBERT E. OGILVIE

Applications of the Solid State X-Ray Detector to the Study of Art Objects

The liquid nitrogen cooled solid state X-ray detector provides a new technique that can be applied to a wide variety of problems associated with the study of art objects. The solid state X-ray detector has many advantages over other means of detection conventionally used in X-ray spectroscopy and X-ray diffraction. It will become obvious that the advantage of the solid state X-ray detector is the simultaneous analysis of the complete X-ray spectrum that is emitted and/or diffracted from the specimen. In X-ray spectroscopy we can use a variety of excitation sources, which include X-rays, gamma rays, electrons, or other charged particles. Here we will concern ourselves only with X-rays and electrons, although the principles of analysis are the same no matter what type of excitation source is used. Probably the most interesting use of the solid state detector in the study of art objects, or in fact the study of many other types of polycrystalline materials, is the energy dispersion X-ray diffraction technique developed by Giessen and Gordon (*Science,* 159 [1968], 973). With this technique it is possible in many cases to obtain X-ray spectrograms which identify the phases present in the specimen in a matter of a few minutes.

In the techniques that will be described here, the solid state X-ray detector must be coupled with a multichannel analyzer, which has the capability of displaying the entire energy spectrum received by the detector on a cathode ray tube. Other means of readout include teletype, tape (magnetic or paper), or an X-Y plotter. The advances of energy-dispersive X-ray spectroscopy in recent years have been due to the fantastic improvement in the resolution of the solid state semiconductor and its associated low noise preamplifier, linear amplifier, and other power supplies.

The Solid State Detector System

The solid state detector is in some ways very similar to a gas-filled ionization chamber; that is, a photon enters the detector and produces a number of free charge carriers which is proportional to the energy of the photon. The choice of detector materials is limited to silicon or germanium. However, silicon has proved to be the better choice because of the deterioration of the germanium detector at room temperature.

The silicon detector is illustrated in fig.1. The high purity silicon single crystal, which is usually between 4 mm to 10 mm in diameter, has lithium diffused across its 3 mm thickness. The purpose of the lithium is to neutralize the charge of impurity centers. This produces an intrinsic zone where the X-ray photons produce the electron-hole pairs. The X-ray side has 200 A of gold evaporated on its surface to allow a negative voltage to be applied. This voltage will vary between 1000 and 2000. There will be a narrow region between the gold and the intrinsic region which is called the dead layer. The X-ray

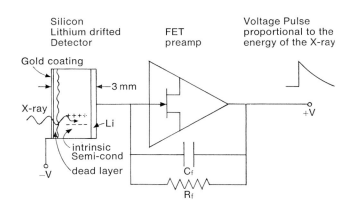

1. Schematic of the silicon lithium drifted X-ray detector.

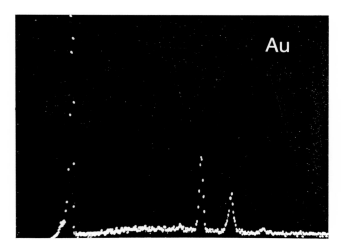

2. X-ray spectra from a Lydian gold coin, minted in Sardis about 550 B.C.

photon must pass through this layer before the photon can produce an active photoelectron, which in turn produces a series of electron-hole pairs. The number of electron-hole pairs will be given by the equation

$$N = E_p/\varepsilon$$

where E_p is the energy of the photon (eV) and ε the average energy necessary to produce an electron-hole pair. The value of ε at liquid nitrogen temperature is taken as 3.8 eV. We see that Cu K_α (8.04 keV) will produce 2115 electron pairs. This process is subject to statistical fluctuations and also a broadening in the final pulse distribution due to noise in the detector and preamplifier.

The free charge carriers will then migrate toward the collection electrodes under the influence of the applied electric field.

The electron pulse will go to the cooled field effect transistor, which is located in the cryostat. In addition there are several states of gain outside the cryostat and this makes up the pre-amplifier. The pulse is then shaped and amplified in the main amplifier and made compatible with the multichannel analyzer. The pulse height measurement consists of an analog-to-digital conversion by charging a capacitor to the peak voltage of the input pulse and then discharging it at a constant rate. During this period of discharge the address register counts pulses derived from an oscillator, and this register subsequently designates which memory address is to be incremented. Every pulse delivered to the analyzer adds "one" to the appropriate memory location. During the time of measurement of the X-rays the spectrum is continually being stored and the results can be viewed at any time on the cathode ray tube display.

A typical spectrum from a Lydian gold coin is illustrated in fig. 2. The resolution of the system is usually measured by the full width at half maximum intensity (FWHM). The width at 0.1 maximum has proved to be a better judge of the system. Assuming that the spectral line has a Gaussian distribution, then the total broadening that we observe is given by the following:

$$FWHM \text{ (volts)} = \left[\left(\begin{array}{c} \text{statistical} \\ \text{fluctuations in} \\ \text{electron} - \text{hole prod.} \end{array} \right)^2 + \left(\begin{array}{c} \text{electronic} \\ \text{noise} \end{array} \right)^2 + \left(\begin{array}{c} \text{detector} \\ \text{noise} \end{array} \right)^2 \right]^{1/2}$$

Fig. 3 illustrates that electronic noise becomes the major influence on resolution below 11 keV and detector statistics above this.

It is also important to know the efficiency of the silicon detector. Fig. 4 shows how the low absorption of silicon for X-rays above 40 keV results in a low efficiency and below 1.0 keV the absorption in the detector window determining the lower limit. The dead layer in the detector also contributes to a lower limit of detection.

The Electron Microanalyzer

The electron microanalyzer has proved its worth as a high spatial resolution quantitative instrument. However, its use as a tool for examination of art objects has been very limited. The reason for this of course is that with the EMA we can examine only small objects, and usually one is reluctant to remove a small sample from a valuable art object. But an interesting example of a suitable specimen that will fit into the standard electron microanalyzer is illustrated in fig. 5. This Lydian gold coin, upon close examination, was found to contain small,

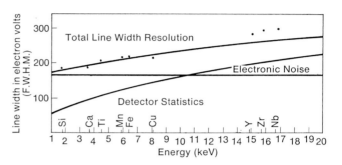

3. Full width at half maximum of X-ray lines as a function of energy.

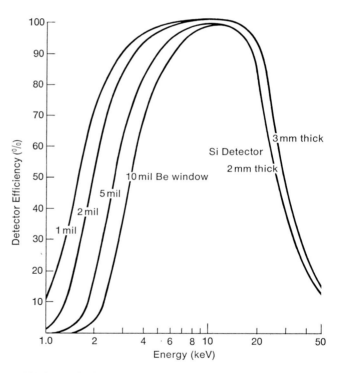

4. Efficiency of solid state X-ray detector as a function of energy.

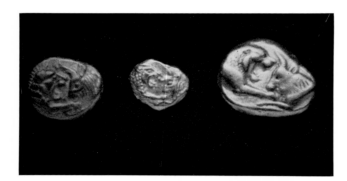

5. Lydian gold coin.

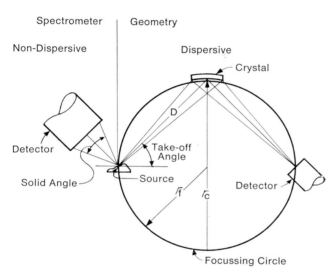

6. Geometry dependence of solid state detector and X-ray spectrometer.

bright metallic particles imbedded in the gold matrix. Analysis of these particles proved that they were a platinum—40 % iridium alloy. The results indicate that the coin was stamped, in the Sardis mint, from a gold nugget.

The time needed to get an X-ray spectrum with the electron microanalyzer is usually less than one minute. However, when one tries to detect low concentrations, longer times are needed, although the time is still much less than that needed for a scan with the X-ray spectrometer. Another important point is that the specimen is usually very irregular and with the X-ray spectrometer the X-ray source must lie on the focussing circle. With the solid state system, however, this is not the case. Fig. 6 illustrates this point.

The scanning electron microscope has the unique capability of focussing the electron beam down to 200 A in diameter, and

the specimen stage is usually better adapted to handle larger specimens. Most of the SEM's today have been fitted with a solid state detector just for the purpose of obtaining some qualitative information in a very short time. Our SEM with the Ortec solid state detector is illustrated in fig. 7.

X-Ray Excitation

Since most art objects will not fit into the electron micro-analyzer or scanning electron microscope, it is better to use an X-ray source to produce the excitation of the characteristic X-rays within the specimen. We have adapted an Ortec detector to the General Electric diffractometer. With this system we can do normal X-ray fluorescent analysis with the detector placed at a high 2θ value or X-ray diffraction by the Giessen-Gordon technique at low 2θ values. In the diffraction technique the

7. Cambridge scanning electron microscope with Ortec solid state detector.

$$\lambda = 2d \sin\Theta$$
$$d = \lambda / 2 \sin\Theta$$
$$d = 6.2 / E \sin\Theta \qquad \lambda(\text{Å}) = 12.4 / E(\text{keV})$$
$$d = K / N \qquad E = \frac{dE}{dN} N + E_o$$

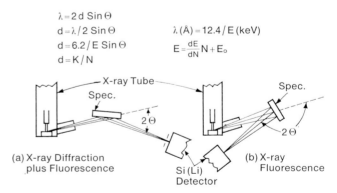

8. Schematic of the X-ray detector position for (a) X-ray diffraction plus fluorescence and (b) X-ray fluorescence.

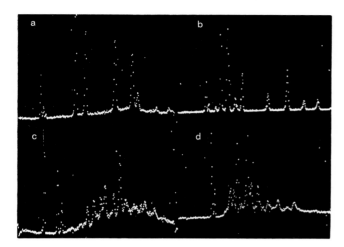

9. X-ray diffraction patterns from (a) Al, (b) W, (c) $CuCl_2 \cdot 2H_2O$ (d) $2PbCo_3 \cdot Pb(OH)_2$.

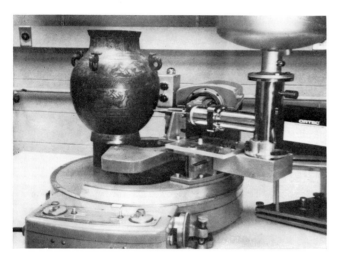

10. Examination of Chinese bronze with solid state X-ray detector.

detector is fixed at a 2 θ value of about 20° to 25°. Since the *d* spacing of the *(hkl)* planes in our specimen is fixed and with the fixed detector position we have fixed θ, therefore, from Bragg's law we see that the specimen will detect particular wavelengths (λ) from the continuous spectrum. Therefore different λ's will diffract which have different energies and will then appear as peaks in our multichannel analyzer. The geometry of this method is illustrated in fig. 8. Several simple diffraction patterns are illustrated in fig. 9.

The standard X-ray diffractometer is not well suited to handle large specimens, but fig.10 illustrates a fairly large Chinese bronze that was quickly analyzed at a large number of places. A specially designed system has been put into operation at the Boston Museum of Fine Arts which is capable of analyzing very large paintings which are placed on an easel and the area to be examined is easily moved in front of the X-ray collimator. The normal collimator is 1.0 mm in diameter, but areas as small as 0.1 mm in diameter can be analyzed. However the time for analysis becomes very long.

Conclusions

The solid state X-ray detector has proved to be very well suited to rapid chemical analysis from selected areas on a wide variety of art objects. The detector has also proved useful for the determination of phases present in paint pigments and to obtain information about the texture of metal objects; that is, one can easily show a cold work, recrystallized, or cast texture.

When all of this information is brought together the museum curator can more easily determine the materials used, the technique of fabrication, and the thermal treatments used in making the art object.

Acknowledgments

Would like to acknowledge the help of Ortec Incorporated, in particular Mr. Lee Munz and Dr. Dale Gedcke, for their assistance in obtaining a high resolution solid state X-ray detector, and also the help of Mr. William Young of the Boston Museum of Fine Arts for supplying not only many art objects but information concerning their source and other information that only a museum curator could supply.

FLORENCE E. WHITMORE and **WILLIAM J. YOUNG**

Application of the Laser Microprobe and Electron Microprobe in the Analysis of Platiniridium Inclusions in Gold

In the past the museum analyst has encountered a great reluctance on the part of some museum curators to routinely submit objects for analysis. The curator is responsible for the well-being of the object and fears the analyst will demand a sample that will disfigure it. Classical methods of analysis demand a fairly large sample and, while a curator may be sympathetic to science, in that he feels all possible information should be obtained from an object, he has been in a constant dilemma, weighing the results of analysis against the care in handling and possible damage from sampling.

Most objects with which the museum scientist deals are of great value. The ideal is a nondestructive method of analysis giving good accuracy and producing a chart or photographic record which can be filed for future reference. Before a museum analyst adopts a particular procedure, certain questions must be asked. What type of analysis will produce the most useful result? Is a good quantitative analysis called for—one that would include the trace elements? Are the inclusions in the matrix important? Can a sample be removed from the object or must the analysis be produced from a sample of the smallest dimension possible? Does the object demand a completely nondestructive procedure? Each method has its own limitations. Today nondestructive analysis is a reality.

Spectrochemistry is an instrumental method for performing chemical analysis. Optical emission is produced by energy perturbations of the outer or valence electron shells of the atom. Energy applied to the atom disturbs the natural orbiting of the electrons. This energy state is not natural, and to restore itself the atom picks up a free electron to maintain a state of energy balance. When a photon is emitted, the light ray has a wavelength characteristic of the energy transmission. The optical emission spectra of the elements are available whereby the presence of an element in an unknown sample can be identified. The optical spectrograph, in conjunction with the laser microprobe, is fast becoming one of the most versatile tools in analyses of works of art.[1] A laser is a device which produces a coherent ray of light. The light obtained from an arc or a spark is incoherent. The laser is relatively nondestructive, as it removes a sample approximately 20 microns in diameter and 80—100 microns in depth. When an area is selected by the aid of a microscope using cross-hair motion adjustments, the laser is energized and a pulse of coherent radiation is received by the sample. The density of light photons is so great that it causes local vaporization of the material which rises from the sample as a small luminous plume. An auxiliary spark gap is positioned above the sample which has been pressured by a stored electrical charge of 1500 volts. On reaching the spark gap, the luminous plume creates a short circuit and the electrical charge is dumped into the vapor. The resulting bright beam of incoherent radiation is optically re-

layed into the spectrograph. Not only can the laser be used in this method for spectrochemical analysis, it can also be used as a sampling device for other methods of analysis. In such case, the spark gap is removed and the coherent beam of laser light is allowed to penetrate through a thin Mylar film which has been positioned over the surface of the object to be analyzed. The burst of laser light is allowed to vaporize the surface of the sample and the resulting vapor plume is collected on the Mylar film, which then can be analyzed by other techniques such as X-ray fluorescence.

As early as the Bronze Age, man found riches prospecting for gold, silver, and other metals. The ancient prospector may perhaps be visualized using a sheepskin to separate the gold from the quartz sand from placer deposits in alluvial streams.

According to Herodotus,[2] a development of great importance took place at Sardis in Lydia. Considerable quantities of gold were extracted from the alluvial sands of the Pactolus River in about 700 B.C. and were collected by the founder of the Lydian Empire, Gyges. By means of his gold hoard and his successful trading ventures, Gyges gained in wealth and power, and he became the first despotic ruler over the Lydians. Most significant from the point of view of this study, Gyges realized the importance of establishing a sound currency. During his rule, the first stamped, authenticated gold coinage of the Western world was produced. The last of Gyges' successors is thought to have been Croesus, whose wealth was vast enough to justify a legend and who is credited with the introduction of silver and electrum coinage as well as gold coinage. At a very early date, the Greeks adopted this form of currency. Strabo recorded that the gold in the Pactolus Valley had been virtually exhausted by 500 B.C.[3]

Close examination of a number of Lydian coins (fig.1) has revealed small, rounded or angular silver white inclusions in the gold matrix (fig. 2). These inclusions, measuring approximately from 80—150 microns in diameter, were subjected to analysis by the laser microprobe (Table I), which indicated a high percentage of platinum, a lower percentage of iridium, and a still lower percentage of osmium. The inclusions also were found to contain trace amounts of tin, ruthenium, rhodium, and nickel. These elements were not detected in the gold matrixes. Because spectrographically it was impossible to obtain an accurate quantitative analysis of the high percentages, the inclusions in the gold matrix of the Lydian coins were subjected to electron microbeam probe analyses, which indicated approximately 60% platinum, 40% iridium, and traces of osmium, proving the inclusions to be an alloy of platiniridium with some osmium. Platiniridium is a very rare alloy and is found in gold placer deposits in only a few parts of the world: the Ural mountains, Brazil, and the Ava River near Mandalay in Burma.[4]

Table I

Semiquantitative Analyses of Gold Matrixes and Inclusions in Lydian Coins, Achaemenian Earring, Bronze Age Jewelry, Egyptian Cylinder Seal

Standards and Objects	Pb	Hg	Au	Pt	Ir	Os	Rh	Ba	Sb	Sn	Ag	Pd	Ru	Zr	Cu	Ni	Fe	Mn	Cr	Ti	Ca	Si	Al	Mg
1. Gold 24 K	—	—	VS	—	—	—	—	—	—	—	—	—	—	—	W	—	—	—	—	—	T	—	—	VFT
2. Platinum — Urals	—	—	—	>VS	—	W	M	—	—	—	W	M	T/W	—	M	—	W	FT	—	T	FT	—	—	T
3. Platinum	—	—	—	>VS	—	W	—	T	—	—	FT	T/W	M	—	W	—	T	—	—	W	W/M	T	—	W
4. Iridium pellets	—	—	—	T/W	>VS	FT	—	—	—	W	—	—	FT	—	W	FT	W	—	—	—	M	W	—	M
5. Iridosmine	—	—	—	M/S	S	M/S	M	W	W	W	W/M	—	W/M	—	T/W	—	T/W	—	—	T	T	M	—	T
6. Gold: Lydian coin 04.1163	—	—	VS	—	—	—	—	—	—	—	S	—	—	—	W/M	—	T/W	—	—	T	M/S	—	T	M
7. Inclusion 04.1163	—	W	—	VS	VS	S	W	—	W/M	W/M	W/M	T	W/M	—	M	T	T/W	W	—	T	W/M	M	FT	M
8. Gold: Lydian coin 04.1160	—	—	>VS	—	—	—	—	—	T	—	S	—	—	—	M/S	—	—	—	—	—	M/S	W	—	T
9. Inclusion 04.1160	—	W	—	VS	S	>S	W/M	—	W	W/M	W/M	T/W	M/S	—	M	T	T/W	FT	—	T/W	W	M	FT	W/M
10. Persian gold earring 1971.256	T/W	—	>VS	—	—	—	—	—	M	—	>S	—	—	—	VS	—	T/W	W	W	M	S	M	W/M	W
11. Inclusion 1971.256	M	—	—	VS	S	>S	W/M	T	M/S	M	W	—	M	—	W/M	W	W/M	T/W	W/M	W/M	S	S	—	S
12. Inclusion 68.127 Hair ring triangle ornament	—	—	—	VS	S	S	W	—	—	M	M	W/M	M/S	W/M	W/M	FT	T/W	FT	—	W	W	T/W	—	W
13. Roundels and lunettes**	—	—	VS	—	—	—	—	—	—	—	S	—	—	—	W/M	—	T	VFT	—	T	M	T/W	T	T/W
14. Solders***	VFT	—	VS	—	—	—	—	—	—	—	M/S	—	—	—	W/M	—	T	T	—	W	W	W	FT	T/W
15. Bracelet 68.122	—	—	VS	—	—	—	—	—	—	—	VS	—	—	—	M	M	T	—	—	T	M	W	VFT	W
16. Bracelet 68.123	—	—	VS	—	—	—	—	—	—	—	VS	—	—	—	T/W	M	T/W	—	—	T	S	W	VFT	W/M
17. Bracelet 68.124	—	—	M/S	—	—	—	—	—	—	T/W	T/W	—	—	W	M	T/W	T/W	—	—	T/W	W/M	W	T/W	W/M
18. Egyptian cylinder seal 68.115	—	—	VS	—	—	—	—	—	—	—	VS	—	—	—	M	—	M	—	—	W	M/S	W/M	—	W/M

Key: FT = <.001%
T = .001–.01
W = .01–0.1
— = Not detected

M = 0.1–1
S = >1
VS = >10

* Elements looked for and not detected: Bi, Cd, Rb, As, Zn, Co

** This is an average analysis from 104 analyzed samples of roundels and lunettes

*** Average analysis of 4 solders from roundels

The Museum of Fine Arts recently purchased a gold earring of the Achaemenian period, circa fifth century B.C. (fig. 3). Of superb workmanship, the earring was undoubtedly made for a person of the hierarchy. The design was created by inlaying precious stones on each side of a gold disc in the form of crescents of red carnelian, blue turquoise, and blue lapis lazuli. A technique similar to cloisonné inlay outlines the design. The earring was made for pierced ears, with the lobe of the ear fitting into a V-shaped slot.

The craftsman formed seven circles with crescents on each side of a gold disc, standing them on edge and soldering them to a back plate of gold. Inside each circle he formed a crescent, on top of which, fastened by soldering, is the cut-out figure of the king, or Ahura Mazda.[5] He then incised these small profiles with delicate circles and crescents. The outer edge of the earring was formed into palmettes by soldering small arched pieces of gold of a thickness of 2.6 mm, with no fewer than 168 solder joins. Into the design was fitted lapis lazuli, turquoise, and carnelian. The color of the carnelian was enhanced by underlaying the natural thin stone with red cinnabar, a practice still in use today.

When the earring was examined in the museum's Research Laboratory under a binocular microscope using a power of 40 x, minute silver-white particles embedded in the gold matrix were discerned (fig. 4). These inclusions were submitted to a similar laser microprobe analysis, which proved the inclusions to be almost identical to those found in the Lydian gold coins, platiniridium. Because of the important implication of these small white inclusions of platiniridium and the rarity of the alloy of which these particles are composed, it was felt that it would be fruitful to trace it to its source.

Another fine Achaemenian piece is a small stamp seal, made of bluish white chalcedony (fig. 5). The design is composed of

5. Persian stamp seal. 66.1077. Achaemenian, 5th century B.C., chalcedony with gold mount. Diameter 1.5 cm.

two rearing affronted lions with heads turned backward. Two duck's heads in gold form the clasp. Examination of the clasp under magnification revealed that the gold contained platiniridium inclusions, indicating that, in all probability, it was from the same source as the gold of the Achaemenian earring.

The Hermus and the Pactolus valleys were an important source of native gold, not only in the Persian period but also in the early dynastic periods. The fine workmanship of the gold in the early dynastic royal tombs of Ur in 2600 B.C. would suggest a long history and experience in goldsmith's art and an early contact with gold producing areas. The Museum of the University of Pennsylvania granted us permission to examine microscopically various gold objects from the Royal Cemetery at Ur. These consisted of a fluted gold beaker, large saucer earrings, a necklace with pendant leaves with the veined design produced by tracing with a tool or stick, a necklace of lapis lazuli and rounded gold beads, spiral rings and a gold bracelet from the grave of Queen Shub-ad (ca. 3000—2500 B.C.) (fig. 6).

The microscopic examination proved that all these objects from Ur contain platiniridium inclusions in the gold matrix.[6] The collection of gold objects from Ur, excavated by the late Sir Leonard Wooley, now in the collection of the British Museum, were found to contain minute silver-white inclusions which have the characteristics of platiniridium. These inclusions were also found in the gold Achaemenian period Oxus Treasure in the British Museum (fig. 7). The inclusions vary from about 50 to 150 microns in diameter. From this, one may infer that native gold was used and that the Sumerian goldsmith did not practice gold refining in the early dynastic period. The presence of platiniridium inclusions strongly suggests that the gold of the various objects from the Royal Cemetery at Ur originated and was transported from the Pactolus Valley.

Another important ancient source of gold was Astyra in the Troad. According to Strabo, it was from this gold that the legendary king Priam of Troy derived his immense riches.[7] A small hoard of jewelry in the University of Pennsylvania Museum is said to have come from this region.[8] The collection consists of an ornamented pin, basket earrings, bracelets, pendants, necklace, diadem, and a number of shell earrings. There is similarity between these pieces and the gold objects from Troy published by Heinrich Schliemann in *Ilios: The City and Country of the Trojans*.[9] The University Museum also permitted us to examine their collection of gold from Troy, and we found that in comparison with the reddish gold from Ur, the Troy gold is of paler color, as it is electrum. Moreover, it was found to be lacking in the characteristic inclusions of platiniridium, indicating that it did not originate from the Pactolus area.

As a centennial gift, the Boston Museum of Fine Arts received an Early Bronze Age funerary hoard of 125 pieces, which includes 69 gold roundels in two sizes (each with five

1. Lydian coins. 04.1163, 04.1162, and 04.1161 H. L. Pierce Fund.

2. Platiniridium inclusions in Lydian coins.

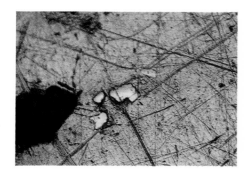

4. Platiniridium inclusions in Achaemenian earring.

3. Achaemenian earring. 1971.256. 5th Century B.C., gold with inlays of lapis lazuli, turquoise, and carnelian. Diameter 5 cm.

6. Gold objects from Ur from the University of Pennsylvania Museum.

7. Armlet from the Oxus Treasure.

8. Gold jewelry of the Bronze Age. Centennial gift to Museum of Fine
Arts, 1968. 68.116—139.

concentric circles with a raised center boss), 35 lunettes, as well as hair rings, a diadem, 3 gold bracelets, and an Egyptian seal (figs. 8, 9). The hollow gold cylinder seal is incised with Egyptian hieroglyphs precisely indicating two Egyptian pharaohs, Menkawhor and Djedkare, who reigned successively in Dynasty 5 (ca. 2490–2450 B.C.)[10]

A microscopic examination was made of the 125 pieces, and platiniridium was observed in most of the gold matrixes. These inclusions were particularly evident in the gold hair rings, the roundels, and a gold bracelet with lion finials. It was found that the gold from which the cylinder seal was made was lacking in platiniridium inclusions, and analysis showed it to be a gold-silver alloy. It is evident that the seal was first incised in the flat and then made into a cylindrical form by soldering. What appeared to be a core inside the hollow gold seal was dated by thermoluminescence.[11] If the cylinder seal had been formed over a clay core, the thermoluminescence time clock would have been turned back to zero at the time the cylinder was heated during the soldering. But the thermoluminescence date indicated an approximate geologic age of 250,000 years for the "core" material, which strongly suggests that what appeared to be a "core" was in fact silt that filtered into the hollow cylinder during burial. X-ray diffraction analysis indicated this deposit to be mainly calcite with some quartz.

The gold funerary hoard must have originated from the tomb of a person of high rank, perhaps a princess, who was buried in her royal finery. In all probability, the roundels were fastened across the princess' chest in a pectoral design. The circles and crescents appear to be solar-lunar symbols. It is likely that the Egyptian gold seal was carried by a courier from Egypt. Although the name of the bearer is not recorded on the cylinder, it is quite evident from the inscription what his duties were under his two royal masters. Under Menkawhor he was "Inspector of Tenant Farmers of the Pyramid called Netjer." He also served Menkawhor's successor, Djedkare, as "Master of Secrets and House Official of the Palace."[12]

Since the location of the tomb from which the hoard originates is not known, it is impossible to indicate how great a distance the gold from the Pactolus Valley was transported. We do know from the characteristic inclusions of platiniridium that the gold must have come from the same source as the Lydian coins, although, as has been mentioned, Strabo wrote that the gold in the Pactolus River had run out by 500 B.C. The identification of platiniridium in the early Bronze Age jewelry clearly indicates that the Pactolus was an extremely important source and that this gold was available in the Pactolus Valley as early as 2400 B.C.

9. Egyptian gold cylinder seal. 68.115.

Acknowledgments

The authors would like to acknowledge the collaboration of Prof. Robert Ogilvie, Department of Metallurgy, Massachusetts Institute of Technology, in making the electron microbeam probe analysis of the platiniridium inclusions of the Lydian coins. We would also like to thank Professor Cyril S. Smith, Department of Humanities, Massachusetts Institute of Technology, for drawing our attention to the platiniridium inclusions in the fluted gold beaker from Ur in the University of Pennsylvania Museum collection, and Dr. Anthony Werner, Research Laboratory, British Museum, London, for making available to us for study the gold objects from Ur and the gold Oxus Treasure.

Notes

1. Brech, Frederick, and Young, William J. "The Laser Microprobe and Its Application to the Analysis of Works of Art," *Application of Science in Examination of Works of Art, Proceedings of the Seminar: September 7–16, 1965,* Boston, Museum of Fine Arts, 1967.

2. Herodotus 1.93, v.101, v. 49.

3. Pliny, *Naturalis Historia* 33.66; Strabo 13.4.5 and 13.1.23.

4. Palache, Charles, Berman, Harry, and Frondel, Clifford. *Dana's System of Mineralogy,* 7th ed., New York; John Wiley, 1944, vol. I, 1.110.

5. Simpson, William Kelly. "Acquisitions in Egyptian and Ancient Near Eastern Art in the Boston Museum of Fine Arts, 1970–71," *Connoisseur 179* (February 1972), 120; McKeon, John F. X. "Achaemenian Cloisonne-Inlay Jewelry," *Alter Orient und Altes Testament* (in preparation).

6. The gold fluted beaker was examined with the aid of a magnifier through the glass of its exhibition case, and platiniridium was thought to be seen. Professor Cyril Stanley Smith of Massachusetts Institute of Technology had the opportunity to examine this piece more closely and found that platiniridium exists on the side and bottom of the beaker.

7. Strabo, 12.2.323.

8. Bass, George F. "Troy and Ur: Gold Links between Two Ancient Capitals," *Expedition* 8, no. 4 (Summer 1966), 26–29; idem, "A Hoard of Trojan and Sumerian Jewelry," *American Journal of Archaeology* 74, no. 4 (October 1970), 335–341.

9. Bass, "Troy and Ur," p. 28.

10. Vermeule, Emily T. "Golden Links to the Bronze Age," *Horizon* 13, no.1 (Winter 1971), 51.

11. Thermoluminescent dating can be achieved on most ceramics, cores, and lava materials that have been heated in the recent past. Thermoluminescence results from the fact that radiation, by alpha, beta, or gamma rays, may displace certain electrons in some of the crystal lattice, such as quartz or felspar, which is found in most clay fabrics. Once pottery has been heated to a temperature greater than $400°$ C, and its electrons have emitted their thermoluminescent light, the thermoluminescent time clock will be turned back to zero. All ceramic material from archaeological sites shows thermoluminescent glow. This energy is proportional to the total radiation dose that has been absorbed by the material during use or burial. Consequently, recently fired ceramic wares show little thermoluminescent glow, and it is, therefore, possible by measuring the amount of thermoluminescent glow to indicate the approximate age of the material.

12. Vermeule, "Golden Links," p. 52.

CYRIL STANLEY SMITH

An Examination of the Arsenic-Rich Coating
on a Bronze Bull from Horoztepe

At the last scientific conference held under the auspices of the Museum of Fine Arts, Brech and Young[1] used as one of their examples of the use of the laser in spectrochemical analysis a bull that had large areas plated with a whitish metal which, in contrast with the adjacent bare bronze, was relatively uncorroded. The bull (fig.1) was said to have been found at Horoztepe in Northeastern Anatolia in a chieftan's grave attributed to the Hattian culture, about 2100 B.C. Mr. Young's spectrographic analysis showed the presence of over 10 % arsenic in the coating but less than 0.001 % in the underlying bronze. X-ray fluorescence analysis confirmed the presence of large amounts of arsenic in the surface material. Moreover, Young reported that on a metallographic examination of a section cut from the leg where it had been broken "one could readily observe the plated surface merging into the bronze casting." On cleaning the bull cathodically in 2 % sodium hydroxide, it was found that the high arsenic areas were smooth and virtually uncorroded while the low-arsenic areas were swollen, for they had been deeply attacked and mineralized.

Mr. Young's discovery is of considerable importance for the light it throws on early metallurgy. The technique of local plating with arsenic has not been recorded elsewhere, although the decoration of Anatolian cast bronze animal figures with a true inlay of silver or electrum is well known.[2] Özgüç and Akok in their original report of the excavation at Horoztepe[3] illustrate two bulls very similar to the present one except in the distribution of the silvery areas. Supposedly because of the simple outline of the plating which terminates on an essentially vertical plane, though in the middle of each animal, Özgüç was led to believe that the plating had been applied by immersing one end or the other of the bull in a bath of molten alloy. In the first report, he says, "The bull figures are of bronze. One has a silver-lead plating on head, horns, forelegs in the front part of the body, the other on hind legs, tail and hindpart of the body ... The technique of plating is that of dipping a core of bronze in a mixture of molten lead and silver. The triangular piece in the forehead of the bull is pure silver inserted in a prepared cavity." He gives, however, no evidence for the composition of the silver-lead coating, and in a later report it is referred to even more equivocally: "the plating has been made secure by dipping the core of bronze into molten lead."[4] The photographs, however, leave no doubt that these bulls originated in the same workshop as those in Boston, for they are very similar in general style as well as in all the characteristics of the coatings and their corrosion. They should be tested for arsenic. The early use of this element in metallurgy and the decorative arts is more widespread than has been suspected. Many white coatings, so easily classed as silver because they are silvery in appearance, may turn out on reexamination to be arsenic.[5]

Through the courtesy of Mr. Young and Mr. Cornelius Vermeule, and the Museum of Fine Arts, it has been possible to examine microsamples of the Boston bull in more detail. The microstructure of the base metal was quite typical of a normal cast bronze, with dendritic coring and a little residual eutectoid. The surface of the uncoated parts was heavily corroded, and beneath the totally mineralized corrosion products on the surface, the grain boundaries and connected intragranular eutectoid areas were corroded to a depth of about 2 mm. The plated part was relatively uncorroded, though some intergranular attack had occurred.

In the cross-section of the plated part, the microscope revealed a sharply defined layer of a bluish-grey intermetallic compound, in thickness varying between about 0.005 mm and 0.15 mm (figs. 2 and 3). The outside of this layer of compound is regular and smooth, except where it has been mechanically damaged. The interface with the underlying bronze is somewhat irregular and scalloped in the manner which is almost invariably associated with the formation of a layer of intermetallic compound by a diffusion reaction in the solid state. The external appearance of this layer and the lack of relation between the inside and outside contours on the section suggest that it had once been thicker and had been reduced to its present surface by working, supposedly with abrasives.

The white alloy coating was not excessively brittle, for slight deformation ridges were formed around the impressions of accidental impacts on the bull surface; moreover, it had not cracked severely or flaked off anywhere. However, an unsupported edge crumbled when pushed with a needle and revealed a dark metallic crystalline fracture. An X-ray diffractometer record was prepared by Miss Florence Whitmore in the museum laboratory on the coating on the hip of the animal after cleaning. Some strong lines are compatible with those given in the American Society for Testing and Materials catalogue for the solid solution of arsenic in copper known to mineralogists as whitneyite (F.C.C.) while the principal lines corresponded to the intermediate phase beta domeykite, which is approximately Cu_3As. There were, however, many lines that could not be identified. A new analysis by X-ray fluorescence showed the presence of some tin which escaped detection in the 1965 analyses.

This superficial layer, therefore, is assumed to be the compound Cu_3As (28.2 wt % As), which, according to the constitution diagram (fig. 4), is the phase in equilibrium with the copper-rich solid solution (about 5.4 to 7.9 wt % As) at temperatures between 300° and 685° C.[6,7] The presence of tin would undoubtedly affect the constitution somewhat, but the ternary diagram is unknown.

If the compound on the surface of the Boston bull is actually the compound Cu_3As, how was it applied? The coating is

1. Bronze Bull with local white metal plating. Hattian Culture,
Anatolia, *ca.* 2100 B.C. Length, 12.2 cm, height, 9.1 cm. William E.
Nickerson Fund. Courtesy Museum of Fine Arts, Boston.

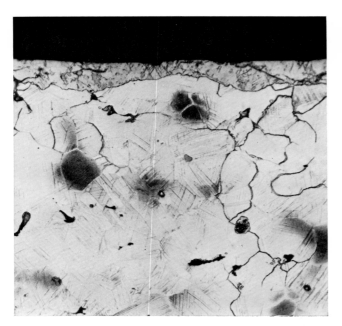

2. Microstructure of a section cut from the right rear leg of the bull. Etched with potassium bichromate reagent. x 500. The band at the top is the white metal coating.

3. Same as figure 2, another area.

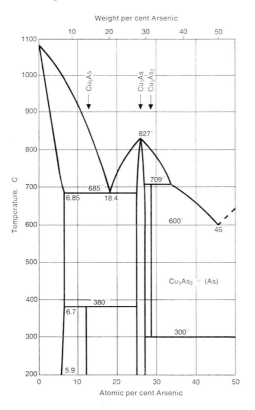

4. Constitution diagram of copper-arsenic system (from Hanson and Elliot[6]). In a recent study of the diagram at 350° C. and below, Skinner and Luce[7] show that alpha domeykite (Cu_3As exactly) decomposes at 90° C to beta domeykite with the composition $Cu_{3-x}As$, where x is about 0.5 at 90° C but decreases to 0 well below the melting point. Algodonite is a solid solution ranging at its maximum between $Cu_{5.2}As$ and Cu_8As. At 300° C, as Cu_8As, it decomposes to the alpha solid solution (5.4 wt $^0/0$ As) and beta domeykite, which are the only two phases that would be expected to be present in any artificially prepared sample.

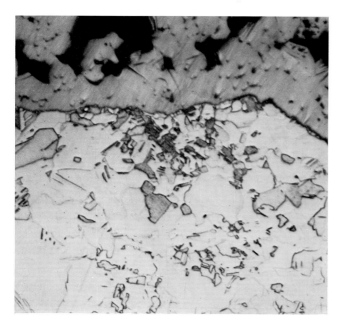

5. Layer of arsenic compound formed on pure copper by reaction at 450° C with the white arsenic mixture described in the text. Etched. x 125.

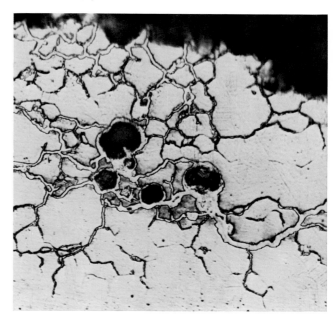

6. Copper-arsenic alloy needle from Chan Chan, Peru. Chimu period. Microstructure showing corroded area in which intergranular cracks have been filled in with what is thought to be electrochemically redeposited algodonite. Lightly etched with potassium bichromate. x 700.

somewhat malleable, but nevertheless far too brittle to have been applied by hammering into pre-cut grooves, as is usually done when inlaying with more ductile metals. Moreover, although the bronze immediately beneath the coating has recrystallized (indicating that it had been worked over with a tool before its final heating), there is no evidence of a mechanical interface, and in any case inlay is improbable for covering such large curved surfaces. The alloy could perhaps have been applied in the molten state, but this is unlikely, for the microscope reveals no sign of the duplex eutectic structure between α and Cu_3As, which would have formed on cooling from the liquid state above 685° C., and there is no evidence of intergranular penetration of liquid into the underlying bronze.

There remains little alternative to the diffusion hypothesis, and we must assume that the arsenic was applied in some kind of a cementation process involving arsenic vapor. The parts to be left bronze color would have been coated with some impermeable stop-off material, if the whole object was packed in a cementation pot, or possibly a paste containing arsenic could have been locally applied.

It is unlikely that metallic arsenic would have been available to the Hattians, but white arsenic could have been known as a condensed fume from the roasting of arsenical copper ores. Though As_2O_3 sublimes at 193° C, there are stable arsenates of the alkali metals (available in plant ash) which are easily reduced with charcoal at moderate temperatures. If, therefore, a mixture of white arsenic, an alkali carbonate, and charcoal is heated, arsenic vapor will be formed which will react with any metallic copper present to produce a superficial layer of Cu_3As. An attempt to produce such a coating in the laboratory was made by Mr. Jonathan Sachs at M.I.T. The reaction went fast at temperatures above 350° C, producing large amounts of loose crystals of Cu_3As and some patches of an underlying coherent layer like that on the bull (fig. 5). The mixture used was 4 parts As_2O_3, 1 part dry K_2CO_3, and 0.3 part carbon black, all finely powdered, heated with the copper for one hour at 450° C. A mixture that evolved arsenic vapor less rapidly would be preferred.

Is it unreasonable to propose the use of controlled cementation with arsenic in the third millennium B.C.? As is well known, cementation was used in Roman times for the case hardening of semifinished iron (steel) objects and in the making of molten brass. Both of these involve the transfer of material in gaseous form (C as CO, Zn as vapor). By the 6th century B.C., if not earlier, the removal of silver and other impurities from gold by cementation with clay and salt was an important refining process, and somewhat related processes have been used for "coloring" gold ever since, but these work by removing something from the material being treated rather than adding to it.[8]

There is only one antecedent of the suggested cementation process that I know of, but it is an interesting one: this is the blue-glazing of quartz stones and objects loosely molded from quartzite sand that began in Sumeria before the end of the fifth millennium B.C. and became widely known as one form of Egyptian faience (frit). Its true nature as the product of a kind of cementation process was not suspected until 1966, when a modern survival of it was observed by Hans Wulff in Iran, making the blue "donkey" beads so popular with tourists.[9] This process involves an alkaline plant ash high in soda mixed with copper oxide to give the blue color, and with lime as an inert carrier. The alkali melts and soaks into the lime, through which it runs to react with the surface of the embedded silica objects, so forming a layer of glassy silicate to which (for reasons of interfacial energy) the lime does not stick.[10] If indeed this process had been used in making the earliest blue glazes, the type of experimentation that gave rise to it would have undoubtedly been tried to produce decorative coatings on other materials, including metals such as our bull. It is even conceivable that, much earlier, it had provided a means of reducing arsenical copper ores in a highly alkaline environment to give low-sulphur metal. Perhaps an experimental attempt to coat solid copper using other minerals, such as cassiterite, in place of an arsenic compound, first gave a liquid bronze. *There is not, of course, the slightest evidence to support these speculations,* which are introduced here only to promote consideration of this type of process by those concerned with the origin of metallurgy.

Appendix: Notes on Copper-Arsenic Metallurgy

It is, of course, well known that the use of copper-arsenic alloys with up to about 6 % arsenic preceded true bronzes in both the Old and the New Worlds.[11] Key[12] describes some cast mace heads and other objects found in the Dead Sea region (dating from about 3000 B.C.) which contained up to 12 % arsenic.[13] Marechal[14] emphasizes that arsenic-copper alloys are far easier to cast than pure copper as well as being harder and adequately malleable. Though softer than bronzes with high tin content, they are superior to copper for most purposes. It is, if anything, strange that the copper-arsenic alloys were so little used once the tin alloys became known. Arsenic did, however, continue in a very minor way in making castings of white copper alloys. Recipes for such copper appear in almost all the manuscript collections of recipes from Pliny on into the 19th century. For example, one of the more intelligible recipes in Leyden X (third century A.D.) reads: "For whitening copper, . . . so that no one can recognize it. Taking some Cyprian copper, melt it, throwing on it 1 mina of decomposed sandarach, 2 drachmas of sandarach of the color of iron, and 5 drachmas

of lamellose alum and melt (again) . . . It is heated and then poured." (Translation by E. R. Caley.)[15] Medieval interest in these alloys was almost alchemical, as a color-change trick rather than for serious exploitation in industry or art. Few examples of it have survived, and most white copper objects are of the Chinese Cu-Ni-Zn alloy paktong or its successor, German silver.[16] Arsenic was, however, regularly used in speculum metal (containing about 30 to 35 % tin) to improve both the castability and the color. In the 19th and early 20th centuries, about 0.5 % arsenic was added to copper for locomotive boiler tubes to improve its strength at slightly elevated temperatures, and very minor amounts are used today in brass condenser tubes to prevent the type of corrosion known as dezincification.

There is one application of the alloy in a form aesthetically somewhat similar to our bull. This is the Japanese material *shirome,* which was used as inlay on Japanese iron sword guards of the 18th century and later.[17] Its warm white color contrasts beautifully with the black patina on the iron. According to Gowland,[18] shirome separates out during the desilverization of impure copper by liquation. It is actually a speiss, containing up to 11 % of arsenic, with minor amounts of antimony and sometimes lead and traces of other elements. It was applied to the iron by fusing into an intaglio cut design and then polishing to a surface that is flat and continuous with that of the adjacent iron: It is more akin to niello or champlevé enamel than to inlay. Tsuba makers often used a copper-tin alloy called *sawari* as a substitute for it.

The alloys with higher arsenic content deserve renewed study by modern metallurgists. The phase Cu_8As, corresponding to the mineral algodonite, is known only to mineralogists. Though it is only stable below 300° C., it is quite ductile and is considerably more resistant to corrosion (at least under archaeological burial conditions) than the alpha solid solution. By coincidence I have recently encountered malleable copper-arsenic microconstituents in two widely different archaeological contexts. It now seems that (despite the earlier failure of analysts to find arsenic chemically), the mysterious rapid-etching and deformable clearly defined second phase in Iranian native copper and artifacts hammered from it[19] is probably algodonite. Secondly, a phase with appearance and etching characteristics identical with this has recently been found by Heather Lechtman in a slightly corroded copper needle from Chan Chan in Peru, believed to date from the Chimu period. Wet chemical analysis showed that the metal of which the needle was made contained 2.55 % arsenic and 0.79 % silver; the spectrograph revealed traces only of Bi, Fe, Ni, Sb, and Sn. The structure is shown in fig.6. The phase that surrounds some of the grains in a geometry that suggests connected stress-corrosion cracking is nearly invisible on the unetched section, though it is slightly lighter in color than the matrix.

Etching in potassium bichromate very rapidly defined it. This phase is believed to be algodonite. It is highly resistant to corrosion, for, near the surface, it persists for some distance into the area where the metal in the grain bodies has changed completely into cuprite. Microprobe scanning photographs confirmed the existence of arsenic in the matrix, and showed almost an order of magnitude greater concentration of arsenic in the intergranular regions. The formation of the phase was highly localized. It seems to be related both to local stresses which produced intergranular cracking and to local electrochemistry, which simultaneously or subsequently filled in the space with cathodically redeposited algodonite as the more anodic alloy corroded. The electrolytic deposition of copper in cavities in corroding bronzes is well known.[20] The mechanism is clearly related to the formation of the minerals in native copper deposits — mineralogists and archaeologists should work together more.

Addendum

Some additional information on copper-arsenic alloys should be recorded. H. McKerrel and R. Tylecote in a paper entitled "The Working of Copper-arsenic Alloys in the Early Bronze Age..." (*Proceedings of the Prehistoric Society,* 38 [1972], 209–18) study the loss of arsenic under various smelting, melting, and annealing conditions and conclude that copper-arsenic alloys have a very low partial pressure of arsenic vapor in a nonoxidizing atmosphere at any reasonable temperature. They point out that castings of copper-arsenic alloys are subject to considerable segregation, which greatly complicates the problem of analysis of archaeological material. Moreover, they show that the surfaces of castings are often completely coated with thin layers of once-liquid alloy of near eutectic composition (21 % As) forced out during solidification by inverse segregation (more often called exudation or sweating in bronze founders' parlance). This can give an almost uniform silver surface to the alloy and may be the origin of some intentional plating.

In a paper of considerable importance, Dr. Hugh McKerrel (private communication, July 1972) examines this "silver plating" of axes in considerable detail. He reports that very many Early Bronze Age weapons excavated in Scotland have a clearly defined surface layer of silver-colored metal, sometimes as much as a millimeter thick. Axes cast from metal containing 9 to 13 % tin and 0.3 to 0.7 % arsenic had white surfaces analyzing between 23 and 45 % tin, 0.7 to 2.4 % arsenic. McKerrel shows that alloys containing arsenic (with or without tin) are particularly subject to exudation, and he consistently obtained fairly uniform white coating of low-melting-point arsenic-rich alloys on castings made under laboratory conditions. He suggests that the production of such "silver" coatings

was a consistent part of the bronze-age metallurgist's repertoire and that it was the origin of the recipes for white copper that appear in Leyden papyrus X, Zosimos, and later manuscripts, eventually to provide alchemists with reliable silver-making transmutations and optical instrument makers with improved specula. (The microstructure of the Scottish EBA axes shows unmistakably that the white surface layer had been melted, and is therefore different in origin from the solid-state diffusion coating on the Horoztepe bull. Dr. McKerrel thinks that the coating on his bronzes was not applied by hot-dipping.)

McKerrel discusses at length the behavior of arsenic and antimony during smelting and inclines to the belief that ores containing these elements would have been roasted and some of the volatile trioxides collected as a condensate on adjacent cold surfaces. An arsenic-rich master alloy could be made by heating copper in a mixture of this oxide and charcoal. His analyses show that high-arsenic alloys were used for halberds long after the period when tin became available, and he suggests that the founder may have regarded silvery tin and the silvery arsenic-copper alloy as virtually equivalent hardeners for alloy-making. McKerrel's paper is of importance not only for the broad technical implications of the processes involved but also for its use of metallurgical clues to indicate extensive contact between different parts of Europe in the Early Bronze Age.

Acknowledgments

I am grateful to Mr. W. J. Young and the Museum of Fine Arts for making the microspecimen of the bull available for study. The photomicrographs are the work of Katherine Ruhl and James Howard. My work on archaeological metallurgy is supported in part by grants from the National Endowment for the Humanities, the Sloan Fund for Basic Research (M.I.T.), Mrs. Dominique de Menil, and the Wenner-Gren Foundation.

References

1. Brech, F., and Young, W. J., "The Laser Microprobe and Its Application to the Analysis of Works of Art," in *Application of Science in Examination of Works of Art,* Boston, Museum of Fine Arts, 1967, pp. 230–237.

2. See, for example, the standard no. 30 in the catalogue of the exhibition *Art Treasures of Turkey,* published by the Smithsonian Institution, Washington, D.C., 1966. Also the superb Proto-Hittite stag illustrated on page 120 in Wooley, Leonard, *The Art of the Middle East,* New York, 1961.

3. Özgüç, Tahsin, and Akok, Mahmut, "Objects from Horoztepe," *Belletin Türk Tarih Kurumu* (Ankara), 21 (1957), 211—219.

4. Özgüç, Tahsin, and Akok, Mahmut, *Horoztepe: An Early Bronze Age, Settlement and Cemetery,* Ankara, 1958.

5. The arsenic plating process appears in Egypt at about the same time as in Anatolia. In 1933, Fink and Kopp described a white metal plating on an Egyptian bowl and ewer of thick hammered copper in the Metropolitan Museum of Art, dating from the fifth or sixth dynasty (2500—2200 B.C.). (Fink, Colin G., and Kopp, A. K., "Ancient Egyptian Antimony Plating on Copper Objects," *Metropolitan Museum Studies,* 4 [1933], 163—167. Summary in *Industrial and Engineering Chemistry,* 26 [1934], 236). The coating was found after electrolytic cleaning and was identified as antimony. Fink believed that some form of electro-deposition was involved, perhaps involving contact with iron strips, as in his own attempts to duplicate the coating. Lucas and Harris utterly reject the idea of Egyptian plating, suggesting instead that Fink's antimony had been deposited at the time of the cleaning operation in the museum laboratory. (Lucas, Alfred, and Harris, J. R., *Ancient Egyptian Materials,* London, 1962, pp. 197—199). Few people have accepted Fink's claims, which is understandable but unfortunate, since the plating is real though misidentified, and Fink's discovery was an important one. A recent examination of these objects made by me showed that the coating, though very thin and worn entirely away on most high spots, is identical in general characteristics and microscopic appearance with the coating on the Boston bulls. Moreover, neutron-activation analyses were kindly made by Dr. Pieter Meyers on surface rubbings from both the Egyptian objects, and these indeed confirm that the coatings are rich in arsenic and that antimony is not detectable. In retrospect, it is easy to account for Fink's analytical error. He identified antimony by the formation of an orange sulphide precipitate and by the stibine reaction. Working with traces it would be easy to confuse yellow arsenic sulphide with the yellowish orange of the antimony compound, and arsenic yields a gaseous hydride that thermally decomposes even more readily than does antimony. This error has delayed for forty years the recognition of an interesting facet of early metallurgy.

6. Hansen, Max, *Constitution of Binary Alloys.* First supplement, ed. R. P. Elliott, New York, 1965.

7. Skinner, B. J., and Luce, F. J., "Stabilities and Compositions of alpha-domeykite and algodonite," *Economic Geology* (in press).

8. On superficial gold enrichment in South American metallurgy and elsewhere, see the paper by H. Lechtman in this volume. When discussing plating in general, mention must be made of "electroless" plating by chemical deposition methods, some of which are clearly within the reach of early technology. Silver-plating by rubbing a copper object with a paste containing silver chloride, and tin-plating by boiling objects with granulated tin in an alkaline solution of tartar are of respectable antiquity, while zinc and especially nickel deposition by such means are processes in wide use today. For Gallo-Roman tin-plating, supposedly with tartar, see Aimé Thouvenin, "L'étamage des objects de cuivre et de bronze chez les anciens," *Revue d'histoire des mines et de la métallurgie,* 2 (1970), 101—109.

9. Wulff, Hans E., et al., "Egyptian Faience: A Possible Survival in Iran," *Archaeology,* 21 (1968), 98—107.

10. An alternative process has been suggested by Noble. (Noble, J. V., "The Technique of Egyptian Faience," *American Journal of Archaeology,* 73 [1969], 435—439). In this, the alkali and copper are incorporated in the objects themselves, which are molded of damp silica sand. The coating is formed by efflorescence on drying and subsequent firing. Noble beautifully duplicated Egyptian frit in this way, and it seems likely that a process of this kind was used in Egypt. However, the earliest frit was probably done by Wulff's process — an astounding survival — and the blue glaze on solid quartz crystals could not possibly have resulted from efflorescence. Moreover, Noble's process does not explain the absence of support marks on most Egyptian material.

11. Charles, J. A., "Early Arsenical Bronzes — A Metallurgical View," *American Journal of Archaeology,* 71 (1967), 21—26.

12. Key, C. A., "Ancient Copper and Copper-arsenic Alloy Artifacts," *Science,* 146 (1964), 1578—1580.

13. Before these analyses are accepted, the manner of sampling should be examined. A superficial sample such as is often taken for analysis gives totally misleading results on plated objects.

14. Marechal, Jean R., *Reflections upon Prehistoric Metallurgy,* Lammersdorf, West Germany, Otto Tunker, 1963. See also Coghlan, H. H., "Prehistoric Working of Bronze and Arsenical Copper, *Sibrium,* 5 (1960), 145—152.

15. Caley, E. R., "The Leyden Papyrus X — an English translation with brief notes," *Journal of Chemical Education,* 3 (1926), 1149—1166.

16. Bonnin, Alfred, *Tutenag and Paktong,* Oxford, Oxford University Press, 1924.

17. Robinson, B. W., *The Arts of the Japanese Sword,* London, Faber & Faber, 1963, p. 64.

18. Gowland, William, "A Japanese Pseudo-speise (Shirome)..." *Journal of the Society of Chemical Industry,* 13 (May 31, 1894), 436—471.

19. Smith, C. S., "Metallographic Study of Early Artifacts Made from Native Copper," *Actes du XIᵉ Congrès International d'Histoire des Sciences,* part VI, Warsaw, 1968, pp. 237—252.

20. Gettens, R. J., *The Freer Chinese Bronzes, vol. II, Technical Studies,* Washington, D.C., 1969, pp.136—137. Massive redeposited copper has been found in corroded bronze axes by H. H. Coghlan, *Archaeologia Austriaca,* 41 (1967), 48—65. I cannot accept the theory mentioned in the appendix to this paper that the copper was produced by thermal treatment rather than as an electrochemical by-product of corrosion.

ARTHUR STEINBERG

Joining Methods on Large Bronze Statues: Some Experiments in Ancient Technology

It should be made clear from the start that this is merely a brief introduction to a complex and tantalizing problem that might be characterized as the development of the conceptions and practices of the foundry and its related operations in classical antiquity. I have selected randomly from a sampling of ancient statues that is in itself random owing to the chance of survival; the conclusions from such data can, at best, be sketchy. Examples have been chosen from the Greek, Etruscan, and Roman world, dating from the sixth century B.C. to the third century A.D., because this was presumed to be a homogeneous tradition; I am not even sure of that anymore.

It is quite apparent from ancient descriptions such as Pausanias' that Greek sanctuaries and marketplaces were literally packed with large bronze statues; the Romans carried off many when sacking Corinth in 146 B.C.,[1] and Verres did a fine job of pilfering the Greek cities of Sicily of their bronze riches during his illustrious term as governor there.[2] For obvious reasons, such as the scarcity and resultant high value of bronze in the Middle Ages and later, its usefulness for machines of war, its ability to be easily reused simply by remelting, and the greed of a peasantry who destroyed ancient bronzes to find the gold they believed hidden inside them, very few of these precious bronzes have come down to us. Furthermore, those that are preserved are now the highly treasured and costly possessions of museums who are most reluctant to have these art objects tampered with. The inaccessibility of these statues to close scrutiny, such as the examination of the microstructure of the bronze, has severely limited me from providing as full an account of the different methods of joining the parts of these statues as is desirable. But on the basis of a few close examinations and some experiments we are able to make some reasonably educated guesses.

Though the casting of copper and copper alloys is already attested in the fourth millennium B.C., the casting of large objects is probably not known much before the middle of the second millennium (the paintings in the tomb of Rekh-mire, Thebes[3]), and it is not clear that much large-scale casting was done before 1000 B.C. (The 13th century B.C. headless statue of Napir-Asu, consort of a Cassite king, is an exception.[4]) At that time, however, we hear of a massive industrial operation in the Phoenician castings for Solomon's Temple in Jerusalem (I Kings 7:13—47 and Chron. 4:2, 4, 5, 17), and a few centuries later Sennacherib's (705—681 B.C.) description of casting giant bulls and lions for his palace is worthy of note, though the technological language (and its possible interpretation) leaves a great deal to be desired.[5] To judge from these descriptions all these early castings were made in one piece. It is from roughly the time of Sennacherib on that we begin to get a picture of large-scale bronze casting in the classical area of the Mediterranean. Whether the tradition came to the West from

Egypt or the Syrian-Phoenician coast or Anatolia is not clear, but the written tradition speaks of Samos as the Greek cradle of this new art: Rhoikos and Theodoros are mentioned by Pausanias (XVII, xiv, 8) in connection with the invention of large, hollow bronze castings which they may have learned about in Egypt (Diodorus Siculus I, 98, 5—7). Interestingly enough, the same two artists are credited elsewhere with possibly inventing the art of modeling in clay (Pliny, N. H. xxxv, 152). The coupling of modeling in clay and casting large bronzes is striking,[6] and it would be very interesting to piece together again exactly what these Samian artists did, in fact, do. Nevertheless, the heart of the matter is that building the model to be cast and constructing the molds from this model, are in fact, the real art of the bronze-founder. In some ways the casting of the metal is — once the complex geometry of the molds is worked out and the behavior of the gases and liquids understood — the easiest part of the operation. It is also worth noting that the descriptions alluded to above are primarily concerned with the mold-building stage of the operation rather than the actual casting and finishing, and in dealing with the history and development of ancient bronze-casting it is essentially the mold-building that must interest us, for in it lies the real documentation of the technique. But the building of the mold is difficult to document from finished bronzes[7] and, in fact, all that is left to us as clues of the actual technique of the foundry are such details as the internal surface of the bronze, traces of joins, and the number and division of pieces of the statue. From these data we can make suggestions about the process of an individual bronze, but it must be stressed that these are mere guesses, and until ancient foundry-sites have been carefully excavated by people who are aware of the nature of the evidence, these will remain guesses.

I have enumerated elsewhere the kinds of problems confronting the foundryman in the process of casting.[8] Included among these problems are the soundness, dryness and evenness of mold surface, careful juxtaposition of sections of different thickness, and ample provisions for adequate feeding of molten metal and escapement of gases during pouring. Important during the actual pouring of the metal is a constant and sufficient flow of metal at a reasonably even temperature, and lack of dross and slag in the metal. If the mold is designed well, and the foundryman has taken care, all should go well. From the products of the foundry that remain to us it is clear that all did not always go well, and we can only guess at how many pieces were melted down again because of faulty casting, or needed to be heavily repaired to make up for inadequacies in the foundry operation.

Since all the problems of the mold-building and foundry operations are immeasurably compounded in the manufacture of a large bronze statue (such as a life-size human) the ancient foundryman's ingenuity was heavily taxed when making these large bronzes. It apparently was soon obvious to the Greek foundryman and his successors in Italy that it would be easier to make a large statue by casting separate smaller parts and then joining them rather than casting it all in one piece. Thus, if any part turned out poorly it could be cast again without having to melt down and recast the whole statue. In avoiding the complexities of large castings, the foundryman now was faced with the task of finding effective ways of joining the sections of his statue. It is with an examination of some of these joining techniques that this report is concerned.

1. *Berlin Foundry Cup.* The artist has shown the interior of a workshop with a statue being assembled.

2. *Berlin Foundry Cup.* On the other side of the cup, the artist has shown the final dressing of the finished statue by scraping.

The earliest evidence from Greece for casting a large statue in several pieces appears to be the early fifth century B.C. illustration on the red-figure Berlin Foundry cup showing in an unclear, abbreviated, artist's conception the assembly and finishing of a large bronze statue.[9] In the shop stands a tall bellows-operated furnace in which bronze is presumably melted either for the actual casting or for the joining procedure.

On the workshop walls hang some tools (planishing [?] hammers, a saw, molds for making plaques [?]) and some feet that are either models for making feet for large statues or actual pre-cast feet to be fitted to a statue. A boy is assembling a statue of which it appears at least the hands, feet, and head were cast separately. He is using a hammer either for making mechanical joins on the statue (pins, dowels, or some sort of "tongue and groove"[10]), or for finishing and smoothing the surface around the joins which had been made with molten bronze in one of the ways noted below. We simply cannot tell. What is significant about this illustration is that we see for the first time a large statue made in several pieces. The painting on the reverse of the cup shows the statue being scraped with a rasp or scraper of some kind to remove tell-tale marks of the workshop. Like so many operations described in writing or pictures by people not deeply versed or even interested in the depict, the result is more tantalizing and ambiguous than informative, and we must rather turn to the actual monuments than to descriptions or illustrations of them.

The logical pieces to examine at this point in our chronological view would be the *Poseidon* from Artemisium and the Delphi *Charioteer*.[11] We know virtually nothing about the technique of the former, nor have I been able to study it carefully. I have not been able to look at the Delphi *Charioteer*, but we are told by Chamoux that it was cast in seven pieces and that the joins, except for that on the neck, were carefully masked by the overhanging drapery which could well cover a multitude of sins, as we shall see later.

We do know that at this time, the first half of the fifth century B.C., a kind of fusion welding known as *flow-welding* was attempted. Flow-welded joins were made in a number of different ways to be described below, but the main principle involved is that molten (filler) bronze of similar composition to the casting was poured on the parts to be joined in order to bring about a fusion between them, with the molten bronze acting both as filler and as heat source. In some instances excess filler metal remains on the interior of the join, though it was usually scraped away from the visible exterior; in other instances virtually all of the filler was merely flowed over the area and channeled off again, resulting in a weld with very little excess metal remaining. These differences are due merely to the geometry of the operation and the amount of metal used rather than any physical properties of the materials. The Chatsworth head (containing about 89 % copper and 10 % tin) was fastened to the neck of the statue by some such method: excess metal from this process still remains in large lumps on the inside of the neck. Since this metal is identical in composition to that of the casting, we can assume that some form of flow-welding was in fact employed.[12] Haynes reports that the arms and legs had also been cast separately and attached to

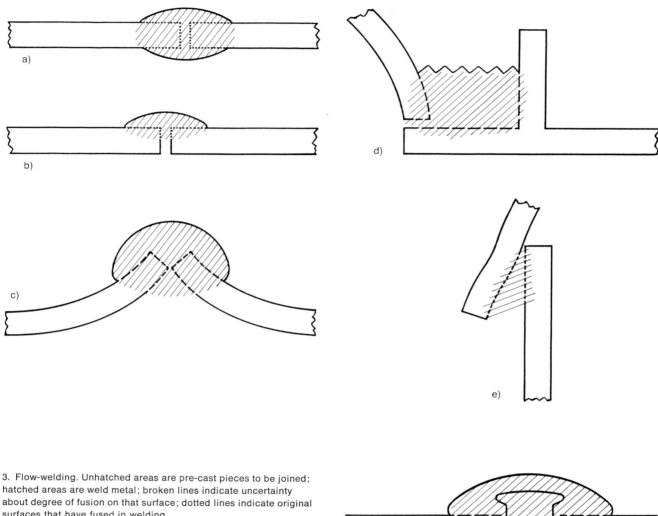

3. Flow-welding. Unhatched areas are pre-cast pieces to be joined; hatched areas are weld metal; broken lines indicate uncertainty about degree of fusion on that surface; dotted lines indicate original surfaces that have fused in welding.

a) Spot weld, in which a weld-through occurred and fused the surfaces of the join area; this is generally done in discrete spots.

b) Running together, in which only partial fusion occurred (no weld-through); this is generally done in a continuous band along the line of the join.

c) Casting together, in which a lump is cast over two surfaces so as to clamp them together; it is not clear whether there is any metallurgical bonding in this process, or if the bond is purely mechanical.

d) Sticking together, in which a pasty lump of metal is made to adhere to several surfaces; the degree of metallurgical bonding is unknown.

e) Filling, in which pasty metal is used as a space filler to keep two large sections of a statue rigid. The degree of metallurgical bonding is unknown.

f) Locking in, in which the dowel-like end of one casting is inserted through a hole in another casting and molten metal is built up over the end of the dowel so that it will not slip out of the hole; the degree of metallurgical bonding is unknown.

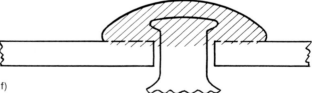

perature may cause hot-short cracking during cooling which may also jeopardize the soundness of the weld. But it is obvious from the examples of flow welding that we have been able to examine that the ancient foundryman was aware of these difficulties and overcame them with great ingenuity in a number of different ways.

By the fourth century B.C. Greek workshops had not only perfected the technique of melting or fusing pre-cast pieces of bronze together in a manner something like that described above, but they used molten or pasty bronze in a number of different ways to secure complex castings. The three over life-size statues of women found in the Piraeus in 1959 are fine examples of some of these approaches; their composition is all similar, with about 87 % copper, 11—12 % tin, and about 1 % lead — probably merely an unintentional impurity.[13] All three statues were cast in many pieces, with some form of

5. *Chatsworth Head*, detail of interior of neck, showing irregular lumps of excess weld metal. *Photo reproduced by courtesy of Bernard Ashmole, Oxford.*

4. *Chatsworth Head,* British Museum. *Photo reproduced by courtesy of the Trustees of the British Museum.*

the body of the statue, of which only this head now remains.

This kind of flow-welding of a copper-tin bronze will work if the area to be joined is heated sufficiently (preferably under non-oxidizing conditions) and enough new filler metal is poured over the area to be joined so that a fusion in the liquid or pasty state may take place between the base metal and the filler metal. The major problem in effecting such a join is the initial wetting of the base metal surface by the liquid filler metal: this wetting is easily jeopardized by the propensity of hot bronze to form impenetrable oxide skins. If such an oxide skin should form on the surfaces to be wetted the weld will not take. The highly refractory tin oxide (SnO_2, with a melting point of 1630° C.) especially complicates this process. If however the oxide can be fluxed or the bronze under it can be molten enough so that the oxide skin is mechanically broken by the force of the flow of hot metal on it, then a fusion can take place, and the join will hold. Moreover, there will be none of these problems if the whole operation is accomplished with the exclusion of oxygen from the weld area, by covering the melt and packing the weld area with charcoal. Finally, it should be noted that localized heating of a large bronze to a high tem-

6. *Athena,* Piraeus Museum, general view. Reproduced from S. Me-latzis and H. Papadakis, *National Museum of Archaeology, Athens,* Munich and Zurich, 1963.

7. *Athena,* exterior, showing deep inward projection of drapery folds.

8. *Athena,* general view of interior, looking from bottom up toward waist and beyond. In the upper portion of the picture are horizontal joins; the extensive chiseling in the foreground of the photo was probably done to remove excess metal from the castings in order to make the sections to be joined thinner and easier to work with.

9. *Athena,* exterior, detail of drapery. The horizontal darker line across the middle of the photo is a welded join of the running-to-gether type (cf. fig. 3 b).

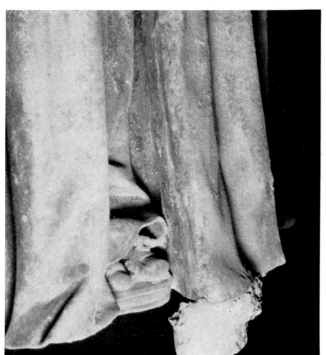

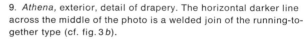

Table I

Composition of bronze statues from the Piraeus, presently in the National Museum, Athens, percentages by weight*

	Cu	Sn	Pb
Kouros	91	8	1
Athena	87	11	1
Artemis	86	12	1
Mask	85	12	3

* Wet chemical analyses done for Bruno Bearzi and reproduced here by his permission.

piece-molding,[14] from models that may, in part, have been wax-dipped. The long vertical sections of drapery that were all cast separately and then joined were not taken by piece molds from a solid model, since they have portions projecting much too far to the inside of the statue to be mere surface reflections of a solid model. Rather these sections of drapery were modeled in order to be joined on the inside of the statue after they had all been modeled, molded, and cast separately. Such a procedure might well have been possible if the model was built of sections of actual stiffened cloth, disassembled, and cast separately.[15] In addition to the vertical lower parts of these statues, the two that could be more closely observed (the *Athena* and the *Large Artemis*) were also cast in several large horizontal sections, with major joins across the waist, skillfully masked by the foundryman with the overhanging folds of the upper garments. The heads were also cast separately, inserted into the upper portions of the garments, and held in place by running them together.

At least four variants of flow-welding are apparent on these statues. The first is a kind of *running together* (cf. fig. 3b): this is used on a number of horizontal joins in the Athena. On the exterior, there is a raised band of weld metal apparent on the seam. On the interior, the two edges of the joined sections are quite distinct, whence it would appear that this kind of join did not melt all the way through the bronze from the outside to the inside, but merely "tacked" the two portions together on the surface. On the *Large Artemis* the same technique was used to join the head to the upper portion of the garment and to attach the lower arms at the biceps on this piece as well as on the *Small Artemis*. A variant of this technique appears to have been used on some of the vertical joins of the *Large Artemis* drapery, where bronze was apparently poured in a channel on the apex of the two folds.

A second method of joining portions of these statues is by a kind of *casting together* (cf. fig. 3c), where two sections especially the bottom of sections of drapery, which are so designed that they have projecting edges for this purpose) are held to-

gether by a large lump of bronze that was poured over the whole area, effectively clamping the pieces together. In some cases some metallic bonding may have taken place between the cast-on metal and the original castings, but, to judge from the cracks on these joins, they were secured mechanically owing to the massive amount of metal deposited over the area rather than because of metallurgical bonding. There are good examples of this on the *Athena*. A variant of this method is casting a whole separate molded piece on to a junction to hold the various parts together; a good example of this is to be found on the *Large Artemis*.

Temporary molds built up against the castings appear to have been used in the foregoing methods for holding the molten bronze against the area to be joined. It is not quite so clear that molds were employed in an operation that appears to be *sticking* two surfaces *together* (cf. fig. 3d). In the best illustration of this technique (on the *Athena*) a projection had been cast onto one of the drapery sections; in order to join this section to another a pasty lump of metal was somehow pushed between the projection and the other surface — it seems to have stuck, with, presumably, a minimum of bonding taking

10. *Athena*, interior, detail of drapery. The horizontal line across the middle of the photo is the interior of the welded join in fig. 9; there is no evidence of weld-through (cf. figs. 38, 56—58).

place. A similar form of *sticking* is apparent on the *Large Artemis*. Whether molds were used to cast together the sandals and garments of these statues is not clear; but on one of them a casting fin remains which indicates a mold was used here, although it may have been part of the operation illustrated in figs. 19—20.

Another variant of adding pasty or molten metal is widely illustrated on these two large statues in the area under their

11. *Large Artemis,* Piraeus Museum, general view of upper half. The identification of this figure is uncertain; the smaller female seems to be an Artemis with quiver; this larger figure might also be one. Reproduced from Melatzis and Papadakis, *National Museum of Archaeology, Athens,* Munich and Zurich, 1963.

12. *Large Artemis,* detail showing attachment of head-neck portion to upper edge of garment; the edge of the filler metal shows clearly against the lower portion of the neck.

13. *Large Artemis,* detail of arm, exterior. The horizontal crack in the bronze is where the join was made; in this particular place the two sections did not fuse together on the exterior.

14. *Large Artemis,* detail of arm, interior. Some filler metal (indicated by arrow) remains in the join here. The light gray material below is some of the refractory which was either part of the core of the casting or was added when the welding was done in order to channel the filler metal.

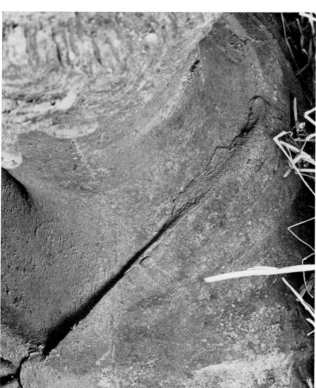

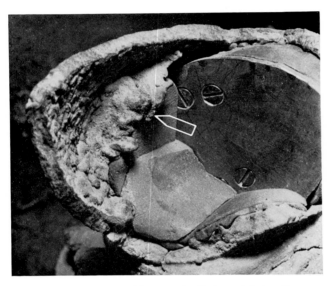

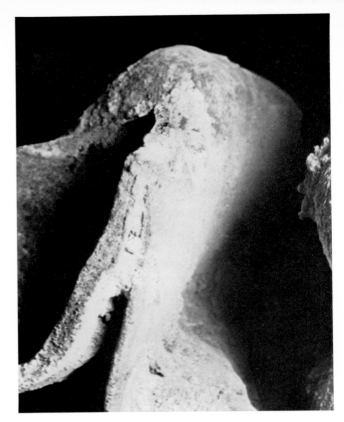

15. *Small Artemis,* Piraeus Museum, detail of arm, interior. The irregular lump of metal (indicated by arrow) projecting from the broken stump of the casting is excess weld metal from a flow-welding operation. The screws, metal plate, and plasticene in the lower portion of the arm are all parts of the modern consolidation of this statue.

16. *Large Artemis,* detail of lower portion of drapery, interior. The vertical band in the center of the photo is the weld on the edges of two folds of drapery.

17. *Athena,* detail of piece cast over projecting edges of drapery folds.

18. *Athena,* detail of piece cast over a number of surfaces to hold them together.

19. *Large Artemis,* detail of exterior, bottom of two drapery sections joined by a piece cast over them. The uneven edge of the weld metal is apparent at the right. At the top of the photograph is the vertical sharp dark outline of the upper part of the cast-on piece which has not bonded well to one of the drapery sections. The blurred crack in the center, lower foreground (indicated by arrow) is where the cast-on piece has broken away from the other drapery section; nevertheless, the join has held.

20. *Large Artemis,* detail of interior, same area as fig.19. The crack in the lower foreground is the same as that indicated by arrow on fig.19. The casting fin near the lower edge of drapery fold (indicated by arrow) may be a remnant from the casting-together operation. The lumps of excess metal on the right side are probably irregularities of the original casting; they are in stark contrast to the more carefully molded and cast area above the casting fin.

21. *Athena,* detail of exterior, bottom of two drapery sections. The curved piece at left is one section, the projection facing the viewer is cast integrally with the horizontal section below; between the projection and the curved piece has been pressed a lump of pasty (note the irregular sharp contours on top) filler metal (indicated by arrow).

22. *Large Artemis,* detail of exterior, bottom of two drapery sections, joined by a lump formed between them.

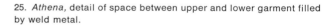

25. *Athena,* detail of space between upper and lower garment filled by weld metal.

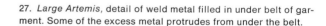

23. *Large Artemis*, detail of interior of attachment of sandal to bottom of garment. It is not clear whether the irregular metal at left of sandal is a remnant of the original casting operation, or a sticking together operation.

24. *Large Artemis*, detail of interior of sandal (upper left) attachment to bottom of garment. The folds in the background and crack at lower right are those illustrated in figs. 19—20. The casting fin (indicated by arrow) running horizontally near the bottom edge of the drapery might be connected with the sandal attachment or the joining of those drapery sections.

26. *Athena*, detail of selective use of filling weld metal between a corner of upper garment and main body of lower. The dark slightly raised band running over the lower garment appears to be a long, continuous flow-weld of the running-together variety illustrated in figs. 3*b*, 9, and 10.

27. *Large Artemis*, detail of weld metal filled in under belt of garment. Some of the excess metal protrudes from under the belt.

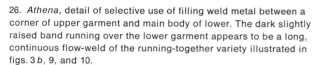

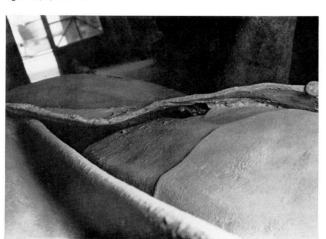

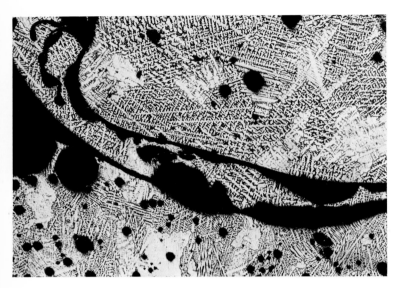

28. Photomicrograph of an experimental flow weld of an alloy of 84 % copper, 16 % tin. The long wavy black regions running across the micrograph are broken up oxide skins displaced by the force of the molten filler metal hitting them. x 50; etch: potassium bichromate.

29. An unetched detail (x 200) of fig. 28 shows the skin of oxides (grey, fine-structured borders) along the edges of the dark regions.

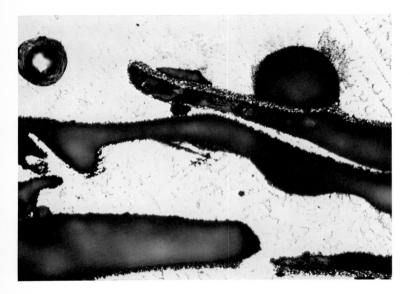

overhanging upper garments. It was noted before that these overhangs are important for masking the horizontal joins of the upper and lower halves of the statues. They apparently serve another purpose as well, which is to help keep the two sections better attached by means of metal added in the hollow area under these overhangs so *filling* up the space that there is no sideways play left (cf. fig. 3c). There is no evidence of any bonding between the surface of the upper garment and the lower drapery by means of this added metal, but the mere mechanical filling of this space probably serves to give some security to the statue.

To what degree these various joins represent successful metallurgical bonds in which some of the filler metal has wetted the surfaces to be joined and actually alloyed with those surfaces remains to be seen; unfortunately this can only be properly attested by metallographic examinations which require removal of a sizeable section of metal across the join. But judging from their surface appearances alone, little bonding seems to have occurred except in the first *running together* technique (cf. fig. 3b). The joins have held because of their geometrical design, which has insured a mechanical bond, rather than the metallurgical qualities of the weld. It should be recalled again here how difficult it is to weld a copper-tin bronze because of the easy formation of skins of oxide which must somehow be fluxed away or broken by the force of the hot metal before the base metal surfaces can be wetted by the new filler metal.

Experiments in flow-welding bronzes in the laboratory are summarized in the accompanying table (table II). Small pairs of plates $3/8$ inch thick were made of a given alloy; several pairs of these plates were set side by side in sand molds and covered over except for a circular area $5/8$ inch in diameter over the join; a channel led from the circular area to a hole through which the excess molten metal could run off. Molten bronze of the same composition as the plates was poured on them at various temperatures above the melting point of the alloy to determine the flow-weldability of the bronze. This procedure was repeated for several different alloys.[16] Thus a bronze of composition 93 % copper, 7 % tin (melting point 1050° C) required 4 $3/4$ pounds of bronze at 1125° C poured for 12 seconds to attain enough surface wetting for even a partial bond; 1150° C (100° C superheat) was required for a complete weld-through. No advantage was obtained when small amounts of lead (1—5 %) were added to the alloy, even though the melting point was lowered; in fact, weld-through did not occur even as much as 150° C above the melting point. There would appear to be some reaction of the oxides here that we need to study more carefully. When the lead content becomes 11% and higher bonding and weld-throughs do occur in the 100° C superheat range. It is, moreover, significant that with the 73 %

copper, 5% tin, 22% lead alloy weld-throughs occur exactly at 1050° C and above, in other words, 100° C above the melting point of the alloy and at a temperature where important reactions between the lead oxide and tin oxide may be taking place (see below). Finally, with an alloy of 84% copper, 16% tin (melting point 950° C), it was again possible to attain weld-throughs at 100° C superheat (as with the ternary alloy of identical melting point). In this last instance the oxide skin was apparently not as deleterious as in alloys with lower tin content and small amounts of lead, for though the tin oxide (probably SnO_2) is probably particularly coherent with 16% tin, it is thin and easily pierced by the force of the molten metal hitting it.

Greek bronzes (like those from the Piraeus that we have discussed above) tend to have 10—12% tin in them, along with

Table II

Flow-welding experiments done at the research laboratory for archaeological materials at M.I.T.

Alloy (by weight percent)			Melting point (°C)	Temperature of pour (°C)	Amount of pour (lb.)	Length of pour (sec.)	Success of weld
Cu	Sn	Pb					
93	7	0	1050	1080	2⁹/₁₆	12	No
				1125	4³/₄	24	partial weld
				1150	3¹/₂	14	weld-through
92.6	6.4	1	1035	1125	4	12	No
				1150	4	15	No
				1175	4	12	No
91.7	6.3	2.0	1025	1125	2³/₄	13	No
				1150	3⁵/₁₆	13	No
				1175	3³/₄	15	No
88.9	6.1	5.0	1015	1125	3³/₄	15	No
				1150	4³/₄	13	Weld slightly fused to surface
				1175	3³/₈	13	No
82.4	6.6	11.0	980	1080	4	16	All bonded, but not certain if complete weld-through
				1100	4¹/₄	16	
				1125	4¹/₂	16	
73	5	22	950	1000	4¹/₄	15	No
				1025	4¹/₈	13	No
				1050	3¹/₂	12	weld-through
				1085	1¹/₈	4	weld-through
84	16	0	950	1050	2¹/₄	15	weld-through
				1100	1¹/₄	7	weld-through
				1150	1¹/₄	6	weld-through

some impurities such as lead. From the still sketchy evidence of our experiments (they were actually directed at examining the flow-weldability of the ternary alloy with high lead content) we might expect that by flow-welding with weld metal at least 100° C above the melting point of the alloy (for 10—12% tin bronzes the melting points are about 1020—1000° C) one could wet and partially bond these surfaces provided they are sufficiently free of oxides. The depth of the fusion, once the oxides are penetrated, would be determined by the length of the pour, or rather, the amount of heat brought to the join, since the molten metal acts at once as heat source and filler metal for the weld. Far more careful examination is now needed to understand more fully the deleterious role of oxides in this operation. Nonetheless, it is apparent from the numerous examples of flow welds we have examined on the Piraeus bronzes that the Greek foundrymen were able to attain sufficiently high temperatures, keep the bronzes relatively free of oxides at crucial moments, and achieve at least some bonding in a good number of flow welds. Because of difficulties they may have encountered in the past with oxide formation and broken joins, they tended to rely more heavily on the geometry of the join, and the mechanical advantage to be gained from its design, rather than on metallurgical bonding: we have shown this clearly where large lumps have been cast over the edges of two sections to join them (the cracks on these are highly significant in showing their lack of bonding), or where bronze was poured between two pieces to produce a filling effect. On the other hand, the added lumps of metal between two planes, and the patently run-together joins do seem to have accomplished more than just minimal bonding and the joins have withstood corrosion for 2000 years.

A striking combination of these various joining techniques is found on the fourth or third century B.C. *Lady from the Sea.* The complex construction of this piece is remarked by Mrs. Ridgway, and she illustrates well the various sections in which the statue was made.[17] Again, I presume that the drapery sections have been cast separately from a model that may have been stiffened textile and could be disassembled easily for molding. She notes (p. 332, n. 27) that the head pieces were joined by "nails... or a tongue-and-groove system." I have seen no evidence of this and cannot discuss it. Though the inside of the piece is rather heavily corroded and covered with accretions from the sea there do remain some telltale signs of the joining methods employed.

Repairs have been made at the top of the right breast by simply pouring molten bronze into the defective area, attaining some kind of fusion, and then subsequently dressing the outside of the piece so that virtually no sign of the repair appears. This process is much clearer on the interior where there are several lumps of excess metal still protruding. The vorious

30. *Lady from the Sea,* Izmir Museum, general view. Reproduced from Ridgway, *American Journal of Archaeology 71 (1967), pl.97, fig.1, by her permission.*

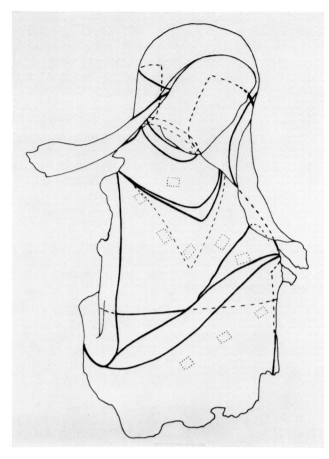

31. *Lady from the Sea,* drawing showing the pre-cast pieces from which the statue was assembled.

ends of drapery sections were secured by a combination of mechanically *locking* them *in* and actually fusing them to the surrounding bronze. The ends of these sections were inserted through holes in the piece to which they were to be attached. Molten bronze was then poured around these projecting ends until it built up a lump, keeping this projection from slipping back out through the hole, but sufficient bronze was also poured to achieve a slight bonding. The effect is a combination of mechanical *(locking-in)* and metallurgical bonding. On the interior some square areas are apparent near the center of the chest that might well be the ends of some of the drapery fragments that have merely been hammered over flat to hold onto the main portion of the casting, but it should be added that this is still mere conjecture. Finally there is a major seam apparent running through the middle of the figure across the two breasts. It appears to have been "tacked" with molten bronze

in several places, including, on the left side, a junction point of several sections of drapery. This statue illustrates the technical ingenuity of the foundryman, who had to use a variety of joining methods, most of which required the use of metal at temperatures of 1150° C poured into carefully designed molds, in reasonably restricted areas.

An important piece illustrating a kind of transition from the varied ad hoc procedures of the Greek foundryman to the almost assemly line efficiency of the Roman foundry is the *Arringatore.* This Etruscan sculpture of the third or first century B.C. appears to be the earliest piece studied in detail with an appreciable lead content (about 5 %, with about 11.5 % tin; melting point of alloy around 960° C).[18] According to Dohrn, the *Arringatore* was cast in seven pieces (two legs, left hand, right arm, head, upper and lower body halves), which were subsequently "welded" together. The legs, as he observes, bore

32. *Lady from the Sea*, detail of statue's proper right side. The dark patches on and above the right breast are the remains of patching by flow-welding. A comparison of this photograph with fig. 31 will show that the drapery folds running across the middle of the bust are made in several separate pieces which are apparent only from an examination of the interior of the statue.

33. *Lady from the Sea,* general view of the interior of the statue. The lumps on the interior of the right breast (indicated by a hatched arrow) are the excess metal from the repairs illustrated in fig. 32. The large lump (indicated by a white arrow) farther up on the right side is the excess metal from a lock-in weld; another lock-in weld, for the end of a sliver of drapery, is indicated by another white arrow below the center of chest. Note especially the lack of correspondence between the contours of the drapery folds on the interior (this picture) and the exterior (fig. 32) of this statue, indicating that much of the drapery detailing on the exterior was applied in separate pieces.

34. *Lady from the Sea,* detail of exterior of proper right side. At the center of the photo is the junction of several drapery fragments.

35. *Lady from the Sea,* detail of interior of proper right side. At the right is the locked-in junction of drapery fragments illustrated in fig. 34. The arrow indicates the end of one of the drapery fragments, but the whole oval area above it is part of the join.

the whole weight of the bronze and were securely fastened by: (1) providing them with long projections which were inserted in appropriate holes in the figure's garment, and then hammered over and "welded"; (2) directly "welding" their upper edges to the garment; (3) securing them with dowels. It is the "welding" in which we are particularly interested; Dohrn illustrates it by good detailed photographs, but, unfortunately, he does not describe it adequately. This "welding" is used for attaching all the other extremities, and notably, for joining the upper and lower halves of the body. Whether this is a *melting together,* using a filler metal of the same alloy as the base metal of the casting by means of flowing in large quantities of molten metal, or whether it is a more abbreviated form of *flow spot welding* (to be illustrated on the Roman pieces below) is not clear. It is, however, significant that the main seam of this piece runs straight across the various vertical drapery folds without the slightest regard for masking the join. This is a striking departure from the Greek drapery we have discussed so far, in which all the joining is done as inconspicuously as possible under overhanging folds, or at the bottom of sections of drapery. Had the need for masking the seam been impressed upon the Etruscan foundryman he could easily have cast most of the body in one piece (except for the extremities), or better still he might have cast the drapery in several large vertical panels (like the Piraeus bronzes), joining them by their edges inconspicuously on the sides of the figure either with *cast-on* lumps, or with projecting tongues fitted into corresponding holes on the other portion of the drapery which could then be *locked-in* by hammering and/or pouring bronze on them (as was done on the *Arringatore*'s legs, or on the *Lady of the Sea*). The foundryman did not choose any of these methods but preferred to cast top and bottom separately and join them horizontally across the middle. Whether we see here the first step in a new conception of how to assemble large statues — a conception that does not shrink from showing where the work was done, but rather makes a point of sectioning the statue in a manner most

Table III

Compositions of various parts of the *Arringatore* in the Museo Archeologico, Florence, percentages by weight*

	Cu	Sn	Pb	Zn
Body (lower part)	82.20	11.48	5.41	0.26
Body (upper part)	82.75	11.78	5.15	—
Right arm	82.84	11.53	5.10	0.27
Left hand	82.20	11.03	5.98	0.31
Head	83.28	8.46	7.36	0.33
Clavus	93.00	4.59	2.06	—

* Wet chemical analyses done for Bruno Bearzi and reproduced here by his permission.

36. *Arringatore,* Museo Archeologico, Florence, general view.

37. *Arringatore,* drawing of left leg, showing projections that insert into lower part of figure's garment. *Drawing taken from Dohrn, fig. 33, p. 113 (see note 18).*

38. *Arringatore,* detail of join of left arm on interior of statue. The thin dark line across the middle of the picture is the space between the two castings that are joined here; the small lump at the center (indicated by arrow) is a weld-through; at the left of the join is another weld-through. *Photo taken from Dohrn, fig. 5c, p. 102 (see note 18).*

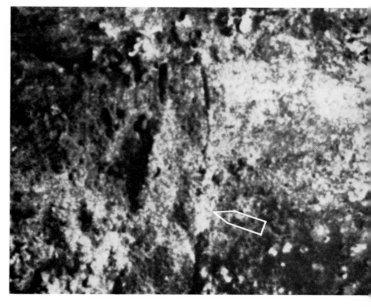

39. Life-size *Youth* from Agde, Louvre, general view. *Photo reproduced from S. Delbourgo, fig.1 (see also her note 21) by her permission.*

40. *Young Athlete,* style of Polykleitos, Toledo Museum of Art, gift of Edward Drummond Libbey. This Roman copy of a Polykleitan original exhibitis the characteristic oval bordered welds on the left leg around the knee, at the left wrist, and across the middle of the torso above the waist. The break on the proper right arm shows a join made with rectangular patches and lead. *Photo reproduced by courtesy of the Toledo Museum of Art.*

41. Fragment of over life-size draped figure, *polygatus,* Museum of Fine Arts, Boston, general view. This fragment may have been part of a large relief of bronze figures applied to a stone or wood background.

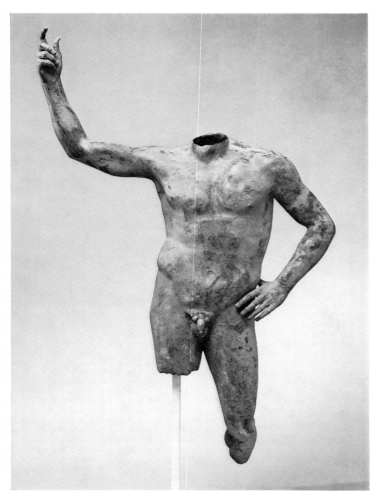

42. Over life-size bronze statue of Hellenistic *Ruler* type, Museum of Fine Arts, Houston, reproduced here by courtesy of the museum.

43. *Houston Ruler*, detail of line of oval welds on small of statue's back.

44. *Polygatus,* detail of concentric ovals in one of welds along main join. The cracks to the right of the larger oval are hot-short cracks due to the cooling properties of this high lead alloy. The sample for metallographic study was removed from the right edge of this area.

convenient to the mold-builder — or whether this piece is merely a matter of foundry chance, cannot be determined. What follows in Roman foundry practice is somehow previewed by the Etruscan *Arringatore.*

We come finally to the finest examples of ancient *flow-welding,* as illustrated on Roman bronzes, all of which have notably high lead contents (ranging from about 11.5 % to 25 %).[19] I will first describe the appearance of these welds on large statues and then discuss the metallurgical properties of this technique, which is one of the most impressive examples of the expertise of Roman metallurgy that I know. A number of statues will be examined that illustrate several variants of this technique.[20] They all date in the first three centuries A.D. and come from various provinces of the Roman Empire. The earliest example of this technique that has been well studied is found on a statue newly dredged up from a river in Agde, France.[21] A fine bronze youth, thought to be a Hadrianic copy of a Polykleitan original, now in the Toledo, Ohio, Museum of Fine Arts, also illustrates this technique,[22] though I know it only from pictures. A fragment of a draped figure from southern Italy referred to as a *polygatus* (in the Boston Museum of Fine Arts) was the piece that inspired this study.[23] It dates from sometime in the second century. Finally there is a superb group of Severan pieces from the late second and early third century thought to come from a single large dedication in southern Turkey — these pieces are now dispersed in the Houston Museum of Fine Arts, a number of private collections, and the art market.[24] This collection forms the epitome of this extraordinary welding technique.

The positioning of the seams on the statues and their general uniform outward appearance are the most striking characteristics of this joining method. Apparently the Romans were not too deeply concerned with where their joins appeared on statues: many examples are found on nude figures, with seams at the neck, arms near the shoulders, middle of the torso or waist, somewhere across each thigh, and often at the ankles and wrists, so there are anywhere from 7 to 11 pieces joined in this way. The welds themselves now appear as circles or ovals of varying sizes with slightly raised borders. It has been observed in a least one instance that these borders are lower in lead content than the rest of the alloy,[25] apparently because of metallurgical segregation: this causes differential corrosion which makes these borders stand out so clearly. Occasionally the borders are concentric; in other instances the raised borders are not too clear, and it becomes very difficult to detect the welds. The circles and/or ovals appear either individually as repairs of poorly run castings or as spot welds of seams that do not require extensive welding — in this form the line of the abutting surfaces of the two parts are generally apparent between welds. In other instances, mainly on the major (and

Table IV

Compositions of various parts of two Roman bronze statues, percentages by weight

	Cu	Sn	Pb
Agde youth, Louvre*			
(1) Average of casting alloy	67.3	7.8	22.2
(2) Weld metal	65.8	8.15	22.25
(3) Raised borders of welded areas**	?	?	ca. 10
Toledo youth, Toledo Museum of Art			
Cast alloy of left hand***	78	4	17

 * Wet chemical analyses done at Laboratoire du Musée du Louvre.

 ** Analysis done by ultraviolet emission spectrography at Laboratoire du Musée du Louvre.

 *** Semiquantitative analysis done by emission spectrography and X-ray diffraction at Research Laboratory, Museum of Fine Arts, Boston.

Table V

Composition of various parts of the *polygatus*, Museum of Fine Arts, Boston, percentages by weight*

	Cu	Sn	Pb
Weld metal on inside of left shoulder	68.5	4.8	19.5
Weld metal from interior of main join	67.7	3.1	19.9
Upper part of casting, interior	65.6	3.5	21.9
Lower part of casting, interior	65.7	6.6	23.8
Upper part of casting, from section of join	65.5	6.6	24.8
Lower part of casting, from section of join	54.1	3.7	38.5

 * Wet chemical analyses done by Donald L. Guernsey at the Central Analytical Laboratory, Department of Metallurgy and Materials Science, M.I.T.

Table VI

Composition of various parts of statues from a Severan group, percentages by weight

	Cu	Sn	Pb
Draped figure, private collection	81.0	7.58	11.5
Houston "Ruler," Museum of Fine Arts, Houston*			
(1) Section of casting from neck	75.8	5.3	15.4
(2) Lump of weld metal, inside left leg	67.4	7.8	17.4
(3) Lump of weld metal, inside right leg	68.0	7.9	21.2

 * Analyzed at M.I.T. Central Analytical Laboratory by wet chemistry.

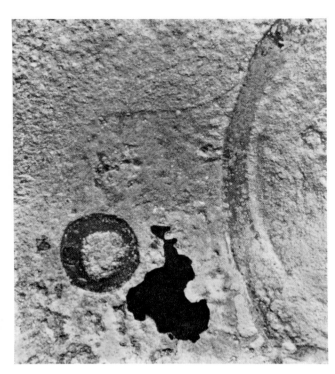

45. Separate leg from Severan group, private collection, detail of exterior of join. The large rectangular patches are in the area of a flow-welded join (see fig. 55 for interior view), but none of the characteristic ovals or circles are evident.

47. *Agde Youth,* detail of proper left side at waist height. Both the dark bordered circle and the lighter raised border to the right are from flow spot-welded repairs. *Photo reproduced from S. Delbourgo, fig. 5 (see note 21) by her permission.*

48. Over life-size male figure of ruler type, probably *Septimius Severus,* private collection, detail of left leg. The straight horizontal white line marks the abutment of two sections of the leg. The separate oval areas are individual flow spot-welds. Note that each of these welds has at least two raised borders, indicating perhaps two or more pours for each spot.

46. *Houston Ruler,* detail below buttock. The circle with a dark border (partly covered by a sandy incrustation) is a flow spot-welded repair.

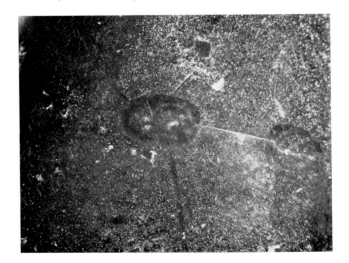

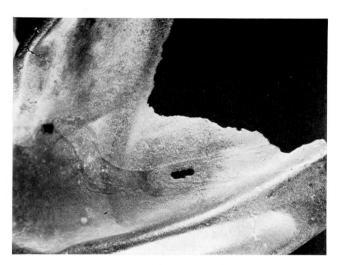

49. *Septimius Severus,* detail of another part of same join illustrated in fig. 48, showing clearly four individual spot welds along the line of the join. The horizontal faceting apparent above and below the join is due to extensive scraping of the surface, probably in order to remove all traces of the welding operation (cf. fig. 2).

51. *Polygatus,* detail of left end of join on exterior. The long uneven oval on the left follows the curved contours of the drapery, from which it takes its irregular shape. At the center of this area two weld spots overlap each other, which is unusual in this technique. The rectangular holes are apparent in this portion of the join, too.

50. *Polygatus,* detail of right side of join on exterior. The line of the join is clear as a series of irregular ovals with raised borders; in the middle, below this line, is a large oval repair. The hot-short cracks along the join are due to rapid cooling. The square holes in two of the spot-welds along the main join may be connected with some kind of clamping device used to hold the two pieces in place as they were being welded.

52. *Houston Ruler,* detail of exterior of main join on small of back. The contiguous ovals are apparent in the middle of the photograph.

final) seam of these statues through the middle of the torso, the circles and ovals are arranged contiguously, forming a continuous zone of individually executed spot welds with the original surfaces completely obliterated. Some of these welded areas appear rather porous and cracked owing to excessive heating and shrinkage: hot-short cracking is especially liable to occur in bronzes of such high lead contents.

Fortunately, we have also been able to observe the interior of many of these joins, either at breaks near the joins or through holes in the statue in such places that one can see the interior opposite. On the *individual* noncontiguous *spot welds* the weld metal melted all the way through the casting and is deposited in lumps or slightly spread out pools on the interior of the join. This would seem to indicate that some clay or other refractory material was packed fairly close to the interior surface of the joining area as a mold to restrain the molten metal when it ran through. The abutment of the two edges of the castings is clearly apparent except in the immediate area of the weld.[26] In the case of *contiguous spot welds* the interior shows whole runs of metal not clearly distinguishable one from the other (unlike the appearance on the outside of the piece). In these instances it appears that there had been a continuous run of metal on the inside, though the outside clearly shows that the welds were discrete operations. This would seem to indicate that a single channel of mold material was placed under the seam on the inside of the statue, while metal was applied locally to individual molds built over the weld spots on the exterior. In these cases it is significant that none of the original abutment of the two castings is any longer apparent on the interior, since the whole join area was fused together by the welding process. In short, even the surface or macro-appearance of these welds indicates that there had been complete weld-through and bonding in the welded areas, and that there is no question of the solidity of the join here, whereas the flimsier appearance (and reality) of the fourth century B.C. Greek flow welds raises questions as to their soundness. (An obvious comparison can be made between the short horizontal flow weld on the drapery of the Piraeus *Athena* [figs. 9–10, where the abutment of the two castings is apparent along the full length of the interior of the join] and any of the weld-throughs described above.)

The microstructure of these bronzes corroborates what we have just observed and goes still further in explaining how and why these joins are so successful. I should add a word of warning, however: the careful scrutiny of these microstructures and attempts at reproducing them experimentally have, as is so often the case, raised more questions than we can yet answer, so that here too, we can only point the direction in which more work needs still to be done.

A section through one of the welded circles on the Boston

53. *Agde Youth,* detail of left leg before it was restored. Note that the leg broke above the welded join, which is again marked by the raised borders of spot welds. Further down on the leg are clear traces of welded repairs of the faulty casting. *Photograph reproduced from S. Delbourgo, fig. 4 (see note 21) by her permission.*

54. *Polygatus,* detail of large welded patch below join. Not only are there hot-short cracks above this large patch, but the patch and area below it are very porous (filled with blow-holes) and are in turn repaired with small rectangular patches which were hammered into appropriately chiseled out areas to fill particularly badly damaged spots.

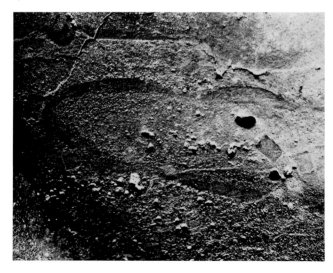

55. Separate leg, detail of welded join on interior. Discrete lumps of weld-through, with the abutment of the two cast edges between them, are apparent here.

57. *Septimius Severus,* detail of join at waist on interior of side of statue. Here the weld-through spilled over more unevenly than on figs. 55 and 56, indicating that an excess of filler metal had been poured. The edge of the upper casting projects inward over the edge of the lower one by several millimeters, though on the exterior the two castings are perfectly flush — this gives some indication of the amount of carving and dressing that must have been done to obtain a clean fit for the pre-cast pieces; the high lead content of this alloy greatly aided this cutting operation.

56. *Septimius Severus,* detail of join at waist on interior of front of statue. Discrete lumps of weld-through obliterate the abutment of the edges of the castings in only two places. Note the jog in the line of abutment of the two castings. The square hole at the upper right corner of the photograph once contained a chaplet, which was removed and the hole plugged when the statue received its final dressing.

58. *Polygatus,* detail of left end of join on interior (cf. fig. 51, exterior of same area). The lumpy excess weld metal forms a continuous line here, obliterating the original abutment of the edges of the two castings. The extensive chiseling on the lower portion of the figure was probably done to facilitate the fitting of the two sections and their welding (cf. fig. 8, where I noted the same operation).

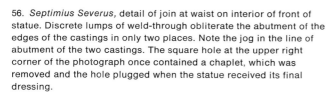

polygatus shows that the as-cast portion is basically the alpha solid solution of copper and tin, with moderate coring; large and small globules of lead have segregated as irregular shapes along the copper-tin grain boundaries, or in completely separate large, round globules; there are also areas of alpha-delta eutectoid rich in tin. As we approach the weld area the structure becomes finer (cooled more rapidly), the lead is dispersed more finely (though there are still large globules) and the eutectoid is more frequent and also more finely distributed. At the edges of the weld zone itself appear some anomalous lines of continuous alpha phase accentuated by lead globules behind them. We have called these lines "stringers" for want of a better word. Our feeling is that they represent some kind of "fossilized surfaces" that formed momentarily during cooling: when more molten bronze came into contact with the surface the lead was somehow removed from the immediate surface, and these fossilized surfaces resulted (see below our attempts at reproducing them). We should stress that in the various examples of Roman welds that were examined we have found these fossilized surfaces only on this one piece, but here we have noted them not only at this main seam but also on some of the excess weld metal from the neck of this figure, and on some other excess metal on the interior of the statue. This was the first piece to be examined, and the stringers constituted a major red herring across the course of this study!

Though I have sampled the marvelous *Houston Ruler* extensively, I cannot clearly identify an actual junction of cast and weld metal, but have looked at several examples of excess weld metal from the inside of the statue. The structure is much like that of the *polygatus,* with the notable absence of the fossilized surfaces, very little eutectoid, and one sample showing extensive oxidation, which we have not found on the *polygatus.* Clearly this one weld (at the bottom of the leg) was kept hot for some time under oxidizing conditions. It is difficult to distinguish between filler metal and base metal on the one section we have made through a join; the lack of bonding apparent in this region is probably because we have here an example of weld metal that spilled over the join and did not actually fuse with the casting.

The examination of the Agde bronze shows another baffling variety of structures (the work on this statue was done in the Louvre Laboratory — see note 21). Mrs. Delbourgo identified fairly large, extensively cored, alpha-phase grains, interspersed with lead of globules, of various size, of which some are lighter than others. Amidst all this is very finely dispersed alpha-delta eutectoid. Many of the larger lead globules seem to be surrounded with alpha-phase borders that are similar to those that we have reproduced (see below), and that we assume to be metallurgically related to the fossilized surface, but it is sig-

59. *Houston Ruler,* detail of broken end of left leg, interior. The break, below the join, reveals a continuous band of excess weld metal (weld-through) around the interior of the join.

60. *Polygatus.* The mounted and polished section of the join removed for metallographic study (cf. fig. 44); the dressed exterior surface of the statue is at the top. The two dark diagonal zones are the edges of the weld.

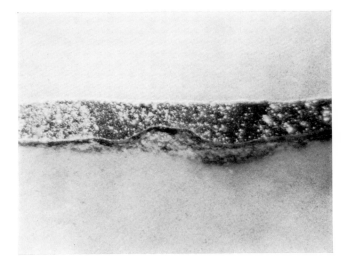

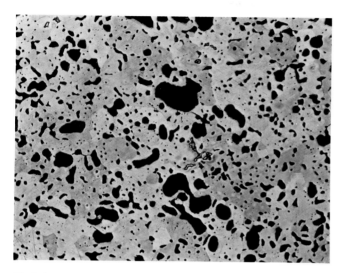

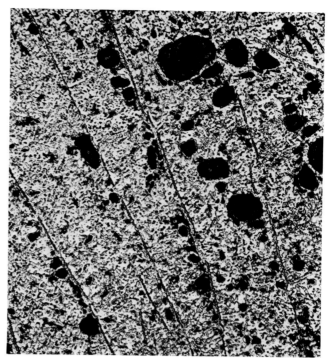

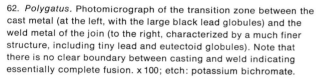

61. *Polygatus*. Photomicrograph of the cast structure shows (in grey) alpha solid solution of copper and tin with moderate coring, irregularly dispersed lead segregated in small and large globules (appears black). At the center is a small zone of alpha-delta eutectoid. x 100; etch: potassium bichromate.

62. *Polygatus*. Photomicrograph of the transition zone between the cast metal (at the left, with the large black lead globules) and the weld metal of the join (to the right, characterized by a much finer structure, including tiny lead and eutectoid globules). Note that there is no clear boundary between casting and weld indicating essentially complete fusion. x 100; etch: potassium bichromate.

63. *Polygatus*. Photomicrograph of weld metal showing fine structure characterized mainly by tiny eutectoid and segregated lead particles, though some of the lead has also segregated in large globules. The long chains running vertically thorough the photomicrograph are the "fossilized surfaces." x 100; etch: copper ammonium chloride.

64. *Houston Ruler*. Photomicrograph of excess weld metal from inside left leg showing the basic alpha solid solution of copper and tin with heavy coring, segregated lead globules of various sizes, and moderate amounts of alpha-delta eutectoid (one concentration indicated by hatched arrow), though the latter is not as dense as in the *polygatus* weld (cf. fig. 63). x 200; etch: potassium bichromate.

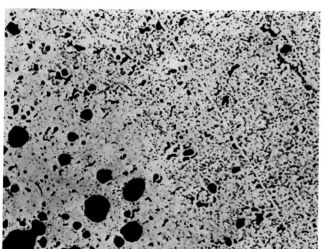

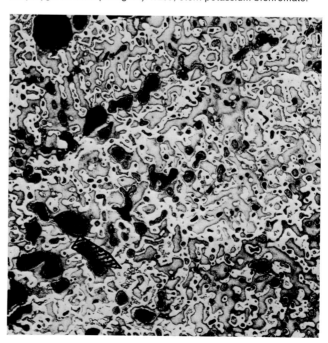

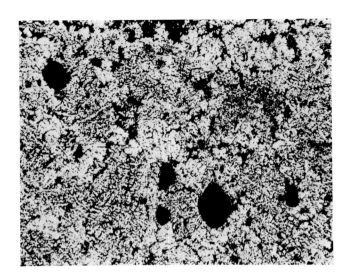

65. *Houston Ruler*. Photomicrograph of excess weld metal from inside right leg showing heavy oxidation (fine black network) which gives nice visual emphasis to the dendritic structure of the alpha solid solution. X 100; etch: potassium bichromate.

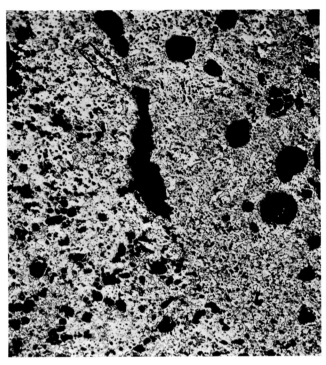

67. *Houston Ruler*. Photomicrograph of part of section removed from neck. The discontinuous black zone (indicated by an arrow) is the boundary between weld metal (left of zone) and casting (right of dark zone). Some fusion has taken place (below large dark area) but not along the whole surface. The crystal size, lead dispersal, and amount of eutectoid are similar in both metals, except that some of the lead has formed in exceptionally large globules in the cast metal on the right.

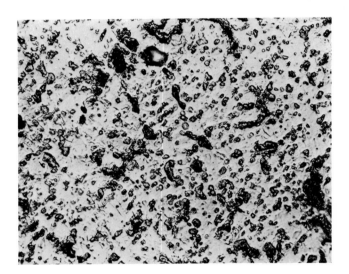

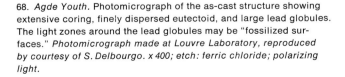

66. *Houston Ruler*. Photomicrograph of heavily oxidized portion (cf. fig. 65). x 500; etch: potassium bichromate.

68. *Agde Youth.* Photomicrograph of the as-cast structure showing extensive coring, finely dispersed eutectoid, and large lead globules. The light zones around the lead globules may be "fossilized surfaces." *Photomicrograph made at Louvre Laboratory, reproduced by courtesy of S. Delbourgo. x 400; etch: ferric chloride; polarizing light.*

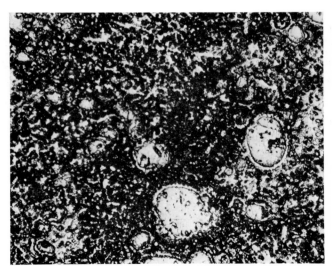

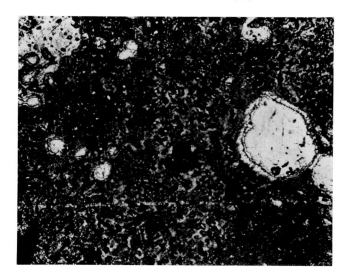

69. *Agde Youth*. Photomicrograph of weld metal showing less coring than as-cast metal, but essentially a similar structure. *Photomicrograph made at Louvre Laboratory, reproduced by courtesy of S. Delbourgo. x 400; etch: ferric chloride; polarizing light.*

70. *Agde Youth*. Photomicrograph of the raised border of a spot weld showing unusually large grain size, finely dispersed alpha-delta eutectoid and a singular absence of lead. *Photomicrograph made at Louvre Laboratory, reproduced by courtesy of S. Delbourgo. x 400; etch: ferric chloride; polarizing light.*

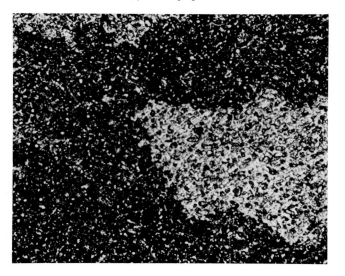

nificant that Mrs. Delbourgo does not identify these fossilized surfaces anywhere in her samples. (We should note that her microprobe analyses of the gray lead areas show them to be rich in tin.) The middle of the welded join shows a structure similar to the foregoing. The border of the weld, on the other hand, shows large grains and little lead except some dispersed finely over the very surface of the section. This latter is quite different from any structure of the *polygatus* or the *Houston Ruler,* and seems to indicate that this area was cooled particularly slowly, though the presence of considerable eutectoid is hard to explain then. Mrs. Delbourgo observes that these borders are poorer in lead than the rest of the alloy (only about 10 %), and we can then probably conclude that they are richer in tin, which would account for the eutectoid, and also that they are more corrosion resistant than the rest of the alloy.

It should be perfectly apparent from the above descriptions and attempted interpretations of the microstructures that we do not fully understand the effect of heating and cooling on the structure of this alloy, and therefore cannot properly explain what happened in the course of welding these statues. To gain a fuller understanding of this alloy we have done a number of experiments with it, attempting to reproduce the microstructure found on the ancient bronzes. This has proved to be difficult.

I have settled on an alloy of a composition that is an average of the Agde and *polygatus* bronzes: 73 % copper, 5 % tin, 22 % lead, and proceeded as described earlier. There is no problem in melting through this alloy in 12 seconds, with 3 pounds of melt, at 1050° C (100 degrees above the melting point of the alloy). No wetting occurs below this temperature, but as the temperature of the weld metal rises, less is needed and shorter times of pouring will affect complete weld-throughs. A structure occurs that is similar to that of the Roman welds in the general dispersal of small and large lead globules, and a finer structure in the area of the weld than in the base metal. But here the similarity ends. We generally do not produce any eutectoid, or only tiny quantities in a few samples, and the fossilized surfaces have caused us a great deal of grief! We do however find these lead-depleted zones appearing on the surfaces of annealed samples. There they appear either as surfaces from which the lead has withdrawn down along the grain boundaries, or they may be surfaces deposited from lead reservoirs rich in tin from which the tin has diffused out and alloyed with the copper to form these surfaces.[27] These alpha-phase areas also appear as borders around larger lead globules (as noted on the Agde bronze too) where they may be the result of diffusion out from the lead. On one experiment we produced extensive fossilized surfaces by stirring a plate in the pasty state while it was cooling; again, there are extensive pools of lead near these lines as though they were somehow

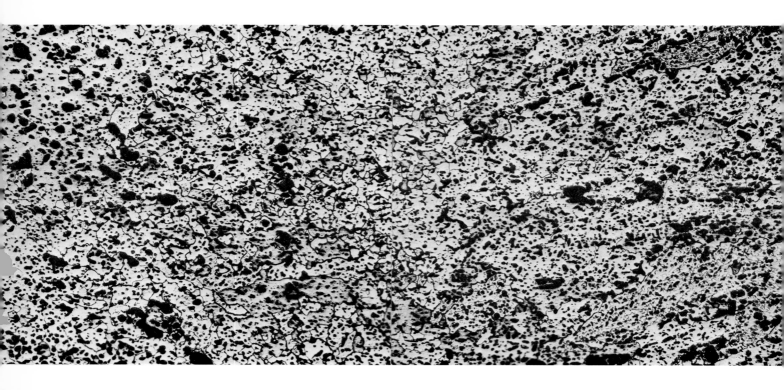

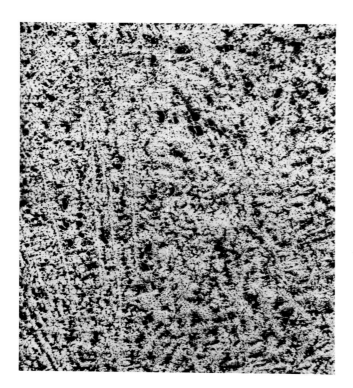

71. Experimental weld with an alloy of 73 % copper, 5 % tin, 22 % lead, poured 7 ³/₈ pounds at 1090° C. Large grains of alpha solid solution with regularly dispersed lead globules in right third of photomicrograph indicate the as-cast structure of the plate. The much finer grain size of the middle third of the micrograph indicates the transition zone of the weld, where the filler metal has melted back the casting and recrystallized selectively rapidly. The more heterogeneous grain sizes in the left third of the micrograph indicate the filler metal where the portion nearest the casting (the transition zone) cooled most rapidly, but the part of the weld nearer the source of the filler metal cooled more slowly because of the prolonged heating from the large amount of filler metal poured, resulting in this variation of grain sizes. The segregated lead globules are dispersed evenly throughout. x 100; etch: potassium bichromate.

72. Experimental weld, same as in fig. 71, photomicrograph of upper portion of weld area. The lead is extremely finely broken up and dispersed through the solid solution. At the left are long vertical lines that look like the "fossilized surfaces" in the *polygatus* section (cf. fig. 63). x 50; etch: potassium bichromate.

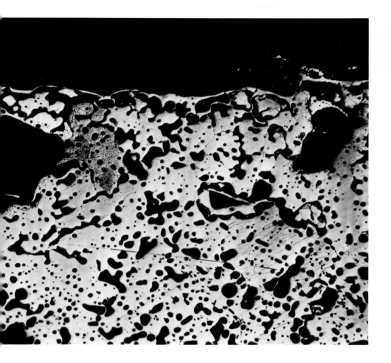

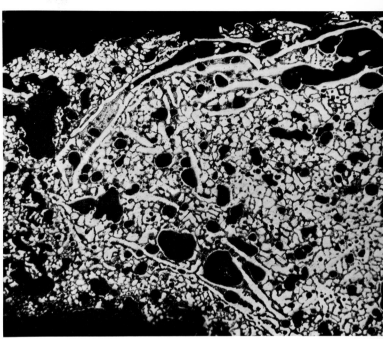

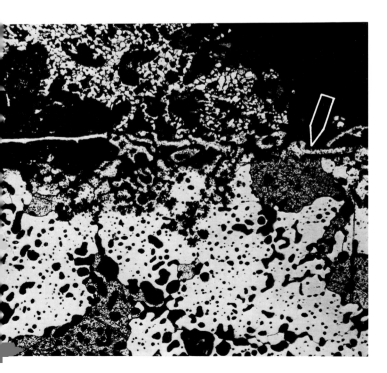

73. Experimental sample of alloy of 73 % copper, 5 % tin, 22 % lead. A cast plate was set on a graphite slab, annealed for 8 minutes at 775° C and cooled at room temperature. The upper edge of the sample, in this photomicrograph, rested on the graphite slab and was cooled in a non-oxidizing context. Running the whole length of this edge is a "fossilized surface" of the alpha solid solution; it appears here that the lead has withdrawn into pools below this surface. x 100; etch: potassium bichromate.

74. Experimental sample of the same alloy as foregoing. A cast plate with lead in a small hole in the center of it was set on a graphite slab, annealed for 8 minutes at 775° C and cooled at room temperature. There is again a "fossilized surface" along the edge (disturbed in part here by a projection), but this one is unusual because of the oxidation on part of it (indicated by arrow) and in large adjacent areas. Though we had supposed "fossilized surfaces" to occur only under non-oxidizing conditions (cf. fig. 73), this seems not to be the case. x 100; etch: potassium bichromate.

75. Experimental sample of the same 73-5-22 alloy as foregoing. This cast plate was heated to the pasty state with a torch and then mixed about with a rod as the metal cooled down at room temperature. The large pronounced "fossilized surfaces" are evident running from the upper right corner in an arc down to the left side and curving around to the lower right side. x 50; etch: potassium bichromate.

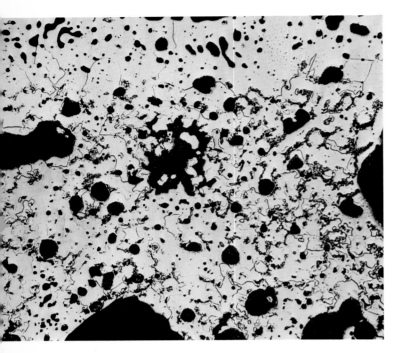

76. Experimental sample of the same 73-5-22 alloy as foregoing. A cast plate about 1 inch square and $^3/_8$ inch thick was clamped between two iron plates so that about $^1/_2$ inch of the bronze protruded above the iron plates. This protruding portion of the bronze was heated with an oxyacetylene torch until it slumped and was then quenched. One edge of the bronze plate shows small clumps of the alpha-delta eutectoid (the small grainy gray islands throughout the middle of the photomicrograph) similar to those found in the welded zone of the *polygatus* (cf. fig. 63). x 200; etch: potassium bichromate.

connected with the formation of these surfaces. We have produced a moderate amount of eutectoid on one experiment where the heat was dissipated quickly away from the plate, and an area rich in tin developed along a surface, but we are still at a loss to explain this mechanism fully. The eutectoid is not an equilibrium constituent in an alloy of our low tin content but forms as a result of micro-segregation, producing first areas of liquid enriched in tin, which solidify to give the beta-phase, and this in turn decomposes (at 520° C) to the eutectoid.

Another important characteristic of this alloy is a result of the fact that the liquid lead phase (in the otherwise solid alloy) will absorb oxygen — about 0.4% at 750° C, more at high temperatures. In annealing experiments done in air we found that the lead phase, which is continuous, carries oxygen deep into the alloy to form minute crystals of SnO_2 within the parts of the immediately contiguous alpha phase. This oxidation requires a fair amount of time, even at temperatures above 750° C. However, lead has a beneficial effect, for it readily

forms lead oxide, which is a highly efficient flux, above its melting point (884° C), dissolving most other metallic oxides. At 1000° C it will dissolve 10% of SnO_2. An intermediate compound, Pb_2SnO_4, which melts at 1060°, may form, and we have noticed an abrupt improvement in the wettability of oxidized bronze at this temperature. At lower temperatures a continuous SnO_2 skin seems to form on the surface of the bronze, even when lead is present, but above about 1060° the oxide film either breaks up or does not form at all, so that the wetting and welding can then easily occur. On heating the solid alloy, lead sweats out of the metal long before the base metal becomes pasty, covering the surface with a kind of natural flux.

To summarize, lead gives the alloy several important advantages which the Roman foundrymen exploited in the production of extraordinarily strong joins. Not the least is that lead

77. Experimental sample of the same 73-5-22 alloy as foregoing. A cast plate, with lead in a small hole in center of it, was set on a graphite slab, annealed for 8 minutes at 775° C and cooled at room temperature. The gray fine-grained area around the large black lead pool, and within several larger crystals, is the oxidized zone. This oxidized zone is at some depth below the surface of the plate which is at the top of the photo, and we assume from its location that the oxygen was carried in and dispersed by the lead. x 100; etch: potassium bichromate.

makes the alloy far more easily sawn, chiselled, and otherwise cut. In the large quantities in which the Romans added lead it appreciably lowered the melting point and made the alloy very fluid (among other things by preventing the formation of tenacious films of solid SnO_2 on the molten alloy); it served to de-oxidize the melt and give less gassy castings; moreover, it wetted the surface to be welded, and though the lead oxidizes readily its oxide liquifies easily and takes other oxides, including SnO_2 when present, into solution.

From these kinds of data we should now be able to make some informed guesses about the technique used by the Roman foundrymen for joining parts of statues with high lead contents. The parts were cast separately in pieces, and the edges were dressed and fitted with great accuracy. To judge from the ease and necessity of working on the inside of statues, I assume that the outer extremities were joined to the trunk and lower portion first, and finally the whole statue was welded together at the middle in one major joint. We have noted variations in microstructure in: globule size, position, and form of distribution of the lead; the degree of coring; and the presence of oxides on some samples. All these variations probably indicate that the techniques employed varied some in such details as: exposure of weld to oxidizing conditions, amount and superheat of weld metal, amount of pre-heating join, and rate of cooling and annealing. In some instances we can determine which of these variables affected the particular characteristics of the microstructure, but combinations of these variables could produce effects that we still do not understand.

Taking the macro- and micro-appearance of these joins together, but keeping in mind that anomalies have been found in the microstructures that still cannot be explained, I think a procedure of the following sort can be inferred for this welding technique. The sections to be joined were so positioned (possibly with the aid of some clamping device) that the edges abutted; clay or some other refractory material was packed on the inside of the statue so as to leave a slight well into which the weld-through would run. On the outside of the statue an open mold (or dam) of refractory material was built over the area to be welded. This was constructed in such a way that a weld button would build up over the weld and the excess metal would be channeled off. The area to be welded may have been preheated, though we do not know to what temperature, or what effect several such heatings might have had on the bronze; from our experiments it is not clear that preheating was necessary. Several of these welds could be made at one pouring, with a careful system of individual or connected molds built up in advance. Positioning the statue so as to facilitate this procedure was itself no mean feat (it is far easier to pour on a flat, level surface than over a curved surface), especially for the execution of the final and longest join through the middle of the statue, but obviously this difficulty also was overcome. After one set of welds was made the molds were broken off, a new set was built, and the whole procedure was followed again. Finally, the weld buttons would be chiseled off and the whole statue was dressed down and possibly patinated.

There is no question that this alloy and the ease with which it could be flow-welded made the assembly of large statues very much easier than it had been previously. It is also apparent that the technique falls in an evolutionary line from the kind of flow-welding we described on Greek bronzes, but the ease of this Roman operation, facilitated as it was by the high lead content of the bronze, is an important new step in the development of ancient metallurgical techniques. Whether its use was restricted to the joining of statues or spread to other genres we do not yet know; certainly it is a technique pleasing both for its simplicity and for its great efficiency. (It is striking that the Chinese also employed bronze with a high lead content and they made vessels in many parts joined together by casting-on methods. However, they never superheated the molten metal, and metallurgically fused welds are never seen.[28]) Though I am wary about seeing specifically national characteristics in ancient technology I cannot resist from observing that the logic, efficiency, and simplicity of this welding technique is typically Roman!

We saw Greek foundrymen fusing statue parts together in a number of different ways all of which required relatively high temperatures (in excess of $1100°$ C) and large amounts of metal — they did not fusion weld individual spots but partially welded whole seams, or they built up lumps of bronze which made mechanical joins, not relying on much metallic bonding at all. We saw an Etruscan piece that seemed possibly to form a transition from these clumsy Greek attempts to the immensely proficient technique of flow-welding of Roman foundrymen. There seems to me to be a qualitative world of difference between these technologies: Greeks carefully hid their joins on their nude figures; on draped figures they executed all the joins in such a way that they were hidden by overhanging drapery or were done on the inside of the statue. Not so the Romans: they boldly cast large nude figures in several pieces, fitted them carefully and simply welded them together; draped figures were done in a similar fashion. There is no hesitation or concern here about outward appearance. Is this a changed aesthetic that we might characterize as sloppier and less exacting because this was imperial propaganda art meant for the people (frequently for the provinces), rather than private dedications meant for the gods? Or is this an example of technological development, uninfluenced by aesthetic considerations, due merely to increased knowledge about materials and improved foundry practice?

It is not possible to draw firm conclusions yet about the practice of Greek and Roman foundries or the aesthetic considerations that governed the choice and development of different joining methods on large statues. But we can point to some kinds of differences in Greek, Etruscan, and Roman practice and indicate that when more work has been done on statues and other bronzes, and when foundries have actually been excavated, we may gain a better sense, feeling, and knowledge of the balance between cultural and physical features in the development of ancient technology.

Acknowledgments

This paper could not have been written without many hours of thoughtful discussion with Cyril Stanley Smith and Heather Lechtman, but I will not blame them for any errors or opinions expressed here, only for extraordinarily stimulating cooperation. The experiments were run by Perry Prince; the metallography (except where noted) was done by James Howard. Much thanks also goes to Linda Sayegh for typing an almost undecipherable manuscript. As always, much useful information was kindly offered by Florence Whitmore and William F. Young of the Research Laboratory of the Museum of Fine Arts, Boston. This work was made possible by generous grants from the National Endowment for the Humanities and the Sloan Basic Research Fund of the Massachusetts Institute of Technology, which is gratefully acknowledged.

Additional Remarks

Since this paper was written in the summer of 1970, I have looked at more Greek bronze statues and find that the views expressed then need now to be modified; I will allude to some of those changes here but publish them more fully elsewhere. Close examination of the *Poseidon* of Artemisium (ca. 475 B.C.), the *Marathon Boy* (4th century B.C.) and the *Antikythera Horse and Jockey* (1st century B.C.), all in the National Museum, Athens, reveals that the contiguous spot-welding technique described on the *Arringatore* and Roman statues was already practiced on Greek bronzes as early as the fifth century B.C. and forms, apparently, an integral part of Greek foundry practice down into the Hellenistic period. Examination of the Piraeus bronzes of draped female figures did not then show the full repertoire of Greek welding practices and caused me to draw too sharp a dichotomy between Greek and Roman methods. (The Piraeus *Kouros,* probably late sixth century B.C. in date, is said to have only its head and arms cast separately and then attached by some kind of flow-welding; I have no opinion about this since I could detect no traces of these joins in the heavily corroded surface of the bronze.) It seems now that one should examine further the reasons for the differences among the various Greek techniques. Contiguous spot-welding,

the epitome of good flow-welding, may have been improved on and facilitated by the Romans with the addition of large quantities of lead, but it was already used centuries earlier by Greek foundrymen welding alloys with no lead and having higher melting points than those used by the Romans.

A word of correction about eutectoid formation in these leaded alloys of fairly low tin content also seems in order. The welds were generally cooled fairly rapidly, though probably not quenched. Alloys of such low tin content (ca. 5 %) would not be expected to produce such large amounts of the alpha-delta eutectoid. The presence of lead in a bronze markedly changes the relations between copper and tin. As the molten metal solidifies, the lead is rejected by the growing copper-rich crystals and concentrates in the liquid, eventually reaching the point where two liquid phases are formed in the intercrystalline spaces, one liquid rich in copper and the other rich in lead. The tin is more concentrated in the copper-rich liquid and the regions of the alloy resulting from its solidification consequently contain more tin. The borders of the large lead drops, on the other hand, appear to be unusually rich in copper, but relatively free of tin, so again the tin is concentrated elsewhere in a limited area, giving rise to the eutectoid (cf. figs. 63, 64, 68–70).

Also when first preparing this paper, I was fascinated by the appearance of the "stringers" and overemphasized their general significance. They were rarely found in other welded statues, and I have not been able to duplicate them exactly in the laboratory. I am confident that they represent the surface of crystallization at some stage of solidification which is momentarily disturbed, but am uncertain whether this disturbed solidification is delineated as a result of the presence of a lead-rich liquid surrounding the solid or whether molten metal flowing across a solidifying surface under rather critical conditions of temperature gradient and shear rate can produce them. The shells of copper-rich material which form around large separate globules of lead (fig. 69 and comment above) almost certainly were deposited during the transformation of the copper-rich liquid to a lead-rich one along the monotectic line.

References

1. Pausanias, *Description of Greece,* VII, xvi, 7–8; Pliny, *Naturalis Historia.* XXXIV, 5–7, 36.

2. Cicero, *Verrine Orations,* passim, but especially the *Second Verrine,* IV.

3. Davies, N. de Garis. *The Tomb of Rekh-mi-re,* Metropolitan Museum of Art Expedition XI, 1943. The relevant Egyptian sources are commented on in H. H. Coghlan, *Notes on the Prehistoric Metallurgy of Copper and Bronze in the Old World,* Oxford, 1951, pp. 67–69.

4. Maryon, H , and Plenderleith, H. J., "Fine Metal-Work," in C. Singer, E. J. Holmyard, A. R. Hall, eds., *A History of Technology,* Oxford, 1954, vol. I, pp. 631–632.

5. Ibid., pp. 632–633, quoting D. D. Luckenbill, *Ancient Records of Assyria and Babylonia,* Chicago, 1927, vol. II, pp. 162–169.

6. Though the making of clay statues surely preceded the casting of large bronzes, the association of two such different processes with the same craftsmen might indicate some sense of a technological association of these processes. Is it possible that the making of clay statues here refers to the building of clay models and molds for the casting of bronzes?

7. D. E. L. Haynes has made a valiant attempt at reconstructing the various steps from model to finished casting, but he is forced to conclude that though he can exclude certain processes, he cannot say with certainty which processes were, in fact, employed: "The Technique of the Chatsworth Head," *Revue Archéologique,* 1968, 101–112.

8. Accommodation of mold-building technique to the configuration of the model is one of the most interesting of these problems. Most of the pieces from classical antiquity that we have examined were probably cast either by the direct or indirect lost-wax method, though multiple piece molds are a possibility for some. These techniques are discussed in my technical introduction to S. F. Doeringer and D. G. Mitten, *Master Bronzes from the Classical World,* Cambridge, Mass., 1967; and my "Technical Note" in Doeringer, Mitten, Steinberg, eds., *Art and Technology: A Symposium on Classical Bronzes,* Cambridge, Mass., 1970, pp. 107–108. Some of the other problems confronting the foundryman in the casting of bronzes are discussed in H. Lechtman and A. Steinberg, "Bronze Joining: A Study in Ancient Technology" in the latter book, pp. 5–35.

9. Recently discussed by H. A. Thompson, "A Note on the Berlin Foundry Cup," in *Essays in Memory of Karl Lehmann,* L. F. Sandler, ed. Locust Valley, N.Y., 1964, 323–328; illustrated in Furtwängler-Reichhold, *Griechische Vasenmalerei,* Munich, 1910, III, pl.135.

10. Ridgway, B. S., "The Lady from the Sea: A Greek Bronze in Turkey," *American Journal of Archaeology,* 71 (1967), p. 332, n. 27, refers to such a join but does not illustrate it.

11. Poseidon (or Zeus) from Cape Artemisium, no.15161 in the National Museum, Athens: extensively published by Ch. Karousos, in *Deltion Archaiologikon* 13 (1930–31), 41 ff.; frequently illustrated, e.g., R. Lullies, M. Hirmer, *Greek Sculpture,* New York, 1960, pls.130–132, VI; J. Boardman, J. Dörig, W. Fuchs, and M. Hirmer, *Art and Architecture of Ancient Greece,* London, 1967, pls.174–175, XXVIII. Charioteer in the Delphi Museum: extensively published by F. Chamoux, L'Aurige, *Fouilles de Delphes,* IV, 5, Paris, 1955; frequently illustrated, e.g., Lullies–Hirmer, op. cit., pls. 102–104, IV; Boardman et al., op. cit., pls.172, XXVII.

12. The head had previously been analyzed by emission spectroscopy in the British Museum Research Laboratory, reported by Haynes (cf. note 7, his p. 110); at my request Mr. Harold Barker undertook an analysis of the weld metal and reported to me in a personal communication that the composition of the weld metal is identical to that of the head.

13. Wet chemical analyses done for Bruno Bearzi, cited in *La fonderia italiana,* 15 (1966), 65–68.

14. Piece-molding here refers to a step in indirect lost-wax casting in which a negative mold is made in a number of interlocking pieces from the positive model so that the mold can be disassembled, coated with wax, cored, and reassembled for casting without damaging the model.

15. Biringuccio, V. *Pirotechnia,* Venice (1540), VI, 4 (English translation by C. S. Smith and M. Gnudi, Cambridge, Mass., 1966, p. 231) discusses this procedure for modeling bronzes in the Renaissance.

16. These experiments were originally designed to determine the properties of the alloy 73 % copper, 5 % tin, 22 % lead, which is the average composition of a number of large Roman statues (see below). Because we wanted to retain the ratios of that original composition we used a 93:7 bronze, and added lead (adjusting the copper and tin proportionately) to determine more precisely the effect of lead on the weldability of bronze. It is in the course of those experiments that the importance of tin oxide and its fluxability by lead became apparent; we are still studying that phenomenon at this time.

17. Ridgway, cf. note 10, pp. 329–334. Drawing fig. 31, by Richard De Poma of Bryn Mawr College; detailed photos of the statue by Karl Dimler, Bryn Mawr College Photographer for Art and Archaeology.

18. Dohrn, T. "L'Arringatore, capolavoro del Museo Archeologico di Firenze," *Bollettino d'Arte,* 49, 4 (1964), 97–116; similar text and illustrations in *Archäologischer Anzeiger,* 1965, pp. 123–142. The analyses were done wet chemically for Bruno Bearzi, who reported them to me by letter.

19. Pliny, *N. H.* XXXIV, 95–98, remarks extensively on the Roman practice of adding lead to bronze.

20. Some of these statues also exhibit other methods of joining than flow spot-welding. A peculiar kind of mechanical bonding is used by arranging small rectangular patches in a sawtooth pattern along the exterior of the join and wiping the interior with lead. This kind of joining is found, among others, on the *Septimius Severus* in Nicosia, Cyprus, the *Toledo Youth* (cf. note 22), and some of the Roman bronzes from Turkey discussed below (private communication from the man who restored them).

21. Delbourgo, S., "L'étude au laboratoire d'une statue découverte à Agde," *Bull. du Laboratoire du Musée du Louvre,* 1966, pp. 7–12; the statue was previously illustrated: Charbonneaux, *La Revue du Louvre* 16 (1966), 1ff.; *Gallia* 24 (1966), 464, pls. I–III.

22. Vermeule, C. C., *Polykleitos,* Boston, Museum of Fine Arts, 1969, pp. 23–29, figs. 20 A–F.

23. Doeringer, S. F., and Mitten, D. G., *Master Bronzes from the Classical World,* Cambridge, Mass., 1967, no. 237.

24. Only the *Houston Ruler* has been published so far. The whole group, unfortunately hopelessly dispersed throughout American and European private collections, seems to be a monumental dedication of the Severan imperial family made at a temple somewhere in southern Turkey. Since the early 1960's pieces from this group have been coming on the market after fairly extensive cleaning and restoration. There are now at least six whole, or nearly whole, over life-size figures in private collections, several more on the art market, and assorted heads and limbs that pertain to the six noted above and probably to some others as yet unknown.

25. Delbourgo (cf. note 21), p. 10.

26. The offset of the edges on the inside of the join shows how extensive must have been the chiselling and carving on the exterior of the join to match the two surfaces; the weld button must also have been removed as a part of this dressing operation. The lead in the alloy makes it soft and relatively easy to carve.

27. This latter process was suggested by Professor John Elliott of the Department of Metallurgy and Material Science, M.I.T. It is an ingenious idea that needs yet to be studied to verify its plausibility.

28. Gettens, R. J., *The Freer Chinese Bronzes, II: Technical Studies,* Washington, D.C., Smithsonian Institution, 1969. In all his careful studies of joins, pp. 76—98, 114—118, Gettens never notes any kind of fusion caused by superheating the metal. In the one instance of a carefully studied solder, pp.134—139, there also appears to be minimal wetting. It is noteworthy that the solder has more tin but less lead than the casting (his table XX, p.138), which seems to indicate that the foundryman was not aware of the effect of lead on the fusibility of this alloy.

ERHARD M. WINKLER

Salt Action on Stone in Urban Buildings

Natural stone often contains water-soluble salts trapped in the pores of natural rock and stone. These salts may be indigenous to stone but may also have migrated into the stone after it was set into place, either from the ground or from the street, or they may have formed by the interaction of polluted air with the stone, whence the salts start circulation within the masonry wall into different directions. The salt transport may be either by capillary transport or by diffusion.

Ionic Diffusion

Ionic Diffusion through water-saturated rock at room temperature and atmospheric pressure was experimentally determined by Garrels et al. (1949) for a few ions. The rate of diffusion depends upon both the temperature and the molecular concentration; the diffusion rate increases with the increase of the molecular gradient. Diffusion explains ionic migration in water-saturated rock, from areas of higher ionic concentration toward areas of lower concentration; osmosis reverses the flow of water, during which process a semipermeable membrane is passed.

Ionic, Osmosis, and Osmotic Pressures

Osmosis of salts through a solid occurs when a solution is separated from its pure solvent by a semipermeable membrane, like leather. Fig.1 shows the principle of osmosis as follows: the pure solvent, n_1, attempts to enter and dilute the solution, n_2, through a semipermeable membrane like leather, with the tendency to equalize the solutions whereby an osmotic pressure, p, ensues against the walls of the vessel; the magni-

1. Principle of ionic osmosis across a semi-permeable membrane. Adapted from Mahan (1964).

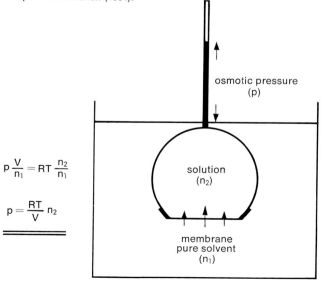

tude corresponds to the height of the meniscus multiplied by the density of the solution. Vant' Hoff's equation was modified by Mahan (1964), as follows:

$$p = \frac{R \cdot T}{V} \cdot n_2$$

R is the gas constant 0.082 liter atmospheres per mole degree, T the absolute temperature in degrees Kelvin, V the unit volume, n_2 the number of moles in solute. I have made calculations for solutions of $MgSO_4$, Na_2SO_4, and $MgCl_2$. The plots of fig. 2 consider the maximum solubility of the salts as well as the

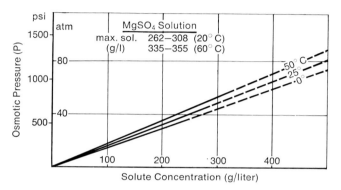

Fig. 2 a

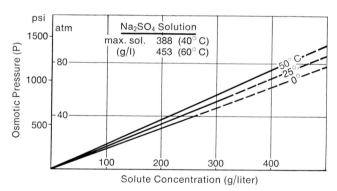

Fig. 2 b

temperature of the rock substance. Theoretical pressures may be well scaled off for various temperatures and solute concentrations; solid line shows undersaturated conditions and dashed line, very rare conditions of super-saturation. Maximum osmotic pressures are very difficult to evaluate in stone, as osmotic pressure is superimposed on pressures caused by expanding water, the possible action of "polywater," as well as crystallization and hydration pressures of entrapped salts. The process progresses in very small openings remote from human observation; controlled experiments are therefore not able to sepa-

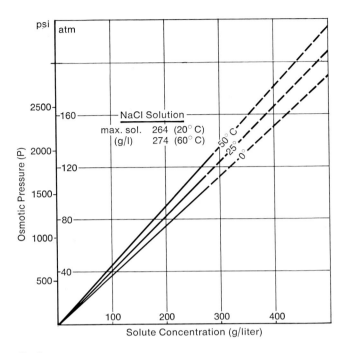

psi atm

Osmotic Pressure (P)

NaCl Solution
max. sol.   264 (20° C)
(g/l)   274 (60° C)

50° C
25°
0°

Fig. 2 c

Solute Concentration (g/liter)

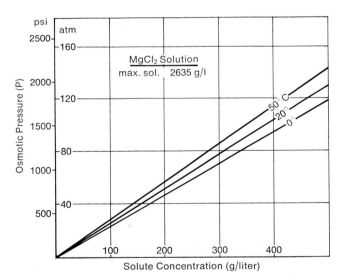

psi atm

Osmotic Pressure (P)

MgCl₂ Solution
max. sol.   2635 g/l

50° C
20°
0°

Fig. 2 d

Solute Concentration (g/liter)

rate osmosis from other processes. The diagrams offer a model and theoretical evaluation of the highest possible pressure developed by osmosis. The following geological implications are involved: rock temperatures in cities, diurnal temperature changes, and mole concentration of pore waters in stone. The question of osmotic membranes is also pertinent.

Salt concentrations in closed pore systems have given rise to much speculation, since very little is known about the molar concentration of salts in closed pore systems. In general, entrapped salts are not expected to form concentrations in excess of the maximum solubility of the dissolved ions. Kaiser's (1929) cross-section through a corner stone from the Regensburg Cathedral suggests that the content of soluble salts in a sandstone should not be expected to exceed 5 %.

Resistance to osmotic pressures should not affect the tensile strength of sound stone which qualifies as construction material. Only partly weathered rock had tensile strength of near 100 atm. in which Heidecker (1968) could observe spalling. Surface spalling is an important component in salt weathering, generally summarized as "salt fretting."

Osmotic conditions are believed to exist within partly weathered igneous rocks, possibly in isolated vugs of carbonate rocks, by soil-osmotic-like conditions whereby ordered water and surface adsorbed ions replace a semipermeable membrane in microcapillaries.

Gels of silica and alumina in partly weathered igneous rocks are believed to form semipermeable membranes in the classical sense with Liesegang. Most scaling and spalling associated with spheroidal weathering in igneous rocks should be explained by osmosis. Isolated vugs in carbonate rocks, mostly in dolomites, may concentrate carbonates of calcium and magnesium, sometimes the sulfate, in solution within the vug. I do not believe that enough salts can be concentrated within the vug to develop destructive osmotic pressures. Fig. 3 shows a vug in dolostone.

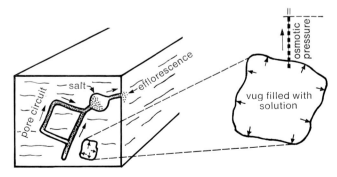

3. Osmotic conditions in a vug of probably dolomite. The vug is separated by dense rock substance. The pore circuit is adapted from Mamillan (1966).

Osmosis by ordered water and adsorbed ions creates conditions in argillaceous carbonates and shales; these appear to be related to soil osmosis, which is responsible for much of the swelling of clays. Both non-swelling and swelling clay crystals can hold water at their surface so tightly that it becomes ordered ("polywater"?) in micropores less than 10 microns in diameter. The great rigidity of such ordered water can well function as an ionic screen or membrane, as this water is much denser and about 20 times more viscous than ordinary water, nor does it freeze above –40° C.

In the field, the source for osmotic pressures in stone and concrete is difficult to establish, as the various factors leading to osmosis overlap; osmosis again overlaps with other disruptive forces such as frost action, expanding water, and others.

Efflorescence on Stone Surfaces

Blotches and patches as margins of white salts on masonry form unpleasant-looking coatings. Limited soluble salts crystallize at the surface at the open end of capillary systems to where outward-moving moisture is the vehicle of transport. Efflorescence across a calcareous sandstone is shown in fig. 4 and in fig. 5 in more detail. The fluid motion during evaporation

4. Mechanism of efflorescence on stone surface from capillaries interrupted by vugs. After Laurie and Milne (1926).

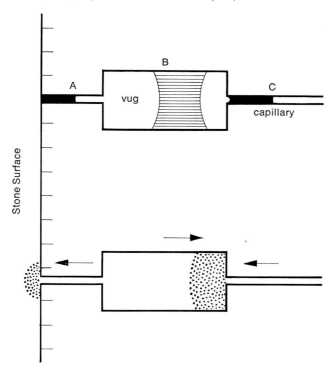

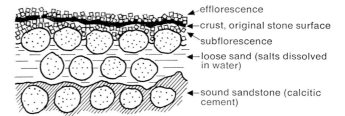

5. Efflorescence and subflorescence of salts in a sandstone with calcareous matrix. From Schmidt-Thomson (1969).

and subsequent crystallization of the fluid is shown by arrows in fig. 4. In general, the fluid migrates from the narrow capillary toward the vug and from there on to the surface. Salts on the surface generally do not harm the masonry but rather inform us of salt migration, and upper fringes of moisture travel whatever the origin of the salts. The mechanism of efflorescence is discussed by many authors but was summarized best by Kieslinger (1957, 1963). Brick walls show this phenomenon best because of the contrast of color in the white salts on the red background. Curing and firing of the clays supplies more sources for efflorescence in bricks than is found in stone masonry — sulfates from the disintegration of pyrite or from sulfur in coal are thus common ingredients. Lamar and Schrode (1953) report on the content of water-soluble salts in natural stone; the sulfates of calcium and magnesium, as well as their chlorides, were the most important constituents. Their presence is important in concentration at or near the surface, since it may lead to efflorescence or subflorescence, though these salts rarely exceeded 0.7 %. In buildings mortar or mortar joints are an important potential source for soluble salts.

Subflorescence

Subflorescence is closely related to efflorescence, as the salts are also moved toward the stone surface but without actually reaching that surface. Instead, they crystallize beneath a crust of dust and soot and weathered rock substance, forming a thin, indurated skin which readily peels off after a few years, or centuries. The stone surface is now ready for another skin, which again will start peeling as a result of the work of the salts accumulated underneath. Subflorescence is commonly found on stone in urban humid areas but is found in deserts as well. Fig. 5 shows a hypothetical cross-section of a fine-grained sandstone that has developed both efflorescence and subflorescence.

Crystallization Pressure of Salts in Stone

The crystallization process of salts from solutions is known to produce pressures by one-directional crystal growth in small pores of rock, which leads to disruption. A crystal under linear pressure has a greater solubility than an unpressed crystal. Correns (1949) summarizes the state of knowledge and presents a workable equation which is based on the Riecke Principle. Fig. 6 gives the equation. The state of supersaturation is

Pressure by Crystal Growth

$$P = \frac{RT}{V_S} \cdot \ln C/C_S$$

P = Pressure by crystal growth
R = Gas constant, 0,082 (liter-atm/mole-degr)
T = Absolute temperature, degree Kelvin
V_S = Molecular volume of solid salt
C = Concentration, actual
C_S = Concentration, saturated

6. Equation for crystallization pressure, after Correns (1949).

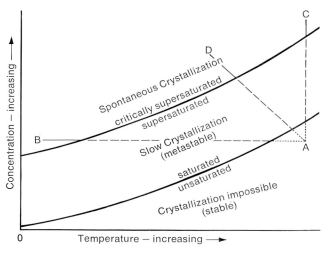

7. Indefinite temperature-solution concentration plot. Obtaining supersaturation by cooling (A to B), by dilution and concentration (A to C) or a combination of temperature drop and dilution. Modified from Mullin (1951).

an essential feature for all processes of crystallization. Fig. 7 plots the temperature T of the solution against the concentration ratio of the solution C/Cs in the indefinite graph (after Mullin, 1961). Crystallization can thus occur only between the state of saturation and supersaturation. No crystallization takes place in unsaturated solutions; no salt is left in solution in case of critical supersaturation. Three theoretical situations are plotted onto the graph of fig. 7.

A to B: At constant concentration the temperature drops from A toward B during a daily temperature cycle whereby the zone of saturation is entered. Supersaturation is thus reached, and crystallization can occur in this metastable state. With higher concentration of the solution, crystallization is more rapid and the crystals are larger than with lower concentrations.

A to C: The concentration rapidly increases with constant temperature by evaporation from ends of capillaries, but also reverts readily to much less concentration by dilution through rainwater.

A to D: Change of both the temperature and the concentration leads to supersaturation where crystallization occurs.

Crystallization pressures were calculated and plotted by Winkler and Singer (1972) as a three-dimensional diagram utilizing Correns' equation as the most practical thermodynamic approach, since it correlates well with actual laboratory tests. Complete curves were drawn for gypsum and halite in fig. 8 a and 8 b, with the degree of supersaturation as the abscissa on a log scale, the pressure generated by crystal growth as the ordinate on a linear scale. The pressure-concentration relationship is a straight line with the natural logarithm of C/Cs for a given temperature. Lines of equal temperature are drawn for 0°, 25°, and 50° C, temperatures which have been observed to occur in nature near the surfaces of stone and concrete. The maximum saturation on the diagrams is $C/Cs = 100$, which is the critical supersaturation for many salts, beyond which no salt should be left in solution. The curves are given for ideal conditions of crystallization which are never found in nature as such. Table I summarizes calculations for salts commonly found as dissolved ingredients in pores of rock, stone, and concrete. The table gives the density D, the atomic weight and the molecular volume as the basis for the calculations; pressures were calculated for supersaturations C/Cs of 2, 10, and 50 times. At $C/Cs = 10$, halite can exert a maximum pressure of 2190 atm. It is my opinion that the actual salt concentrations are below this figure; the destructive effect should be rather sought in pressures caused by salt hydration. This is my conclusion from observations I made (1965) on Cleopatra's Needle of New York City. I compiled the records for this monument from the days of erection 3500 years ago till today. After the Persian king Cambyses had toppled this and similar other monuments about 500 B.C., Cleopatra's Needle laid on the floodplain silts of the Nile River near Heliopolis till 35 B.C., when the Roman Emperor Augustus transported it and re-erected it in Alexandria on the Mediterranean. Thorough salt infiltration occurred toward the upward directed stone surface by both microcapillaries and diffusion. The monument was still in very good condition and the outlines of the hieroglyphics were still sharp in 1880, when the American Captain

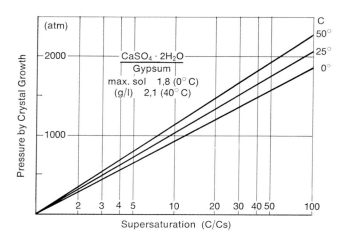

8 a. Plot of crystallization pressures of gypsum; for various temperatures and degrees of supersaturation. From: Winkler and Singer, Geol. Soc. America Bull. 83 (11), 3509–3514.

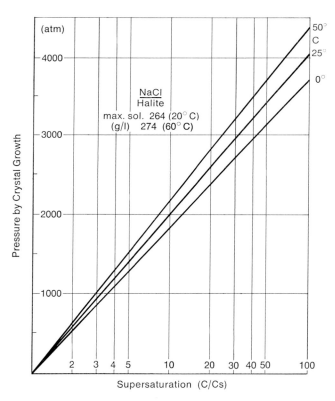

8 b. Plot of crystallization pressures of halite; for various temperatures and degrees of supersaturation. From Winkler and Singer (in press).

Gorringe brought the needle to New York City. After a few years of exposure to the moist atmosphere of New York, part of the stone surface was reduced by spalling to such a degree that the inscription on the present west side disappeared entirely, whereas the east side is still sharp and clearly visible. The north and south sides gradually grade from sharp to almost nil, as seen in fig. 9. During the spring months of the first few years in New York, 800 lb of scalings were reported cleaned up from the base of the monument. Elsewhere, I have discussed (1965) the direct effect of salts on the needle, which I believe to be the result of the history of the monument in Egypt, where salts moved upward from the river silts toward the upper surface of the monument in 500 years of continuous exposure to salt absorption. Repeated hydration and dehydration of the entrapped salts has much accelerated the rapid disintegration; it could therefore not have been the effect

9. Detail of Cleopatra's Needle, New York City. The east face appears to be undamaged while the south face shows the transition from poorly preserved towards total destruction on the present west face. From: Winkler (1965).

of salt crystallization in Egypt. The process of salt hydration may have been aided by frost action. Considering an approximate tensile strength of granites ranging from about 1000 to 3000 atm., gypsum and anhydrite could not have exceeded a concentration of $C/Cs = 50$; the presence of halite would have had to be less than $C/Cs = 10$. Cleopatra's "sister" needle in London underwent much less scaling than the New York needle, according to Burgess and Schaffer (1952). The difference in damage is ascribed to treatment of the London needle six months after exposure to the moist atmosphere of London, whereas the New York needle was not coated with hot paraffin till 10 years after it had been set up. I feel that besides the quicker treatment of the London needle, the much stronger contrast of temperature and the lower temperatures of New York City were instrumental in the development of stronger hydration pressures in New York, probably combined with frost wedging.

Hydration Pressure

Some common salts readily hydrate and dehydrate if the temperature and humidity of the atmosphere change; they will adjust to the new environment by changing to a more stable form. The absorption of water increases the volume of the salts and thus develops pressure against the pore walls. The geomorphologist Mortensen (1933) first recognized the importance of salt hydration as a disintegrating factor in desert weathering and attempted the calculation as hydration pressures. Monuments in cities of semi-humid moderate clime may be readily saturated with salts which are introduced from polluted air, mortar, and groundwater sources. Winkler and Wilhelm (1970) calculated the hydration pressures of some important common salts at different temperatures and relative humidities. The following equation is used to calculate salt burst pressures. Curves are drawn as three-dimensional contours within the fields of stability for each salt. The abscissa gives the relative humidity of the atmosphere which the salt contacts, the ordi-

Equation Used to Calculate Saltburst Pressures by Hydration

$$P = \frac{(n\,R\,T)}{V_H - V_A} \times 2{\cdot}3 \log \frac{P_W}{P'_W}$$

P = Hydration

n = Number of moles of water gained during hydration

R = Gas constant, 82·07 (ml-atm/mole-degr)

T = Absolute temperature, degree Kelvin

V_H = Volume of hydrate, cc/gm mole of hydrated salt $= \frac{\text{Mol·Wt·of hydrate}}{\text{Density}}$

V_A = Volume of original salt, cc/gm mole $= \frac{\text{Mol·Wt·of original salt}}{\text{Density}}$

P_W = Vapor pressure of water, mm Hg given temperature

P'_W = Vapor pressure of hydrated salt, mm Hg at given temperature

Table I

Hydration pressures of some common salts, simplified

$CaSO_4 \cdot \frac{1}{2} H_2O$ to $CaSO_4 \cdot 2 H_2O$ (plaster of Paris to gypsum)

Rel. humidity (%)	Temperature (°C)			
	0°	20°	40°	60°
100	2190	1755	1350	926
90	2000	1571	1158	724
80	1820	1372	941	511
70	1600	1145	702	254
60	1375	884	422	0
50	1072	575	88	

$MgSO_4 \cdot H_2O$ to $MgSO_4 \cdot 6 H_2O$ $MgSO_4 \cdot 6 H_2O$ to $MgSO_4 \cdot 7 H_2O$

Kieserite to hexahydrite   Hexahydrite to epsomite

Rel. humidity (%)	Temperature (°C)				
	65.3° C	10°	20°	30°	40°
100	418	146	117	92	96
90	226	132	103	77	69
80	13	115	87	59	39
70		97	68	40	5
60		76	45	17	
50		50	19		
40		20			

$Na_2CO_3 \cdot H_2O$ to $Na_2CO_3 \cdot 7 H_2O$; $Na_2CO_3 \cdot 7 H_2O$ to $Na_2CO_3 \cdot 10 H_2O$

Thermonatrite to heptahydrite   Heptahydrite to natron

Rel. humidity (%)	Temperature (°C)							
	0°	10°	20°	30°	0°	10°	20°	30°
100	938	770	611	430	816	669	522	355
90	799	620	457	276	666	504	350	185
80	637	455	284	94	490	320	160	
70	448	264	88		282	112		
60	243	46			60			

Source: Winkler and Wilhelm (1970).

nate the pressure P in atmospheres, called the hydration pressure; contours are drawn from 0° to 60° C at 10° intervals which permit the exact theoretical determination of the maximum pressure at a given relative humidity and temperature of the salt during the hydration process. At 0° C and 90 % relative humidity the maximum pressure during hydration is about 2000 atm, at 30° C only about 1480 atm, etc.

The pressure-temperature-humidity curves are theoretical and present maxima under idealized conditions of closed pore systems, unlimited moisture access toward the hydrating crystals in the pores, etc. Indicated temperature stability ranges of the hydrated minerals are theoretical as metastable conditions may exist for a long time at much lower tempera-

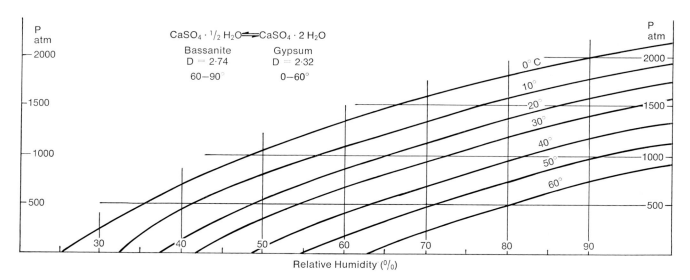

10. Hydration pressures for gypsum at various relative humidities and temperatures. From: Winkler and Wilhelm (1970).

tures than indicated. Some of the calculations were extended to temperatures where metastable conditions may well exist. Calculations were performed with the sulfates of calcium, sodium, magnesium, and sodium carbonate. Fig. 10 presents the complete pressure-relative humidity-temperature diagram for the hydration of plaster of Paris, the half-hydrate of calcium sulfate, to the double hydrate gypsum. Table I summarizes the pressures for several common salts.

In general, low temperatures and high relative humidities produce the highest pressures, high temperatures and low relative humidities low pressures. The hydration of the hemihydrate (plaster of Paris) has been observed to be a rapid process, whereas going from the anhydrite to the hemihydrate is very slow. Engelhardt's experiments with anhydrite powder contrast the previous statement and general belief: in the laboratory anhydrite powder readily re-crystallized to gypsum within a week. Sulfates of calcium form quite readily in carbonate rocks; these reach a maximum bursting pressure similar to that of ice at $-22°$ C. The hydration pressure of anhydrite to gypsum directly may produce a maximum pressure of 2800 atm at $0°$ C and 100 % relative humidity. The hydration of the magnesium sulfates from kieserite ($MgSO_4 \cdot H_2O$) to hexahydrite ($MgSO_4 \cdot 12 H_2O$) to epsomite ($MgSO_4 \cdot 10 \, 10 H_2O$) and to the dodekahydrate ($MgSO_4 \cdot 12 H_2O$) is somehow limited in nature and exerts low pressures. Hexahydrite was reported by Foster and Hoover (1963) as a common efflorescent salt in dolomite stone quarries of northern Ohio, where the metastable hexahydrite has crystallized from solution at the stone surface at

temperatures well below the minimum of its stability. Mortensen (1933) has observed the hydration of the metastable kieserite to epsomite to occur in a single day. The hexahydrite stage was probably skipped during Mortensen's observation.

All three hydrates of sodium carbonate are commonly found in nature. Sufficient stress may develop in their conversion at low temperatures and high relative humidities to destroy stone at nearly 1000 atm pressure, from thermonatrite to heptahydrite and from the heptahydrate to the ten-hydrate. Hydration of the sodium sulfates thenardite to mirabilite is more rapid than hydration of other salts; their hydration and dehydration may repeat several times in a day; the low hydration pressure may then still become effective. At $39°$ C dehydration of mirabilite to thenardite does not take longer than 20 minutes. The calculation of the hydration pressures should merely serve as a guideline for possible maximum stresses which may only be expected under ideal conditions for hydration and dehydration. A full evaluation of the behavior of salts in very narrow capillaries is extremely difficult and the salt action complex and involved. The case of Cleopatra's Needle in New York City was discussed before and the photo presented. There is strong evidence, however, that this precious monument is a victim of hydration pressures of entrapped salts.

Disruption of stone may also be possible by considerable differences in thermal expansion of entrapped salts in the pores of stone. Cooke and Smalley (1968) assign great importance to the high degree of expansion of halite at temperatures below $100°$ C as compared with the rock substance

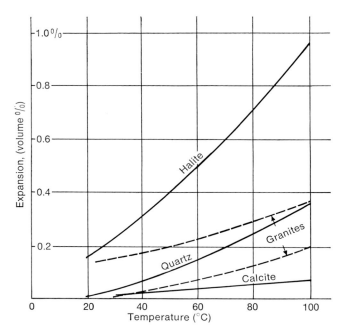

11. Expansion of halite as compared with quartz, calcite, and the expansion ranges of granites.

References

1. Burgess, S. G., and Schaffer, R. J. "Cleopatra's Needle" *Chemistry and Industry* (1952), pp.1026—1029.

2. Correns, C. W. "Growth and Dissolution of Crystals under Linear Pressure," *Discussions of the Faraday Society,* no. 5 (1949), pp. 267—271.

3. Foster, R. F., and Hoover, K. V. "Hexahydrite ($MgSO_4 \cdot 6H_2O$) as an Efflorescence of Some Ohio Dolomites," *Ohio Journal of Science,* 63 (4) (1963), 152—158.

Heidecker, E. "Rock Pressures Induced by Weathering and Physiochemical Processes," Proceedings of the Australian Institute of Mining and Metallurgy, no. 221 (1) (1968), 43—45.

4. Kaiser, Er. "Über eine Grundfrage der natürlichen Verwitterung und der chemischen Verwitterung der Bausteine in Vergleich mit der in der freien Natur," *Chemie der Erde,* 4 (1929), 291—342.

5. Kieslinger, A. "Feuchtigkeitsschäden an Bauwerken," *Zement und Beton,* 9 (1957), 1—7.

6. Kieslinger, A. "Verwitterungseinflüsse an Ziegelmauerwerk," *Die Wienerberger,* 3 (1963), 3—9.

7. Lamar, J. E., and Schrode, R. S. "Water Soluble Salts in Limestones and Dolomites, *Economic Geology,* 48 (1953), 97—112.

8. Mahan, B. H. *Elementary Chemical Thermodynamics,* Amsterdam, W. A. Benjamin, Inc. (paperback).

9. Mortensen, H. "Die Salzsprengung und ihre Bedeutung für die regional klimatische Gliederung der Wüsten," *Petermann's Geographische Mitteilungen* (1939), pp.130—135.

10. Mullin, J. W. *Crystallization,* London, Butterworths, 1961.

11. Winkler, E. M. "Weathering Rates as Exemplified by Cleopatra's Needle in New York City," *Journal Geological Education* 13 (2) (1965), 50—52.

12. Winkler, E. M., and Singer, P. C., "Crystallization Pressure of Salts in Stone and Concrete," *Geol. Soc. America Bull.* 83 (11), 3509—3514.

13. Winkler, E. M., and Wilhelm, E. J. "Saltburst by Hydration Pressures in Architectural Stone in Urban Atmosphere," *Geological Society of America Bulletin,* 81 (2) (1970), 567—572.

14. Winkler, E. M. *Stone in Man's Environment, Properties, Durability,* Vienna, Springer-Verlag (in press). Much of the information in this article will be covered in the book.

surrounding the salts entrapped in capillaries. The difference of expansion of calcite, quartz, granite, but also of halite is shown in fig.11. If we assume a stone temperature of 60° C, halite expands 50 % and granite not more than 0.2 %. The disruptive expansion of the salt may participate in physical disintegration in stone weathering.

Summary

Salts may be derived from ground moisture, stone weathering, and from polluted air; they travel in stone both by diffusion and by capillarity. Surface efflorescence, near-surface subflorescence, salt crystallization, and salt hydration on stone can produce considerable pressures, in excess of 30.000 psi for halite and gypsum. Differential expansion of entrapped salts during stone heating is probably less important. Stone disruption by salt action is destructive because low tensile strengths of rocks amount to only one-fifth to one-tenth of the compressive strength. Osmotic pressure may affect partly weathered silicate rock and soft shale.

Desert weathering conditions are very similar to those in urban environs. The process of damage due to moisture with or without the presence of salts is extremely complex and thus very difficult to analyze.

B. H. VOS

Moisture in Monuments

I do not think it is an exaggeration to say that if one could prevent the penetration of water into a structure, many ancient and valuable objects and monuments would be saved. It is well known that much damage is caused by water. Therefore, it is strange that the behavior of moisture and moisture transfer in relation to this damage has never been a serious subject of fundamental research. The subject of heat and moisture transfer, which is a part of the physics of building, is still in its infancy. This does not change the fact that making more and better use of the studies in this field can help architects who are in charge of the renovation of valuable buildings. In this paper it is clearly impossible to do more than touch lightly on the problems.

Humidity of the Air

The ambient air always contains a certain amount of water vapor. The vapor concentration generally is expressed in grams per cubic meter of air. This vapor concentration cannot exceed a maximum value. The maximum vapor concentration increases when the temperature rises.

The relative humidity (φ) of the air is defined as the relation between the actual vapor concentration (c) and its maximum value (c'):

$$\varphi = \frac{c}{c'}$$

The result is usually expressed in percentages. If the air is not saturated — in other words c is smaller than c' — saturation can be reached in two ways. In fig.1, we start from the situation indicated by point P. Vapor can be added, while the temperature is kept at a constant value. The situation moves into the

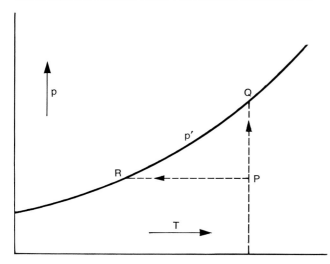

1. Maximum water vapor pressure (p') as a function of temperature (T); P: nonsaturated situation; saturation can be obtained by adding vapor (PQ) or by decreasing the temperature (PR).

direction of point Q. When such an amount of vapor has been added that Q has been reached, the air is saturated. If more vapor is added, condensation will occur.

Instead of adding vapor, one also can decrease the temperature (in the direction of point R). If R has been reached, the air is saturated. The temperature related to R is called the dewpoint. Further decrease of the temperature leads to condensation. If in a vapor-air mixture the vapor concentration is not the same at every place, water vapor will move from places where the concentration is high to places where it is low. This process is called diffusion. It should not be confused with streaming or flow. The latter phenomenon takes place if the total pressure is not the same everywhere. Air and water vapor move together in the same (low pressure) direction. Diffusion can also take place through porous materials.[1] As a matter of course the amount of vapor being transferred is determined by the concentration differences and the internal structure of the material. Often the latter property is given by its μ-value, i.e., the diffusion resistance factor.[2] The μ-value of air has been fixed at 1. A μ-value of 30 means that the resistance against vapor diffusion is 30 times as high as that of pure air.

Hygroscopic Moisture

If a dry material is placed in a room with a certain constant relative humidity, water vapor will penetrate by diffusion into the pores of the material. The moisture is bounded in the small pores.[1] In course of time an equilibrium is established. The amount of moisture being absorbed in the latter case is called the hygroscopic moisture content; the name equilibrium moisture content is also used.

At a temperature of 20° C and a relative humidity of 60 %, 1 m³ air contains about 10 gm water. A cubic millimeter of wood placed in this air can contain 100 kg moisture under equilibrium conditions. Every value of the relative humidity corresponds with a definite moisture content of the material. Fig. 2 shows how the hygroscopic moisture content of wood (800 kg/m³) depends upon the relative humidity. This hygroscopic moisture is to a high degree responsible for *dilatation* and *shrinkage* of materials. In fig. 3 the change of length of pine wood in the direction of the fibers as a function of its moisture content has been sketched.[3]

In winter the relative humidity indoors in many countries is low; let us suppose it is 30 %. From fig. 2 we read that moisture content of wood in that case is about 7 mass %. In summer the relative humidity indoors often is on the order or 80 %, which corresponds with a moisture content in the wood of about 15 %. Therefore, if no special measures are taken, we may expect that moisture content in wooden objects will vary between 7 and 15 %. Fig. 3 shows that the length of such an object will undergo a change of 1.5 %. Such changes can also

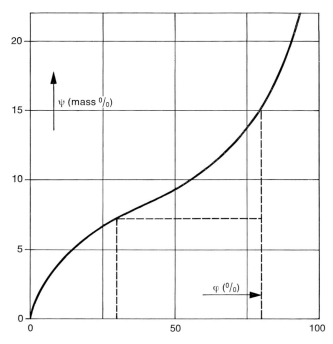

2. Hygroscopic moisture content (ψ) of wood (800 kg/m³) as a function of the relative humidity of the air (φ).

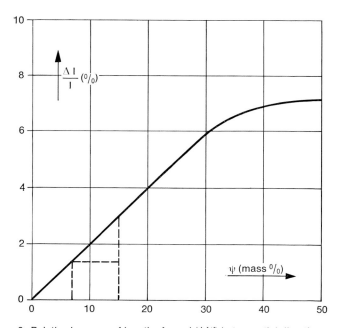

3. Relative increase of length of wood (Δl/l) in tangential direction as a function of moisture content (ψ).

be expected for other organic materials. It will be clear that this is why in museums one cannot do without air conditioning. Paintings and other valuable objects must not be exposed to great changes of relative humidity.

The hygroscopic moisture content of a material is influenced by the presence of salt in its pores. Normal brick, for instance, is hardly hygroscopic. If the relative humidity is 90 %, it contains about 1 % per volume water. As long as the relative humidity is below 75 % the presence of sodium chloride does not have any influence. Above this percentage, however, a steep increase of moisture content takes place, as illustrated in fig. 4. As a consequence, in countries where the relative humidity outside is usually high, danger can develop if sodium chloride has penetrated into the pores. Brick walls will not dry easily if this is the case. Information about hygroscopic moisture content is found in the references 2, 4, and 5.

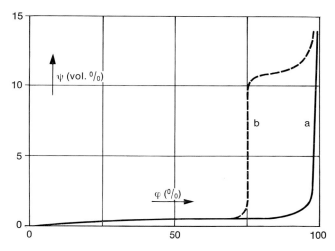

4. Hygroscopic moisture content (ψ) of brick as a function of the relative humidity (φ); *a*: normal brick containing no salts. *b*: item containing 0.04 g NaCl per cm³.

Water Absorption; Rain Penetration

If a material is in contact with free water this water is absorbed by capillary forces. During this absorption process the water distribution looks as it has been sketched in fig. 5. A waterfront is formed, which moves through the material. At this front the water content remains constant at its so-called critical water content ($ψ_c$). This water content is a characteristic property for a material. For brick (mass per unit volume 1700 kg/m³) it is 6 to 8 % per volume, which is about 25 % of its maximum water content; for heavy weight concrete it does not differ much from its maximum water content, that is, 12 to 15 % per volume. If a water film is formed along a wall, for instance if

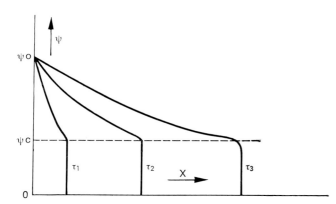

5. Water penetration into a material at different times (τ); at the surface ($x = 0$) a water film is present; here water content (ψ) is maximum (ψ_0); ψ_c = critical water content.

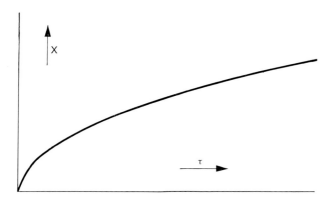

6. Penetration depth (x) as a function of time (τ) during free water absorption into a material or structure.

a heavy driving rain is striking a wall, the place of the water-front (x) as a function of time can be found from:[6]

$$x = B \sqrt{\tau}$$

The proportionality constant (B) is called the *water penetration coefficient*. It is a measure of the absorptive capacity of a material. A high value of B means that the water is absorbed rapidly. Fig. 6 shows how x depends upon time. The more water has been absorbed, the slower the suction process takes place. This can easily be understood: when the front has penetrated deeper, the resistance against flow has increased.

The penetration coefficient of soft brick, as it is often found in ancient buildings, is on the order of 10^{-3} m/s$^{0.5}$; for comparison, the B-value of heavy weight concrete is 10^{-6} m/s$^{0.5}$. This penetration coefficient is a measure of the tightness of a structure. The lower the value of B, the longer it lasts before

the front has reached the opposite side. As easily can be checked, the front will reach the opposite side of a soft brick wall, 25 cm thick, after about 20 hours. A wall of heavy weight concrete of the same thickness will show water at the opposite side after about twenty million hours!

Suction of Water from the Ground

In the previous section we did not take into account the influence of gravity. This force can be of great importance if water rises from the ground into the walls of buildings. This process is initiated by the capillary forces; on the other hand, gravity acts as a brake. As a consequence, after a certain time, the absorption process comes to a stop: maximum height has been reached. Gravity and suction keep each other in balance.

Under normal conditions this theoretical maximum height is never reached, as evaporation from the surfaces to the ambient air also counteracts the rising process. The height of the front usually is outlined sharply. Here water content is critical; above this front of course some hygroscopic moisture will be found. Fig. 7 shows the water distribution in a wall of the San Sebastiano cathedral in Venice, as it has been measured by a team of our institute. Above 3 m the wall was nearly dry. Below that level, water content increased until maximum water content is reached near the bottom.

In some countries many firms are engaged, with more or less success, in the fight against the rise of subsoil water. The most efficacious method is establishing water barrier near the bottom of the walls, if possible in the foundations. One has to take care that these layers pass through the total cross-section. One should not plaster the wall afterward to hide this

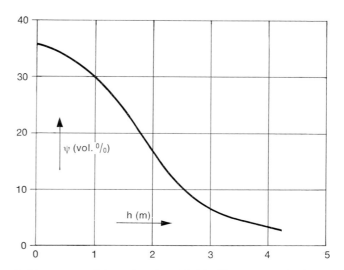

7. Water content (ψ) as a function of height (h) in a wall of the San Sebastiano cathedral in Venice.

layer, since by so doing a new route for water transfer is created.

Sometimes for drying of walls the principle of electro-osmosis is applied. Use is made of the fact that electrical potential differences can cause a movement of water. In spite of a large number of publications mentioning good results, I am not convinced that this system really works. Several firms propagate the use of a special type of tube which has to be pushed into holes in the wall. If this method of drying really worked, which has never been proved, merely drilling holes would have the same result. One should always advise against use of these tubes.

Finally, it should be noted that plastering a wall in such a way that the wet part is hidden generally will have no success. After some time the front will rise again above the plaster layer, as evaporation to the ambient air is prevented. Moreover, there is a chance that in course of time the plaster will fall as a consequence of the action of the water.

Condensation

As we have seen in the foregoing, condensation occurs if the temperature somewhere is lower than the dewpoint of the air. We have to make a distinction between two kinds of condensation: on a surface touching the air and in the interior parts of a structure. We deal first with the former type, which is called surface condensation.

Surface Condensation

The chance that condensation occurs on a surface is greater as the temperature of the surface is lower. We shall deal with two cases, condensation indoors on heavy thick walls, especially in a maritime climate, and condensation on the outside that can take place in a continental climate.

Fig. 8 shows how the outside temperature of the air changes during a warm sunny day in summer. As a consequence of the great heat capacity of the thick walls the surface temperature of these walls inside will show a lag and a flattening. Between 8 and 20 hours it is lower than the outside temperature. During the other part of the day the inverse is the case. The greater the heat capacity of the walls, the greater the difference between the two temperatures will be.

Fig. 9 shows how the maximum vapor pressure related to the surface temperature varies with the time of the day. Whether condensation occurs depends in a large measure upon the climate of the region. In a region with a *maritime climate* a larger amount of water is available for evaporation. When the temperature rises the vapor concentration will increase quickly (curve c). As a consequence of the normal ventilation this vapor concentration will also be found inside the building. During a certain period — in this case about 9 hours — the vapor

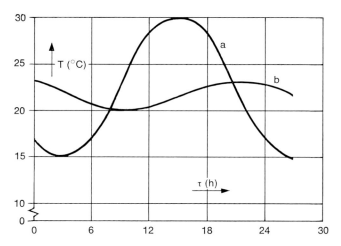

8. Outside air temperature (curve *a*) and inside surface temperature (curve *b*) of a thick wall (curve *b*) during 24 hours on a sunny summer day.

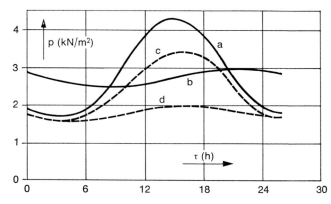

9. Vapor pressures (*p*) during a 24 hour period of a sunny summer day. *a.* maximum pressure of the outside air. *b.* maximum vapor pressure belonging to the inside surface temperature of a thick wall, *c.* vapor pressure of outside air in a maritime climate (condensation), *d.* item in a continental climate (no condensation).

concentration of the air is higher than the maximum vapor concentration at the inner wall surface: condensation will occur. Probably much damage, especially of frescoes, is caused by this type of condensation.

Theoretically, insulating the walls can prevent condensation. However, it works efficaciously only if the insulation is put inside the walls and in practice, this is seldom possible. Drying of the inside air will also be helpful, but the cost is usually high.

In a *continental climate* this type of condensation will not occur: only a small amount of water can evaporate. The vapor concentration can increase but slightly (curve d) and will not rise above the maximum concentration. Another sort of surface condensation can take place in continental climates with great differences between day and night temperatures; it can even occur in deserts.[7] During clear nights as a consequence of the irradiation of walls and roofs to the unclouded sky, the outside surface temperature can become much lower than the temperature of the ambient air: vapor condenses on these cold surfaces. This also can lead to severe damage.

We note that insulating these structures on the inside does not have any effect. The irradiation during the night only can be reduced by sheathing the structures with polished metals, which generally will not be acceptable for aesthetic reasons. All that can be done is to impregnate the materials so that condensed moisture cannnot penetrate.

Internal Condensation

Internal condensation in a structure takes place if the dewpoint of the air is somewhere in the interior of the structure. This type of condensation usually occurs unnoticed. It often manifests itself by its ill effects, when it is too late. This phenomenon often occurs in the boundary plane between two layers of different materials. If the material on the inner side (warm side) has a low resistance against diffusion, vapor can penetrate easily into it. If the material on the outer side has a high resistance, the chance that vapor may condense between the two layers is present.[8] Frost damage can originate in this type of condensation. In this respect we must advise against the fixing of glazed tiles on a brick wall.

Also rotting of wood is often caused by internal condensation. This can occur in wooden roofs. The ceiling usually is pervious to vapor. The roofing, however, is as good as vaportight. Condensation occurs in the wood under the roofing. Here in some cases vapor barriers on the warm side and ventilated cavities in the structure can be of help.[9]

Moisture Distribution

From the foregoing it will be clear that preventing penetration of water into a structure can only be done efficaciously if the origin of the moisture is known. It is of course nonsense to make a water barrier in a wall if the damage is caused by a leaking gutter. Ascertaining the origin of moisture is often anything but a simple problem. In some cases the water distribution can give insight in to what really happens. Fig.10 shows the theoretical water distribution for different cases. The first picture (a) relates to condensation on a surface; water content falls from the inside to the outside. Picture (b) shows the water distribution in case condensation against a vapor-tight layer occurs. The third picture (c) refers to rainwater that has penetrated into a structure. If water from the ground is

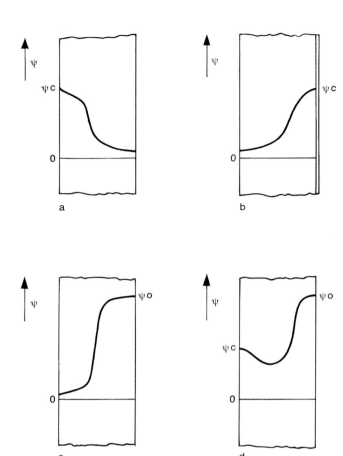

10. Water distribution in a structure (ψ): a. condensation on a surface, b. condensation against a vapor barrier, c. rainwater, d. rainwater and condensation.

rising in walls, water content near the bottom always is high; it decreases at greater heights (compare fig. 7).

Unfortunately in practice many secondary phenomena often obscure the picture. If for instance moisture content in a structure is increased by rainwater, the thermal insulation decreases. This causes a lower inside surface temperature and an increasing chance that condensation will occur (fig.10 d).

Measuring Methods

Measuring moisture content and moisture distribution in structures is a difficult and in some cases nearly impossible thing to do. The most accurate method is to take samples from the structure and determine moisture content by drying and weighing. This method, however, is destructive and cannot be repeated.

Several nondestructive techniques have been developed

11. Apparatus for the determination of moisture content and moisture distribution in structures.

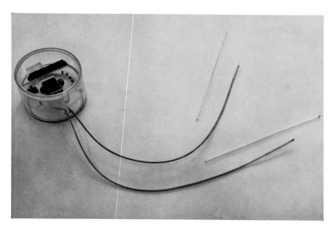

12. Probe for determining moisture content in structures.

during the last decades. Some of them are based upon the scattering of neutrons;[10] other methods make use of the fact that the electric resistance or dielectric properties are changed by water.[11, 12] The accuracy of these methods is not great. Besides we generally get only an indication of the overall moisture content; we do not find anything about the distribution of moisture. Add to this that these methods do not work automatically and that registration usually is not possible.

As far as I know, the only method that is not subject to these failings has been developed by our laboratory.[13] It it based on the fact that thermal conductivity depends to a high degree upon water content. The apparatus (fig.11) works completely automatically; the measurements are nondestructive and can be repeated as often as necessary. With the aid of probes (fig.12) which are connected with the measuring device a clear idea of the moisture distribution can be obtained, while the migration of moisture through the structure can be studied. Unfortunately this way of measuring cannot be used in all materials. Moreover it is fairly expensive.

Conclusion

The problems connected with moisture in materials and structures are a field of work for many commercial firms. Many of them are selling preparations which should be a cure-all for all sorts of moisture. From the foregoing it will be clear that such cure-alls do not exist, no more than in the medical world.

The situation in the world of architects, at least in regard to this field of science, is backward when compared with what has taken place in the world of medicine. If a family doctor is faced with a case that is not quite clear to him, he will not ask a pharmaceutical chemist to have a look at the patient and to cure him. This, however, is exactly how things proceed in the world of architects. If they are faced with damage, instead of consulting a specialist in this field they ask a commercial firm to advise them and to cure the building. This is why there are so many disappointments. Of course this comparison is not entirely valid. In the medical world there is a rigid organization: family doctor, specialist, and druggist have a well-determined function; in many countries their tasks are prescribed by law. Besides, their objects are human beings, who are of greater value than objects of art.

This does not alter the fact that also in the field of moisture problems a better and more efficacious way of working must be found. It is not a cause for shame for an architect not to be able to solve every problem he meets. He has, however, to discern the problems before he can consult a specialist. I hope and expect that this manner of co-operation will lead to a better approach to the problem of moisture in monuments. I am convinced that then more monuments and other valuable objects of art can be saved and retained for posterity.

References

1. Vos, B. H., and Tammes, E. *Moisture and Moisture Transfer in Porous Materials,* Report 69—96, Institute for Building Materials and Building Structures-TNO, Rijswijk Z. H. (Netherlands), 1969.

2. Krischer, O. Die Wissenschaftliche Grundlagen der Trocknungs-technik, Berlin, Springer Verlag, 1963.

3. Kollmann, F. *Technologie des Holzes,* Berlin, Springer Verlag, 1951.

4. Tveit, A. *Measurements of Moisture Sorption and Moisture Perme-ability of Porous Materials,* Oslo, Norwegian Building Research Institute, 1966.

5. Vorreiter, L. "Untersuchungen über Masonite und Kapag Hartplat-ten," *Holz als Roh- und Werkstoff,* 4 (1941), 178 ff.

6. Vos, B. H., and Tammes, E. *Flow of Water in the Liquid Phase,* Report 68—38, I.B.B.C.-TNO, Rijswijk Z. H. (Netherlands), 1968.

7. Kidder, B. P. *Causes and Effects of Moisture in Old Buildings in Desert Regions,* Rome, Icomos Colloquium, 1967.

8. Vos, B. H. "Internal Condensation in Structures," *Building Science* 3 (1969) 191—206.

9. Vos, B. H.: *Ventilation of Flat Roofs,* Report 65—13, I.B.B.C.-TNO, Rijswijk Z. H. (Netherlands), 1965.

10. Waters, E. H., and Moss, G. F. "Estimation of Moisture Content by Neutron Scattering," *Nature* 209 (1966) 287 ff.

11. Künzel, H. "Elektrische Feuchtigkeitsbestimmung in Baustoffen," *Ges. Ing.* 75 (1954), 296 ff.

12. Mamillan, T., et al. *Détermination de la teneur en eau par mesure de la constante diélectrique* C.I.B. — activities in the field of building, no. 3, 1960.

13. Vos, B. H. Measuring Moisture Content and Distribution in Con-structions, *Build. International* 3 (1970), 51—54.

LEONETTO TINTORI

Scientific Assistance in the Practice of Mural Conservation in Italy

It is not my intention to trace here the history of science's contribution to mural conservation — a specialized area involving a large part of the work of the greatest artists. Nevertheless, I feel obligated to present what I have learned of the matter and also to point out how good intentions of competent and conscientious individuals have met with resistance from just those who should have most appreciated its utility.

Until the middle of the last century, the standard treatment for damaged murals was to demolish the affected area as soon as the first signs of decay appeared and to replace that part with a new painted substitute which attempted to reproduce the lost imagery.[1] Often no effort was made to save even the less damaged sections and the entire fresco was demolished. This is how entire cycles have been lost. Of many others only a few torn and abraded scraps survive — uncovered with great effort from under the whitewash which protected them from total destruction.

With the reunification of Italy, awareness of the country's great artistic patrimony was reawakened. For the first time, attention was given to organizing the means of protecting it. From this time on there are many fascinating accounts which testify to the appreciation and respect accorded to murals and the seriousness of the efforts then made to protect them.

In the archives of the *Opera Primaziale* of Pisa there is a large file documenting the anxious concern for the state of the Camposanto frescoes. Recorded here are the care, caution, and diligence exercised to preserve these paintings. The most salient feature of these accounts is the fear of seeing the paintings defaced by retouching. Although they permitted the murals to be consolidated with a wax process (the so-called *cera punica,* the authorities warned the restorer "not to make use of the brush, so that these precious remains of the Italian genius would not be adulterated by retouching and by restoration of any kind which would in consequence remove one of their greatest qualities: their originality" (June 5th, 1858). References to what the sources of the damage might be were of little significance and what decisions were made of a scientific order are characterized by excessive casualness and superficiality.[2]

Padua was more exigent and in the civic commission presided over by Professor Pietro Selvatico we find among the most active members a professor of chemistry — Francesco Filippuzzi. He was asked to follow the repair of Giotto's paintings in the Scrovegni Chapel "so as to guarantee that the substance employed for re-attaching the plaster and removing the grime would not be sources for future damage to the famous frescoes." In another document, a letter of Selvatico's to Andrea Gloria complains that the writer does not have a complete committee at his disposal: "Without a chemist," said Selvatico, "the committee is crippled."[3] Without going on with more quotations of this kind, which are easy enough to find,

1. Giotto, detail from the *Annunciation,* Scrovegni Chapel, Padua: the loosening of the color and the efflorescence of calcium sulphate are due to atmospheric pollution (E. Sayre) and changes in the rate of the relative humidity. Only the purification of the air and the stabilization of humidity can lessen the danger of the further spread of this phenomenon.

these few are, I believe, sufficient to demonstrate how over a century ago there already was a keen awareness of the need for scientific assistance — besides the moral and historical support needed in this particularly delicate and complex task of conserving murals.

It is, however, very important to point out that assistance of this kind was limited to campaigns involving works of exceptional value. As for the rest, a very general briefing snatched at random from the restorer or an administrative official was usually thought to be sufficient as a preliminary to the actual work.

As a result, the restorer was armed only with his own sensitivity and personal experience, guided by a vigilant conscience fearful of being misled by painful and mistaken alternatives. This practice is still too often the case today. The solace offered by help of a purely theoretical or moralizing kind leaves the restorer all the more alone in his desperate fight against the subtlest kinds of material degeneration. Alone, he assumes a responsibility which was, and often still is, beyond his competence. The first seeds of caution were not, as might have been hoped, developed in the next decades; on the contrary, at the beginning of this century, any enthusiasm in this regard was so enfeebled that work was done in the most weary empirical fashion — even in cases involving the gravest responsibility. Sporadic consultations satisfied the more scrupulous spirits. Esthetic dissertations were made instead of more solid efforts to find ways of preserving the fragile material. When read today, some of these consultations turn out to have been surprisingly accurate in their identification of the causes of decay. But search as one may for any evidence in the treatments decided upon during this period, one is astonished to find that the very individuals who most scrupulously urged that research be made utterly ignored the diagnoses.

In Siena, in 1923, Professor Bargellini, a chemist of the University of Siena, found in the wall supporting Simone Martini's *Maestà* abundant quantities of sodium chloride at all heights and all depths. The quantity traced varied from a minimum of 0.12 % to a maximum of 0.69 % — an amount sufficient to double the movement of moisture in the wall. The mural was cleaned with care so that the grime, dust, and smoke stains were removed. Then paraffin was smeared all over the surface.[4] A decade later, the same phenomena reappeared: there was a change of tone in various zones, crumbling off of old as well as modern temperas, and a general whitening of the whole painting. The use of wax in the preceding restoration was severely criticized, and according to the restorer Silvestri's report, wax and repaints were removed. But fresh paraffin was spread over the surface again.[5]

In this, the second campaign on the *Maestà* of Simone in our century, not only were the existing documents regarding the mural's state ignored but no one even bothered to consult an expert in either chemistry or physics in an attempt to find less dangerous methods and materials of treatment, or even to get the most rudimentary advice for the reduction of the flow of moisture. Whether Florence, Siena, Milan, Venice, or Naples — in short, in the whole of Italy — this situation was the same. The best that can be said is that as far as the *Maestà* was concerned, the choice of restorer was made from among the most sensitive and conscientious.

The absence of a regular and unbroken scientific check became with time increasingly critical until the founding of the Istituto Centrale del Restauro in Rome. The institute was endowed with modern equipment for scientific research and with technicians trained in various specialized fields (chemistry, biology, physics, etc.). All were dedicated to fulfilling this great

2. Ambrogio Lorenzetti, *Madonna della Loggia,* Palazzo Pubblico, Siena: the fresco had already undergone transfer in the last century. But use of a poor method and unsuitable materials almost destroyed the painting.

need. Because of the great backlog of work facing the founders of the institute, and because it had been set up in a world unprepared, deaf, and hostile to innovation of any kind (even to the simplest requests for collaboration), solid progress regarding mural conservation was at first slow to develop. The research, though extensive, was not particularly profound, and tended toward establishing rights of authority and precedence over an increasing number of projects. The restorers remained the same as before, and even the techniques and materials used did not differ significantly. This was the period of the restorations of Giotto at Assisi, of Paolo Uccello in the Chiostro Verde and of Lippi in the Carmine — all in Florence. Nevertheless, the era of the analysis of cross-sections had begun.

According to an article concerned with the Tomb of the Chariots at Tarquinia (*Bollettino del Istituto Centrale del Restauro,* no. 2, 1950), "during the war period, not only was all research regarding the problem suspended, but the condition of the paintings became noticeably worse due to the lack of

3. Lorenzetti, *Madonna della Loggia*.

4. Lorentino d'Arezzo, *Episode from the Life of San Bernardino of Siena,* San Francesco, Arezzo: humidity rising from the ground and climatic conditions threaten the complete destruction of this fresco.

even the most ordinary precautionary steps as well as to the use of the tombs as habitations by refugees and as anti-aircraft emplacements by German troops." It was only after the war that it was possible to resume these studies. These led to careful analyses of the plasters and of the extraneous materials superimposed upon them by the institute chemist, Dr. S. Liberti, and others. In the same issue of the *Bollettino,* the results of the analyses were published, which led to the decision to detach the murals.

The ingenious work of the restorer Pigazzini made it possible to transfer these Etruscan paintings satisfactorily, considering the precarious condition of the colours and the support. Following this success, more decorations were removed from

other tombs: the Tomb of the Triclinium, that of the Funeral Bed, and the Golini tombs I and II at Orvieto.

After the campaign among the Etruscan tombs, it was decided also to detach the mural decorations of the Palatine. Here again, science was forced to capitulate before uncontrollable humidity, which fostered the most complex and lethal transformations.[6]

At the same time, elsewhere in Italy, restoration work proceeded in the traditional manner — that is, on the basis exclusively of experience. The rare consultations with nonspecialized chemists, or the occasional contact with the institute in Rome, were insufficient to guarantee an effective scientific check and, as a result, they were of slight help. Quarrels among the various administrative authorities did not improve matters. Between 1950 and 1960 there was great activity in repairing the damage caused by the war. The ferment provoked by the discussions stemming from the initiatives of the Istituto Centrale made every laboratory strive to improve its own methods and to expose the defects of those used elsewhere. Since inorganic fixatives of assured strength and reversibility were then unavailable, it was often decided to detach those murals which were already beyond the initial stage of decay. The existing techniques were steadily improved as a result of the great number of works handled; many small defects were eliminated with a more stringent selection from the available fixatives. Stability and reversibility were required. The canvas and glue were applied with new methods, assuring better adhesion. The adhesives were chosen from among those which met the requirements of greater strength, elasticity, and reversibility — qualities considered indispensable in every case. The problem of supports, which was then among the most troublesome, was continually discussed, and from year to year experiments were made with new materials. As far as one can tell now, there was no visible tendency toward general agreement concerning solutions of these difficult problems; each seemed to barricade himself behind his own conclusions, and the methods used were those thought to be the most suitable.

With regard to this independence of action, for which no limiting provisions were made by the competent authorities, it must be admitted that each method had its advantages and disadvantages, and granting the fundamental exigencies of the situation, it is usually possible to see the reasoning which led to the choice of method in each particular case.

During all these various modifications developed for the conservation of murals, whether treated on the wall or after detachment, the scientific contribution was still external and occasional. In 1963, greater ease and breadth of consultation led to the possibility of having more institutions contribute studies and analyses to define the sources of deterioration in various sections of Giotto's frescoes in the Scrovegni Chapel at Padua. The Istituto Centrale of Rome, the chemistry department of the University of Padua, and the Conservation Center of New York University's Institute of Fine Arts competed in an admirable race to find the best means of protecting the celebrated scheme. There were grave difficulties in the *Paradise,* in the *Birth of the Virgin;* and even more severe in the *Marriage Procession* and in the *Mission of the Angel Gabriel.* Blistered crusts of color were visible in the angel of the *Annunciation* and in the *Last Supper.* Especially disfigured were the heads of the personages who received Enrico Scrovegni's gift of the chapel on the entrance wall. Furthermore, aside from these more obvious and dangerous deteriorations, there was spread over the entire surface a myriad of tiny blisters which were des-

tined to break, causing destructive craters of microscopic size. The plurality of research conducted contemporaneously in Rome and in New York allowed us to profit from the comparative results.[7]

In certain details, the reports are not in perfect agreement, but in the main, all contributed to show that the most deleterious transformation was that of calcium carbonate into sulphate. A part of the investigations made by Doctors Sayre and Majewski was published in *Studies in Conservation* (vol. 8, May 2, 1963). From it, we gleaned helpful advice on the qualities needed for the fixatives which were to consolidate the particles of broken paint, and above all, on the *quantity,* which had to be reduced to a minimum so as to avoid chromatic repercussions, aside from the natural reluctance to introduce any organic materials.

Since the time of occasional contacts between scientists and restorers, during the end of the 19th century and the first decades of the 20th, we have finally come to collaboration. Unfortunately, it is still not of a continuous kind. Nevertheless, meetings are frequent, and there is readiness for further ones in order to cope with new problems. The more we proceed, the clearer it becomes that, generally, murals are in a desperate state and that there is an urgent need to establish a research center entirely devoted to fresco problems.

The urgency for such a center was felt intensely after the flood suffered in Florence in 1966. Even those who first regarded the presence of a chemist as an intrusion and scientific participation a waste of time gave in before the exasperating multitude of destructive phenomena, even renouncing their hitherto passive resistance to help of this kind. In the first months after the flood, there was no grave concern for the murals involved. Attention was concentrated on the pictures, statues, and furniture, where the marks left by water and mud were more obvious. However, before long, the gravest symptoms of tragic consequence appeared among the frescoes too. Hardly had the walls begun to dry and the effects of their saturation began to show. In the lower area of Castagno's *St. Jerome* in SS. Annunziata, the color swelled in a shapeless mass, as if under pressure from a yeast of some kind. In the Spanish Chapel of Santa Maria Novella, in the scenes painted by Andrea da Firenze, areas blistered and scaled in an increasingly alarming way. The *Last Supper* of Taddeo Gaddi in the refectory of Santa Croce was covered with salt crystals, which as they increased pushed off innumerable particles of paint. In the church of S. Maria Maddalena dei Pazzi, in the chapel decorated by Poccetti, the plaster disintegrated as a result of uncontrolled development of salts.[8]

This rapidly growing ruin, which involved works by the greatest Tuscan painters, such as Giotto, Botticelli, Ghirlandaio, Paolo Uccello, Pontormo, and Allori, summoned the most

5. Fourteenth century follower of Duccio, Cappella dei Nove, Palazzo Pubblico, Siena: use of an unsuitable fixative has caused the surface to crumble, pulling off the color from the plaster. Only detachment and choice of a support adapted to the traction of the hardened paint layer can assure the conservation of the remains.

eminent experts from all over the world. Present and active were chemists, physicists, and biologists from Florence, Rome, London, New York, Boston, and Munich in a race of proposals, meetings, and discussions which were more or less dispassionate and constructive. All outdid themselves, often at great personal sacrifice, in efforts to be helpful in the defense of these threatened masterpieces. The goodwill of all was evident, but what also became clear was a grave lack of adequate scientific preparation in dealing with these problems.

The neglect, or to be more precise, the bland interest shown until then in the problems of mural conservation now betrayed its own weaknesses. It was not merely unusual elements, such as the presence of fuel oil and layers of mud which found us unprepared, but also the recurring phenomena caused by molds and salts. An enormous effort was made to try to identify as quickly as possible the exact source of all the single phenomena which always differed from case to case, so that the necessary provisions might be made in time before the mo-

ment of extreme crisis arrived. At first, no one knew how to remove the fuel oil which had already invested the entire thickness of the plaster layer; no one knew which were the salts which effloresced and caused the color to crumble and which were the ones responsible for the holes; or what provoked the swelling of the plaster, and so on. Without exact information, the restorer, faced with all these different manifestations, risked using the wrong method or the least suitable material. For instance, tributyl phosphate, useful in confining the action of nitrates on glues, turned out to be ineffective against sulphates — although no one knew this at first. The most volatile solvents, which had proved so useful in dislodging fuel oil from frescoes still in solid condition, proved to be dangerous when tempera colors were present or when the fresco was fragile. From beginning to end it was a state of perpetual doubt, anxiety, and courageous — often desperate — experiment.

Still, as a result of research stimulated by the flood, we have recently had an important suggestion which in many cases may eliminate the use of organic substances in the consolidation of frescoes: namely, use of barium hydroxide.[9] Although the properties of this material were already known and various attempts to use it in conservation had been made without any clear advantage, it now seems that the method perfected by Professor Ferroni and Dr. Malaguzzi has succeeded. The means of applying it were presented at the congress in Pistoia held on September 29, 1969, accompanied by precise explanations which have been scientifically tested showing that frescoes could by this means be given a greater solidity than they had even before the sulfation process of the murals began their decay. This development has interested the entire world of mural conservation and has restored hope that works may be preserved on the wall which otherwise could only have been given prolonged existence by detaching them.

This finding is most important, but unfortunately it belongs to the category of chance discoveries — discoveries snatched with sacrifice from the scientist already burdened by heavy obligations elsewhere. Every day the most unexpected phenomena may occur in the difficult effort of protecting frescoes, and one must be able to count upon immediate studies conducted by specialized personnel dedicated exclusively to this end.

Today, most of the worst damage caused to murals by the flood has been almost entirely repaired, and it is a comforting thought that we have been able to prevent even greater damage. But what cheers us most is the hope that we have overcome the resistance to new contributions and that in future we can count on continuous and ever-increasing scientific help. Such aid must be continuous and in direct contact with the restorer and with the works themselves. Occasional diagnoses are not enough: at every moment during treatment,

6. Domenico Ghirlandaio, *Mourning of Christ,* Vespucci Chapel, Ognissanti, Florence: the flood waters of 1966 caused a rapid efflorescence of calcium sulphate crystals (Malaguzzi and Young) destroying large areas of color and causing the rest to be in a precarious condition.

complications can arise, and it is indispensable to have someone near to whom one can turn, aware that only over long experience at this level can sufficient data be collected which can offer certainty to the technician and safety to the mural. In every frescoed wall there is a jungle of questions to which it is not easy to find the correct answer. Often the least obvious evidence of decay proves to be the most dangerous. It is not with prudence and precautionary postponements (often designed to protect those responsible rather than the works of art themselves) by which these problems are to be resolved.

About thirty years ago, the Giottesque frescoes in the Upper Church of San Francesco at Assisi were restored. I know of no reference to details regarding any dangerous areas there. The restoration did not meet with universal approval. Here and there the usual dissenting voices were heard criticizing excessive cleaning, the materials used, the tones inserted in the areas where original paint was gone. However, this campaign was among the generally good restorations of the time.

Today, the cycle as a whole appears dull and stained as it must have before 1935. Naturally, in the large uncleaned areas which were left as samples of the unrestored state, dust and salts have redoubled, so that one should not be confused when these are compared with the rest of the work. The frescoes now need to be cleaned again and stringently examined. Needed above all is a study to show with precision the losses suffered during the last decades, the causes which year by year weaken and destroy the painting and the treatments best suited to protect them.

These are questions regarding Giotto of Assisi and cannot be dealt with lightly, nor is a simple cleaning sufficient. As far as appearances go, everything would seem to suggest an easy job. The supporting walls are of a notable thickness, which protects against thermal variations; infiltrations of water are not noticeable, and apparently humidity via capillary action is to be excluded, nor is the neighborhood particularly infested by industrial fumes. In this respect, one could call this one of the best locations for the well-being of a mural. Furthermore, the fresco technique in which the paintings were done is among the most impeccable known — especially if one compares them to other frescoes in the same church. Light and air are given discrete entry via the large stained glass windows, and the doors are almost always shut. The marble pavement within and the lawn outside limit the amount of bothersome dust. Then what explains the deterioration which is visible even to the most uninstructed visitor?

Even without scaffoldings and special lighting one notices that in the *Miracle at Greccio* pale colors have faded and dark tones have vanished. One often finds the same phenomena in the *Confirmation of the Rule, St. Francis Receiving the Stigmata,* the *Death of St. Francis,* and in the *Apparition to Gregory IX.*

Few are the scenes where this deterioration is not active which leads eventually to the complete disappearance of the colors. Other phenomena disturb many of the scenes: scales of color raised because of an expansion of the surface; tiny blisters, the harbingers of new craters in both paint and plaster; and, most mysterious of all, the decoration of some areas where just those pigments usually believed to be strongest become faded and pale, as in the cassocks of the *frati* in the *Ecstasy* or in the *Approval of the Rule.*

At this point it is possible to foresee soon a decay of the Franciscan cycle which will reduce it to a state similar to that of the Old Testament cycle above it. It is truly frightening to think that the *Miracle of the Spring* or the *Saint Giving his Mantle to a Poor Knight* may eventually be reduced to a state such as the *Mourning of the Dead Christ* or *Isaac Blessed by Jacob.*

The recent restorations in the transept and in the Magdalen Chapel of the Lower Church did not have the same problems as did the Franciscan cycle, but both give the impression of

7. Ghirlandaio, *Mourning of Christ.*

having been carried out according to criteria aimed more toward esthetic effect than toward the frescoes' conservation.[10] To be honest, this judgment could be baseless because of the lack of exact information scientifically collected during the work there. It is, in fact, very difficult to obtain any data concerning the results of scientific research there from which one might draw any conclusions concerning the methods used by the restorers.

The restorations recently done in the Magdalen Chapel and on other Giottesque frescoes such as those in the crossing vault of the Lower Church are described with clarity and precision by Enzo Pagliani in his report published in *Giotto e i Giotteschi in Assisi* in the series edited by Padre Palumbo. Here we learn of other agents afflicting the murals in the basilica: molds which partially weaken the colors. The restorer refers to the difficulty of cleaning the surface in a uniform fashion, of the materials used to fix the colors, and he cites the solvents employed to remove the repaints, but one searches in vain for information on any scientific research done to identify the causes of the deterioration and any steps taken to stop the phenomena. There is only a brief reference that "as to this subject it is better to leave the way to the microbiologists and wait for the results of their studies." This was said at the *end* of a restoration! We ought not to be scandalized then if the same thing occurred with the scenes of the Magdalen and those in the crossing vault that happened in so many other restorations, namely, that scientific study was limited to a mere suggestion.

I have cited Giotto at Assisi, but I could just as well have referred to Piero della Francesca at Arezzo, Simone Martini at Siena, or even to Giotto at Padua again. But even a list of awesome length would be pointless unless one wished to keep in mind the importance of the scientific contribution and to be able to apply its results to actual restorations in hand.

Before a restoration is begun, all the necessary research should be done, and on the basis of this, plans should be drawn up, keeping in mind all the materials as well as the esthetic requirements. The contrary must be avoided — that is, to get involved in the restoration before one has a complete picture of the patient's state. Chemists and physicists should be called in to participate more actively and more directly. Only in this way is it possible for them to gain a clearer idea of the tragic state mural painting is in, and to involve them in a methodical process whereby they obtain insight based on reality in this very difficult task.

A beginning has been made at the research center in Florence which is partially financed by the *Consiglio Nazionale delle Ricerche* and equipped (as a result of the flood) with instruments presented by America, England, Germany, and the Scandinavian countries. But insufficient encouragement has limited its development and nourished the fear that one will not always be able to count on its support.

I would like finally to discuss a few suggestions of some urgency for better results in the common effort to improve the conservation of murals. In the first place, there is a lack of common agreement on technical definitions. This, the basis for a more complete utilization of aid of all kinds, must be studied and organized as soon as possible. The compilation of a brief but precise dictionary clarifying the terms which until now have varied from one personal interpretation to another would be of exceptional importance. The confusion which, for example, exists in the use of terms such as fresco, tempera, fresco-secco, mezzo-fresco, encaustic, etc., could be facilitated by the publication of a table where one could find the appropriate definitions, and above all, an explanation based on scientific demonstrations of the nature of each type.

The existence of so many different kinds of mural techniques requires an equally rich store of ready definitions. Fresh plaster has been painted with pigments dissolved solely in water, but also colors bound with glues and mixed with emulsions have been used. Insofar that in all of these cases the carbonatization of the lime always functions as the primary binding agent, it would be useful to have terms to explain the differences.

Another much debated subject is that of painting on the wall partially in fresco and partly refreshed by saturation with lime water. Of course, to clarify these particular techniques and to find suitable terminology, bibliographic research is not sufficient. A group of researchers ought to be organized which would add from their own direct experience to the body of knowledge handed down by tradition.

I have cited two examples, but there are many more themes about which there is little agreement regarding temperas and pigments. In conservation, that is, in the measures to be adopted to protect or cure a particular painting, it is especially important to know what material one is working with, and in any preliminary discusion of the problem terms must be used in which there is no risk of misunderstanding.

Another area which might prove useful for research for the protection of mural painting is the lack of precise information concerning the phenomena of condensation and the absorption or evaporation of the moist portion of the support material. It has been found that much damage suffered by murals derives principally from this hydric action. However, we still have floundered on the uncertainty which surrounds the argument, thus rendering the result hypothetical.

It should not seem strange that in a congress where one awaits the exposition of positive results, one should also hear so many questions such as I have presented here. My capacity as restorer obliges me to point out the weaknesses and lacunae in which our work is done and to expose these weaknesses in the hope that help may be obtained for better solutions.

Notes

1. Among the most distinguished examples of this concept of restoration which dominated the 19th century; the following may be cited: the Bardi and Peruzzi chapels in Santa Croce, Florence. The restoration of Giotto's frescoes in the former were executed by Professor Gaetano Bianchi (Cesare Guasti, *Gli affreschi di Giotto nella Cappella de'Bardi in S. Croce,* Florence, 1853). For the Peruzzi Chapel, the restoration was begun in 1848 by Professor Antonio Marini, and after his death in 1861 work was continued by his pupil, Pietro Pezzati (Tintori, L., and Borsook, E. *Giotto: The Peruzzi Chapel,* New York and Turin, 1965.

2. Botti, Guglielmo. "Sulla conservazione delle pitture del Camposanto di Pisa," *Memorie e lettere.*

3. *Bollettino del Museo Civico di Padova,* No. I in vol. XLIX (1960).

4. Archives of the Soprintendenza alle Gallerie di Siena. Folder on the *Maestà* by Simone Martini.

5. Loc. cit.

6. *Bollettino dell' Istituto Centrale del Restauro,* nos. 17–18 (1954).

7. Tintori, L. "The State of Conservation of the Frescoes and the Principal Technical Restoration Problems," *Studies in Conservation,* 8 (May 1963), 37–41; Sayre, E. V., and Majewski, L. J. "Technical Investigation of the Deterioration of Paintings, *Studies in Conservation,* 8 (May 1963), 42–54.

8. Abundant photographic documentation is preserved at the Gabinetto Fotografico della Soprintendenza alle Gallerie di Firenzi.

9. Speech of Professor Ferroni and Dr. Valerio Malaguzzi-Valerj at the International Council of Museums conference at Amsterdam in 1969.

10. Pagliani, Enzo. "Note sui restauri degli affreschi giotteschi nella Chiesa inferiore di S. Francesco," in *Giotto e i giotteschi in Assisi,* 1969.

VALERIO MALAGUZZI-VALERJ

Ancient Fresco Technique in the Light of Scientific Examination

During the last three years that I have dedicated to my new activity as a chemist in the fine arts, I have had the possibility of reading and, above all, of hearing a great deal about mural paintings in general, and fresco paintings in particular, and about the pigments and the techniques used by the old masters. I want to describe briefly some of the fascinating experiences I have had during frequent meetings with restorers so as to tell you as much as possible about what we learned of this type of painting: about its technique and the conservation problems we encountered. In this way it may be easier to begin a useful discussion about difficult aspects of mural conservation to which I am sure that many of you can contribute valuable suggestions.

What induced me to present this report was the great confusion of terms and, sometimes, even of ideas, extant in the literature concerning mural techniques. In fact, very often one finds reference to certain pigments used "*also* for wall paintings." Even if this expression is not wrong, it is misleading, because someone dedicated to the technique of fresco painting might wonder whether this pigment is usable for frescoes, simply because painting *a fresco* is completely different from any other kind of mural painting.

As this point, everything will become very complicated, if we do not explain briefly the execution of fresco painting to those who do not clearly remember it. Perhaps this will astonish you, but many people understand little about frescoes because either they are not to be found in the immediate neighborhood, or they are situated in sites difficult of access, making close inspection possible only with a scaffolding. The "fresco" is a special type of mural painting. The word "fresco" means fresh: the fresco painter spreads the pigments (suspended in water) without adding any medium, over the fresh plaster. As you know the plaster (in Italian, *intonaco*) consists of an *impasto* (mixture) of calcium hydroxide and sand; the hydroxide in combination with the carbon dioxide of the air is transformed into carbonate, which incorporates the sand particles and forms, in this way, a hard and resistant layer.

It is evident that the carbonation takes place first on the surface and then in the interior; consequently, the complete carbonation of plaster requires a long time. Among others, the sand has the function of giving porosity to this layer, so that carbonation is possible even in the interior. If one spreads pigments over the not yet carbonated but still fresh, even if not wet plaster (when it draws), a certain quantity of water saturated with calcium hydroxide appears on the surface. In this, the pigmented particles become immersed. With carbonation, the particles remain embedded in this layer, which consists of calcium carbonate in formation. This is the birth of a fresco; now we shall see the details of the whole process, starting from the preparation of the wall.

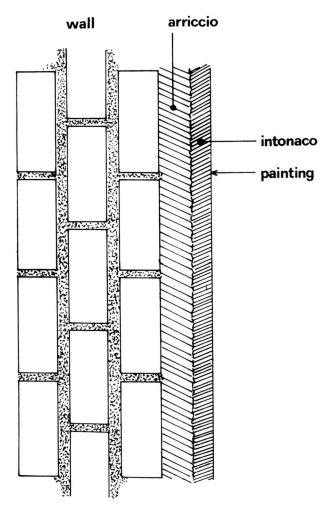

1. Cross-sectional view of a frescoed wall.

The fresco is a mural painting, and its fundamental support is a wall built of bricks or stones or both; the wall is covered by a layer of plaster about 1 or 2 cm thick and remains rough, in order to improve the adhesion of the second layer (this first layer is called *arriccio*); when it has dried (after some days), the second layer of plaster (from 0.5 to 1 cm thick) is applied on the morning of the day the painting is to begin, but only on that part which the artist has decided to finish on the same day.

For getting a resistant paint layer with a strong pigment bond with the plaster, it is necessary to carry out the painting during the first hours (from 1 to 8 hours) of the drying period of the plaster. Therefore, the painting has to be finished within the same day. It depends on the ability of the artists to prepare the intonaco in the right way; different factors, like humidity of

2. Cross-section of a fresco fragment.

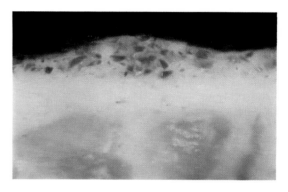

3. Fresco in Via dei Servi. Intonaco, yellow ochre 40 μ.

4. Santi di Tito, S. S. Annunziata, Refectory. Intonaco, red 20 μ.

5. Sodoma, Abbazia di S. Anna in Camprena. Intonaco, ultramarine with S. Giovanni white 50 μ.

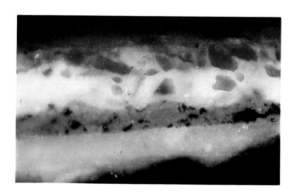

6. Sodoma, Abbazia di S. Anna in Camprena. Intonaco, red ground mixed with black 25 μ, azurite with S. Giovanni white 70 μ.

7. S. Martini — La maestà — Siena. Intonaco, black ground 45 μ.

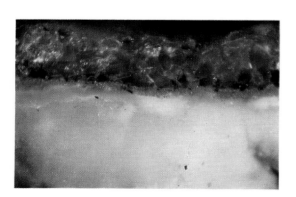

8. Sodoma, Abbazia di S. Anna in Camprena, Enlargement of sample (taken from the garment of Jesus) fresco. Intonaco, red ground 15 μ, azurite 70 μ.

the environment, the type of wall (bricks or stone), the thickness of the arriccio, as well as that of the entire plaster layer are of great importance for this. In fact, the necessary time for the beginning of the drying period (*tirare* the Italian technical term) varies and must be reevaluated with each case.

For the preparation of the mortar, limestone heated to about 1000° C for several hours is used. During this treatment, the calcium carbonate is transformed into calcium oxide. Afterward, water is added to this oxide causing a strong exothermic reaction producing calcium hydrate. The hydrate has the property of reacting with the carbon dioxide of the air, transforming itself again into carbonate. In fact, the latter reaction is used for the setting of the mortar and also for binding the particles of the pigment with the plaster. The calcium hydrate, which must have the consistency of a paste, is mixed with sand and ground bricks. As soon as the mortar has been applied to the wall, the carbonation process begins making the plaster hard and solid.

Now I want to make a short comment about one of the most controversial aspects of fresco painting, which we discussed at length with Professor Procacci,[1] who has long studied mural paintings, with different restorers who are in daily contact with these masterpieces, and also with Mr. W. J. Young of the Museum of Fine Arts during his stay at our laboratory in Florence.

It has been said, and many people still believe this, that in fresco painting the pigments *penetrate* into the fresh plaster, during the time the painter is working on it. It has been thought that it is possible to distinguish between the different techniques (*buon fresco* and *fresco secco*) by imagining that, in one case, the pigments penetrate into the intonaco, and, in the other, are spread on top of the plaster to form a separate crust. It is enough to look at a few cross-sections to see that it is incorrect to speak of "penetration" of the pigment into the intonaco. My opinion is that we never find any penetration. By the very nature of the process in which the pigment gets "bound" to the intonaco it is almost the reverse; it is the calcium hydrate of the mortar which comes to the surface and spreads into the paint layer; so, the pigment cannot penetrate into the intonaco.

We said that there is an ideal period for painting on a fresh intonaco: when it starts to dry. This drying is not so much from the exterior (because of evaporation) but rather from the interior because the stones or bricks of the supporting wall are absorbing the water of the plaster. When the pigment is spread with the paint brush, we notice a rapid absorption of the deposited water suspension; in the same moment, the calcium hydroxide of the intonaco is drawn to the surface and spreads within the pigment layer. During the subsequent carbonation, the pigments become "bound" closely to the intonaco. On the

other hand, it is possible to paint on a dry intonaco (this is called *secco* painting). But then, just as with panel painting, an organic binder is necessary, such a glue, egg, or (more modern) oil, since the natural medium of the wet plaster is lacking.

Midway between these two techniques, we may add another one, generally called *fresco secco,* in which the painting is executed on a no longer moist intonaco (laid some days before). The pigments are mixed and painted with lime water, *not* with clear water (sometimes the intonaco is moistened with lime water, before the painting is begun). Even in this case, the "binder" is calcium hydrate in a state of carbonation; but clearly with this technique the painting does not form a continuous layer on top of the intonaco (as in buon fresco), and, therefore, it is far less durable.

For easel painters, the choice of suitable pigments is not so problematic; but, in fresco painting, the artist's palette is more restricted. It is not possible to use any pigment indiscriminately, because some of them change their color in contact with alkalies, as, in our case, calcium hydroxide. Even if this alkali is rapidly transformed into carbonate, it may, nevertheless, alter the color of certain pigments.

Table I

Pigments Used in Frescoes

Color	Pigment
White	Calcium carbonate (bianco di S. Giovanni)
Yellow, red, brown	Earth pigments (iron oxides)
Green	Green earth: glauconite
Blue	Ultramarine blue natural, Egyptian blue
Black	Charcoal black

Table II

Pigments That Generally Should Not Be Used for Frescoes, Because They Are Subject to Alteration

Color	Pigment	Alteration
White	Lead white $2PbCO_3 \cdot Pb(OH)_2$	Blackens (PbO_2)
Blue	Azurite $2CuCO_3 \cdot Cu(OH)_2$	Blackens or becomes green
Green	Malachite $CuCO_3 \cdot Cu(OH)_2$	Blackens
Red	Cinnabar HgS	Sometimes blackens

There is no doubt that pigments can suffer chromatic alterations caused by certain mediums; for instance, there is a very recent scientific study[2] in this field which has examined the discoloration of smalt, generally attributed to its medium. The old sources[3] on this subject also refer to the alteration of some colors, of course, without explaining the causes. One is merely advised against the use of certain pigments for frescoes (table II). I do not believe that all the explanations (even the recent ones) are necessarily right or definitive.

White lead is one of the pigments considered unsuitable for fresco painting; with regard to this, Cennini says: "One works very well with it on the wall. But beware using it, because after some time it becomes black."[3] Thompson[4] explains this change from white to black by the presence of sulphurized components in the atmosphere, which favor the transformation of the basic carbonate of white lead into black lead sulphide. Even if not considered suitable, white lead has been sometimes used in frescoes, and sometimes, of course, it became black, even if nobody ever identified it as a sulphide. It has recently been reported by Kuhn[5] that the black component to be found in those parts of the mural paintings where the highlights should consist of lead dioxide; but there is no explanation for this alteration. My laboratory is also working on the problem of blackening. We located the black alteration-product in Assisi on the frescoes of Cimabue and also on one of Signorelli's frescoes at Monte Oliveto Maggiore. By means of X-ray diffraction, the black product was identified as lead dioxide.

Examining different cross-sections, we have seen that the alteration does not start from the surface particles exposed to the atmosphere, but rather in the interior, in the contact-area between lead white and calcium carbonate (which was still calcium hydroxide when the painting was done). Within this same zone it is possible to notice yellow and red particles, but so far we have been unable to identify them.

During laboratory tests we verified that the white lead is rapidly transformed into its oxide (PbO) by calcium hydroxide. We obtained a mixture of massicot (yellow) and litharge (red); more accurate determinations showed that the first alteration product is the yellow oxide, which derives directly from the decomposing basic carbonate, but that after a long period of reaction the only oxide present is litharge, which therefore is the more stable crystalline compound. Probably the yellow and red particles which we find between the pigment layer and intonaco are the reaction product of the white lead with calcium hydroxide. It is possible that this alteration takes place at scattered points; this could be caused by the longer exposure of the white lead to the calcium hydroxide (perhaps at just those points where the paint layer was more airtight, favoring slower carbonation). The process of subsequent oxidation in dioxide is harder to demonstrate: perhaps it occurred because of some product used for restoration or it was the result of some other energy source, such as ultraviolet rays. Of course, in the laboratory it was very easy to obtain the dioxide from the mixture of the oxides: a treatment with hydrogen peroxide (or

still easier, with sodium hypochlorite) proved to be sufficient.

Azurite is also one of the pigments that must be avoided in fresco painting; very often it changes into green, becoming malachite. In fact, in many paintings, the parts painted in azurite (generally the color of the sky or the background) have completely changed to green. But in all these cases, the azurite has not been employed in the fresco technique but has been applied *a secco,* that is to say, on the already dry intonaco with some kind of medium, generally a glue. Azurite is one of those pigments which have been used largely for mural paintings but almost never in the *buon fresco* technique.

Let us review for a moment which blues were used in mural paintings and by what technique. After the disappearance of Egyptian blue, we can say that the blue colors commonly used were ultramarine blue (lapis lazuli) and azurite. (Both are of natural origin and especially the latter has always been very expensive.) For their use as pigments, they have to be ground and purified. Cennini gives us a detailed description of the process. Besides these two pigments, since 1500, we also find smalt, a cobaltiferous glass. The ultramarine blue derives from the mineral lapis lazuli, a semiprecious stone that contains besides its blue mineral (lazurite: a silicate of aluminium and sodium) particles of pyrite (iron sulphide), and calcite (calcium carbonate). It is still a very expensive pigment, also because of its long purification process. One of the best methods is that described by Cennini, whereby it was possible to separate particles of different dimensions and naturally of different color. The smallest particles are the bluer ones, in contrast to the azurite, where the big particles are the more vivid ones.

Ultramarine blue has been widely used in fresco painting, because it is a pigment which does not change in the presence of alkalies. Generally, it is mixed with different quantities of *bianco di S. Giovanni* to obtain the various tones of blue.

As far as azurite is concerned, even during intensive research I never succeeded in finding it painted in the buon fresco technique, nor do I know of anyone else having found it. However, the possibility cannot be excluded, because certain equivocal cases exist. Let us review the ways it has been used. In those parts where the artist wanted to paint in azurite, he spread first a fresco a color, usually dark in tone, such as ochre, green earth, or even black. Later, when dry, the same area was painted with azurite tempered with a glue. Nevertheless, the azurite may alter in the presence of alkalies, as said earlier, and thus also in the presence of calcium hydroxide. Personally, I am unconvinced that this should be the sole reason why it has not been used in the fresco technique. One should be able to find some experimental attempts of its use in true fresco, even if the results were failures. We should keep in mind that for a good result in fresco painting the pigments have to be ground very fine (that is why the earth pigments work so well); but the azurite "è forte sdegnosa della pietra" says Cennini,[6] and if the azurite is finely ground, it loses almost all its color. However, using it in big particles, one does not obtain a deep blue, even though the white intonaco would perforce shine through it.

Here, the question naturally follows: supposing they used the azurite always a secco, why did they put it always on a dark preparation and never on the white intonaco? It is not very easy to give a definite answer, but I believe, in any case, that the "transparency" factor (I mean tiny particles which are losing their color, plus the white intonaco that shines through) should be of great importance. Only once I found the azurite put directly on the white plaster, but I suppose not a fresco (it is almost impossible to analyze it, because over that azurite one finds a repaint with glue, which has certainly penetrated into the azurite layer). The azurite in question was discovered on the sky of Fra Angelico's great *Crucifixion* in the San Marco Museum. The background of this fresco was originally painted with azurite over a preparation of red ochre; but in the lower part, where esthetic considerations required a lighter tone, the azurite has been spread directly on the white intonaco. It is interesting to note that during a restoration (probably of the 19th century), a restorer has repainted the whole upper background red (just where the azurite remained on its red preparation) and the lower background white (where the azurite had been employed directly on the white intonaco). As most of the azurite had fallen off, the restorer probably thought that it was good to ameliorate the state of the painting as it was at that time and as everyone then knew it. Therefore, he decided to repaint the red parts red and the white parts white. So it is incorrect to say (as has been written[7]), namely that Fra Angelico never applied any blue to this background; actually he did, and, as usual, in a very refined technique.

As a result of all that has been said concerning the use of azurite and to show that it can also be used in fresco technique, we prepared, together with our friend Tintori, fresco samples where azurite was employed. These samples are not yet sufficiently aged (they are about two years old). So far, they have not changed; even in the area of contact between azurite and intonaco, no alteration is noticeable. This shows that apparently the carbonation of the intonaco is much faster than the possible reaction process of azurite to calcium hydroxide.

As regards our specific research, it is clearly concerned with the conservation of these paintings; therefore, it is essential to have a solid knowledge of the various techniques and of the materials employed, both those used originally as well as those used in subsequent restorations.

The weakest parts of a fresco in which disintegration phenomena are most frequently formed are: the area between pigment and intonaco and between intonaco and arriccio. Very often in these parts, there is a lack of cohesion in the mortar which inevitably causes the color as well as the intonaco to crumble.

Until recently there have been few remedies. All depended upon the practical experience of ingenious restorers. Different adhesives were used: formerly, egg and caseins, then in recent times, products such as synthetic resins. Visibly these materials seemed to consolidate the intonaco and, for a certain time, stopped the detachment of the color. But, in many cases, the situation has complicated the already precarious condition of these masterpieces. In fact, the glues very often formed superficial films and made the phenomenon of the color detachment worse. These glues are ideal breeding grounds for micro-organisms which attack the color and sometimes increase the detachment. These micro-organisms grow even beneath the paint layer and, in this way, they generate an outward pressure, with the result that the color is forced off the wall. Another serious problem often encountered is the presence of soluble salts, which generally penetrate from the interior and crystallize on the surface, causing whitish efflorescences and disintegration of the color. After the flood of 1966, this phenomenon appeared with special violence when, weeks afterward, the waterlogged walls at last began to dry.

Even the origin of these salts has not been completely clarified. In some cases, we know what happened; for instance, the nitrates, usually those of potassium and sodium (more rarely of calcium) appeared on walls resting on a soil containing significant quantities of decomposed organic substances. But, in other cases, such as gypsum (calcium sulphate), our studies have not given clear results. Nevertheless, it is possible to make some simple suppositions, which we may see in connection with the well-known theories concerning the attack of the thiobacillus or of the products of the air pollution.

The calcium sulphate is found very often on mural paintings, and its effects are disastrous. I would like to make a few concluding remarks about what we have done in Florence on this.[8] In those parts where gypsum ($CaSO_4 \cdot 2 H_2O$) crystallizes, not on the surface, but right underneath the paint layer, the surface of the painting generally shows innumerable tiny craters. The pressure of the growing crystals causes explosion of the craters and detachment of the color. In these points we always found calcium sulphate by taking samples from the inner part of the not yet "exploded" craters and analyzing them by X-ray diffraction. After the preliminary laboratory tests, we effected two operations. First, there was a treatment with ammonium carbonate which allows the gypsum to transform itself again into calcium carbonate, from which it presumably derived. Secondly, we treated the wall with barium hydrate in order to neutralize the ammonium sulphate formed in the first reaction and also to give a greater consistency to the whole paint and intonaco layer. Deliberately, an excessive quantity of barium hydroxide was used in order to take advantage of its carbonation.

As the restoration experts said, the results have been really extraordinary; they can be controlled even now, two years after the beginning of the treatment. These results are opening a completely new way of restoration, which has the intention and the desire of working in situ without treatments which prejudice the structure of the pigment and which make later operations (such as the *strappo* detachment) no longer possible.

References

1. Procacci, U. *The Great Age of Fresco,* introduction, New York, the Metropolitan Museum of Art, 1968.

2. Plesters, J. "A Preliminary Note on the Incidence of Discolouration of Smalt in Oil Media," *St. Cons.* 14 (1969) 62—74; Giovanoli, R., and Muhlethaler, B. "Investigation of Discoloured Smalt," *St. Cons.* 15 (1970) 37—44.

3. Cennini, C. *Il libro dell'Arte,* chap. LIX.

4. Thompson, D. V. *The Materials of Medieval Painting,* London, George Allen and Unwin Ltd., 1956.

5. Kuhn, H. "Bleiweiss und seine Verwendung in der Malerei," *Farbe & Lack* 73 (March 1967), 99—105; 209—213.

6. Cennini, C. Op. cit. chap. LX.

7. Thompson, D. V. Op. cit. p. 72.

8. Ferroni, E., Malaguzzi-Valerj, V., and Rovida, G. *Experimental Study by Diffraction of Heterogeneous Systems as a Preliminary to the Proposal of a Technique for the Restoration of Gypsum Polluted Murals* (in press).

G. TORRACA

Deterioration Processes of Mural Paintings

The continuous expansion of the studies on the deterioration of stone has produced a substantial increase of our knowledge on the deterioration of porous materials as a function of their environment. This new knowledge can be applied to the problems of mural painting too. Having reviewed the literature on stone deterioration for a recent Italian meeting[1] on the preservation of open-air sculpture (Bologna, November 1969), I think it useful to attempt to coordinate available information on the deterioration processes of mural paintings, even if the resulting scheme might appear, as is very likely, lacking in completeness and precision. I believe that at the present stage an organized theory is necessary in order to consider the conservation techniques which are applied to mural paintings in a critical light and so to select them on the soundest possible bases. Future discussions and experimental developments will allow correction, or even complete renewal of the present scheme, but this process cannot start if an initial draft is not proposed. This, however, must be based on arbitrary assumptions on some points, since our knowledge is often far from complete.

Evaporation and Crystallization

Evaporation of water from the surface of mural paintings and crystallization of the soluble salts contained in it is one of the most widespread deterioration processes of porous materials. Crystallization of soluble salts and its disruptive action has been carefully studied by Schaffer[2] and Iniguez.[3]

As a conclusion of the review of the problem presented by Schaffer (p. 71–72), the disruptive force of growing crystals must be attributed to capillary forces which act by suction of fresh solution into the crevices opened between the crystals and the inner surface of the pores by differential thermal expansion. This process allows a crystal to grow even when it is filling a pore completely.

On the other side Iniguez shows that some soluble salts can first crystallize in an anhydrous form and then be hydrated when climatic conditions change; hydration results in increase in volume of the crystals and in possible disruptive action of the surrounding material. In both processes a contrast of forces is determined between the expanding crystal and the inner surface of the pore, the final outcome depending upon the strength of the materials involved; if the crystal is weaker it is extruded from the pore, if it is stronger the walls of the pores are crushed. Crystallization can thus result either in efflorescence, i.e., growth of needle-like crystals out of the porous material, or in disgregation of the porous material.

Sometimes the phenomena take place simultaneously on the same surface, since both the strength of the porous material and the chemical composition of the crystals vary from point to point. It is interesting to know that, according to Schaffer's argument, capillary forces are enabled to act by temperature changes which cause differential expansion effects. As a consequence these forces should be inactive if the temperature is kept constant. On the other side, the variation of the hydration state of the salt requires a change of humidity conditions. These considerations can explain the remarkable state of preservation of mural paintings which are kept at constant temperature under very high but relatively constant humidity (e.g., Lascaux, Tarquinia).

Solutions of soluble salts can reach the surface of a wall either because water rises from the soil within the masonry drawn up by capillary forces (rising damp), or because rainwater penetrates from the outside. Water rising from the ground carries along salts contained in the soil, in the foundations, or in the masonry itself. A typical example is the case of the Florentine frescoes endangered by the 1966 flood because water carried up the walls soluble nitrates formed from the decomposition of corpses buried under the floors of churches.

Rainwater, which contains a relatively small amount of salts, dissolves salts contained in bricks and mortars used in the masonry and carries them to the inner surface. Another cause of access of water to the surface of mural paintings is condensation. Condensation interferes with the crystallization processes and very likely favors their disruptive action; but since condensation also causes other deterioration processes, it will be considered separately in the next paragraph.

Condensation

Direct condensation of water vapor takes place on a surface when the relative humidity of air in its vicinity reaches 100 %. It can also happen that water droplets can be formed in the air, when humidity reaches 100 %, and remain dispersed in the air; we shall, however, deal with this case in the paragraph on aerosols.

A typical condition of condensation on wall surfaces inside a building is one in which the temperature of the walls is lower than that of air entering from outside. If the temperature difference is large enough, air may show relative humidity below 100 % in the center of rooms, while it reaches 100 % in the region near the cold surface of walls, even if its absolute water content remains the same. A thin veil of water is thus formed on the wall surfaces. Besides interfering with hydration-dehydration processes and capillary effects, condensation can cause chemical reactions of the surface materials, because condensed water is not pure but contains some acidic gases which are present in the atmosphere. Carbon dioxide is always present in the atmosphere, its concentration being larger in polluted areas. It dissolves in water, forming carbonic acid, a very weak acid. Carbonic acid solutions can affect mural paintings in which carbonated lime acts as binder of the pigment particles, i.e., fresco and lime techniques. As is well known, carbonic acid solutions can dissolve calcium carbonate by converting it into water-soluble calcium bicarbonate. Calcium bicarbonate in turn reverts to calcium carbonate upon evaporation of the solution, but obviously calcium carbonate is not re-precipitated in exactly the same position it had before nor does it exert the same binding action.

The paint layer can thus be affected by the process and lose its cohesive strength while an efflorescence of calcium carbonate may appear. Since carbonic acid is a weak acid this is a very slow process. But air in polluted areas also contains sulphur dioxide, which is readily oxidized by a catalytic process to sulphur trioxide. Sulphur trioxide, in turn, dissolves in water, forming sulphuric acid, a strong acid.

Deterioration processes caused by sulphuric acid solutions proceed at a fast rate and affect most materials. Calcium carbonate is converted to calcium sulphate, which is sparingly soluble and can form surface crusts that are extremely dangerous because they have a tendency to expand, to detach themselves from the plaster, and to flake off in the last stage of the process. Also, organic mediums, like glues, casein, or egg, and fixatives, both natural and synthetic, are affected by sulphuric acid solutions and are unable to protect the plaster on which they are laid, because organic films are porous and seldom form a surface layer which is absolutely impervious to water.

Since reactions caused by sulphuric acid progress at a much faster rate than in the case of carbonic acid, condensation becomes an extremely dangerous source of damage in polluted atmospheres. It is not at all easy to determine whether the surface of a porous material is damaged by condensation or by evaporation of water solutions. Porosity and density of the material can give an indication of the most likely process, but definitive proof can be obtained only through a complete hygro-thermic study of each single case. In general, heavy materials with low porosity, like marble and compact limestones or sandstones, are more prone to be affected by condensation than by evaporation.

The reverse should be true in the case of lightweight porous structures like most plasters, but it would be very dangerous to jump to conclusions. For instance, Massari[4] cites the case of mural paintings on vaults which were believed to be damaged by rain penetrating through the roof. Addition of a concrete roof on top of the other not only did not stop the damage, which was due to condensation, but made it worse. Also, the *Last Supper* by Leonardo da Vinci was damaged by condensation and not by rising damp; condensation in this case was due to the fact that the room behind the painting was not heated in wintertime, so the wall carrying the painting was colder than the others in the same room (Massari[4]).

If hygrocopic salts are deposited over the surface of a mural, a liquid layer can be formed at relative humidities below 100 %, the actual limit depending upon the nature of the salt. For instance, sea salt particles become droplets of water at 75 % relative humidity (Green and Lane,[5] p.101). So in areas where sea spray is present, condensation can take place on surfaces reached by the spray at 75 % relative humidity instead of 100 %, and its control is far more difficult.

Condensation is caused also by visitors, particularly in monuments that are visited by large crowds. Lacy[6] calculated that in King's College Chapel, Cambridge, the amount of moisture which passed from the visitors to the structure during the summer of 1961 should have been around 16 tons of water vapor. Condensation of water vapor produced by visitors would take place on the coldest surfaces of the building; therefore, the paintings on the vaults and the high registers of the side wall would be affected preferentially.

Aerosols

The word "aerosol" designates liquid or solid particles which are light enough to remain suspended in the atmosphere for some time. In nonpolluted areas particulate matter in the air is composed mainly of dust raised from the ground (carbonates, feldspar and clay, quartz, etc.) or salt drawn up by winds from seawater (sea spray).

In the atmosphere over the sea aerosols contain mainly chloride and sulphates; the chlorine-sulphur (Cl-S) ratio is close to that of seawater (21.5:1). These particles are liquid or solid depending upon relative humidity: at 75 % r.h. the crystals of salt absorb a large amount of water and dissolve in it, the particles increase in size and become droplets. In the reverse transformation, hysteresis phenomena usually take place, causing some delay in the return of the particle to the solid state after relative humidity drops under 75 %.[7]

When liquid aerosols drift over the mainland, a modification of their chemical composition that has been studied in detail by Eriksson[8] takes place. The value of the Cl-S ratio drops, and pH is shifted toward acidity (over the sea it shows a slight alkalinity, as in seawater). Cl-S values from 8 to 14 for giant particles (over 1 micron) and as low as from 0.5 to 0.9 for large particles (0.1 to 1 micron) have been reported by Junge.[9] Sulphur is always present as sulphate.

Eriksson shows that the most probable cause of the modification of aerosols is catalytic oxidation of sulphur containing gases (hydrogen sulphide and sulphur dioxide), which results in the formation of sulphuric acid. While sulphur content of aerosols increases, chlorine content drops because some hydrochloric acid can be formed and evaporated.

In nonpolluted areas the presence of sulphur-containing gases over the land is explained by Eriksson by the formation of hydrogen sulphide in intertidal flats, as a consequence of biological reduction processes. In inhabited areas sulphur dioxide is produced by combustion of sulphur-containing fuels. Its oxidation was studied by Junge and Ryan,[10] who found that it is catalyzed by iron, carbon dust, and metallic oxides, which are common constitutents of urban atmospheres. Junge and Ryan found also that oxidation of sulphur dioxide stops when pH drops below 2.2; therefore, the production of large amounts of sulphuric acid requires continuous neutralization of excess acidity. Neutralization can be effected by calcium and magnesium carbonate suspended as dust in the atmosphere, or by ammonia, another gas present in polluted areas, but it can also take place directly on solid surfaces containing calcium carbonate which are hit by the aerosol drops. These drops would remain on the impact area acting as microscopic reaction vessels for the production of sulphuric acid which is immediately neutralized by reaction with stone or plaster.

Research carried out in Italy[11] on industrial smoke showed that a major portion of the sulphur content of industrial fumes comes out of the chimney as droplets of sulphuric acid solution which possess a long enough life to affect considerable areas around the pollution source. These droplets often escape detection in the usual air pollution controls that determine gaseous sulphur dioxide only. Aerosols can thus be powerful means of destruction for many materials, among which are murals. Eriksson, for instance, speaks of liquid particles with a salt concentration ten times larger than seawater and a pH close to 1.

In urban atmospheres giant aerosol particles also contain carbon black, metal oxides, tar-like substances, etc., which make their path visible, since they cover the surface they hit with dark soot. However, smaller, invisible particles (which, as Junge shows, contain more sulphur) are more dangerous. They have a longer life and can follow currents of air around several obstacles; it is extremely probable that they can enter buildings, where the doors are frequently open, as in the case of churches. In fact, it is often noticed that the most damaged stones or paintings are situated in the path of obvious air drafts. It is more difficult to understand the action of aerosols in other cases; however, some properties of aerosols must be kept in mind, in order to better understand their action and to provide clues for defense against them. In the first place, aerosols move from warm areas toward cold spots; therefore, the coldest part in a building is the most likely to be attacked, as in the case of condensation. Second, the life of aerosols increases with relative humidity and decreases with temperature; therefore, they can follow longer paths in cold, damp environments. Finally, their life is greatly increased by the presence of hygroscopic salts, so it must be expected that

their action is more important in coastal areas where the salt content of the air is higher.

Surface Incrustations

Murals found in caves or in buried buildings are frequently covered by very hard incrustations, which are in most cases extremely difficult to remove. There are three different processes which lead to the formation of incrustations: (a) percolation of water through the mural; (b) deposits from water running over the surface of the mural; and (c) deposition of dust, which is then cemented by condensation. Processes (a) and (b) are rather obvious. In the first, water containing calcium salts, mostly as calcium bicarbonate, passes through the mural spreading on its surface as a fine veil and finally evaporating. A thin layer of calcium carbonate is formed upon evaporation and becomes thicker as the process is repeated.

It is also well known that calcareous water running over a surface leaves a hard deposit. On the other hand, if the water contains an excess of carbon dioxide over calcium, it can exert a corrosive action on materials containing calcium carbonate.[12] Thus the effect of water running over a mural will depend upon its calcium-carbon dioxide ratio, the final result being either corrosion or incrustation (equilibrium would be a very unlikely event, resulting in perfect preservation of the mural painting).

Case (c) may occur when the cave, or buried building, is in contact with the external air. It was recently detected by a Rome Centre mission in the tombs of Beni Hassan, Egypt.[13] In the case of Beni Hassan, an extremely hard incrustation had formed over mural paintings of the twelfth dynasty, painted over a gypsum plaster which also contained calcium carbonate. It was thought that incrustations should consist of calcium sulphate and calcium carbonate, but X-ray diffraction of the surface showed that feldspar, quartz, and calcium carbonate were the main components. Chemical behavior of the crust, which is soluble only in strong, concentrated acids, confirms this result. The conclusion that could be drawn was that the incrustation was formed by dust cemented in place by calcium carbonate, which is dissolved and re-precipitated by a periodical condensation process.

This kind of process might have a general importance and be responsible for incrustations which usually are attributed to percolation processes.

The formation of incrustation (or efflorescences) in a cave or buried building implies always that an equilibrium condition is never reached in the enclosed space. This may happen because there is a continuous inflow and outflow of air or because the equilibrium is disturbed by the intermittent presence of visitors which cause temperature and humidity variations resulting in evaporation or condensation of humidity over the surface of the murals.

The ideal condition of conservation for these murals would be that of an airtight chamber which reaches a hygrothermic equibilrium with the natural or artificial walls confining it. All factors disturbing such an equilibrium are potential causes of deterioration of the paintings.

Dehydration

It used to be said by restorers years ago that extreme dryness could damage murals, causing disintegration of the paint layer and so allowing pigment particles to dust off (in Italian *spolverare*) under the slightest mechanical action. This has never been proved for fresco paintings, nor is there any theoretical basis for accepting the fact that calcium carbonate formed by carbonation of lime could be damaged by dryness. Some organic mediums, like gums or glues, might indeed become brittle if totally dehydrated, but it is unlikely that this might happen in any climate in view of the fact that tempera paintings of the pharaonic age resisted quite well in the desert climate of the Valley of the Kings.

Often the loss of cohesion in the paint layer, which appears upon drying of murals, is the result of a disintegrating process which took place in the damp stage, for instance, because of condensation and evaporation of water. In the dry condition flaking pigment particles dust off more easily because liquid films no longer hold them in place. Dehydration processes, however, can be important in gypsum and clay plasters. Recent research carried out by the Rome Centre in the tomb of Queen Nefertari, in the Valley of the Queens, Egypt,[13] shows that the gypsum plaster lost cohesion and adhesive strength because of complete dehydration in the local environment ($28°-29°$ C, $30-40\%$ relative humidity).

The fundamental study on gypsum by Van't Hoff and co-workers[14] indicates that at $30°$ C calcium sulphate bihydrate is not stable below 75% r.h. Usually transformation of gypsum into snhydrite at low temperatures is not noticed because it must be extremely slow, but after a very long time the stable phase is finally formed. Also the force of clay plasters must be affected by dehydration, although no accurate study of the strength of clay plasters in various environments appears to have been carried out in the past. Clay plasters are normally considered extremely weak and in need of reinforcement regardless of the climatic conditions to which they are exposed.

Direct Action of Rain, Sunlight, Oxidation, Temperature Variations, Frost, Wind

Murals which are directly exposed to weathering agents usually undergo much heavier damage than those which are protected inside buildings. Direct action of rain is one of the main destructive agents, since rainwater contains dissolved carbon dioxide in fair amounts and so is able to dissolve small amounts of calcium carbonate. The result of this process is a light etching of plasters and stones which, if tolerable on statues and decorative elements of façades, is totally destructive for frescoes in which the image of the work of art is carried by the outermost $10-30$ microns of the solid material.

Also, paintings done by tempera techniques are heavily damaged by rainwater, while clay and gypsum plasters are completely disintegrated. Hydrophobic mediums, instead, should withstand rain well while they are in good condition, but after the destructive action of oxidation, light, and thermal expansion has modified their chemical structure, weakened their mechanical properties and impaired their adhesion to the support, they are also easily washed away.

Sunlight, particularly ultraviolet radiation, acts on painting materials, fading non-light-fast pigments and triggering oxidation and cross-linking reactions of the organic medium. So the overall effect of radiation and oxidation on fresco paintings, where no organic medium and only light-fast pigments are used, should be small (however, some archaeological finds show that dyes were occasionally used in murals). Tempera and oil techniques, on the other hand, must be greatly affected by light and oxidation processes, which usually result in embrittlement and loss of adhesion between the paint film and the inorganic support. Strong variations of temperature favor the detachment of paint films from plasters because all organic substances have larger thermal expansion coefficients than inorganic ones. Heating and cooling of the surface of the painting results, therefore, in the setting up of mechanical stresses between the paint film and the support.

The processes of deterioration of organic mediums used in mural paintings obviously also affect organic fixatives that are used on fresco paintings to protect them or restore adhesion of the pigment particles. In some circumstances the creation of a film of an organic adhesive on mural paintings can result in serious damage if the destructive effects of light and temperature variations are not foreseen and somehow controlled.

Frost obviously has a destructive action on murals as on any other porous material. It is very rare, however, that a mural is damaged by frost, the reason being that if a mural is exposed to conditions which allow soaking with water and freezing, there is no chance for it to survive but for a very short lapse of time.

For sake of completeness, erosion by wind must also be taken into account. As in the case of stones, we must distinguish two destructive mechanisms involving wind: the first is a straightforward abrasion carried out by airborne sand particles; that is a natural sandblasting process. In the second case, wind interferes with evaporation processes taking place from a wet porous surface; as the rate of evaporation of water

increases with the speed of air circulation, when it is sufficiently high, evaporation and crystallization of soluble salts
takes place inside the pores and not any more on the surface
of the material.[2] So the destructive power of the crystallization
process is enhanced by the wind, and it can result in a cavita-
tion process (eolic corrosion) because the wind is channelled
in the attacked areas, causing further activation of the process
of evaporation and crystallization.

Biological Attack

Fungus, algae, and lichens are frequent causes of deterioration of murals. Their action is always tied to the presence of
water in the wall structure; in my experience, biological attack
is likely to take place only on walls which are permanently
soaked with water, and even in this case other contributing
conditions, such as the presence of nutrient materials or light
(for some types of algae), must be fulfilled to make the life of
such organisms possible on murals.

Nutrient material can be contained in the original paint layer
(mediums in non-fresco techniques) or introduced by restoration processes (fixatives) or finally produced by the breath of
large numbers of visitors, as in the case of the Lascaux cave.[14]
The main studies on biological alteration of mural paintings
have been conducted by the Commission for the Preservation
of the Lascaux Cave[15] and the Istituto Centrale del Restauro.[16]
Biological sulphation processes, such as those reported by
Pochon for stone in tropical climates, are possible in theory,
but no actual occurrence has been reported as far as I know.

Conclusions

A list of deterioration processes is hardly a practical tool in
the hands of conservators to orient them in their preservation
work. A step forward should consist in the introduction of
some correlation between the environmental condition of
murals and the probability that a given deterioration process
might appear. I shall try a first sketch of such a scheme, divid-
ing the murals into five groups according to their environment
and listing the most probable deterioration processes.

(a) *Temperate climate — murals inside buildings.* Evaporation
(due to rising damp or rain infiltration) and condensation.
Aerosols should be taken into account, particularly in marine
climates and damp, polluted areas.

(b) *Temperate climate — external murals.* Direct rain, condensation, rising damp. Aerosols in marine climates and damp, polluted areas.

(c) *Temperate climates — caves, buried buildings.* Evaporation
and condensation produced by visitors. Evaporation due to air
circulation. Incrustations. Biological attack.

(d) *Arid zone.* Evaporation and consequent salt crystallization.
Dehydration (gypsum plasters).

(e) *Humid climate — tropical area.* Biological attack. Evaporation and condensation. Aerosols in marine climates.

The main purpose in codifying our knowledge of deterioration of murals is that of convincing conservators and restorers
that identification of the causes of deterioration is imperative
before any restoration process is adopted. Materials and techniques can be continuously improved by the ingenuity of
restorers, but a real improvement in the conservation of murals
will be realized only when the right materials and the right
techniques are applied after identification of the disease which
affects the mural to be preserved.

The best fixative cannot protect a mural subject to a heavy
evaporation process, particularly if light and temperature
variations are great; conversely, detachment of a painting
affected by rising damp or condensation is an unnecessary
massacre which could be avoided by taking care of the patient
(i.e., the wall) instead of tearing off its skin.

References

1. Torraca, G. "The Present Knowledge of Stone Deterioration. Causes and Conservation Techniques" in *Sculpture all'Aperto Ferrara–Bologna 1969,* Soprintendenza alle Gallerie di Bologna, 1969 (in Italian).

2. Schaffer, R. J. "The Weathering of Natural Building Stone," London, Her Majesty's Stationery Office, 1950.

3. Iniguez, J. "Alteration des calcaires et des grès utilisés dans la construction," Paris, Eyrolles, 1967.

4. Massari, G. "Hygienic Rehabilitation of Damp Buildings," Milan, Hoepli, 3rd ed., 1968 (in Italian); "Humidity in Monuments," Rome Centre, 1969, 1971 (in English).

5. Green, H. L., and Lane, W. R. "Particulate Clouds," London, Spot. 2nd ed., 1964.

6. Lacy, R. E. "A Note on the Climate inside a Medieval Chapel," *Studies in Conservation,* 15, no. 2, 1970, p. 78.

7. Junge, C. E. "Air Chemistry and Radiochemistry," New York, Academic Press, 1963.

8. Ericksson, E. "The Yearly Circulation of Chlorides and Sulphur in Nature," *Tellus* 11 (part I) (Nov. 1959), 375–403; *Tellus* 12 (part II) (Dec. 1960), 63–109.

9. Junge, C. E. "Recent Investigations in Air Chemistry," *Tellus* 8 (1956), 127–139.

10. Junge, C. E., and Ryan, I. G. "Study of the SO_2 Oxidation in Solution and Its Role in Atmospheric Chemistry," *Quarterly Journal of the Royal Meteorological Society,* 84 (1958), 46–55.

11. Vittori, O. and Nucciotti, F. "Concentration of Sulphur Dioxide and Total Sulphur at Low Levels and Temperature Inversion," *Rivista di Meteorologia Aeronautica* 27 (3) (1967), 3–9 (in Italian).

12. Weyl, P. K. "The Carbonate Saturometer," *Journal of Geology,* 69 (1961), 32–44; "The Solution Kinetics of Calcite," *Journal of Geology,* 66 (1958), 163–176.

13. Plenderleith, H. J., Mora, P., Torraca, G., and de Guichen, G. "Conservation Problems in Egypt," report of UNESCO Consultant Contract 33.591, Rome Centre, 1970.

14. Lefevre, M., and Laporte, G. S. "The *maladie verte* of Lascaux — Diagnosis and Treatment," *Studies in Speleology,* 2 (part L) (July 1969), 35–44.

15. Van't Hoff, J. H., et al. "Gypsum and Anhydrite," *Zeitschrift für Physikalische Chemie,* 45 (1903), 257–306.

16. C. Giacobini, "Problems of Microbiology in Mural Paintings," *Bollettino Istituto Centrale del Restauro,* 1965, 83–103 (in Italian).

EDWARD V. SAYRE

Investigation of Italian Frescoes, Their Materials, Deterioration, and Treatment

Important among the many factors that contribute to the deterioration of fresco mural paintings is the transport of water through the paintings accompanied both by solution of portions of the painting support and by deposition of destructive efflorescences upon or beneath the paintings' surface. The destructiveness of such water transport, of course, will be increased if the water carries with it in solution acidic gases derived from the atmosphere. In addition, when the surface of the painting is moist, either because of transport of water or because of condensation upon it, the painting is likely to be directly corroded by these acidic gases. Purely mechanical, thermal and photochemical processes, and biological attacks also are significant contributors to deterioration.

In the case of Italian Renaissance fresco paintings all of these processes of deterioration have been taking place throughout the four to six centuries of their existence. It has been noted, however, that the rate of deterioration of these paintings has in many instances greatly increased during the twentieth century. This is seen in the Giotto frescoes in the Scrovegni Chapel at Padua, where a careful review of the conservation records going back for many years reveals that a preponderant fraction of the total visible changes that have occurred have taken place within the twentieth century.[1] One might ask whether the progressive deterioration has just recently become increasingly visible or whether new destructive elements recently have been introduced. There is good reason to believe that the rapid increase in concentrations of acidic air pollutants, particularly sulfur dioxide, during the twentieth century has been a major contributor to this accelerated decay. Certainly the overall conditions of the paintings within the Scrovegni Chapel, together with the state of the atmosphere at Padua, indicated this conclusion to Professor Lawrence J. Majewski and myself when we examined them in collaboration with Professor Tintori in 1961.[2]

This paper will be concerned in part with a more recent examination of Italian frescoes that I again undertook in collaboration with Professor Tintori in 1966, which has shown additional evidence of atmospheric attacks, although in some instances the nature and effects of this attack have been different from that experienced at Padua. Since the entire question of atmospheric attacks upon frescoes remains a subject of debate it might be well to review briefly the bases for the conclusions arrived at in the case of the Scrovegni Chapel. The more fundamental reasons for implicating atmospheric attack as a predominant decay mechanism in this instance lay in the quantity, nature, and distribution of calcium sulfate dihydrate, the mineral gypsum, found in and upon the paintings rather that the simple observation of the presence of sulfate itself. In fact I had observed the presence of sulfates in preliminary samples provided by Professor Tintori before going to

Padua to study the overall condition of the paintings, without reaching conclusions as to its origin. In the chapel it was found that all surfaces tested were covered with a layer of sulfate, ranging from those near the bottom of the cycle to those near the ceiling, including both regions in which there was evidence of penetration by water and those where the plaster appeared to have remained dry and also including the original painting surfaces and the surfaces exposed within deep cracks. In fact every surface tested which had been exposed to the air had accumulated a sulfate coating. In contrast to this, no specimens of subsurface, solid unattacked intonaco or arriccio showed X-ray diffraction lines of calcium sulfate dihydrate. The sensitivity of these diffraction measurements was such that it could be deduced that the concentrations within unattacked plaster were well under one percent. The accumulation of calcium sulfate in major regions of decay was extensive, representing many times the amounts that could possibly have been derived by transport from the original arriccio and intonaco together. On the other hand the concentrations of sulfur dioxide in the air in the vicinity of the Scrovegni Chapel, as measured by a research group at the University of Padua, were so great as to easily account for the greatest quantities of sulfate found as being the direct product of reaction between the affected plaster and the air. Indeed, in light of the fact that it is known that a sizable concentration of highly reactive sulfur oxides, calcium carbonate, and moisture existed together for many years in the areas in which the most extensive deterioration occurred, one might ask how they possibly could not have reacted together. Finally the nature of the decay, i.e., the development beneath the pigment layer of extended "blisters" containing a soft nonconsolidated powder, rich in calcium sulfate dihydrate, which when they grew to an unstable size broke open to expose regions of the bare carbonate of the intonaco that then spread rapidly in size, was quite consistent with what one would expect from direct reactions between the carbonate support and sulfur oxides in the air.

The More Recent Investigation of Fresco Deterioration

In all, six northern Italian mural paintings were studied in collaboration with Professor Tintori in early 1966. The collection of specimens for laboratory investigation occurred some months before the devastating flood of that year. Since that time several of the paintings have been transferred by the strappo technique and others cleaned and partially consolidated in situ. Hence in some instances the direct alteration products which we were able to observe have now been fully removed. The selection of specimens was a matter of joint consideration, although the careful removal of the very small specimens required for analysis was left entirely to Professor Tintori's skilled hands.

The following specific paintings were investigated: in Padua the Giusto dei Menabuoi cycle in the Baptistry of the Duomo, in Pisa the Nicolo Gerini paintings in the refectory of the Chiesa San Francesco, in Florence the Masaccio and Filippino Lippi frescoes in the Brancacci Chapel of St. Maria del Carmine, the Ghirlandaio Last Supper in the refectory of the Chiesa di Ognissanti, and the Del Sarto murals in the Chiostro dello Scalzo, and at Montesieppi near Sienna the Ambrogio Lorenzetti paintings in the Chapel of San Galgono. In each instance specimens of surface efflorescence and of intonaco in both a well-preserved and a deteriorated condition were taken. In addition, in some instances, specimens of pigments were taken for identification. Although this pigment identification is somewhat extraneous to the main purpose of this paper, it has seemed worth while to provide a record of our findings at this time. Therefore an appendix describing the results of pigment analyses is attached. Most interesting and unusual among these observations is the occurrence of ultramarine blue in the dei Menabuoi frescoes and lead white in the Lorenzettis.

With the exception of the frescoes in the relatively remote chapel of San Galgono all of the paintings studied showed evidence of extensive sulfatization. Surface efflorescences when examined by X-ray diffraction proved to be almost pure gypsum, and sizable concentrations of gypsum were found in deteriorated intonacos. Intact intonacos, however, produced only diffraction lines of calcite and silica, indicating that a rather pure lime plaster had been used for the intonaco of all of these paintings. With two exceptions there was little to indicate that the deterioration of these paintings was qualitatively different from that observed in the Scrovegni Chapel. These exceptions were the paintings in the San Galgono Chapel at Montesieppi and in the Chiostro dello Scalzo at Florence.

The Chapel of San Galgono stands on a hilltop in the countryside southwest of Sienna. Although the Lorenzetti paintings of this relatively remote location had a light covering of efflorescence, this powder was nearly pure calcium carbonate, containing only a small trace of gypsum. The same was true of the intonaco even in regions where it had somewhat disintegrated. Also the appearance of the surface of the painting in regions where visible decay had occurred was distinctly different from what we had observed before. There was no evidence of swellings in structure such as occurs when calcium is converted to calcium sulfate dihydrate; instead small pits were prevalent in attacked regions (see fig. 1). It would seem very likely that both the deposition of a calcium carbonate efflorescence and the dissolution of surface pits could

be primarily just the result of the action of carbon dioxide and water upon the painting and its support. The windows of the chapel are unglazed and the building unheated. Condensation of moisture upon the surface of the paintings must be a fairly frequent occurrence. Such periodic wettings plus the fact that some transport of water through the walls is also likely could explain the observed deterioration. There was in addition some question as to whether the paintings might not have been periodically washed. However that may be, these paintings provide evidence that buon fresco may still deteriorate considerably even in a structure well isolated from the high concentrations of the very corrosive sulfur oxides present in urban and industrial centers.

The second exceptional condition of decay was found on the del Sarto paintings in the Chiostro dello Scalzo at Florence. Here there was extensive evidence of sulfatization, all outer layers being very rich in gypsum. What was unusual was that in certain rather extensive areas nearly the entire outer layer seemed to have been converted relatively uniformly to a sulfate-rich structure. In these regions the whole outer surface had expanded, causing extensive cracking, buckling, and general scaling off. Fig. 2 shows such regions. For such a relatively uniform conversion to sulfate to have occurred moisture must have reached the surface so affected to a relatively uniform degree. It would seem unlikely that transport of water through the walls would moisten the surface this uniformly. In most instances where it is apparent that sizable amounts of water have come through the walls preferential paths seem indicated as spots or streaks of extensive decay occur. However, surface condensation would have tended to wet the surface uniformly and also would have resulted in localized wetting of the outer layer. General surface wetting of this type in the presence of sizable concentrations of sulfur oxides could have led to the surface scaling in evidence here.

A general conclusion that can be drawn from these observations is that although attack by the acidic sulfur oxides is not the only mechanism of deterioration taking place in Italian Renaissance frescoes it appears to be a major contributor to the deterioration of frescoes present in all major cities. Only those in some remote location such as at the Chapel of San Galgono seem to have largely escaped its ravages. A treatment that would specifically protect frescoes from this acidic attack and also consolidate the weakened portions that have already developed without essentially altering the appearance of the paintings would be very useful.

The Barium Ethylsulfate Treatment of Frescoes

The treatment process which has recently been tested on small specimens of Italian frescoes at the New York University Conservation Center involves the impregnation through the

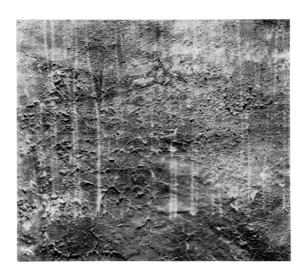

1. Surface of wall paintings by Ambrogio Lorenzetti at the Chapel
of San Galgono, Montesieppi, showing typical surface pitting.

2. Areas of the Andrea del Sarto frescoes, in the Chiostro dello Scalzo, Florence, in which the surface layer has expanded and is scaling off.

fresco pigment layer into the intonaco and perhaps the even deeper-lying arriccio with colorless barium sulfate by direct precipitation from a homogeneous aqueous solution. The barium sulfate is grown slowly from solution within the painting and support structure in such a way that well-formed cohesive crystals are developed. The net result is to bind the structure together with a material that is nonreactive toward acidic atmospheric gaseous components, that is itself extremely insoluble and will remain indefinitely chemically stable. Barium sulfate exists in nature as the stable rock mineral barite. The fact that this newly deposited inert material will surround and cover the reactive carbonate remaining in the painting structure should protect the structure from continued corrosion. Also any relatively soluble sulfates already present in the painting structure which might migrate with water to form destructive efflorescences will be converted by the treatment to insoluble barium sulfate, the metal ions present being eventually converted to their carbonates. The porosity of the entire structure will be lowered by a partial filling in of its pores and cavities without sealing the structure to the passage of water vapor. These results are accomplished by saturating the painting structure with an aqueous solution of the water-soluble salt barium ethylsulfate together with a slightly more than equivalent amount of barium hydroxide. These components will react together slowly, over a period of several weeks at normal room temperatures, to form the barium sulfate plus ethyl alcohol which evaporates away. To prevent the solution from drying during the period of reaction, a humectant such as glycerine, up to 20 % by volume, is included in the

solution or the surface is covered with protective coverings, which are afterward removed. The barium ethylsulfate process as applied to stone is described in detail in a paper presented at the 1970 meeting of the International Institute of Conservation of Artistic and Historic Works.[3]

It has been recognized since the late nineteenth century that a limestone that was either naturally soft and friable or had become so through deterioration when treated with an alkaline barium solution underwent a marked hardening in structure. A treatment of this type has recently been applied to frescoes by E. Ferroni, V. Malaguzzi-Valerj, and G. Rovida.[4] In their approach the fresco specimens were first treated with a solution of ammonium carbonate to convert any calcium sulfate present to calcium carbonate and ammonium sulfate. A following treatment with barium hydroxide converted the soluble ammonium sulfate to insoluble barium sulfate. Portions of the frescoes in the Spanish Chapel of Santa Maria Novella have been successfully treated by Malaguzzi-Valerj by this technique. In the treatment of these frescoes a layer of a thin but strong paper, such as Japanese mulberry paper, was first laid upon the frescoes and a cellulose pulp wet with treatment solution placed upon this. The cellulose pulp was kept moist with treatment solution for the desired period of reaction, during which time any extrasurface precipitation occurred in the paper and pulp exterior layer. Following treatment when the paper and pulp were removed the pigment layer was found to be free of any dulling or covering deposit.

The barium ethylsulfate treatment of frescoes is best carried out in a manner similar to that described above, except that the final treatment would be with a solution of barium ethylsulfate combined with an equivalent excess of barium hydroxide rather than with a simple solution of barium hydroxide alone. The treated fresco must then be kept in a moist condition until the chemical reaction between the two solution components has been essentially completed. The inclusion of barium ethylsulfate in the last step of treatment will substantially improve the effectiveness of consolidation and protection against atmospheric corrosive gases for the following reasons. Because barium sulfate is so very insoluble, barium and sulfate ions in solution react together almost instantaneously and precipitate as a finely divided powder; hence when a barium hydroxide solution is applied to a fresco structure containing soluble sulfates the barium sulfate that comes down is in the form of a fine, noncohesive powder. However, if barium ethylsulfate is also present in the treatment solution an additional slow precipitation of barium sulfate occurs. Because this deposition occurs slowly the new barium sulfate grows upon that already deposited and upon the carbonate and other particles present to form well-developed crystals which (1) contribute to the cohesive strength of the structure and (2) tend to cover the chemically reactive carbonate particles with a protective inert coating.

A preliminary testing of the effectiveness of the barium ethylsulfate treatment on Italian frescoes was made possible through the generosity of Professor Leonetto Tintori in providing small samples, a few square centimeters in area, 2 to 3 mm thick, from the decorative edge areas of the very severely deteriorated frescoes in the refectory of Santa Maria del Carmine in Florence. He provided specimens with uniform white, blue, and red surface pigment layers. The specimens were extremely soft and friable. The very softest of the Venus pencils 5B and 6B would scratch the surface of these fragments.

Two sets of these fragments were treated with an aqueous solution containing 20 % glycerine by volume in which barium ethylsulfate dihydrate and barium hydroxide octahydrate were dissolved to concentrations 4 and of 3.5 grams per 100 milliliters respectively. A third set of samples was left untreated as a control. In the treatments, the specimens were first covered with Japanese mulberry paper to which was applied a thick layer of cellulose pulp wet with the barium ethylsulfate solution. One set of treated specimens was allowed to stand at room temperature for a period of three weeks. The second set was positioned vertically in front of an infrared heat lamp. Thermocouples imbedded below the cellulose pulp next to the pigment layers of the specimens reached temperatures close to 50° C during the period of irradiation. This temperature-accelerated treatment was continued for a period of twelve hours. In both treatments an effort was made to keep the superficial pulp layer moist with treatment solution. However, in the higher temperature treatment the composite structure did come close to dryness at one time. After treatment the moist paper and pulp layer was carefully stripped from the specimens, which were then allowed to dry thoroughly. The results of the room temperature and infrared-heated accelerated treatments were nearly identical, the most immediately obvious change being a pronounced hardening of the total structures of the treated specimens. This change in hardness was most easily measured in a roughly quantitative manner by the graded hardness pencils already mentioned. The change in hardness essentially spanned the entire range of these hardness pencils. After treatment only the hardest of the pencils, 5H or 6H, depending upon the region tested, would scratch the surface of the specimens, while before treatment even the softest of them would cut through the plaster structure in many regions. It is to be noted that the backs of the treated specimens as well as the faces to which treatment had been applied were hardened.

Neither treatment visibly affected the hue of the pigment layers. There was no discoloration of the white specimens, and the only observable alteration in appearance of the red and blue specimens was a slight increase in color intensity. This enhanced brightness is the expected result of consolidation of structure around the pigment particles. There will be less random scattering of light from the well-consolidated structure than from the powdery deteriorated structure. Thus it can be concluded that the treatment could strengthen and consolidate a fresco pigment layer and underlying intonaco without affecting the painting other than to tend to return it in part to its original intensity. Of course it should be stressed that all pigment areas of a specific wall painting to be treated should first be tested for stability toward the treatment solution before proceeding to an overall treatment. It is to be hoped that this method of treatment can soon be field tested on a sizable area of deteriorated fresco painting.

Appendix
Identification of Pigments from the Giusto dei Menabuoi Frescoes of the Baptistry at Padua and the Ambrogio Lorenzetti Frescoes at Montesieppi.

In all fifteen specimens of inorganic materials were taken from various regions of the baptistry frescoes at Padua. Nine of these specimens were of pigments used at different locations, and the remainder were of efflorescence, intonaco, and supporting materials. These specimens have been studied primarily by the methods of emission spectroscopy and X-ray diffraction. A general statement to be made concerning the X-ray diffraction patterns of the pigment specimens is that in every case the lines of calcium carbonate, silica, and calcium sulfate dihydrate were present. This was to be expected because, of course, the pigment was laid onto lime plaster, which would likely have contained some fine sand, hence the pigment would have been embedded in calcium carbonate with silica. The original plaster when originally set might have contained some calcium sulfate dihydrate, but it is even more likely that this substance would have been generated on the fresco surfaces through chemical reaction with the sulfur oxides known to be present in the atmosphere at Padua. Diffraction lines arising from the pigment, therefore, appeared superimposed upon the fairly complex diffraction pattern arising from these three relatively uniformly present crystalline substances. Despite this, it was usually possible to resolve clearly a number of lines characteristic of the pigment itself.

Blue Pigments

Two specimens of blue pigments were taken, one from a figure clothed in blue at the right edge of the painting on the left wall of the altar, and the second from the sky in the painting immediately over the doorway. The diffraction lines of ultramarine were observed in the diffraction pattern of samples of both of these specimens. Confirmation that ultramarine was present in both specimens was provided by arc spectra of samples of both; in each case sodium and aluminum, which are metallic components of ultramarine, showed up with relatively strong intensity, while copper, which would have indicated the presence of azurite, showed up only very weakly.

Red Pigments

Two specimens of red pigments were taken, one from the bottom right of the robe of Christ from a panel to the left of the altar, and the second, a composite specimen, taken from the Madonna enthroned, from the robe of St. John, and from the panel *Entrance into Jerusalem,* which is the lower left of the wall facing the entry door. Spectra of these pigment samples showed relatively strong iron lines with weak copper and aluminum lines. It both instances strong clear lines of ferric oxide, Fe_2O_3, are present in the X-ray diffraction patterns of these specimens. Red ocher, or a burnt earth rich in red ocher, is indicated as the red pigment in these specimens.

Yellow Pigments

A yellow pigment specimen was taken from the lower edge of the robe of St. Peter in the *Kiss of Judas* on the right wall of the baptistry. Its diffraction pattern contained lines corresponding to yellow ocher. The arc spectrum of this specimen contained small amounts of lead, aluminum, and titanium in addition to iron.

Green Pigments

A specimen of green was taken from the lower edge of the female figure to the left of Christ in the painting to the left of the altar. The X-ray diffraction pattern of this specimen shows very little in addition to the ever-present calcium carbonate, silica, and gypsum. No malachite lines were in evidence, and only weak copper lines appeared in the arc spectrum of a sample. Relatively weak lead, aluminum, sodium, and tin lines also showed up in the spectrum. The presence of aluminum and an indication of weak lines corresponding to terraverte indicate that the pigment is a green earth.

Black Pigments

Two specimens of black pigment were taken (1) from the figure of Christ in the panel to the left of the altar and (2) from trees in the *Entrance into Jerusalem* panel. The X-ray diffraction patterns showed lines which are observed in raw umber. Copper and weak lead lines were observed in the arc spectra of these specimens. A dark earth pigment is indicated.

Among the samples taken at the Oratory of San Galgono at Montesieppi near Sienna was some of the pigment layer from a strip of blue above the left side of the Annunciation of the Lorenzetti frescoes. Microscopic examination of this specimen showed it to be largely composed of a white powder in which a relatively few grains of a bright blue and one grain of bright green color were observed. Any arc emission spectrum of a portion of this specimen showed significantly large concentrations of lead and copper. The X-ray diffraction pattern of this material was dominated by lines of basic lead carbonate, i.e., the pigment lead white. Although the use of lead white in fresco painting is not unknown, its presence has been observed in relatively few instances. Unfortunately the diffraction lines of the copper pigment were so overpowered by those from lead white that they could not properly be observed. However, the presence of copper, the presence of some green particles among the blue, and the confirmatory observation that the blue particles dissolved in dilute acid with effervescence left little doubt that the blue pigment in this instance was azurite.

References

1. Personal communication from Professor Leonetto Tintori.

2. Leonetto Tintori, Edward V. Sayre, and Lawrence J. Majewski, "Studies for the Preservation of the Frescoes by Giotto in the Scrovegni Chapel at Padua," *Studies in Conservation* 8, no. 2 (May 1963), 37–54.

3. Edward V. Sayre, "Direct Deposition of Barium Sulfate from Homogeneous Solution within Porous Stone," pp. 115–117, in *Conservation of Stone and Wooden Objects,* G. Thomson, ed., London, International Institute of Conservation of Artistic and Historic Works, 1970.

4. "Experimental Study by Diffraction of Heterogeneous Systems as a Preliminary to the Proposal of a Technique for the Restoration of Gypsum Polluted Murals, report presented at the ICOM Conference, Amsterdam, September 1969.

LAWRENCE J. MAJEWSKI

Interim Report on an Investigation of Processes of Disintegration of Frescoes

Some frescoes of great antiquity have survived in many parts of the world in remarkably good condition despite the vicissitudes of time, water damage, air pollution, and neglect. However, many of our greatest artistic treasures in the form of wall paintings have disappeared through chemical and physical deterioration of a variety of causes. Floods and water seepage, attacks of plants and animals, air pollution, and natural and man-made disasters have all taken their toll.

International conferences and committees have studied individual problems, and ad hoc examinations have provided much information about the processes of decay of the various parts of wall painting structures. The wall, roof, and foundation providing the fundamental support as well as the lime, sand, and other ingredients of plasters form complex structures of the painted wall surface. Any one part of such a structure may undergo a chemical or physical change which can be disastrous.

The mechanism of many of these processes of fresco disintegration have been observed and described by several scientists and conservators.[1] However, further study is needed on the behavior of the individual causes of decay, and quantitative measurements of types of chemical and physical reactions on fresco materials need to be observed. For the purpose of this investigation, only a few types of conditions which could lead to destruction of frescoes have been considered. These preliminary observations have been made on the following types of attack: (1) The cycling of moist and dry air through samples of fresco materials. (2) The effects of an atmosphere of a high concentration of moist sulfur dioxide gas on similar fresco samples. (3) The effects of capillary seepage of distilled water into similar samples. (4) The effects of capillary seepage of a 3 % solution of potassium nitrate in distilled water into similar samples. (5) The effects of capillary seepage of a 3 % solution of sodium sulphate in distilled water into similar samples.

Preparation of the Fresco Samples

A quantity of fresco samples was prepared at the Conservation Center of the Institute of Fine Arts of New York University for this investigation. They were prepared during the summer of 1964 in an attempt to simulate four categories of fresco types, namely: (*a*) a Roman-type fresco; (*b*) a medieval-type fresco; (*c*) a true or *buon* fresco; (*d*) a late renaissance-type containing *secco* painting with an egg medium.

Fine-textured ceramic tiles, 10 cm on a side and 0.8 cm thick, were chosen as the primary support for the samples. This particular tile was used because of its convenient small size and rather light weight and its fine texture, which permits a slow transmission of moisture. Also, the textured tile back acted as a mechanical bond to hold applied plaster on the surface. The

lime used for the sample preparation was a commercial lime putty which was aged in water for at least one year. A fine river sand and commercially prepared marble chips and marble dust were used in the plaster. Dry artists' pigments with no medium or vehicle were used for the preparation of the design layer of the samples.

All samples were prepared by soaking the tiles in water and then applying an *arriccio* (first) layer of plaster composed of one part lime putty and three parts sand and sufficient water to make a thick, somewhat dry plaster. A layer about 1 cm thick was spread over each tile. This arriccio was textured with fine scratches and then allowed to dry to prepare it for application of the *intonaco* plaster layer. Intonaco and pigments were prepared and applied with four procedures to provide a variety of fresco types for experimental purposes.

To simulate a Roman-type fresco the following procedure was followed. The intonaco plaster was prepared with one part lime putty and two parts marble dust. This was trowelled onto the wetted set arriccio to form a very smooth, wet layer of plaster about 2 mm thick. A medium was prepared with soap and beeswax and water (that is, a wax emulsion) as follows. The beeswax was melted in a double boiler, and an equal amount of water was added. Ivory soap was introduced in small amounts by stirring until the mixture formed an emulsion. Upon cooling this wax emulsion was of a creamy paste consistency. It was then mixed with skimmed milk to a consistency of cream and was combined with dry artists' pigments and applied to the wet plaster in a single flat tone over the entire surface. Flat tones of a lighter and darker value of the same color were then applied to each tile over the first flat tone. When this paint layer had dried for a few hours, the surface was ironed with a hot iron to produce the very smooth and somewhat waxy surface characteristic of many Roman frescoes.

The so-called medieval-type frescoes were prepared with an arriccio as described above. Then a flat tone of pigment mixed with lime water was applied over the damp intonaco in true fresco manner. This was allowed to dry for one day, after which the surface was wetted before applying the lighter and darker stripes of pigment mixed with thinned lime putty. The third type of fresco samples were prepared in the true fresco manner. The intonaco layer of marble dust and lime putty was applied over the set arriccio of lime and sand. Pigments were mixed with water, and a flat tone of color was applied over the surface followed almost immediately with modeling stripes of lighter and darker tones, that is, all colors were applied while the intonaco was fresh and wet. Finally, a type of fresco was prepared in which the beaten whole egg with a little vinegar and some water was used as a medium and applied to the wet intonaco as a flat tone. After partial drying the modeling stripes

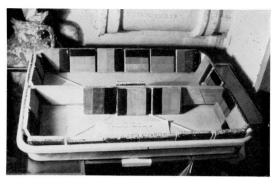

1. Fresco samples being cycled with changes of dry and moist air at 45° C.

2. One of the fresco samples after dry-moist cycling of air, showing no change in surface.

3. Fresco samples in a desiccator jar are being exposed to an atmosphere of moist SO₂ gas.

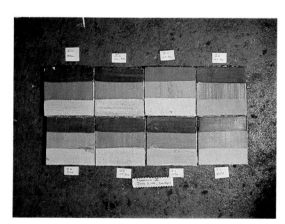

4. After 25 days' exposure to a moist SO₂ atmosphere the samples exhibit a small amount of efflorescence of $CaSO_4 \cdot 2H_2O$ and some microscopic pitting of surfaces.

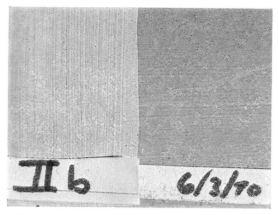

5. The buon fresco sample of fig. 4, which produced the greatest amount of efflorescence.

6. Samples of fresco on edge are immersed in a tray of water to a depth of 1 cm.

7. The samples of fig. 6 being dried in air.

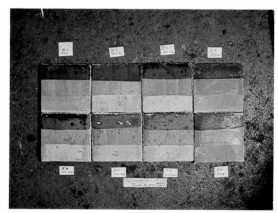

8. The samples treated by a capillary rise of water, showing "water-staining" upon drying but no surface deposit of salts.

were applied, also using the egg, vinegar, and water as a medium. These samples were aged for a period of over six years before the present experiments were begun.

The Experiments

Two tiles of each of the four types described above were selected for each of five experiments in disintegration. The tiles chosen were those made with the following colors: (a) yellow ochre, lime white, and lamp black and (b) green earth, lime white, and lamp black. Experiment 1 consisted of subjecting the eight samples to alternating dry and wet atmospheres of New York City air. The samples were placed in a closed container in an oven with a controlled high but not excessively high temperature of 45° C. Containers of water were set into the sealed tank, and paper humidity indicators recorded a relative humidity in excess of 80% (see fig.1). After four days in this high humidity the water containers were removed and the tank left unsealed so that a dry atmosphere of less than 10% relative humidiy surrounded the samples. After three days of drying, the cycle was begun again with a very high relative humidiy. This cycling was continued for a period of six weeks, that is, six complete cycles. Admittedly, this is not a very long period of cycling. However, the atmospheric differences were quite severe, changes from less than 10% to around 90% relative humidity at 45° C. But there is no apparent deterioration in any of the samples. Changes of humidity alone in this experiment caused no observable decay. Fig. 2 shows a typical tile after the moisture cycling with no change in tonality or structure.

Experiment 2 was designed to test the effect of an atmosphere of a high concentration of sulfur dioxide at 80% RH on a group of eight samples similar to those used in Experiment 1. Sulfur dioxide gas was pumped through a closed container of water (sealed desiccator jar) with an exhaust through a container of water and a container of sodium hydroxide solution to trap sulfur dioxide passing through the system (fig. 3). Thus the atmosphere surrounding the samples was a very high concentration of sulfur dioxide in a high relative humidity at room temperature — about 23.5° C. After five days in this atmosphere the samples were removed and examined and photographed. Already some surface efflorescence had developed — particularly on the buon fresco sample. The Roman fresco showed very little efflorescence, as did the egg tempera fresco.

The samples were returned to the sulfur dioxide atmosphere for a total of 25 days, after which they were removed and rephotographed. The efflorescence on the buon fresco samples had increased, and a small amount had developed on all four types (fig. 4). While most of this crystal growth lies on the surface of the paint, some crystals are growing from beneath,

forming microscopic pits in the paint film. While the deterioration is appreciable, of course, one would expect it to be much more severe if oxygen or just air had also been pumped into the container to oxidize more of the SO_2 to SO_3. Fig. 5 shows a detail of the yellow buon fresco sample after 25 days in the SO_2 atmosphere; note the fine white crystals on the lighter stripe, which is also accompanied by abundant fine pitting. This experiment clearly demonstrates that an atmosphere with high SO_2 alone is quite damaging even over a short period of time.

Experiment 3 was devised to demonstrate the effect of capillary rise of pure water in a fresco structure. Again, eight samples were selected, and they were set on edge in a container of distilled water to a depth of 1 cm so the water could rise by capillary action (fig. 6). After five days the samples were removed from the water and set on the same edge to dry in trays (fig. 7). While the samples were obviously soaked through and somewhat darkened, there was no apparent damage while they were wet. However, the surface plaster was considerably softened and could easily be scratched with the fingernail.

After drying for one week the samples were again photographed, and now the surface had taken on a somewhat mottled appearance (fig. 8). The paint film had not developed any efflorescence of crystalline material but parts of the paint film were water stained, i.e., some areas had darkened and some had lightened in tonality. Water seepage of distilled water can be disfiguring, as one would expect from observation of frescoes in buildings where rainwater has seeped into wall paintings on plaster. Fig. 9 shows the effect of water staining on a buon fresco sample painted with tones of yellow ochre.

Experiments 4 and 5 were intended to demonstrate the effects of seepage of dissolved salts into fresco structures. A 3% solution of sodium sulfate in distilled water and a 3% solution of potassium nitrate in distilled water were prepared and as in Experiment 3 the samples were set on edge to a depth of 1 cm for a period of five days. These particular salts were chosen for this experiment since they had been found on the flood-damaged frescoes of Florence after the flood of November 4, 1966,[2] and had also been observed by Tworek on frescoes.[3]

Upon removal of the samples from the capillary soaking, they appeared wet but undamaged, and as long as the samples were kept wet no deterioration took place. However, upon drying, salts began to form through the structure of the fresco, pushing flakes of paint away from the surface (fig.10). It is interesting to note the character of the surface formation of these crystals. The KNO_3 solution has produced pale white translucent crystals that branch out like a tree from a single point (figs.11 and 12). These crystals are soft to the touch and appear almost like a mold growth. They form in patterns which

9. The buon fresco sample of fig. 8 with pronounced discoloration.

12. Detail of fig. 11 showing soft, white translucent crystals of KNO_3 forming like a "mold growth."

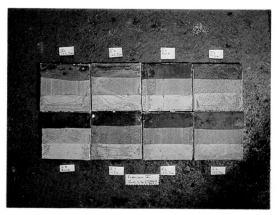

10. Samples of fresco treated by capillary action of a 3% solution of KNO_3 and dried in air. Salts have formed on the paint surface and just below the paint layer and are pushing paint from the plaster.

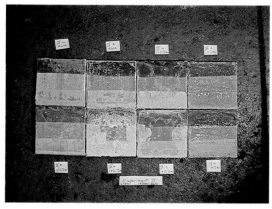

13. Samples of fresco treated by capillary action of a 3% solution of Na_2SO_4 and dried in air. The salts formed are pushing the paint off the plaster.

11. The pattern of capillary flow of KNO_3 solution is evident in this buon fresco sample from fig. 10.

14. The buon fresco sample of fig. 13, which developed the greatest amount of efflorescence.

15. A detail of fig.14, showing heavy salt formation and flaking areas of *intonaco* as well as paint.

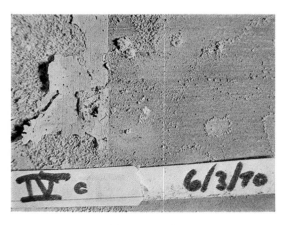

16. Damage from Na_2SO_4 salt formation, most pronounced in the *secco* layer of paint in egg medium.

characterize the flow of the water. The central area of each sample developed only a small amount of crystals as the water flowed outward carrying salts to a point of maximum evaporation. Note in fig.11 how a "triangle" of thick crystal growth has formed. It is in the areas of thick growth where the damage is most pronounced.

While the damage is considerable from the migration of KNO_3 in solution to points of evaporation and crystallization, it is not nearly so destructive as that from similar action of a Na_2SO_4 solution. Fig.13 shows the eight samples after the Na_2SO_4 solution had evaporated. The deterioration is particularly devastating in the buon fresco samples and in the samples painted with an egg medium. A heavy, fluffy white efflorescence has developed both on the surface and just below the surface of the paint layer. The result is extensive flaking of the paint film and even to some extent the intonaco layer of plaster.

Fig.14 shows the yellow ochre buon fresco sample after formation of the crystals of Na_2SO_4. In the dark stripe particularly one notices the loss of paint into the plaster itself (fig.15). In fig.16 the damage to the upper layers of paint of the egg medium fresco (the modeling *a secco*) is most pronounced — whole areas have flaked away in large scales.

These experiments are the beginning of a series which will be continued at the Conservation Center of the Institute of Fine Arts of New York University to gather more detailed information on processes of disintegration of frescoes through various agents of deterioration. With a greater knowledge of the mechanism of such decay and with more information on the rate at which various reagents attack fresco materials, perhaps specific treatments can be devised for specific ailments.

Acknowledgments

I should like to acknowledge the assistance of two advanced students at the Conservation Center, Ruth Bones, who prepared the samples, and Paul Schwartzbaum, who helped prepare the experiments and made the photographs. Thanks are also due to Dr. E. V. Sayre, Dr. N. S. Baer, Dr. R. L. Feller, and Leonetto Tintori for advice and encouragement.

References

1. Sayre, E. V., and Majewski, L. J. "Technical Investigation of the Deterioration of the Paintings," Article II of "Studies for the Preservation of the Frescoes by Giotto in the Scrovegni Chapel at Padua," *Studies in Conservation* 8, no. 2, pp. 42 ff. Philippot, P., and Mora P. "Deuxième Partie: Causes d'Altération," *Technique et Conservation des Peintures Murales,* Rome Centre and ICOM, 1965.

2 Feller, R. L. "Special Report on Visit of Assistance to Florence, Italy, February and March, 1967," National Gallery of Art Research Project no. 4345–17 (Nov.1969), p. 8 ff.

3. Tworek, D. "The Destructive Effect of Inorganic Salts on Wall Paintings," unpublished paper, ICOM Conference, Amsterdam, 1969.

HAROLD BARKER

Scientific Criteria in the Authentication of Antiquities

It is an inescapable fact in this far from perfect world that many antiquities and objets d'art offered for sale to museums and private collectors carry with them no well-documented evidence of their age or place of origin. In many cases there are legitimate reasons for this, but at a time when antiquities are in great demand purely as a source of investment, there exists a situation which is ripe for exploitation by those unscrupulous enough and skilled enough to augment the supply of genuine antiquities by means of clever forgeries. In the past the assessment of objects which carry with them no well-documented evidence of origin has depended principally on stylistic considerations, but in more recent years the natural sciences have been called upon increasingly to provide other criteria to set against the stylistic evidence. In carrying out this task the scientist quickly realizes that the application of absolute dating methods such as radiocarbon is often subject to such restrictions and limitations that recourse has to be made to what is essentially the method used by the archaeologist and art historian, i.e., comparison with objects of known provenance. There is a difference, however, in that science allows for examinations through different eyes and from different viewpoints aided as it is by the sensitive methods of analysis and examination which have been developed during this century and particularly since World War II.

In carrying out the task of comparison, the museum laboratory is in a particularly advantageous position, for its major functions concern both the scientific examination and the conservation of antiquities. For example, systematic studies of museum collections provide information on the materials and methods of fabrication of artifacts which not only is of value to the scholar in the antiquities department but also can be directly relevant to problems of authentication. In dealing with the problems of conservation, a body of experience is accumulated concerning the state of corrosion and deterioration of antiquities which can also prove of particular value when assessing the probable age of an object. In addition, a large national museum may well be required to meet the demand for absolute dating in the form of radiocarbon or thermoluminescence methods, and as we shall see, such techniques can have direct, if somewhat limited, application to problems of authentication.

The establishment of criteria by which the authenticity of an object is to be judged can thus be considered under three main headings: (1) studies in ancient technology, (2) studies of corrosion and deterioration, and (3) absolute dating methods. In the course of its normal function of providing a service to the other departments of a large museum, a museum laboratory must conduct research and development in all three fields, and while the information obtained is usually intended in the first place to elucidate problems not directly connected with authentication, the accumulated data provide a valuable pool of information which can be drawn upon when required for specific problems in this field. All three areas of study depend very much on the application of modern techniques of scientific examination and measurement, and it is perhaps appropriate at this stage to consider some of these very briefly.

The Techniques of Examination

In many cases, the examination of antiquities is hampered by restrictions arising from the fact that the objects are valuable and often unique whereas the most effective methods of examination and analysis usually demand the abstraction of a sample and therefore some damage to the object. As a result there has been a natural tendency on the part of laboratories engaged in such work to adopt where possible the so-called nondestructive methods of examination and also those sensitive methods of analysis which demand a minimum of sample. Optical microscopy in its many forms is of course an essential tool, so much so that one takes it for granted and tends to overlook its value. A good low to medium power binocular microscope is indispensable in this work, and one quickly finds it necessary to supplement this with facilities of more specialized instruments for metallography, mineralogy, and the examination and identification of organic materials.

X-radiography, ultraviolet fluorescence, and infrared photography have been in use for many years and continue to provide valuable evidence to supplement optical examination in visible light. It is in the field of elemental analysis that the principal difficulties arise and this despite the tremendous advances that have taken place in techniques during the past twenty years or so. Here the problem is one of avoiding damage to the object, so that one concentrates on trying to obtain the maximum information on the composition of the object with a minimum of material. Emission spectrography was perhaps the earliest sensitive technique used for this purpose. It can provide from a single small sample an indication of its total composition, including major and minor trace elements. Its accuracy for quantitative estimates, however, is rather poor, so that nowadays there is a tendency to restrict its use to purely qualitative surveys and to apply such techniques as spectrophotometry, atomic absorption spectroscopy, and polarography where higher accuracy is required. Atomic absorption in particular is proving of great value while the polarograph in the form of the Davis Differential Cathode Ray Polarograph (Davis & Seaborn, 1960) is unique in that it can be operated in several different modes, one of which can yield results of very high quantitative accuracy indeed.

Using one or other or a combination of these techniques, it is possible to provide a complete analysis of the composition of a sample of metal or other inorganic material weighing only a few milligrams. However, this does not in itself settle the analytical problem, since there remains the question of the relationship between the composition of a small sample of an object and that of the object itself. Many materials are not homogeneous at the microscopic level, and thus a sample which is too small may not be representative. The size of sample required may well be determined by this factor rather than any lack of sensitivity in the analytical methods available. Methods which attempt to overcome this limitation include X-ray fluorescence spectroscopy and neutron activation analysis. X-ray fluorescence achieves this by sampling the composition in a nondestructive manner over a wide area of the surface of an object. Its limitation resides in the fact that it provides the composition of the surface only and ideally that surface should be flat. Thus in the case of materials which have suffered surface alteration as a result of burial in the soil it will provide erroneous results unless the surface layers are first removed from about a square inch of the surface and the underlying areas polished flat. The method then of course becomes a destructive one, and it is preferable rather to apply the technique to a small sample taken in the normal way. Neutron activation can provide a result which is based largely on the total composition of an object, providing the object is small enough to be irradiated in a nuclear reactor or neutron generator. In practice this restricts its use to quite small objects such as coins. The method can of course be applied to small samples, in fact to very small samples indeed, as has been demonstrated extensively by Gordus, but it is then subject to the same limitation arising from the size of the sample as the other methods already mentioned.

One cannot conclude this brief summary of analytical techniques without some reference to X-ray diffraction. The Debye Scherrer powder method can be applied to such small samples as to be regarded as almost completely nondestructive and provides invaluable information which, since it is essentially based on structure, is supplementary to the elemental analysis derived from the other techniques. As a means of identifying the mineral constituents of pottery and ceramics and the corrosion products in ancient metals, it is unsurpassed.

These are some of the techniques used in the examination of antiquities, but the list is not by any means complete. In particular no reference has been made to mass spectrometry. Brill (Brill and Wampler, 1967) has already shown the value of isotopic studies of ancient lead, and it may well be that in the next decade despite the high cost of suitable instruments, mass spectrometry will also emerge as one of the most valuable tools available in the field of elemental analysis. The spark source mass spectrometer in its latest form provides a means of obtaining an accurate total analysis of a small sample, including major, minor, trace, and sub-trace constituents as well

as their isotopic composition, and its more widespread use could bring a major revolution to the application of analytical information to archaeological problems including authenticity studies.

Absolute Dating Methods

It is perhaps convenient at this juncture to deal with absolute dating methods, since they are dependent essentially on very sensitive analytical techniques. In the past few years, owing in no small measure to the efforts of the research group at Oxford, we have seen thermoluminescence dating of pottery emerge as a valuable tool in this field (Tite, 1966, Fleming, 1966, Zimmerman, 1967, Zimmerman and Huxtable, 1969). Since Dr. Fleming will be dealing with the method in detail, I shall refer to it only briefly.

The application of the method to accurate archaeological dating would seem to depend on the use of material excavated under strictly controlled conditions, thus ruling out the use of much material already lying in museums. However, Fleming (Fleming, Moss, and Joseph, 1970) has shown that such restriction need not apply where the prime consideration is whether a piece is a genuine antique or has been recently fired. Since the test can be carried out on a relatively small sample (15 mg) one can envisage its application during the next few years to many large museum collections, no doubt resulting in some cases in surprising and somewhat unpalatable results.

Turning now to radiocarbon dating. This is a method which, during the past twenty years, can be said to have completely revolutionized archaeology and archaeological thought. Its basic principles (Libby 1951) are by now, I hope, quite well known. It depends essentially on the measurement of extremely low levels of radiocarbon activity in materials which once formed parts of living organisms, as for example, wood charcoal, skin and hair products, bone and antler, natural fibers, etc., and the date obtained refers to the time of death of the organism which provided the sample. Thus, unlike thermoluminescence dating, the calculated age is not connected directly with a human activity like the firing of pottery, and in applying the method one must therefore be able to infer from other evidence, a close correspondence in time between the date of death of the sample and the archaeological event which one is attempting to date. This condition imposes a major restriction on the application of the method to problems of authenticity.

It means that while radiocarbon dating can reveal the approximate age of the material from which an object is made (providing of course it is organic), it can normally do nothing to date directly the actual fabrication of the object from that material. Thus radiocarbon dating alone cannot expose the type of forgery which is made from organic materials of the correct expected age, although in considering this factor one must also take into account the difficulty the forger must experience in obtaining such closely dated basic materials.

Another factor which has restricted the use of radiocarbon for authentication has been the fact that it is a method which normally requires the total destruction of a sample from the object equivalent to several grams of carbon. In many cases this means that the removal of the necessary sample would result in unacceptable damage to an object. However, the large sample requirement is not an absolute restriction. It arises principally from the use of measuring equipment designed to produce a reasonably high output of dates for normal archaeological or geological purposes. Equipment capable of dealing with quite small samples has been designed and used successfully in the past. For example, de Vries designed a proportional counter capable of dealing with only 0.1 gm of carbon in the form of carbon dioxide, and one very successful application of this instrument was its use in confirming the relatively recent origin of the notorious Piltdown skull (Oakley and De Vries, 1959).

The need for designing, building, and maintaining such special equipment and its very low rate of production of results has certainly been one of the major factors in preventing the more widespread application of radiocarbon dating to authentication. However, with the more widespread adoption of the liquid scintillation technique, one can foresee that the situation is likely to change. This technique allows for a much greater flexibility in the size of sample used for measurement. The equipment at the British Museum, in common with other installations of this type, can deal with samples ranging in size from the equivalent of 0.3 gm carbon to as much as 8 gm carbon, and in authenticity measurement where high dating accuracy is usually not essential, it is quite feasible to use only 0.1 gm carbon. Moreover, since in this technique measurements are carried out on groups of samples rather than on individual samples, as in other methods, an authenticity measurement, which usually requires much larger counting time than normal because of the small sample size, can be carried out quite readily with no restriction on the output of archaeological dates.

Finally, it should also be pointed out that there are also cases where the very size of the object is such as to impose no restriction on sampling for radiocarbon dating. Such an instance occurred some years ago when the age of the Roman Spanish Waterwheel in the Greek and Roman collection of the British Museum was questioned. This object from the Rio Tinto Mines in Spain had since its acquisition been accepted without question as of genuine Romano-Spanish origin. However, its date was questioned some years ago, and in order to settle the matter radiocarbon measurements were carried out. In this case the object was so large that the necessary sample could be provided without causing visible damage. Fortunately for the honor of the British Museum, the result obtained was 2400 ± 150 years BP (BM-85, Barker and Mackey, 1961). In another case, however, the radiocarbon evidence did not support the supposed age of a large object. This was a mediaeval torture rack, the timber of which proved to be modern.

Studies in Technology

In considering the value of the information which can be obtained from studies of the development of technology through the ages, one finds scattered through journals covering many disciplines, a very wide ranging and voluminous literature concerning the scientific examination of antiquities, an activity which has been going on now for over a hundred years. One major difficulty in applying this knowledge to particular cases lies in obtaining rapid access to the required information. The existence of such journals as I.I.C. abstracts is a great help in this respect, but there would seem to be little doubt, in view of the volume of information and the speed with which it is now accumulating, that the problem of information retrieval will soon reach such proportions as to necessitate the setting up of a large-scale computer project, and the Research Laboratory of the British Museum is now looking into this possibility.

One must also consider that the information to be obtained from the literature is sometimes of rather limited value. It is not difficult to find examples where the provenance of the objects examined has not been rigorously established, and others where the analytical information is not sufficiently comprehensive or accurate enough for particular purposes. Thus another major difficulty which arises in applying information from the literature to problems of authentication lies in knowing what value to place upon it. At best it can provide a useful supplement to the evidence obtained by direct comparison with objects of known provenance. At worst it can be downright misleading. However, despite the need for some caution in applying information culled from the literature, reports of technological studies can undoubtedly contribute much information of direct use in questions of authenticity, although one must also bear in mind that such publications also become available to the manufacturer of fakes and forgeries and can provide him with the means of improving his product.

In examining an object for authenticity one must concentrate, aside from determination of age which is often of limited applicability, on the techniques of manufacture and the nature of the materials used. One must ask the questions, "How was this object made and are the methods used typical of the time and place of origin suggested by the stylistic evidence?" One must also ascertain whether the materials used and their present state of preservation are also consistent with the supposed time and place of origin of the object, and it is concerning this aspect of authentication that experience gained in the conservation of antiquities can prove of considerable value.

Studies of Corrosion and Deterioration

Scientific conservation depends increasingly on the initial application of the same techniques of examination and analysis as are applied to studies of ancient technology and authentication. Only the aims are different. Thus in the process of conservation in a large museum laboratory there arises the opportunity to acquire detailed information on the states of corrosion and deterioration which are found in genuine antiquities from many periods in time and widely different areas of the world. In addition, and perhaps of equal importance, there arises the ability to recognize when and to what degree conservation and restoration have been carried out on an object. This can be of considerable value, e.g., where one has to decide whether a metal object is an outright fake or a genuine antiquity which has been drastically overcleaned and then re-patinated in modern times in order to "improve" its appearance.

All who have worked in this field will know that the state of deterioration of an object is no absolute guide to its age. So much is dependent on both its composition and the environmental conditions to which it has been subject since it was made. One has only to compare the state of corrosion of a bronze from the dry environment of an Egyptian tomb with that of one of a similar age from a damp corrosive environment to realize the difficulties in applying such evidence. Nevertheless, scientific conservation does provide a means by which there can be built up a set of norms against which the condition of suspect antiquities may be compared.

Examples of Authentication in Practice

Most fakes and forgeries are carried out for financial gain, and one of the oldest and commonest is in connection with currency. The basic principle here, which has not changed up to the present day, is to deceive the unwary into accepting base metal in the mistaken assumption that it is more noble. The method adopted is usually to produce a coin consisting essentially of base metal covered with a thin coating of a more noble one. This type of forgery is easy to detect by relatively simple analytical techniques. One typical example is a contemporary counterfeit gold Noble of Henry VI from the Fishpool hoard and now in the British Museum. This consists of a silver core covered with a thin layer of gold applied by mercury gilding. The nature of the materials used was easily established by qualitative emission spectrography. Such a piece, relatively worthless at the time it was made, has of course now a considerable rarity value. Turning to more recent times we come to an example of the proverbial brass farthing. One coin, dated

1829 and apparently of brass, would, if made entirely of that metal, be unique and now of value as a collector's piece. However, in one case we examined it was soon established that the coin was slightly heavier and very slightly bigger than normal and that it was in fact a normal bronze farthing which had been electroplated.

Some forgeries, as for example the notorious Piltdown skull to which reference has already been made, do not seem to have been perpetrated for any financial gain. An example in the numismatic field concerns two "bronze" Anglo Saxon coins of Ecgfrith (A.D. 670—685), which were "discovered" in the early part of the last century by a clergyman in Scotland, actually in his own churchyard. He later caused to be erected on the spot a granite monument to commemorate the "find." These coins were interesting in that they were the first example of the bronze coinage of Ecgfrith to be discovered and have remained unique. In recent times their authenticity has been questioned because numismatic evidence now suggests that the coinage of Ecgfrith should have been of silver not bronze. In support of this contention, a recent examination of the coins at the British Museum has shown that their composition is not typical of the bronze alloys of the Anglo Saxon period. They are in fact made of copper of such a degree of purity as to suggest an early 19th century origin. These are examples of forgeries which can be condemned on the ground of wrong composition alone.

Most modern coin forgeries, however, are more subtle in that they set out to provide examples of rare coins which are so valuable that the counterfeiter can well afford to employ the correct metal, and often this is gold. Usually, however, such forgeries fail to meet other criteria, in particular the method of manufacture and/or the condition of the piece. As is well known, coins are made by striking in a die, and in order to avoid the difficulty and expense of making this, recourse is often made to investment casting in the case of gold coins. The results are often very convincing to the naked eye, but under the microscope it is usually possible to distinguish the difference in surface appearance between a cast forgery and a genuine struck coin. If necessary the difference between cast and struck metal can also be established by X-ray diffraction by the back reflection technique, although there can be difficulties here in the case of gold objects owing to the phenomenon of self-annealing. The back reflection technique is of particular value in dealing with very valuable pieces, since it is completely nondestructive in its application. The difference in the appearance of the relevant diffraction patterns between cast and struck (i. e., cold-worked) metal is quite marked, but in applying this technique to coins and to the detection of counterfeit hallmarks which have been cast into forgeries of antique silver, it is particularly important to locate the X-ray beam precisely on the area of metal that could have suffered cold work by striking, since the distortion and stress produced by the application of a die is very localized.

In the case of large metal objects which are unique, this technique may be the only one which can be applied in order to obtain information as to the structure of the metal without causing visible damage. As an example, reference may be made to a large cast bronze plaque of a female figure which was suspected to have been derived by disfigurement of a male figure. Such disfigurement would inevitably result in localized stresses in the metal which could be expected to be revealed by X-ray diffraction. Back reflection examinations carried out on the genital area and on the umbilical area for comparison indicated in fact that there was considerably more evidence of cold working in the genital area than in the umbilical. Thus the X-ray evidence supported the view that the figure may have been originally a male.

We have seen in the case of coins examples of the use of the wrong material and techniques of manufacture. An example in the field of Greek antiquities was a silver myrtle wreath. One significant piece of evidence here was the fact that drawn wire had been used in its construction, whereas there is no evidence that drawn wire was ever used in genuine articles of jewelry from that period. Other evidence which pointed to a recent origin was the absence of corrosion and the use of modern solder containing cadmium in its construction.

In carrying out studies in authentication, the scientific evidence is not always to the detriment of the object. Museum collections often contain objects which for one reason or another, usually lack of complete documentation as to their place of origin, are somewhat doubtful. In these cases scientific examination can often resolve doubts and permit the position of the object in a collection to be made secure.

In contrast to the previous example we have the case of some other pieces of Greek jewelry, this time gold-enameled rosettes in which the scientific evidence helped to resolve doubts as to their authenticity. It had been suggested that the gold stamens on these pieces were made from modern drawn wire on which the spiral pattern was engraved. However, it was clearly shown by microscopic examination and practical demonstration that the wires had been cut from sheet and block-twisted in a manner quite typical of the period. It had also been argued that the presence of a trace of chromium in the enamel indicated a modern origin. However, there was no doubt that the weathering of the enamel was quite typically that to be expected in ancient glass, and it was shown in other analytical studies that chromium can and does occur as a trace element in ancient glass from the Mediterranean area.

Scientific evidence can also help in resolving wrong attributions. For example in the case of a Cista which had been

judged to be Etruscan, examination produced evidence which did not support this supposed origin of the piece but which could nevertheless be interpreted satisfactorily in terms of a somewhat later but still ancient origin. Unlike other similar objects of undoubted Etruscan origin the object was shown to be of cast rather than worked construction. Moreover, its green patination suggested a copper alloy but the underlying metal was of a silver color. On analysis the metal proved to be a base silver alloy containing copper, similar in composition to Roman coinage alloys of the second and third centuries A.D. and quite unlike the tin bronzes typical of the Etruscan period. Detailed study of the patination and the state of mineralization of the metal established that corrosion was natural and must have taken place slowly over a very long period of time. Thus the scientific evidence established that the piece was ancient and most probably of Roman rather than of Etruscan origin — a conclusion which helped to resolve some inconsistencies in the stylistic evidence.

As a further example one may cite the case of a silver ring from Bosham, now in the collection of the Moyse's Hall Museum, Bury St. Edmunds, which was examined recently in the British Museum Laboratory. Spectrographic examination showed that the metal had a composition typical of the Anglo-Saxon period and X-ray diffraction analysis indicated that the corrosion products in the metal were chiefly silver chloride, as would be expected to occur on an old piece of silver which had been buried in the soil for some considerable time.

This was a case in which there was available a large body of comparative evidence on the composition of Anglo-Saxon silver and conservation experience concerning its expected state of mineralization. It is much more difficult to reach a decision in cases where there is little or no comparative evidence available and no means of acquiring it by reference to museum objects. Indeed, in the past there have been notable instances where some unusual object has at first been rejected on stylistic grounds because it has not fitted into any known framework until subsequent events have shown its true significance. The classic example is the so-called Boss of Tarkondemos. This was offered to the British Museum about the year 1860, and was rejected on stylistic grounds as a fake. Fortunately for subsequent events, an electrotype copy was made at the time. Some years later, in 1880, Sayce recognized from a study of the copy that the object was a miniature crib script for the Hittite hieroglyphs, a sort of miniature Rosetta Stone, but by this time all trace had been lost of the original object. It finally came to light again in the Walters Art Gallery in Baltimore, Maryland, and as a result of scientific examination and comparison with the British Museum copy it was possible to establish its authenticity beyond doubt (Hill, 1937).

Somewhat similar problems arose in the case of the copper

figure of the so-called praying man from Crete. When this first appeared in the 19th century before Evans' excavations had revealed the existence of the Minoan civilization, its antiquity was in some doubt owing to lack of stylistic parallels and its very good state of preservation. Later its relationship to this period was established without doubt and it took its rightful place in the British Museum collections without question as to its authenticity, since at the time it was discovered no forger would have had any documentary evidence on which to base its construction.

On the other hand, the copper figure of a bull and leaping athlete from Crete, originally in the Spencer Churchill collection and now in the British Museum, first appeared after Evans' discoveries and at a time when a forger could just possibly have had access to the necessary stylistic information. That this piece was in fact a forgery seemed rather a remote possibility, since at the time it was first acquired it seems that there would have been little profit derived from the transaction. Nevertheless, in view of this possibility and its excellent state of preservation, the object was subjected to a very careful examination in the Research Laboratory of the British Museum. This case provides a good example of the difficulties inherent in such examinations when comparative material is scarce or nonexistent and the unique nature of the object imposes restrictions on the tests which can be carried out. However, comparison with the "praying man" did produce sufficient scientific evidence to suggest that the figure is authentic. Of particular interest was the discovery that both figures had suffered only superficial corrosion during their long period of burial.

It will be seen from these few examples that the task of detecting forgeries and authenticating genuine antiquities can range from the relatively simple to the very difficult. In the field of absolute dating methods, radiocarbon is of somewhat limited application, but recent advances in thermoluminescence dating have undoubtedly resulted in a major breakthrough as regards the authentication of pottery and ceramics. It may well be that other dating methods, which depend on the detection and assessment of the significance of radiation damage in materials, may emerge in the future. At present however the major portion of authenticity work must remain dependent on comparative studies, and while this is so the laboratories concerned with this work must continue to keep pace with scientific advances in many fields in order to provide increasingly refined techniques of comparison and to support fundamental studies into the relationships between the composition of ancient materials, their environmental conditions, and the nature of their products of corrosion and decay. Only by continued effort to improve and extend its facilities and experience in the field of examination and conservation can

a laboratory hope to foil the efforts of the modern forger of antiquities.

It has been argued that the unrestricted publication of information arising from the scientific study of antiquities, as well as aiding scholarship, makes life easier for the maker of fakes and more difficult for those involved in their detection. However, this may be a rather too pessimistic view. Undoubtedly, such information will allow for the writing of a much more detailed specification involving many more "genuine" criteria, but in meeting such a specification in full, including the employment of an artist capable of satisfying completely the stylistic requirements, it may well be that the costs of production will rise to such an extent that forgery becomes relatively unprofitable and loses its atractions. In any case there can be no turning back now, nor can one see the possibility of any universal agreement on the suppression or restriction of such information. The existence of a few fakes of such superb execution that they defy all efforts at detection would seem to be a small price to pay for the vast reservoir of knowledge concerning the past which is now growing rapidly in size as a result of the increasing application of science in the field of archaeology and the fine arts.

References

Barker, Harold, and Mackey, John. *Radiocarbon* 3 (1961), 39.

Brill, R. H., and Wampler, J. M. *Am. J. Archaeology* 71 (1967), 63.

Davis, H. M., and Seaborn, J. E. *Advances in Polarography,* I. S. Langmuir ed. Elmsford, N.Y., Pergamon Press, 1960, p. 329.

Fleming, S. J. *Archaeometry,* 9 (1966), 170.

Fleming, S. J., Moss, H. M., and Joseph, A. *Archaeometry* 12 (1970), 57.

Hill, Dorothy Kent. *Arkiv Orientalia* 9 (no. 3) (1937), 307.

Libby, W. F. *Radiocarbon Dating.* Chicago, University of Chicago Press, 1951. See also 2nd ed., 1955.

Oakley, K. P., and de Vries, H. *Nature* 184 (1959), 224.

Tite, M. S. *Archaeometry* 9 (1966), 155.

Zimmerman, D. W. *Archaeometry,* 10 (1967), 26.

Zimmerman, D. W., and Huxtable, J. *Archaeometry* 11 (1969), 109.

BERNARD KEISCH

Art and the Atom: Two Dating Methods Based on Measurements of Radioactivity

During the first half of the twentieth century, quite a few paintings have been "discovered" which purport to be the works of the Old Masters, but which in reality are forgeries produced for an increasingly lucrative art market. Through its program of sponsored research at Mellon Institute in Pittsburgh, the National Gallery of Art soon ascertained that, through the application of the most recent and sophisticated technology, there was a method which might be fruitfully exploited for this specific purpose. Thus began the research which culminated in the development of the method we at Mellon Institute refer to as the white lead "dating" method.[1,2,3]

In considering other identification problems involving questioned paintings, it became clear that in more recent years the type of paintings that were the most popular for forgers to produce were those of 19th-century impressionists or even more modern artists. The reasons for this are obvious: compared to forgeries of older objects, the materials are more easily available, great age need not be simulated, the painting techniques were less difficult to imitate, and, since "normal" prices were considerably lower, the objects were more easily foisted upon the unwary buyer with less likelihood of careful checking. In seeking a method which would be appropriate to this more recent time scale, that is, the post World War II period as compared to the earlier part of the 20th century and the late 19th century, we soon conceived the general idea of detecting, in artists' materials of the nuclear era, the presence of certain manmade radioactive materials. These, we knew, would be present only in the most minuscule amounts, and although finding them at all would be conclusive evidence of modernity, the sensitivity with which we could detect such materials would be the deciding factor in the practicability of such a method.

The "Dating" of White Lead
Principle

The theory behind this method is not new. It was stated as early as 1928 by H. Zeigert[4] and its potential was studied in 1939 at the Massachusetts Institute of Technology by a group which included George L. Stout.[5] Unfortunately, the technology of the period was not quite up to the task, and only ambiguous results were obtained. The reasoning, however, was correct. Fig.1 shows, in simple form, the natural radioactive decay series that begins with uranium-238, a scarce but rather ubiquitous element. Almost all rock, including lead ore, contains small amounts of uranium. The individual atoms of this radioactive element disintegrate to become atoms of thorium, which in turn decay further. Eventually, through many such steps, they become nonradioactive isotopes of lead. Nearly all of the uranium (more than 99%) consists of the isotope of mass 238. The main path for the decay of uranium-238 is shown

in fig.1. The most important features to note in the figure are (a) that the nuclide radium-226 has a half-life of 1600 years (half of it disintegrates in 1600 years; half of the remainder, in another 1600 years; etc.); and (b) that the nuclide lead-210, a direct descendant of radium-226, has a half-life of twenty-two years.

The laws of radioactive decay (and growth) state that in time all members of a chain beginning with a long-lived ancestor, such as that shown here, will be present in concentrations having a mathematically precise relationship. This equilibrium relationship exists in the ages-old rocks of the earth. Specifically, in lead ore the radioactivity concentration (here defined as the number of disintegrations per minute [dpm] of a radioisotope per unit weight of sample, or a major constituent thereof; for example, dpm per gram of lead) of lead-210 and of radium-226 will be equal.

The next important point is that, when the ore is smelted, any lead-210 present remains with the lead metal, while most of the radium-226 is removed with the slag. From that moment on, the lead-210, no longer being replenished by its longer-lived precursors, begins to decay with a twenty-two-year half-life and will continue to do so until it once more reaches an equilibrium relationship with the much smaller amount of radium-226 which somehow survived the smelting process.

1. The uranium-238 decay series.

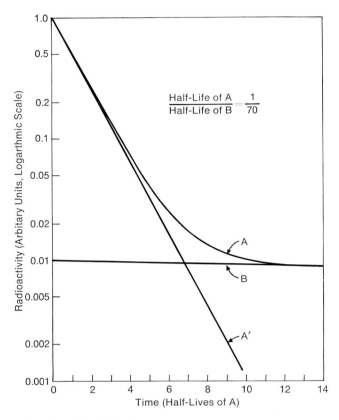

2. Sample radioactivity decay curves.

Fig. 2 illustrates a simplified version of the radioactivity-concentration relationships. The scale along the bottom is the time in terms of the half-life of A, the "short-lived" daughter. The parent, B, has a half-life seventy times longer than A in this illustration. Curve B shows the activity of the parent beginning at a concentration $1/100$ of that of A. (This would represent 99 % removal of B at time zero.) During the period shown, a relatively small fraction of B decays. Curve A' would represent the activity of A, if all of B had been removed at time zero. Curve A shows the actual case; that is, eventually the activity of A "levels off" at the new activity of B.[6]

In the case of lead-210 and radium-226, despite the short-lived nuclides through which the radium must decay before becoming lead-210, a similar relationship holds. Thus, a modern sample of lead, that is, lead produced only a few lead-210 half-lives ago, will exhibit a difference between the radioactivity concentrations of lead-210 and radium-226 in it. In old lead, there will be no such difference. Measurements of the radioactivity concentrations of lead-210 and radium-226 in a sample of lead, therefore, give the information needed to apply the method.

Methodology

The details of the analytical procedure used to obtain the required sensitive determination of these two radioelements, radium-226 and lead-210, have been published elsewhere.[1, 2, 3] Suffice it to say that radioactivity measurements are made in such a way as to minimize any extraneous "background" radiation present in the samples or in the materials of which the radioactivity detector, etc., are constructed.

Fig. 3 shows the equipment used. Samples of polonium-210 (concentration of which directly measures that of lead-210) and radium-226 are prepared from the white lead samples and mounted on special discs which are placed in the detector chamber. The electronic equipment is designed to count only radiations of the type (alpha particles) and energy appropriate to the measured radioisotope.

Results of Analyses of Samples of Known Age

Table I shows the results obtained from a few of the many white leads we analyzed that were produced during the 20th century.[3] Note the large differences between concentrations of polonium-210 and radium-226. Table II shows the results obtained for 19th century samples.[3] Concentration differences still exist, but they are not nearly so overwhelming. Finally, Table III shows data obtained for samples produced prior to the 19th century.[3] Note that the concentrations of the two radioisotopes are identical (within the experimental uncertainties) in all cases.

Although it is fairly obvious from these data that the method is workable, its utility can be more easily visualized by means of fig. 4. In this figure, a function of the concentrations of the two radioisotopes measured is plotted along the vertical axis while the estimated date for the samples is plotted horizontally. One can easily observe the conclusive difference between old and modern samples as well as the ambiguous area between. For those who are statistically inclined the dashed and dotted lines outline two-to-one and twenty-to-one probability areas for use with data obtained on individual samples of unknown production date.[2]

Results Obtained on Problem Samples

Table IV shows the results obtained for a number of paintings of interest.[2] These include five that were produced by the famous forger Van Meegeren (including *Christ at Emmaus*), one pseudo-Hals of unknown origin, and two disputed paintings at the National Gallery in Washington which have been attributed to Vermeer. The last column in this figure confirms beyond doubt the modern origins of all the Van Meegerens and the pseudo-Hals. This includes the *Emmaus,* the source of which has, even in recent years, been hotly disputed.[7] However, the results also show that the National Gallery paintings

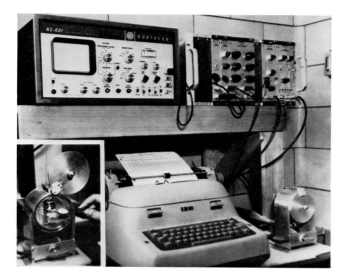

3. Alpha-particle spectrometer and associated electronic equipment. The inset shows a sample being placed into the detector housing for a radium-226 measurement.

contain white lead produced no later than the latter part of the 19th century and could have been produced at the time of Vermeer.

Summary

The method is workable and can be of great utility for the specific purpose of distinguishing between 20th century forgeries and works dating prior to the 19th century. It is also possible, in certain favorable cases, to assign a probability that a painting was produced during the 19th century.

Table I

Polonium-210 and Radium-226 Concentrations in White Lead Produced in the 20th Century

Sample Description	Approximate Date of Manufacture	Po–210 Concentration (dpm/g Pb)*	Ra–226 Concentration (dpm/g Pb)*
Cremnitz white (Holland)	1965	36 ± 2	0.05 ± 0.04
Flake white (U.S.)	1965	15.5 ± 1.8	0.0 ± 0.2
White lead (England)	1965	1.7 ± 0.3	0.04 ± 0.02
Stack Process (Australia)	1948	5.2 ± 0.5	0.1 ± 0.02
Cremnitz white (Germany)	1923	12.3 ± 2.3	0.6 ± 0.5
From Stretcher of John Kane Painting (U.S.)	1921	6.7 ± 1.0	0.03 ± 0.07
Portrait by Logan (U.S.)	1908–13	2.2 ± 0.2	0.0 ± 0.2

* dpm/g Pb = disintegrations per minute per gram of lead

Table II

Polonium-210 and Radium-226 Concentrations in White Lead Produced in the 19th Century

Sample Description	Approximate Date of Manufacture	Po–210 Concentrations (dpm/g Pb)*	Ra–226 Concentrations (dpm/g Pb)*
Stack Process (England)	1884–94	2.8 ± 0.2	0.0 ± 0.1
Cavalry Scene by DeLaunay (France)	1880	1.8 ± 0.2	0.12 ± 0.03
Landscape by Innes (U.S.)	1850–70	5.5 ± 2.0	2.9 ± 2.1
Portrait (France)	1830–40	5.3 ± 2.3	3.9 ± 1.4
Ground by Eicholz (U.S.)	1817	.35 ± 0.8	.13 ± .03

* dpm/g Pb = disintegrations per minute per gram of lead

Table III

Polonium-210 and Radium-226 Concentrations in White Lead Produced in the 18th Century or Earlier

Sample Description	Approximate Date of Manufacture	Po–210 Concentration (dpm/g Pb)*	Ra–226 Concentration (dpm/g Pb)*
Portrait by Earl (U.S.)	1780–1801	1.75 ± 0.62	1.57 ± 0.50
Female Saint (Italy ?)	1750–1800	3.8 ± 0.7	3.0 ± 0.4
Portrait by Claypoole (U.S.)	1746	1.96 ± 0.46	1.82 ± 0.43
Portrait by Badger (U.S.)	1730–50	2.58 ± 0.81	2.70 ± 0.29
Dogs (Holland)	1600–60	0.23 ± 0.27	0.40 ± 0.47
Painting (Italy ?)	Early 1600's	2.81 ± 0.57	2.56 ± 0.47

* dpm/g Pb = disintegrations per minute per gram of lead

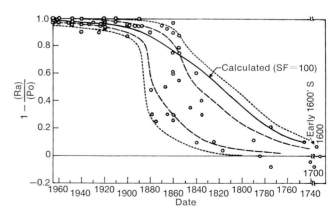

4. A dating curve for lead white.

Table IV

Paintings of Questioned Authorship

Description	Po–210 Concentration (dpm/g Pb)	Ra–226 Concentration (dpm/g Pb)	[1–(Ra)/(Po)]
Van Meegeren[a] – "Washing of Feet" – Vermeer Style	12.6 ± 0.7	0.26 ± 0.07	0.98 ± 0.01
Van Meegeren[a] – "Woman Reading Music" – Vermeer Style	10.3 ± 1.2	0.30 ± 0.08	0.97 ± 0.01
Van Meegeren[a] – "Woman Playing Mandolin" – Vermeer Style			
Pigment Sample	8.2 ± 0.9	0.17 ± 0.10	0.98 ± 0.02
Ground and Pigment Sample	7.4 ± 1.5	0.55 ± 0.17	0.93 ± 0.03
Van Meegeren[a] – "Woman Drinking" – Hals Style	8.3 ± 1.2	0.1 ± 0.1	0.99 ± 0.01
Van Meegeren[b] – "Disciples at Emmaus" – Vermeer Style	8.5 ± 1.4	0.8 ± 0.3	0.91 ± 0.04
Unknown[c] – "Boy Smoking" – Hals Style	4.8 ± 0.6	0.31 ± 0.14	0.94 ± 0.02
Vermeer[d] – "Lace-maker" –	1.5 ± 0.3	1.4 ± 0.2	0.07 ± 0.23
Vermeer[d] – "Laughing Girl" –	5.2 ± 0.8	6.0 ± 0.9	0.15 ± 0.25

a Courtesy of the Rijksmuseum, Amsterdam, The Netherlands, Dr. A. van Schendel, Director-General.

b Courtesy of the Museum Boymans-van Beuningen, Rotterdam, The Netherlands, Dr. J. C. Ebbinge Wubben, Director.

c Courtesy of the Gröninger Museum, Gröningen, The Netherlands, Dr. A. Westers, Direktor.

d Courtesy of the National Gallery of Art, Washington, D. C, Dr. J. Walker, Director.

On the minus side, white lead which happened to have been produced from an ore unusually low in uranium can occasionally yield ambiguous results owing to there being insufficient lead-210 and radium-226 present for this sensitive method to measure in a sample of reasonable size. Care must also be exerted in sampling a painting so as to exclude possible retouched areas. Finally, the sample size requirement is ordinarily approximately 20 milligrams of lead, which might be unacceptably large in some cases.

Carbon-14: Application for Modern Forgeries
Carbon-14 Dating: A Review

The usual meaning of carbon dating using measurements of carbon-14 radioactivity has no real application for works of art produced during the last few hundred years. To understand this point, we briefly review the basis of this invaluable method. The theory behind the method begins with the fact that carbon-14 is produced naturally in the upper atmosphere of our planet by the bombardment of atmospheric nitrogen by cosmic rays. The rate of production has been continuous and at a constant rate (to a first approximation) for at least thousands of years. The carbon-14 thus produced becomes incorporated into the carbon dioxide of the atmosphere and then into growing plants and animals.

The resulting thorough mixing of carbon-14 into every living being is the winding of a clock. The clock starts running for an organism when that organism is removed from participation in the constantly replenished biosphere, that is, when the organism dies. Normally, during its lifetime, the concentration of carbon-14 in an organism is approximately 15 disintegrations per minute per gram of carbon. For example, in each gram of carbon contained in a growing flower, 15 carbon-14 atoms disintegrate each minute. Since the half-life of carbon-14 is approximately 5,000 years, then 5,000 years after the flower is picked, the carbon-14 concentration is halved, that is, it will be only 7.5 disintegrations per minute per gram of carbon (after another 5,000 years, it will be halved again to 3.75 and so forth).[8]

In terms of paintings that are only a few hundred years old, one may calculate, for example, that after 300 years the carbon-14 content will have decreased by only 4 %. As a practical matter, it would take a prohibitively large sample of paint (containing several grams of carbon) to obtain a measurement with sufficient precision to detect so small a change.

Carbon-14 Concentrations During the Twentieth Century

The example of the growing flower that I used for illustrative purposes above is not quite correct during our present century. Mankind began to perturb the natural concentration of carbon-14 early in this century. Fig. 5 illustrates the actual status of the carbon-14 concentration in carbon-bearing materials produced during the last few hundred years. These are the approximate concentrations that one would measure in such samples today.[9]

Prior to 1900, we see that the normal decay of carbon-14 is rather small on this scale. During the first half of this century, however, we note a *decrease* in carbon-14 concentration. This decrease is due to the increased combustion of coal, oil, and gas in our industrial age. Since these materials are millions of years old, the carbon-14 in them is essentially gone. The point

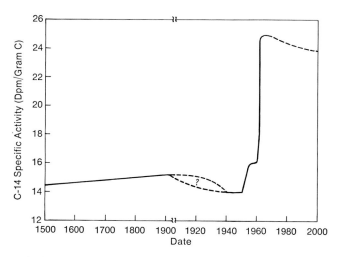

5. Carbon-14 in the atmosphere.

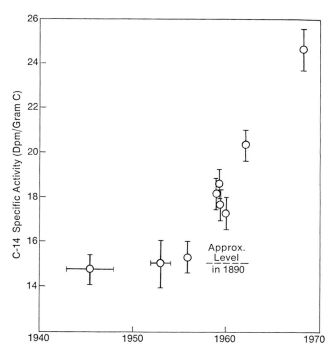

6. Carbon-14 in linseed oil.

is that enough of these fossil fuels have been burned to dilute the carbon dioxide in the "normal" atmosphere measurably. The exact shape of this section of the curve is unknown and thus dotted in the figure.

Then came the nuclear era and the testing of nuclear weapons in the atmosphere. The figure is self-explanatory. From the early 50s, when manmade carbon-14 overcame the dilution from fossil fuel combustion, to 1962, there was a rapid increase in carbon-14 concentration, essentially doubling during that period. The remaining dotted line is the predicted slow return toward "normal" assuming no further atmospheric weapons testing takes place. Note the high level well into the 21st century.

Potential Use for Detecting Modern Forgeries

Since many components of a painting are derived from living organisms, the facts presented here may be put to use to distinguish between production dates since the 1950s and those prior to that time. There is a substantial difference in the problem of measurement: increases of as much as 100 % in this case as opposed to a decrease of a few percentage points for ordinary carbon-14 dating.

A tempting subject for our consideration is that of linseed oil. Produced from the flax plant, the oil is usually manufactured only a few months after the harvest. With its short shelf-life it is also not generally stored for very long periods after its manufacture. The question whether the carbon-14 concentration of oils produced during the last thirty years shows the same increase as atmospheric carbon-14 during the period now had to be resolved.

Carbon-14 in Dated Linseed Oils

We were fortunate to obtain multi-gram quantities of linseed oil produced at various times since 1945. With such large samples, it was a relatively simple matter to measure the carbon-14 content of these materials. We used an instrument called a liquid scintillation counter. A special technique was used to purify the samples for use in this counter, and we were gratified to obtain the results[9] shown in fig. 6. Note the excellent agreement between these results and those presented in fig. 5.

Future Development of the Method: A Problem of Sensitivity

We are presently engaged in constructing a rather special system for measuring carbon-14 concentrations in the relatively small samples available from paintings. With the present state of technology for such a system, we estimate that samples of 50 milligrams of oil paint would be sufficient for our purposes. This is still a rather large sample, but it can be inconspicuously removed from the edge of a painting without regard to pigment content. Other materials that are a part of the painting can be analyzed as well, for example, the material of the support. Ultimately, we believe that the utility of the method will be successfully demonstrated. The successful forgery of items purportedly dating prior to the 1950s will then become prohibitively expensive if not virtually impossible.

References

1. Keisch, B., Feller, R. L., Levine, A. S., and Edwards, R. R. "Dating and Authenticating Works of Art by Measurement of Natural Alpha-Emitters," *Science,* 155, no. 1238 (1967), 1238–1241.

2. Keisch, B. "Dating Works of Art through Their Natural Radioactivity: Improvements Application," *Science,* 160 (1968), 413–415.

3. Keisch, B. "Discriminating Radioactivity Measurements of Lead: New Tool for Authentication," *Curator,* 11 (no.1) (1968), 41–52.

4. Ziegert, H. Z. *Physik,* 46 (1928), 668.

5. Evans, R. D., Farnsworth, M., Brown, S. C., and Stout G. L. "The Detection of Radioactivity in Works of Art," *Technical Studies in the Field of Fine Arts,* 8 (1939–1940), 98.

6. A more complete and rigorous treatment of this material may be found in Friedlander, G., Kennedy, J. W., and Miller, J. M. *Nuclear and Radiochemistry,* 2nd ed., New York, John Wiley, 1964.

7. Kilbracken, J. *Van Meegeren,* London, T. Nelson and Sons, Ltd., 1967.

8. Libby, W. F. *Radiocarbon Dating,* Chicago: University of Chicago Press, 1955.

9. Keisch, B. *Application of Nuclear Technology to Art Identification Problems – First Annual Report,* U.S. Atomic Energy Commission Report no. NYO-3953-1, February 1969.

HERMANN KÜHN

Terminal Dates for Paintings Derived from Pigment Analysis

The Doerner Institute examines about 250 works of art yearly, including some 170 paintings, by scientific methods. These investigations give us a great deal of information — which is stored in a card catalogue system — about the materials used in works of art. The information resulting from the investigation of authenticated paintings gives us insight into the painting materials used in different periods and regions, as well as into changes in painting technique. The main interest of our examinations is to reveal the close relation between style and painting technique and painting materials. This is due to the fact that new artistic ideas can often be expressed only by new materials and by the application of a new, suitable technique. On the other side, new materials may stimulate the artist and may give him ideas for new works. Generally speaking, paint is a mixture of pigments and binding media. The pigment is the coloring matter. The pigment particles are held together and are fixed on the ground by means of the binding medium.

Knowledge about the composition of paint, or also of the ground, may help to give us a terminal date for a painting, or, in some cases, to localize it roughly. A terminal date is either a "terminus post," the earliest date from which a painting can originate, or a "terminus ante," the latest possible date for a painting. The term "terminus post," therefore, covers *all the time after* the earliest date, while the term "terminus ante" covers *all the time before* the latest possible date. Terminal dates are not always absolute and precise dates; in many cases, they have a greater or less degree of probability, often covering a period of time.

A terminus post or a terminus ante can be derived from analysis of the pigments in a painting. If there are pigments which have not been known, introduced, or used before a distinct period of time, a terminus post can be set up for the examined painting. The painting cannot be earlier than the most modern pigment in its paint, or ground layers. However, care must be taken that the paint samples are taken from original parts of the painting. Samples from later additions, over-paintings, or retouchings would lead to completely wrong conclusions. A terminus post related to pigments can generally be fixed more precisely the more it approaches recent times. This is due to the fact that, in the 19th and 20th centuries, many more new pigments were invented than in earlier centuries.

Also, the dates of invention or introduction of rather modern pigments are generally fixed in technical publications. For instance, the date when chromium yellow was first prepared in the beginning of the 19th century is precisely known. A painting which contains chromium yellow or other chromium pigments cannot be earlier than 1809, when chromium yellow was first prepared by Vauquelin. Between the first preparation of a pigment and its introduction as an artist's pigment, a certain period of time has generally passed. The date of introduc-

tion can be found — in the case of the19th century — by studying lists of dealers for artists' materials. We have to consider also the possibility that an artist could have used a pigment before it was commercially available. In this way, a certain terminus post is the date of the first preparation. The date of introduction of a new pigment, however, can be assumed as "terminus post" with a high degree of probability.

If neither a certain date for the first preparation nor the introduction of a pigment is known from literature, such dates can only be derived from systematic examination of authenticated, precisely dated paintings. For instance, the first recipe for the preparation of Naples yellow, that I know of, originates in the 18th century. Systematic examination of paintings at the Doerner Institute, however, revealed that Naples yellow had already been used sporadically by painters in the 17th century. Since the 18th century it has been widely used. Until now, we have had no reliable evidence that Naples yellow was used in European painting before the 17th century. This means that a painting containing Naples yellow is with high probability not earlier than the 17th century. Such statistical conclusions are the more precise the more exactly dated paintings have been studied and the more reference data are available.

A terminus ante can be set up if a paint sample contains pigments which have gone out of use by a certain time, which is generally a longer period of time rather than a narrow, limited, or precise date. In general, there is no literary mention if a pigment ceases to be used. Only from systematic examination of exactly dated paintings do we get information about the gradual disappearance of certain pigments from the painters' palette. In this way, a terminus ante is never absolutely certain, although it has a greater or less degree of probability. An example can elucidate this fact: lead-tin yellow was the most common yellow pigment in the 15th, 16th, and 17th centuries. It was used to a smaller extent before the 15th century, and it was also sporadically found on paintings originating from the first half of the 18th century. Until now, we had never found this pigment on later paintings. This finding enables us to set up a terminus ante of about the middle of the 18th century. However, we should not completely overlook the possibility that a painter could have used lead-tin yellow after the middle of the 18th century, if he had acquired some from an old stock of this pigment.

Up until now lead-tin yellow was not found in any of the numerous forgeries originating from the 19th and 20th centuries which have been examined at the Doerner Institute. Lead-tin yellow in a painting means, therefore, that the painting was done with high probability before the middle of the 18th century; it is more probable that it was done before the 18th century than in the first half of the 18th century. The term "before the 18th century" covers all the centuries before 1700.

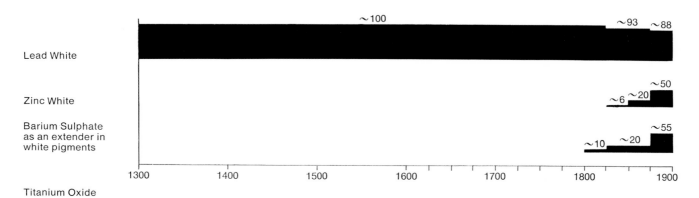

Lead White

Zinc White

Barium Sulphate
as an extender in
white pigments

Titanium Oxide

1. Frequency pattern of white pigments in white paint
in European easel painting.
(Preliminary state)

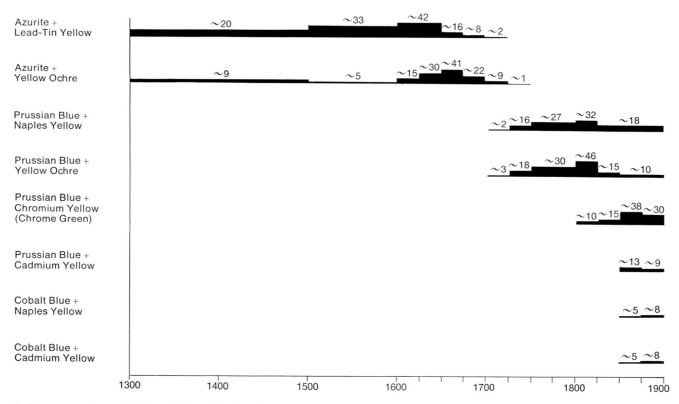

Azurite +
Lead-Tin Yellow

Azurite +
Yellow Ochre

Prussian Blue +
Naples Yellow

Prussian Blue +
Yellow Ochre

Prussian Blue +
Chromium Yellow
(Chrome Green)

Prussian Blue +
Cadmium Yellow

Cobalt Blue +
Naples Yellow

Cobalt Blue +
Cadmium Yellow

2. Frequency pattern of mixtures of blue and yellow pigments
in green paint in European easel painting.
(Preliminary state)

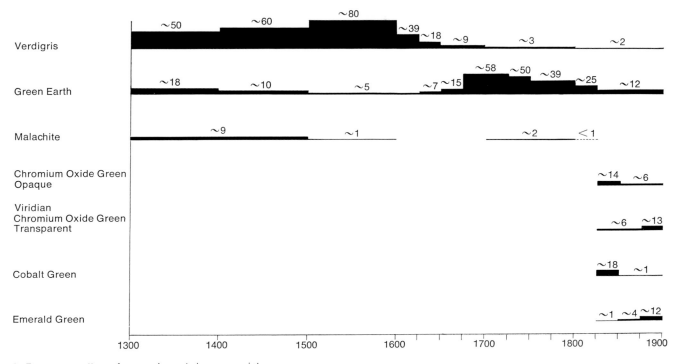

3. Frequency pattern of green pigments in green paint
in European easel painting.
(Preliminary state)

There is also a group of pigments which has been known since classical times, and which have been used until recent times. Such pigments are, i.e., lead white, ochre, umber, green earth, vermillion, and carbon black. If only such pigments occur in a painting, neither a terminus post nor a terminus ante can be set up. It is quite understandable that the terminal dates derived from pigment analysis cannot substitute, in any way, for the dating or localization of paintings on the base of stylistic criteria. If a painting shows significant stylistic features, it can be rather precisely dated or localized by the art historian, much more exactly than by a terminal date related to pigments. However, definite stylistic criteria which enable an exact dating are, in general, significant only on paintings of high quality, which were up to date in the time they were painted. The incertainty of dating or localization on the basis of stylistic criteria increases with decreasing quality. A lot of problems also arise with copies, owing to the fact that the copyist often wants to imitate the original painting as well as possible. In these cases the analysis of paint is often the only way to approach a rough dating or localization.

In spite of the fact that unquestionable paintings of high quality can be well ascribed by means of stylistic criteria, scientific examination of such paintings is necessary in order to collect reference data on the composition of paint, ground, and on painting technique. In some cases, analysis of binding media may also give a terminal date; for example, if a synthetic resin medium has been used. Synthetic resins are not used before the 20th century in painting; to a larger extent, they are used only since about 1950. But nowadays synthetic resin media have not completely replaced the classical media, such as drying oils, natural resins, proteins, and plant gums.

If the date of invention or introduction of a synthetic resin medium is known, analysis of the medium can yield a terminal date for a painting done within the 20th century.

Methods of Analysis Used at the Doerner Institute

Most desirable for the determination of pigments and media would be a method which does not require taking any samples from the paintings and does not cause any damage. Although it is possible to determine some pigments in situ on paintings by means of X-ray fluorescence-analysis and X-ray diffraction-pattern, a complete and precise determination of all pigments (especially small admixtures and minor components) occurring in a painting cannot be done without taking samples. If samples have to be taken, the sample size must be kept to a minimum. The paint losses caused by removed samples should be so small that they can scarcely be seen by the naked eye. This, however, means that only highly sensitive analytical methods can be used. To get reliable results, several methods of analysis should be applied to each sample and a check obtained on the findings.

The samples can be taken by a needle with a lancet-shaped point or a scalpel under a binocular microscope. At a magnification of 10, retouchings or later additions can be easily detected. The application of a laser beam in combination with emission spectrographic analysis is planned at the Doerner Institute, because this technique will be an improvement in reducing "paint losses." Analysis is started by methods which do not destroy the paint sample, for example, microscopic examination, which already gives an indication of the pigments in the sample, and which gives information on the physical character of pigments, as grain size and grain shape. Size and shape of the individual pigment particles which can be observed under magnifications of 100 up to 600, are, in many cases, characteristic for certain pigments. Often they show a typical behavior under polarized light, too. Naturally occurring pigments often contain characteristic accompanying minerals. These, as well as a typical grain size and grain shape, can be important for the distinction of naturally occurring pigments

from artificially prepared pigments. This is the case, for example, with natural and synthetic ultramarine. In order to get a better view on the individual pigment particles, a drop of concentrated ammonia solution, or a drop of potassium hydroxide (5 % aqueous solution) may be added. This agent causes saponification of oil or oil resin media so that the pigment particles "float out." Simultaneously, pigments which are not resistant to alkali are destroyed or altered, which also gives some indication of the nature of a pigment. Another technique for studying the pigment particles is the cross-section. Although a lot of information on pigments can be obtained only by microscopic examination, in many cases it is necessary to confirm the microscopic observations by determination of the elements and/or by X-ray diffraction powder pattern. Determination of elements can be done either by spectrographic or by microchemical analysis. In many cases, especially if there are several pigments in one paint-sample, reliable results can only be achieved if two or three methods are applied on the same paint sample. The second method, the X-ray diffraction powder pattern, is based on the reflection of X-rays on the lattice of crystals. The paint — a few micrograms are sufficient — is fixed on a slightly greased glass fiber, which is placed in the center of the X-ray chamber. The X-rays give a line-pattern on a photographic film, which is characteristic for a definite pigment. The identification of the X-ray diffraction powder pattern can be

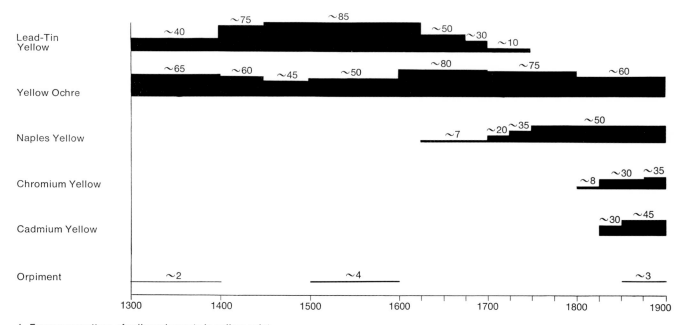

4. Frequency pattern of yellow pigments in yellow paint
in European easel painting.
(Preliminary state)

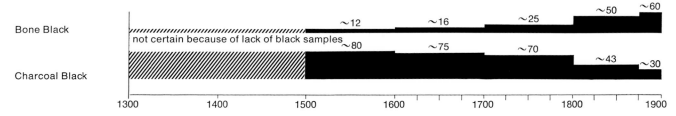

5. Frequency pattern of black pigments in black paint
in European easel painting.
(Preliminary state)

performed either by reference pattern from known pigments or
by means of the ASTM Data file. If there are several pigments
in comparable parts in a paint sample, the identification of the
individual pigments is often difficult. Also the sensitivity of the
X-ray powder pattern method differs greatly from pigment to
pigment. In general, the sensitivity is relatively low compared
to other methods, so that X-ray diffraction analysis is often
suitable only for the detection of those pigments which form
the major part in a paint sample. However, X-ray diffraction
analysis supplies additional information, for example, on crystal structure, which cannot be revealed by other methods.
X-ray diffraction patterns can also be made in situ by a special
type of back-reflecting camera, designed for analyzing pigments on paintings. Although X-ray diffraction analysis is performed before other analytical methods, the identification of
the patterns can be made afterward. This is especially desirable if the result of spectrographic analysis and microscopic
examination is available, as then it is much easier to identify
the X-ray diffraction patterns knowing which pigments could
be actually involved.

The next step in the analysis of a paint-sample is the detection of the elements, which is carried out at the Doerner Institute by emission spectrographic analysis. Although this method
cannot be substituted for all microchemical tests it takes the
place of most of them. There are some reasons why we prefer
spectrographic analysis to microchemical analysis: Only one
spectrographic shot is necessary in order to identify all elements present in a sample. On the other hand, microchemical
analysis requires a specific test for each element which is supposed to be in the sample. Because one often has to look for a
lot of elements, many tests have to be carried out. Each microchemical test requires a very tiny sample which, indeed, can
be smaller than the sample required for spectrographic analysis. However, several very tiny samples together give a larger
amount of material than is required for one spectrographic
analysis. Besides, microchemical analysis detects only elements for which specific tests are carried out. Tests, however,

are performed only for those elements which are supposed to
be in the sample. Unexpected elements are not detected. Careful evaluation of the lines of the emission spectrogram, however, covers all elements present in the sample, expected or
unexpected. The absence of certain elements is also confirmed simultaneously by spectrographic analysis. For some
elements, the sensitivity of spectrographic analysis is much
higher than the sensitivity of microchemical tests; thus, it is
difficult, or sometimes even impossible, to detect minor components and trace elements by microchemical tests. Trace
elements, however, can be an important characteristic for a
pigment.

For spectrographic analysis, we use a quartz prism spectrograph (Optische Werke, Jena Type Q 24). A prism spectrograph
does not have as high a resolution power as a large grating
spectrograph, but it has a higher aperture than a grating spectrograph. A high aperture allows reduction of the sample size
to a minimum. With the aid of a beam condenser, spectrographic analysis can be performed with samples of about
10 micrograms. Detection of trace elements, however, requires
samples of 50 to 100 micrograms. The paint sample is placed
on a carbon rod — without a previous separation of pigments
and media, because there is no interference by the medium —
and burnt up by a direct current arc (10 A). The evaluation of
the spectrum, which is recorded by a photographic plate, can
be done with the aid of either spectral tables or reference
spectra of known elements. The spectrographic analysis of tiny
paint samples does not lead to quantitative results; however,
a rough classification in main components, admixtures, minor
components, and trace elements is possible.

For the quantitative analysis of trace elements occurring in
pigments, neutron activation analysis is a suitable method.
Neutron activation analyses of paint samples for the Doerner
Institute are performed at the radiochemical department of the
Technical High School, Munich. The sensitivity of neutron
activation analysis may be 10 to 1000 times greater (depending
on the nature of the element) than the sensitivity of emission

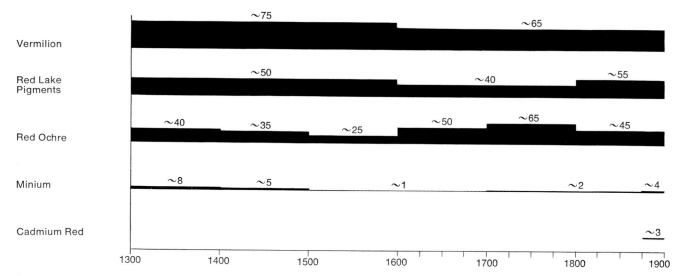

6. Frequency pattern of red pigments in red paint
in European easel painting.
(Preliminary state)

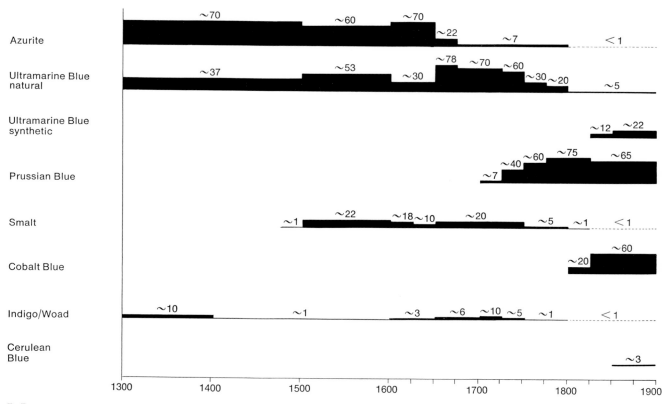

7. Frequency pattern of blue pigments in blue paint
in European easel painting.
(Preliminary state)

spectrographic analysis. The distribution pattern of trace elements in pigments may help to give a rough localization of paintings.

Another method, suitable for the identification both of inorganic and of organic pigments is the infrared absorption spectrograph, which requires about 20 to 100 micrograms of paint. The infrared spectrograms are identified with the aid of reference spectra. For the identification of lakes and organic pigments, gas chromatography, thin-layer chromatography and ultraviolet absorption spectrographic analysis are also very useful techniques.

Appendix

The Use of Pigments through the Centuries of European Easel Painting

The frequency pattern on the following pages is based on the analytical results from scientific examinations of paintings at the Doerner Institute since 1960. It includes only authenticated paintings from 1300 to 1900 which have dates on them or which can be integrated with certainty in a time span of a quarter of a century. It is confined to the more frequently used pigments. The scheme indicates the number of paintings — related to 100 paintings — which contain a certain pigment. However, in each painting examined all colors do not occur, nor have they been analyzed. Therefore, in the reference number of 100 paintings, only paintings are included for which the corresponding color has been analyzed; for example, in the case of blue pigments in the reference number 100, only paintings of which blue colors have been analyzed are included. On the other hand, several shades of one color may occur in a painting which often contain different pigments. That is the reason why the number of paintings added up over all pigments of one color may exceed 100. The steps in the frequency pattern are a graphic simplification, because the use of a pigment during the centuries increases or decreases gradually.

The frequency patterns — as shown here — have preliminary character because of the following facts:
1. The statistic is not based on the same number of paintings in each century. From the 16th to the 19th century, between 80 and 280 paintings could be used for each century. In the 17th, 18th, and 19th centuries, the number of paintings examined allowed a subdivision into quarters of centuries. Only between 20 and 40 paintings were at disposal in the 14th and 15th centuries. In this way, the statistics have a fluctuating degree of probability in different centuries. Continuation of the systematic examination of paintings will increase the degree of probability.
2 The number of examined paintings is not equally distributed over the different schools of European painting. For example, in the 17th century, Dutch paintings are preponderate by far.

It is to be expected that different schools have used different pigments of certain favored color shades.

The alternating use of many pigments through the centuries can be traced back to two main factors. On the one side, there are technical and commercial reasons: new pigments have been discovered and have gradually replaced other pigments; former pigments have become rare and too expensive. On the other side, there is the artistic idea which leads to a preference of certain color shades and also pigments in certain periods of paintings (material style). However, it requires more reference data from different schools of painting than we recently have at our disposal in order to give a comprehensive and reliable interpretation of the frequency patterns.

S. J. FLEMING

Authenticity Testing of Art Ceramics by the Thermoluminescence Method—Some Important Examples

A consequence of the influence of Confucius around 500 B.C. was the proliferation of pottery sculptures ("ming-ch'i") as a morally healthy alternative to the human sacrificial burial rites of the earlier Shang culture. The placement of appreciable numbers of pottery effigies about the body of the deceased within the tomb confines, if anything, became more expansive and ritualistic in later times, despite the general disintegration of Confucian influence at the close of the Han Dynasty (A.D. 220). The art historians of this period of Chinese art no doubt rightly feel that this proliferation was extensive enough not to require subsequent enhancement around 1910, when the first pieces from such tomb retinue appeared in the Western art market and gained such popularity as to warrant widespread forgery to satisfy the ever-increasing demands of collectors.

It would be wrong to presume that such forgeries could be detected easily upon stylistic grounds at that time, since the catalogue of genuine pieces to which comparison could be made was extremely sketchy. The early pottery products of the Chinese had enough charm and grace to permit some detraction during imperfect imitation so that the imitations still appeared attractive to the Western eye. In present times we can only look back with regret at the confusion that imitation has inevitably caused in attempts to piece together a coherent development of the early cultures. Imitation has certainly not been limited to early Chinese pottery ware. All cultures of substance have been through an era of popularity in subsequent times to a level sufficient to justify forgery. This paper describes some of the investigations of pottery from various parts of the world and its limited extent rightly implies that there are still vast amounts of materials as yet unstudied.

The Thermoluminescent Process

Thermoluminescence is the emission of light caused by heating the pottery under study to 500° C, which is observed above a background of red-hot glow which all substances exhibit at such high temperatures. The thermoluminescence (TL) observed represents a release of stored energy from the minerals of which the pottery is constructed. The source of energy that the mineral stores are the minute levels or radioactive impurities (uranium, thorium, and radiogenic potassium) that exist in everything that surrounds us.

Much energy is stored during the geological history of the mineral, but in the case of pottery clay this stored energy is all released during the firing of the pottery or during the preparative stages of the production of a terracotta. Once the clay has cooled it is again able to absorb radiation from its environment and store a proportionate amount of energy. Reheating of such clay in the laboratory today results in thermoluminescence, which is then a measure of the total radiation

history that the pottery has experienced since original kiln-firing.

This thermoluminescence is observed with use of the apparatus shown schematically in fig. 1. During the heating of the sample on a nichrome strip in an atmosphere of nitrogen, the emitted light is detected by a photomultiplier, which converts the light signal to an electrical current that drives the vertical axis of a chart recorder. The temperature of the sample is measured by a thermocouple welded beneath the nichrome strip and recorded on the horizontal axis of the recorder. The curve obtained of thermoluminescence versus temperature is termed a glow curve (fig. 2 B, curve a).

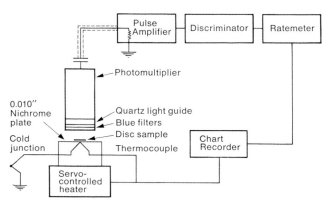

1. Schematic view of the TL apparatus.

The addition of a known laboratory radiation dosage to such a sample of pottery induced further thermoluminescence in all temperature regions between room temperature and 500° C (fig. 2 B, curve b). In this curve some thermoluminescence is observed in the lower temperature regions around 100° C not present in the "natural" thermoluminescence glow curve. This thermoluminescence arises from electron trapping which would not have been stable over archaeological periods. As is apparent from the matching of the natural thermoluminescence glow curve to that of the laboratory-induced glow curve long-term stability of electron trapping occurs at and above 350° C. This conclusion is quite general for most of the pottery studied at the Oxford Laboratory.

A convenient ordinate in the higher temperature region (at 400° C, say) is chosen and a comparison made between the thermoluminescence levels at that temperature of the natural glow curve and of the laboratory-induced glow curve. This allows quantitative assessment of the archaeological radiation dosage to be made. For example, in fig. 2 B for the Chinese Wei

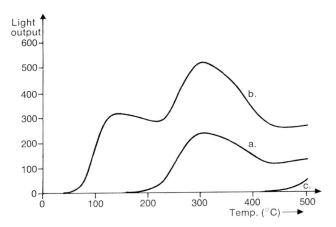

2 B. TL glow curves for the Wei figure of fig. 2 A. Curve a, natural TL; curve b, natural TL + TL induced by 1050 rads of laboratory radiation; curve c, background red-hot glow.

2 A. Figure of a man made of gray pottery. Wei Dynasty in China (A.D. 386–535).

figure (fig. 2 A), 180 units of additional thermoluminescence are induced at 400° C, using 1050 rads (a rad is a measure of the energy absorbed per gram of material subjected to radiation. The typical level of dose rate experienced by pottery in burial is close to 0.5 rads per year) of laboratory radiation. By comparison the 143 units of natural thermoluminescence are expected to have arisen therefore from a dosage of 830 rads of radiation from its burial circumstances.

Pottery Radiation-Environment

The advancement to age determination requires that the annual dose rate (in rads per year) can be determined. This is by no means a simple task, and much of the recent research of the Oxford Laboratory has been involved in clarification of the problems surrounding this dose rate evaluation. The uranium and thorium in the pottery structure emit alpha radiation, which travels only 23 microns on an average through clay fabric. Beta radiation from these isotopes and from radioactive potassium travels approximately 1 mm, on the average, in such fabric. These two forms of radiation are the source of internal dosage in the pottery. The surrounding soil supplies an external dosage through gamma radiation coming from the natural isotopes and effective from as much as 30 cm away from the pottery. Cosmic radiation contributes only a small fraction (on the average less than 3 %) of the total dosage the buried ceramic experiences. The external radiation dosage amounts to between 10 % and 40 % of the total dosage, so that precise dating can be attempted only if appreciable knowledge of the burial conditions of the pottery is available.

Some closer study of the internal dosage components is necessary, as two nonuniformities occur within the structure of the pottery itself. First, the thermoluminescence observed is predominantly emitted by crystalline inclusions (such as quartz) embedded in the clay matrix, while that matrix yields very little thermoluminescence. Second, these crystalline inclusions are free of self-radioactivity, while the matrix of clay bears the natural isotopes that activate the thermoluminescence process. Short-range alpha radiation contributes approximately 40% of the total dosage experienced by the pottery, but much of this radiation is absorbed by the thermoluminescence-insensitive clay before it penetrates into crystalline grains. Further, if the grain radius is greater than the alpha radiation range, there are inner zones of the crystal which suffer no alpha radiation dosage. For a quartz grain of 100 microns in diameter this dilution of alpha radiation dosage is approximately 0.22 times the undiluted clay matrix level.

Precise dating is possible by crushing the pottery in a controlled manner and either extracting fine grains (about 1 to 5 microns in diameter), which are thus known to have suffered an undiluted alpha radiation dosage, or extracting large grains (about 100 to 200 microns in diameter), which are then assumed to have experienced only a small alpha radiation dosage. Accuracy of better than $\pm 8\%$ standard deviation for dating of each pottery fragment studied is now considered possible by either method under such controls.

Application to Authenticity Testing of Ceramics

In the majority of applications of the thermoluminescence method to authenticity problems the accuracy quoted above is neither possible nor necessary. It is not necessary, since we may only need to distinguish between a Chinese Wei figure between 1400 and 1600 years old (if authentic) and a modern reproduction of such ware produced in the present century.

High dating accuracy is excluded, principally for two reasons. To minimize damage to the artistic value of the piece only about 25 mg of pottery powder is drilled from an inconspicuous region. The drilling process immediately contradicts the approach laid down for precise dating, which requires controlled crushing. The powder sample contains a wide spectrum of grain sizes of crystalline inclusions. The drilling action damages and fragments larger crystals and so enhances the concentration of finer grains in the sample collected. The fine grains are extracted from the sample by their suspension in acetone, and about 1 mg of powder is then deposited onto each of a series of thin aluminium discs by way of preparation for thermoluminescence measurement. Some of these fine grains may have originated from the inner volume of a large crystalline grain and so have not experienced alpha radiation dosage, in the original radiation geometry of the pottery structure. They thus act as a diluent to the archaeological

dosage now evaluated by thermoluminescence analysis of these disc-deposited fine grains.

The actual internal dose rate suffered by the grains used for measurement must then be calculated as (f x alpha dose-rate) + (beta dose-rate) where $f<1$. By empirical evaluation, using pottery pieces of known age, an effective value of f has been deduced of about 0.85. A more immediate difficulty in attempting to date art ceramics is the incomplete knowledge of the true level of environment dosage from the burial soil, as the piece is invariably cleaned prior to museum display. A useful average working value of 0.08 rads per year for this dosage has been determined. However, to determine the maximum possible age of the ceramic we must know the minimum possible level of environmental dosage. This is simply the contribution of cosmic rays only, assuming burial of the ceramic in nonradioactive soil and amounts to 0.014 rads/year.

The minimum possible age of the ceramics depends upon the maximum possible level of the environmental dosage. A value of 0.17 rads per year is used at present corresponding to the highest level of radioactivity measured for soil samples studied at the Oxford Laboratory. An imitation is thus acclaimed if the maximum age determined from thermoluminescence analysis is younger than the suggested period of authentic ware for a specific culture.

Practical Application

With this background on thermoluminescence dating, let us return to the Chinese Wei figure (fig. 2 A). The archaeological dosage was determined as 830 rads. Radioactive analysis was carried out on the powder that remained after extraction of the fine grains, and age limits set upon this piece of between 1300 and 2200 years. On the basis of these data, it is concluded that this figure is genuine. As a contrast, consider the data obtained for a Amlash Zebu bull purporting to data circa 1000 B.C. (fig. 3). The "natural" glow curve runs close to the background curve of the sample, glowing red hot around 500° C. Yet the pottery minerals of this piece are sensitive to radiation, as the glow curve for 150 rads of laboratory radiation illustrates. By comparison at 400° C the archaeological radiation dosage is close to 6 rads. Radioactive analysis of the pottery clay yielded a maximum age of 14 years. Thus the thermoluminescence method did not support authenticity of this Amlash piece. It is essential to realize the limitations of the method in its application in the framework of art history. The lady shown in fig. 4 A submitted for study was initially recorded as either of the T'ang period in China (A.D. 618—906) if it were authentic, or of modern origin. The latter possibility was duly rejected when thermoluminescence analysis yielded the glow curves of fig. 4 B, leading to an age determination of between 1090 and 1990 years ago for the

3 A. Pottery vessel in the shape of a zebu bull, in the style of such wares produced by the Mazaderan culture in northwest Persia in the villages of Amlash and Marlik around 1000 B.C.

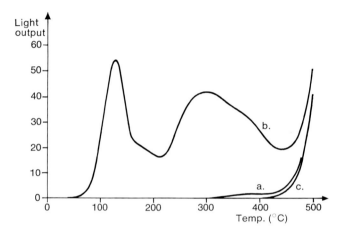

3 B. TL glow curves for the Amlash bull in fig. 3 A. Curve a, natural TL; curve b, natural TL + TL induced by 150 rads of laboratory radiation; curve c, background red-hot glow.

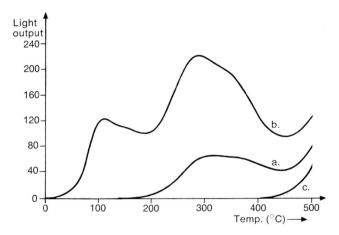

4 B. TL glow curves for the court lady of fig. 4 A. Curve a, natural TL; curve b, natural TL + TL induced by 670 rads of laboratory radiation; curve c, background red-hot glow.

4 A. Pottery figure of the court lady, Yang Kuei Fei. T'ang Dynasty in China (A.D. 618–906). The red clay used for this piece is particularly common among unglazed wares of the 9th century A.D. The surface of the figure was covered with a white slip. Traces of original pigment are still apparent on the figure.

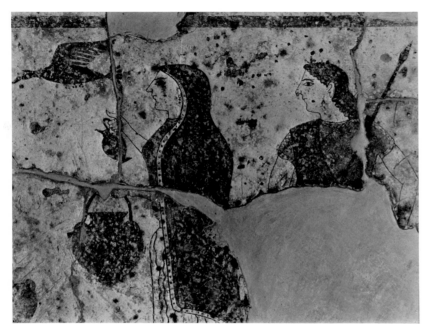

5 *A*. Wall painting on a terracotta plaque, decorated in the Etruscan style. The scene is supposed to depict the ambush of Troilus, son of Priam, as he leads his horse to water. Achilles lies in wait behind the fountain. Troilus is accompanied by his sister, Polyxena.

5 *B*. Fresco of the ambush of Troilus by Achilles painted in the *Tomb of the Bulls* at Tarquinii.

5 *C*. Detail of fig. 5 *A*. Note the similarity of dress of Polyxena and the ladies of the Boccanera group of fig. 5 *D*.

5 *D*. *Procession of women*. Painting of terracotta. One of a series of Etruscan plaques found at Boccanera (near Caere) now in the British Museum. Mid-sixth century B.C.

Etruscan Wall Paintings

In the cases discussed above the method of thermoluminescence analysis has been quite unsophisticated. As an example of one of the inherent difficulties encountered in this method and of how the problem may be overcome by recourse to specialized methods, I have included in here a discussion of the wall painting (fig. 5 A) made on terracotta and purporting to be of Etruscan origin (circa 500 B.C.).

The scene is presumed to depict the ambush and death of Troilus, son of Priam, at the hands of Achilles — comparison is made to the painting in the *Tomb of Bulls,* in Tarquinii, of that "heroic" scene (fig. 5 B). The structure of the water fountain and the presence of the recumbent lion above are direct correlations of the two works.

The basic style of the piece under thermoluminescence investigation is quite different from the Tarquinii painting and follows instead the more sophisticated painting of the Boccanera Slabs from Caere (now in the British Museum) in the style of figure drawing and pigment used — black, maroon, and ochre shades prevail. Figs. 5 C and D illustrate this comparison. Even the small bird in the scene finds direct parallel in that which appears as part of the decoration of the *Tomb of the Augurs,* in Tarquinii.

The large physical size of the terracotta (70 cm x 40 cm x 2 cm) permitted removal of a fragment about ½ cubic centimeter, so that controlled crushing of the sample was practical. However, when the fine grains were used for thermoluminescence analysis, glow curves of the form shown in fig. 6 A resulted. While the light output in the natural glow curve is low and close to the background red hot glow, the thermoluminescence induced by as much as 2000 rads of laboratory radiation is also not overwhelming. The predicted archaeological dosage of less than 290 rads excludes the possibility that the terracotta was last fired in Etruscan times but allows an age of up to 600 years.

The reason for this excess age estimation is that the natural glow curve no doubt contains a component of "spurious" thermoluminescence, meaning that it is nonradiation-induced. The source of this light is obscure, but it has been suggested that it arises from the interaction of trace levels of oxygen or water vapor with an electrical surface charge condition of the grains of clay. Certainly this is consistent with experimental evidence such as (a) its appreciably greater magnitude if the heating of the sample is carried out in air rather than nitrogen, (b) its occurrence correlates to grain size, being larger for smaller grains as the surface area/volume ratio increases. As a fragment of terracotta was available it was practical to attempt removal of this "spurious" thermoluminescence component and so reach a more reasonable age limit for manufacture of this wall painting.

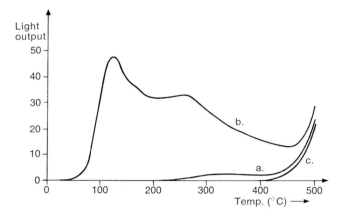

6 A. TL glow curves for fine-grain extract of pottery grains from the terracotta of fig. 5 A. Curve a, natural TL; curve b, natural TL + TL induced by 2000 rads of laboratory radiation; curve c, background red-hot glow.

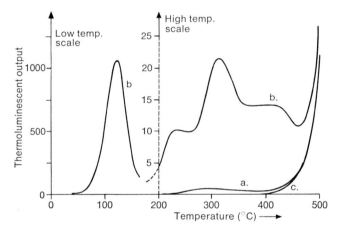

6 B. TL glow curves for the crystalline extract from the terracotta of fig. 5 A. Curve a, natural TL; curve b, b'natural TL + TL induced by 900 rads of laboratory radiation; curve c, background red-hot glow.

figure. With this support for the authenticity of the figure the role of the physical sciences is then complete. The art historian may now eagerly seize the opportunity to narrow the dating of this piece within the limits quoted above, for this lady has by no means an unrecorded past. There is little doubt that she depicts the only fat court lady to be noted among the historical beauties of China, Yang Kuei Fei. As a favorite of the Emperor Ming Hwang, and concubine of the emperor's son, Prince Show, she rose to fame in A.D. 735 and continued to exert much court pressure until her death in A.D. 756. Tomb effigies of her appear in excavated sites between A.D. 744 and 808, tightening the date of the manufacture of the particular piece quite narrowly.

The sample was quite rich in larger quartz grains of the 100 micron size. These were removed by the standard geological method of magnetic separation and cleaned with hydrofluoric acid to free the surface of the larger crystals of minute adhering clay. The result is quite definite. By comparison with an additional laboratory dose of around 900 rads (fig. 6 B) it is suggested that the archaeological dosage experienced by the terracotta was less than 30 rads. Radioactive analysis of the clay, together with the assumption that these large quartz grains experienced little alpha radiation dosage, yielded an age of 130 years, at maximum.

The gain in certainty on authenticity analysis is always a benefit of this more sophisticated approach to a piece, and it is to be hoped that the crystalline dating method will become the rule rather than the exception for study of larger terracottas, for figures as well as wall paintings.

Conclusion

Excluding the cases where the sample emits no thermoluminescence because of absence of sensitivity to radiation (making analysis impossible) and the pieces for which the magnitude of spurious thermoluminescence is excessive and the objects are not large enough to permit fragment removal, the thermoluminescence method may be treated as 100 % certain in matters of authenticity. Only 6 pieces from over 250 studied at the Oxford Laboratory to date could not be analyzed for the foregoing reasons. No case has yet been encountered where doubt has been cast upon the 100 % confidence level, though this could arise if it were believed that a genuine piece has been re-fired to 500° C in modern times, thus negating the tests. Research is now being carried out to determine whether it is possible to detect such refiring by thermoluminescence methods.

References

Thermoluminescence

Aitken, M. J., Zimmerman, D. W., and Fleming, S. J. "Thermoluminescent Dating of Ancient Pottery," *Nature,* 219 (1968), 442—445.
Aitken, M. J. "Thermoluminescent Dosimetry of Environmental Radiation on Archaeological Sites," *Archaeometry,* 11 (1969), 109—114.
Fleming, S. J., Moss, H. W., and Joseph, A. "Thermoluminescent Authenticity Testing of Some 'Six Dynasties' figures," *Archaeometry,* 12 (1970), 59—70.
Fleming, S. J. "Thermoluminescence Dating by the Inclusion Technique," *Archaeometry,* 12 (1970), 135.

Art History

Joseph, A. M., Moss, H. M., and Fleming, S. J. *Chinese Pottery Burial Objects of the Sui and T'ang Dynasties,* Hugh M. Moss Ltd., 1970.
Pallottino, M. *Etruscan Painting,* Skira, 1952.
Stenico, A. *Roman and Etruscan Painting,* Weidenfeld & Nicolson, 1963.

NATHAN STOLOW and **GEORGE deW. ROGERS**

Gas Chromatography and Pyrolysis Techniques to Establish Ageing Characteristics of Works of Art

The gas chromatographic analysis of drying oil paint films, as carried out by this laboratory, has been reported in some detail in the publication arising out of the 1965 Boston meeting.[1] In the interim considerable progress has been made in using this technique to study the deterioration products of aged film fragments which were both artificially prepared and obtained from old works of art. The acquisition of a pyrolysis attachment, as an accessory to the Perkin-Elmer Gas Chromatograph, enable us to broaden our studies by investigating pyrolysis reactions on untreated films — unpigmented and pigmented. This technique, which is most promising in characterizing media of works of art, will be described later on. The object of this paper is then to report on further work in the field of gas chromatography carried out since 1965, and as such is a progress report on the study of the ageing characteristics of drying oils as found in works of art.

The drying oil which has been the subject of our investigations is linseed oil, which is the most important from the point of view of ancient and modern artists' techniques of production. The results reported for artificially prepared films in 1965 were on films of linseed oil pigmented with barium sulphate, iron oxide, and basic lead carbonate. Half of these films were aged up to about one year under room conditions (20° C, 50 % relative humidity, diffuse north light), and the other half were given accelerated ageing exposure (20° C, 50 % R. H., strong ultraviolet light) in a specially designed environmental chamber. The composition, i.e., pigment-medium ratio, of each film was measured as well as the film thickness. Films were also laid down of the unpigmented linseed, oil, and these were also exposed to parallel conditions. A portion of the unused oil was kept in a sealed container under nitrogen for further examination, if necessary. Small samples of films were removed at intervals up to one year exposures, and these were esterified to yield the necessary methyl esters for gas chromatographic analysis. The description of the esterification technique, the gas chromatographic apparatus, and the method of analysis has been described fully in the earlier publication[1] and need not be described again in detail. It was shown in the previous work that certain breakdown products in aged linseed oil films can be measured quantitatively by comparison analysis of the various peaks in the chromatograms. In particular, attention was focussed on the following saturated, unsaturated, and dicarboxylic acid methyl esters derived from esterification of the parent film fragments (see tabulation below).

The methyl esters of the acids with 16 or 18 carbon atoms are listed with increasing unsaturation, i.e., 0, 1, 2, and 3 double bonds. These esters are derived from the triglycerides or triglyceride fragments of the polymerized linseed oil film. The dicarboxylic acids, glutaric, etc., are presumably formed within the dried and aged film as a result of breakdown of the film structure. A useful quantitative criterion established in assessing the ageing characteristics of the various films was to relate the amount of a particular component, e.g., 2C7 or 2C9 methyl ester, as a fraction of the combined amounts of 16:0 plus 18:0 saturated methyl esters. These latter components, palmitic and stearic acid methyl esters respectively, are believed to remain unchanged within the film upon ageing and serve as an internal quantitative standard against which the other components, e.g., the dicarboxylic methyl esters, may be measured. Thus it would be expected that, with ageing, the dicarboxylic acid fragments increase in quantity and therefore the ratios of $2C7/(16:0+18:0)$ or $2C9/(16:0+18:0)$ would increase with time, while on the other hand, $18:1/(16:0+18:0)$ and $18:2/(16:0+18:0)$ would decrease. This was borne out in the studies made on both naturally and artificially aged unpigmented and pigmented (barium sulphate and white lead) films up to about one year of ageing.

Methyl ester	No. of carbon atoms in acid portion	Symbol
palmitic	16	16:0
stearic	18	18:0
oleic	18	18:1
linoleic	18	18:2
linolenic	18	18:3
glutaric	5	2C5
adipic	6	2C6
pimelic	7	2C7
suberic	8	2C8
azelaic	9	2C9

The ageing process has now been studied up to about five years. The graphs in figs.1—4 show the changes in the dicarboxylic acid methyl esters 2C8 and 2C9 and the fall in 18:1 with ageing time. The experimental conditions are given in the captions to the various figures. The iron oxide-linseed oil films (figs. 3a and 3b) show most noticeably the increase in the dicarboxylic breakdown products with ageing. This is also experimentally indicated in the effect of solvents on the film fragments during the esterification process, or in separate studies on the leaching of such films. The films which are rich in dicarboxylic acid breakdown products leach very strongly in solvents and cause marked pigment separation. The iron oxide films as well as titanium white films (not included in the graphs) when drastically aged under strong ultraviolet light are rapidly disintegrated by the esterification solvent mixture, e.g., boron trifluoride/methanol and indeed by most ordinary sol-

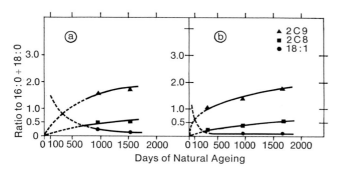

1. Gas Chromatographic studies of dicarboxylic and oleic acids formation with film ageing effect of pigmentation.
(a) Iron oxide (Fe_2O_3)/linseed oil (N-8b), 125 μ thick; aged normally at 20° C, 40—50 % R. H., in diffuse north light.
(b) Linseed oil film (N-1b); 35 μ thick, aged normally at 20° C, 40—50 % R. H., in diffuse north light.
Note: 2C9 — azelaic acid methyl ester; 2C8 — suberic acid methyl ester; 18:1 — oleic acid methyl ester; obtained by esterification of film fragments with boron trifluoride/methanol mixture (see reference 1).

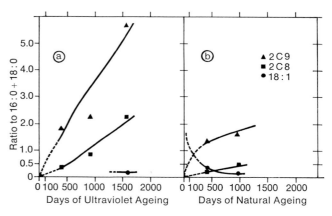

3. Gas Chromatographic studies of dicarboxylic and oleic acids formation with film ageing effect of ultraviolet light.
(a) Iron oxide (Fe_2O_3)/linseed oil (UV4b), 71 μ thick; aged under ultraviolet light, 20° C, 50 % R. H. Ultraviolet intensity incident on sample (200—400 mμ) average 0.2 milliwatts per square centimer (see reference 2).
(b) Iron oxide (Fe_2O_3)/linseed oil (N-8a), 76 μ thick; aged normally at 20° C, 40—50 % R. H., in diffuse north light.

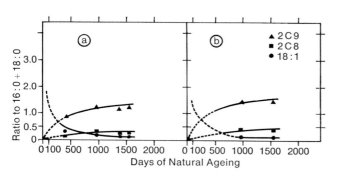

2. Gas Chromatographic studies of dicarboxylic and oleic acids formation with film ageing effect of film thickness.
(a) White lead (basic lead carbonate)/linseed oil (N-7b), 120 μ thick; aged normally at 20° C, 40—50 % R. H., in diffuse north light.
(b) White lead (basic lead carbonate)/linseed oil (N-7a2), 89 μ thick; aged normally at 20° C, 40—50 % R. H., in diffuse north light.

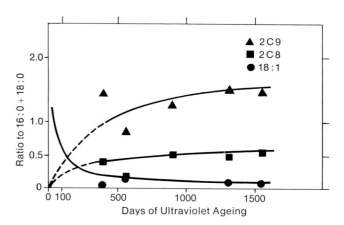

4. Gas Chromatographic studies of dicarboxylic and oleic acids formation with film ageing effect of ultraviolet light.
White lead (basic lead carbonate)/linseed oil (UV3b), 92 μ thick; aged under ultraviolet light, 20° C, 50 % R. H. Same conditions as fig. 3 a.

vents. The naturally aged pigmented films were observed to be less brittle and less prone to solvent action leading to pigment desegregation. The graphs also permit some statement to be made as to the effect of film thickness on the quantities of 2C9 and 2C8. Comparison of the two film thicknesses of white lead-linseed oil in figs. 2 a and 2 b, 120 microns and 89 microns respectively, show that the thicker film builds up 2C9 and 2C8 more slowly, and also the 18:1 component is used up more slowly. This is to be expected in thicker paint films where the oxidative processes, presumably limited by an oxygen diffusion mechanism, take place more slowly compared with a thin film.

Ultraviolet exposure in the accelerated ageing studies promotes film breakdown. The pigment presumably plays a role here, depending on its degree of absorption of ultraviolet radiation. The ultraviolet lamps used in these experiments were of the high intensity type: Hanovia 200 watts, quartz high pressure mercury vapor, with vycor heat-absorbing filter and no other filtration. Measurements made incident to the paint film surfaces gave readings[2] of the order of 0.2 milliwatts per square centimeter in the ultraviolet region 200—400 millimicrons. The strong mercury lines are those at 366, 313, and 302 millimicrons. The ultraviolet reflectance of the films in question was also measured[3] in the region 300—400 millimicrons, and the reflectance curves are given in fig. 5. It would appear from the reflectance curves that at 366 millimicrons the absorption of ultraviolet energy increases in the order: unpigmented linseed oil, barium sulphate, titanium dioxide, white lead, and iron oxide. However, at 313 millimicrons, the order changes: barium sulphate, white lead, iron oxide, and titanium dioxide, and most absorption unpigmented linseed oil. Experimentally, it is observed that for a fixed film thickness the order of increasing film deterioration under the given condition of ultraviolet exposure is white lead, barium sulphate, titanium dioxide, iron oxide, unpigmented linseed oil. It is difficult at this time to correlate the extent of deterioration by ultraviolet exposure with the pigment in question. In early studies by Stutz[4] on the reflectance and transmittance in ultraviolet of a variety of pigmented films he found that the percentage transmission of approximately 1 micron thick pigment layers by the strong mercury line at 366 millimicrons were barium sulphate, 65%; white lead, 61%; titanium dioxide, 18%; iron oxide, 0.5%. If the degree of film breakdown is determined by the extent of ultraviolet absorption at the film surface, then according to Stutz's figures the iron oxide films should be the most affected. This is actually observed experimentally, where these films yield the highest levels of dicarboxylic acids (2C8, 2C9 of fig. 3), and are most prone to solvent leaching (see table I below). The white lead films became extremely brittle upon exposure, but then retained their coherent film structure after

solvent action. The iron oxide and titanium dioxide films were rapidly disintegrated by solvent exhibiting high concentrations of breakdown products. A fuller analysis of the complex problem of the influence of ultraviolet light on the drying process would have to take into account, among other factors, the nature of the pigment-medium bond. Of particular interest here is the possibility of ultraviolet light enhancing or catalyzing the pigment action upon the intimately bonded organic medium, especially in the presence of oxygen.

The results tabulated in table I show clearly that exposure of films to ultraviolet light reduces the concentration of dried oil relative to pigment content, e.g., in (v) and (vi) the dried oil content is reduced from 17.3 to 15,3%, increases film brittleness, and susceptibility to leaching by solvent. Acetone was chosen in this case as the leaching solvent. After leaching there was further film embrittlement, as was to be expected. The reduction in dried oil or organic content upon ultraviolet exposure is an indication that low molecular weight components are formed by photochemical and/or oxidative action and are gradually lost from the film surface to the surrounding air.

Solvent Action and Gas Chromatographic Analysis of Various Pigmented and Unpigmented Drying Oil Films

A number of artificially prepared films, similar to those described in table I, as well as a number of paint samples from dated works of art, were analyzed for amount of leaching, and then with gas chromatography (after preparation of the relevant methyl esters) the leachings were analyzed for various components. Typical results for pigmented, unpigmented, normally aged, and accelerated aged samples are given in table II.

It is apparent from the results, expressed as yields of components as a percentage of the organic medium of the paint film, that the effect of ultraviolet exposure is generally to increase the amounts of dicarboxylic acids. There are no clear trends in the other sets of data. There is a fair spread in percent leaching and percent non-esterifiable in both the normally aged and the artificially aged films. It would be worthwhile to analyze the non-esterifiable portion of the leachings to see whether there are variations in amounts of certain components present attributable to the manner and extent of ageing. For the present the best indicator of ageing is in the amounts of dicarboxylic acids. It is interesting too that the yield of 16:0 plus 18:0 methyl esters (palmitic plus stearic) for the leachings is within the range 4 to 7% for all the linseed-containing films. This tends to confirm the earlier statement that the saturated fatty acid components originally present in the drying oil triglycerides remain unchanged in the film upon ageing. Another identifying factor for linseed oil in addition to the yield for

Table I

The effect of ageing on the leaching of drying oil films by acetone

Film type	Solvent*	Leaching, %*	Film observations
Unpigmented films			
(i) Alkali-refined linseed oil 80 μ thick, aged under ultraviolet light 3.3 yr at 20°C, 50% R.H.**	Acetone	27	Film slightly flexible before leaching, after leaching more brittle
(ii) Open pot stand oil 150 μ thick, aged 187 hr at 65°C, then 2 yr at 20°C, 40–50% R.H., diffuse north light	Acetone	21	Film flexible before leaching (slightly sticky) less flexible and sticky after leaching
Pigmented films			
(iii) White lead-stand oil; 79% pigment; 21% dried oil, 50 μ thick, aged 25 yr at 20–25°C, diffuse light, ambient conditions	Acetone	24	Unleached film moderately flexible; after leaching, very brittle
(iv) White lead-stand oil; 81% pigment, 19% dried oil, 130 μ thick, aged 7 yr, 20°C, 40–50% R.H., diffuse north light	Acetone	21	Unleached film slightly more flexible than (iii) but less brittle after leaching
(v) White lead-alkali-refined linseed oil, 82.7% pigment, 17.3% dried oil, 90 μ thick, aged 3.3 yr at 20°C, 40–50% R.H., diffuse north light	Acetone	28	Unleached film brittle; after leaching, very brittle
(vi) White lead-alkali-refined linseed oil, 84.7% pigment, 15.3% dried oil, 90 μ thick, aged 3.3 yr at 20°C, 50% R.H., under ultraviolet light	Acetone	24	Unleached film very brittle and hard; after leaching, extremely brittle
(vii) White lead-linseed oil artist's palette; 82.4% pigment, 17.6% dried oil, 200 μ thick, aged 48 yr at 20–30°C, ambient conditions	Acetone	21	Unleached film brittle and hard, increased brittleness after leaching
(viii) Titanium dioxide (rutile)-alkali-refined linseed oil; 72.5% pigment, 27.5% dried oil, 90 μ thick, aged 3.3 yr at 20°C, 40–50% R.H., diffuse north light	Acetone	62	Unleached film flexible; after leaching, more rigid
(ix) Titanium dioxide (rutile)-alkali-refined linseed oil; 75% pigment, 25% dried oil, 90 μ thick, aged 3.3 yr at 20°C, 50% R.H., under ultraviolet light	Acetone	84	Unleached film less flexible than (viii), and disintegrated rapidly on solvent contact with dispersion of pigment particles
(x) Iron oxide (Fe_2O_3)/alkali-refined linseed oil; 81% pigment, 19% dried oil, 90 μ thick, aged 3.3 yr at 40–50% R.H., diffuse north light	Acetone	62	Unleached film flexible, after leaching, brittle
(xi) Iron oxide (Fe_2O_3)/alkali-refined linseed oil; 84% pigment, 16% dried oil, 90 μ thick, aged 3.3 yr at 20°C, 50% R.H., under ultraviolet light	Acetone	87	Unleached film less flexible than (x), and disintegrated rapidly on solvent contact with dispersion of pigment particles
(xii) Barium sulphate/alkali-refined linseed oil; 72.3% pigment, 27.7% dried oil, 90 μ thick, aged 3.3 yr at 20°C, 40–50% R.H., diffuse north light	Acetone	52	Unleached film flexible, increase in brittleness after leaching
(xiii) Barium sulphate/alkali-refined linseed oil, 77.5% pigment, 22.5% dried oil, 90 μ thick, aged 3.3 yr at 20°C, 50% R.H., under ultraviolet light	Acetone	30	Unleached film very brittle and yellowed, disintegrated rapidly on solvent contact with dispersion of pigment particles

* The films, or film fragments, were immersed in acetone at 20°C for a period of 24 hours or more to permit leaching to take place. The percentage leaching figures given are calculated as loss in weight due to leaching in acetone based on the dried oil content of the starting film.

** The films were exposed to two Hanovia 200 watt quartz high pressure mercury lamps with vycor (Corning) heat-absorbing filters. The incident ultraviolet on the film surfaces was measured in the 200–400 millimicron region as 0.2 milliwatts per square centimeter. The ageing operation was carried out in a Hotpack Environmental Chamber designed for relative humidity and temperature control over an extended range, i.e., 5 to 40°C, and 0 to 95% R.H.

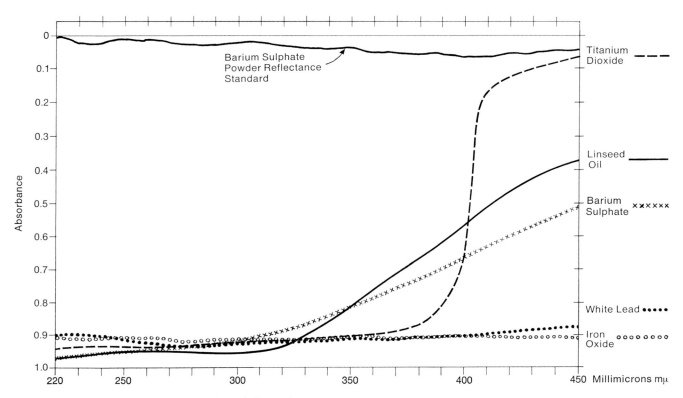

5. Ultraviolet reflectance measurements on linseed oil and pigmented films aged 500 days, 20° C, 50 % R. H. under ultraviolet.
Measurements 220—450 millimicrons by deuterium and tungsten lamp
sources employing the reflectance attachment to the Bausch and
Lomb Spectronic Spectrophotometer.

Table II

Gas chromatographic analysis of methyl esters from leachings of various linseed oil and pigmented films

Film description	Leaching[1] %	Non-ester[2] %	Methyl esters[3]		
			16:0+ 18:0 %	Dicarboxylics %	18:1, etc. %
A. Natural ageing in diffuse light; 20–25° C, 40–50% R.H.					
(i) White lead-alkali-refined linseed oil; 84.3% pigment, 15.7% dried oil; 120 μ thick, aged 330 days	26	12	4.8	4.0	5.0
(ii) Iron oxide-alkali-refined linseed oil; 80.5% pigment, 19.5% dried oil; 76 μ thick, aged 410 days	55	42	3.7	6.4	2.9
(iii) Alkali-refined linseed oil, no pigment; 35 μ thick, aged 340 days	65	46	4.5	9.5	5.0
(iv) White lead-alkali-refined linseed oil; 77% pigment, 23% dried oil; 100 μ thick, aged 14 yr	55	44	5.7	4.0	1.3
(v) White lead-stand oil; 81% pigment, 19% dried oil; 130 μ thick, aged 15 yr	26	20	3.3	1.6	0.9
B. Accelerated ageing[4] under ultraviolet light; 20° C, 50% R.H.					
(vi) Alkali-refined linseed oil, no pigment; 50 μ thick, aged 2.5 yr	27	18.5	3.0	4.0	1.5
(vii) Barium sulphate-alkali-refined linseed oil; 77.5% pigment, 22.5% dried oil; 100 μ thick, aged 2.5 yr	27	11	5.5	8.8	1.2
(viii) White lead-alkali-refined linseed oil; 84.7% pigment, 15.3% dried oil; 100 μ thick, aged 2.5 yr	26	8	5.5	11.0	1.3
(ix) Titanium dioxide(rutile)-alkali-refined linseed oil; 75% pigment, 25% dried oil; 100 μ thick, aged 2.5 yr	84	64	5.0	14.0	1.0
(x) Iron oxide (Fe_2O_3)-alkali-refined linseed oil; 85% pigment, 15% dried oil; 100 μ thick, aged 2.5 yr	85	56	6.0	21.0	2.0
C. Films from old paintings					
(xi) Iron oxide-linseed oil ground from 17th century Dutch painting; estimated 80% pigment, 20% dried oil content, aged 335 yr	–[5]	–	5	15	1
(xii) White lead-linseed oil fragment from same source as (xi)	–	–	7	10	–

[1] The films were leached in methanol and methylene chloride during the course of esterification. The loss in weight (leaching) is expressed as a percentage of the organic (dried oil) content of the starting film.

[2] The non-ester content refers to that portion of the leachings which is not esterifiable as methyl esters, expressed as percentage of the organic (dried oil) content of the starting film.

[3] The methyl esters were prepared by the boron trifluoride-methanol technique referred to in reference 1. The amounts of stearic (18:0), palmitic (16:0), dicarboxylic (2C5–2C9 etc.), and oleic (18:1) methyl esters are expressed again in terms of the organic (dried oil) content of the starting film.

[4] The same exposure conditions under ultraviolet light as noted in table I.

[5] The film fragments were too small to accurately assess the amount of leaching which took place.

$16:0+18:0$ is the more or less constant ratios of $16:0/(16:0+18:0)$ or $18:0/(16:0+18:0)$, which have values of 0.6 and 0.4 respectively. The films fragments tested from old paintings (section C of table II) give results consistent with the younger films in terms of the $(16:0+18:0)$ yield and the relatively high amount of dicarboxylic acids.

It was broadly suggested in the earlier Boston paper[1] that some dating scheme could be arrived at by plotting $2C9/(16:0+18:0)$ ratios for authenticated dated paintings — referring to a consistent choice of pigment. Considering the various factors which tend to alter the production of dicarboxylic acids, it would be premature to make any definite statements regarding dating of linseed oil paint films at this time. In carefully controlled experiments, such as described in figures 1—4, where the pigment, composition, and film thickness are precisely known, where the environmental conditions are fixed, it is possible to see the relationship between the increase in dicarboxylic acids and the time.

Gas Chromatography Applied to Cross-sections of Paintings

The technique of cross-sectioning samples of paint removed from paintings is a standard procedure in this laboratory. The layer structure and the composition of the individual layers is of great diagnostic value in assessing the manner of the artist's work and in correlating or comparing this to that of other artists or with other schools or periods. The emphasis has been almost exclusively on the identification of pigment particles — as to their chemical composition or morphological properties. However, the identification of the medium could perhaps be even more useful in "fingerprinting" the painting. The medium — if linseed oil — would mirror the chemical changes brought about by pigment interaction, environmental conditions, and its particular position in the paint stratigraphy. Paint films lower down would presumably exhibit different degradation processes, perhaps less oxidative breakdown than those layers exposed on the surface. The foregoing discussion indicates that surface exposure and film thickness were important factors in the build-up of such deterioration products as the dicarboxylic acids 2C5 to 2C9. In practice it is difficult to separate the individual layers in a cross-section except perhaps in a micro-manipulator, and then the layer fragments of the order of 0.05 mg or less would be rather too small for accurate quantitative examination of methyl esters. The normal size sample for successful quantitative gas chromatography is approximately 1 mg of pigmented film (containing therefore approximately 0.15—0.20 mg of organic medium). It would be more practical to select areas of the painting in question for which cross-sections have already been made and to scrape away a sufficient sample for gas chromatographic analysis. Con-

siderable thought had been given to the choice of locations for obtaining samples of paint which had been untouched by previous restorations, particularly those areas affected by leaching action in previous cleaning and related restoration processes of the past. It then occurred to us that sampling should be carried out from the back of the painting — boring carefully through successive layers, starting with the ground layer, and segregating the powdered scrapings. This operation, carried out under the binocular microscope, would also be guided by reference to polished sections of paint corresponding to the sampling area. The excavation should of course not penetrate to the front of the painting, but should stop at some intermediate layer, about 50 microns from the surface. The scrapings of paint so removed are likely to be unaltered chemically and physically except by the normal ageing factors peculiar to the painting's environmental history. It is assumed here that no extraneous materials of a penetrating nature, e.g., wax-resin compositions, are present in the region being sampled in the manner described.

This technique of "interior layer" sampling has been applied to the painting *Job* by Jan Lievens in the National Gallery of Canada.[5] This painting had already been sampled and studied by means of cross-sections, by X-ray diffraction, and the X-ray macroprobe.[6] The palette and working method of the artist were therefore already fairly well understood by us. It was now considered worthwhile to analyze the medium of the artist, present in the lower uncontaminated layers of the painting. The site that was chosen was the flesh color in Job's right foot. The cross-section structure for this area is illustrated in fig. 6. For greater clarity and definition of the layer structure, a photomicrograph made under ultraviolet fluorescence is included. Fig. 7 shows in schematic outline the excavating technique for progressive removal of the lower layers, starting with the ground. The hole made in this way is of the order of 1 to 2 mm in diameter or less, and can be readily filled in afterward. Actually three samples were removed from the lowermost layer — reddish-brown ground pigmented with iron oxide and quartz (A); a second grayish layer "ground" containing white lead, lead carbonate, quartz, and probably carbon (B); and a third layer consisting essentially of white lead and lead carbonate (C). The three samples were esterified with boron-trifluoride/methanol in the usual way and were run on the gas chromatograph. The chromatograms for the three layers are shown together in fig. 8. The analytical data are given in table III.

The analytical results show that medium in each layer is quite probably linseed oil, especially since the ratios for $16:0$ and $18:0$ are in the vicinity of 0.60 and 0.40 respectively. The values for the dicarboxylic acid methyl esters, 2C7, 2C8, and 2C9 do not fall in a particular order. They appear to be greatest in the intermediate layer (B). In other words, this layer appears

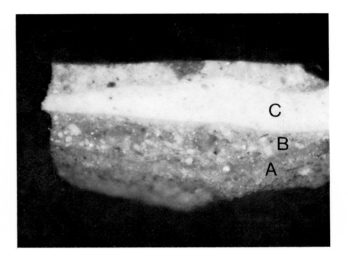

6. Cross-section study of Lievens *Job,* National Gallery of Canada (4093).

(a) The painting was sampled for cross-section and gas chromatographic study in the region of Job's right foot (flesh color).

(b) Cross-section (4093/x2) in ordinary incident light, 160x, of flesh color. The layers studied for gas chromatography (cf. fig. 8) are:

(A): reddish brown ground containing iron oxide, quartz, and dried linseed oil.

(B): a second grayish ground containing white lead, lead carbonate, quartz, carbon-like pigment, and dried linseed oil.

(C): a whitish layer containing white lead, lead carbonate, and dried linseed oil.

The upper layers are flesh tones, terminating in a varnish coating.

(c) Cross-section (4093/x2) in ultraviolet fluorescence incident light, 160x, of same flesh color. The layers A and B are clearly differentiated, and the flesh tones situated above layer C as well as the varnish coating are better defined. The total cross-section thickness is estimated at approximately 325 μ.

Sampling Technique at Back of Painting

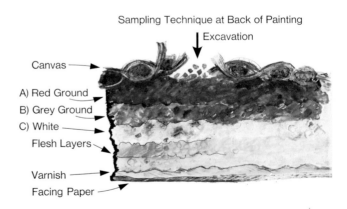

7. Excavation at back of painting to remove layers A, B, and C (reference to cross-section in fig. 6).

Table III

Gas chromatographic analysis of layer samples from *Job* by Lievens

Sample*	Weight, mg	10:0	2C4 or 12:0**	14:0	15:0	2C7	16:0	2C8	2C9	18:0
A (E-176)	10.28	0.55	0.25	0.10	0.06	0.20	0.66	0.67	1.23	0.34
B (E-178)	4.06	0.35	0.37	0.09	0.06	0.14	0.64	0.60	1.67	0.36
C (E-177)	22.71	0.07	0.07	0.02	0.02	0.06	0.61	0.30	0.98	0.39

Ratios to (16:0 + 18:0)

* The samples A, B, C, are from the layers identified as such in fig. 6.
A: reddish brown (ochre) ground containing mainly iron oxide, and quartz, and dried soil.
B: grayish layer, upper ground containing mainly white lead, lead carbonate, quartz, some carbon-like material, and dried oil.
C: whitish layer containing mainly white lead, lead carbonate, and a small amount of organic red pigment, and dried oil.

** It is not certain whether the two peaks superimposed here are 2C4 or 12:0.

to be more deteriorated than A or C. Nevertheless, this kind of gas chromatographic study is valuable from the point of view of establishing analytical data for paint layers in an authenticated and well-documented work of art. It should be evident too that investigations of media would have to take into account location and layer structure of the particular painting; also, assurances would have to be given that the material being studied has not been exposed to restoration processes in the past.

The Technique of Pyrolysis Gas Chromatography

The term pyrolysis may be defined as the transformation of a compound or composite substance into other substances through the agency of heat alone. In the literature on pyrolysis gas chromatography this term has come to mean the thermal breakdown or decomposition of the larger molecular weight substance into smaller components. Zemany[7] was probably the originator of the use of pyrolysis combined with an instrumental analytical technique — in his case the mass spectrometry of pyrolysis products of synthetic rubbers, vinyl polymers, and oil alkyds. Davison, Slaney, and Wragg[8] were the first to apply gas chromatography as an instrumental method for the analysis of pyrolyzates. Since the middle 1950s there has been a progressive and rapid development in the technique of analyzing pyrolyzed substances by the gas chromatograph. The principal applications have been in the identification and study of polymeric and complex organic substances, which lend themselves quite readily to this approach. Thus to cite a few researchers, Ettre and Varadi[9,10] examined the breakdown products of nitrocellulose, poly

n-butyl methacrylate, and polyvinyl alcohol, and the effect of varying the pyrolysis temperature between 300° and 950° C; Cox and Ellis[11] studied the pyrolytic behavior of some 39 polymers, including nylons, polyesters, cellulose acetates, and polyethylenes; Takeuchi, Tsuge, and Okumoto[12] investigated and identified the products of pyrolysis of a variety of urethane foams. There have been comparatively few publications relating to paints and paint products; those published are generally oriented to industrial or forensic problems. Sadowski and Kühn[13] have recorded the pyrograms for a variety of commercial paint vehicles such as urethanes, acrylic resins, linseed oil alkyds, and epoxide resins, and have attempted to identify unknown vehicles by examining characteristic peaks. Cianetti and Grottini[14] have studied the pyrolysis of some 37 natural resins and related products, including some which are of potential interest to the field of fine art, e.g., dragon's blood resin, amber, dammar, mastic, copal, kavri, sanderac, shellac, gum arabic, and colophony. Another publication concerning pyrolysis gas chromatography of paint vehicles is that by Jain, Fontan, and Kirk.[15] These authors examined thirty-four surface coatings, three plastics, and four drying oils. Differences in the pyrograms were established for paint samples containing drying oils, synthetic emulsions (based on polyvinyl acetate), and spirit-type varnishes or lacquers. The results obtained could be applied in forensic investigations, such as in hit-and-run accidents, where the rapid analysis and identification of a trace of paint could produce useful legal evidence. Levy[16] has given an excellent survey of the instrumental side of pyrolysis gas chromatography, describing in detail the various kinds of pyrolysis devices, samplers, and columns, and critically discusses the merits and disadvantages of the various techniques. Brauer[17] in a somewhat different survey details the methods of application to a wide variety of substances and classes of materials, some of which have already been referred to earlier.

The pyrolysis device used in this laboratory is the commercially available pyrolysis attachment for the Perkin-Elmer Gas Chromatograph, which is shown in schematic outline in fig. 9. The principle of operation is based on the rapid insertion of a small sample into a heated area (furnace) under conditions of continuous gas flow to a gas chromatographic column and detector.[10] The kind of samples encountered in our work, small fragments of paint and similar materials, did not permit the use of a flash type of pyrolyzer. As can be seen in the schematic diagram, the experimental set-up is composed of a forked Pyrex tube, which is joined by graded seals to a quartz tube surrounded by a resistance wire wound furnace. The entrance to the loading tube has a screw-on cap with gasket, while the other entry port has a long metal rod fitted through the screw-on cap which functions as a moving device

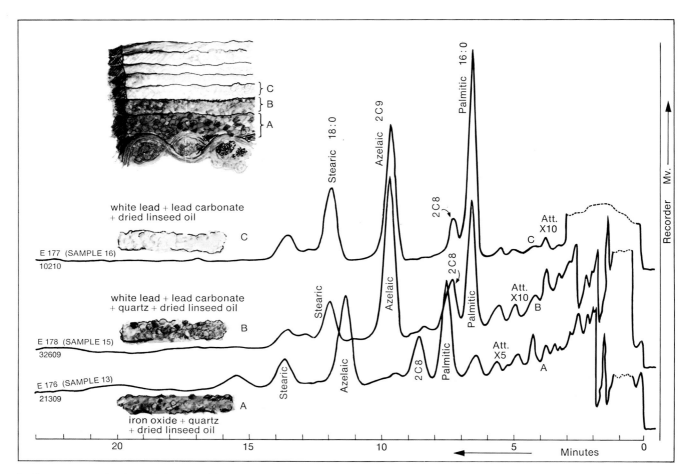

8. Chromatograms for the methyl esters of three layers of paint from Lievens *Job* (National Gallery of Canada, 4093). Samples A, B, C respectively, 10.28, 4.06, 22.71 mg. Column conditions: 2 of $^1/_8$" x 8'. EGSS-X (16 %) on Gas Chrom P-AW/DMCS; 175° C, N_2 = 36, air = 50, H_2 = 20 p.s.i.g. Perkin-Elmer 800 gas chromatograph. F.I.D. detector.

for the porcelain boat sample holder. Beyond the furnace is a fourway gas sampling valve which serves the purpose of distributing the pyrolysis components in the carrier gas flow to the inlet of the chromatographic column. The furnace unit itself has a variable control transformer for controlling the current to the electrical resistance coil, and the furnace temperature sensed by a thermocouple is read directly from a dial in degrees centigrade. The method of operation is as follows. A small porcelain boat (Coors 5/0, 0.5 grams, 17 x 6 x 4 mm) containing the weighed sample (1 mg or less) is placed into the loading tube followed by a small nickel rod; the loading operation is carried out with the sampling valve turned to shunt the carrier gas directly to the gas chromatograph. It is possible to load up a number of porcelain sample boats and nickel rods

in sequence in the loading tube before sealing with the screw-on cap. Now the gas sampling valve (which is heated to some extent by its close proximity to the furnace) is turned to allow the carrier gas to flow through the apparatus and the heated region of the quartz tube in the furnace. The first porcelain boat is moved by means of the external magnet (which pushes on the nickel rod) to an advance "ready" position in the cool region before the furnace. The nickel rod is dropped out of this location through a vertically mounted tube (not shown), again with the aid of the magnet. At this point the metal rod "boat handler" can be used for accurate placement of the porcelain boat into the desired region of the furnace tube. The furnace has been set to the required temperature, say 800° C, and has been on sufficiently long to reach a steady state. The chroma-

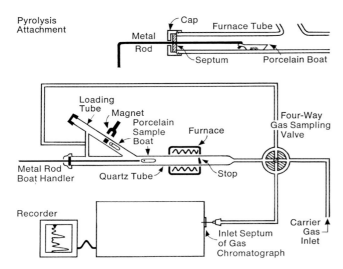

9. Outline of pyrolysis attachment used in pyrolysis-gas chromatography. Detail of method of pushing boat into furnace area shown at top. The apparatus is essentially that of Perkin-Elmer with some modifications by us.

tographic recorder (Leeds and Northrop Speedomax G, 5 mV full scale) is now observed until the base-line has become stabilized, at which time the boat is quickly pushed (1—2 seconds) into the furnace area against the stop built into the quartz tube. The rod is drawn back. The organic products formed by the rapid (5—10 seconds) thermal decomposition of the sample are quickly swept by the carrier gas through the gas sampling valve and into the inlet septum of the gas chromatograph, and subsequently analyzed.

There are a number of parameters which affect the results of a pyrolysis experiment carried out in this way. The extent and nature of the pyrolysis fragments of a given weight of starting substance (e.g., polymer) are determined largely by its initial chemical composition, pyrolysis temperature and its duration, and the speed of removal of the fragments from the thermal zone by flushing action of the carrier gas. The latter is of some consideration if there is the possibility of secondary combination reactions between the fragments. The efficiency of the gas chromatograph in analyzing these pyrolytic fragments rests primarily on the choice of a suitable and specific column packing material, an optimum carrier gas flow rate (and column temperature). Our studies of the pyrolysis of pigmented and unpigmented samples show incomplete combustion at temperatures below 600° C, and by selecting an operating temperature of around 800° C we have arrived at the separation on the gas chromatograph of a number of peaks of appreciable yield. Too low a temperature would produce many fragments of low yield — not too useful for comparison "fingerprint" studies. The pyrolysis studies described below have

been carried out under the following gas flow and column conditions: nitrogen gas at 30 p.s.i.g. and 30 ml/min; hydrogen gas 19 p.s.i.g.; and air at 45 p.s.i.g. for flame ionization detector; column temperature 20° C; column material 10 % UC-W98 (a methyl vinyl silicone gum) on 80/100 mesh chromosorb W acid washed and treated with dimethyl chlorosilane (AW-DMCS). The column was 8 feet long by $1/8$ inch outer diameter stainless steel in coil form. The column temperature was kept at 20° C (isothermal operation), as it was found that the pyrogram peaks were better separated at reduced temperatures.

Results on Paint Films and Various Materials

In fig.10 are shown the pyrograms of a 50-year-old fragment of white lead-linseed oil paint obtained from an artist's palette, and also a sample of white lead-linseed oil paint from a 17th century Dutch painting. It is seen that the number of peaks and their appearance on the time scale are almost identical. Two major peaks marked X and Y are noted for later fingerprinting studies. In fig.11 are shown pyrograms plotted together for three diverse artistic media, linseed oil mastic resin, and egg yolk. Here there appear differences in the numbers of peaks, their relative magnitude (peak height), and their retention times on the column. A convenient method of comparing pyrograms of substances pyrolyzed under identical conditions is to plot the peak heights (noting at the same time attenuations of the vertical scale) against either retention times or relative retention times. The latter is convenient to use when substances within the same chemical class are being considered. Fig.12 has been plotted in this manner and includes three samples of pigmented oil paint and a sample of fresh linseed oil. The relative retention times are based on the time of appearance of a major peak at 17.8 minutes (e.g., Y of fig.10). It is seen that the four pyrograms are nearly identical in peak height pattern and the locations of the peak on the time scale. In the oil sample D, a minor peak is absent at relative retention time 1.63, approximately. The presence of inorganic pigment in samples A, B, and C does not appear to affect the pyrogram, since the pigment does not contribute any appreciable volatile material. The pigments do undergo physical and chemical changes upon heating to the region of 800° C in a nitrogen atmosphere. Thus white lead converts to lead nitride, and some free lead, while red iron oxide, present initially as FeOOH or Fe_2O_3, converts to the black Fe_3O_4. Jain, Fontan, and Kirk[15] have noted in their work on paint vehicles that the pigments had little effect on the quality of the pyrogram. In fig.13 are given the results for a variety of unpigmented films with linseed oil included for comparison. It can be seen that dammar has two peaks at 5 minutes which are missing in the others, that linseed oil has characteristic peaks, e.g., at 2.5, 28, 42.5 minutes. There are also certain differences detectable between

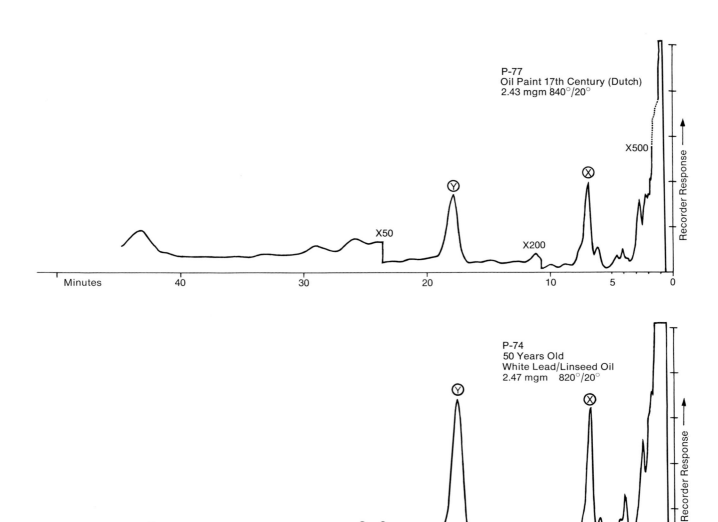

10. Pyrograms for two old white oil paint samples. Upper graph, white lead-linseed oil fragment from Dutch 17th century painting; in lower graph sample of white lead-linseed oil from an artist's palette ca. 1920. Pyrolysis 820–840° C; column conditions — 1 of $^1/_8''$ x 8'; 10 % UC-W98 (a methyl vinyl silicone gum) on 80/100 mesh chromosorb W-AW/DMCS; 20° C, N_2 = 30, air = 45, H_2 = 19 p.s.i.g. Perkin-Elmer 800 gas chromatograph. F.I.D. detector.

gelatin, egg yolk, and egg white. Gelatin has a double peak in the region of 17 to 18 minutes. There are also sufficient differences between gelatin and gum arabic, the latter having peaks at 36 and 48 minutes. Further comparisons are made in the presentation of the results in fig.14. Again these are unpigmented films of mastic, dammar, and various linseed oil samples. Comparison of mastic and dammar shows that there are small but significant differences in the peak pattern in the region of 2 to 5 minutes, as well in the region of 40 to 60 minutes; again the linseed and stand oil films form a consistent group.

The pyrolysis technique was also applied to identify and compare small samples of paint taken from a painting by Rembrandt dated approximately 1650. The samples were weighed and analyzed directly in the usual manner. The pyrograms for the three kinds of paint are given in fig.15. It is seen that the peaks and their retention times are almost identical and correspond very closely to the peak patterns for authenticated linseed oil samples. Again the pigmentation had no noticeable effect on the pyrolysis. The white paint was essentially white lead, the red, white lead with vermilion, and the black, essentially carbon pigment.

An attempt was made to detect any possible relationships between peak heights within the linseed oil pyrograms. Two peaks were selected for special consideration, marked X and Y, consistently appearing at 7.0 and 17.8 minutes respectively according to the given pyrolysis and column conditions. It was assumed that these peaks are consistent chemical species and their yield could be assessed in some way. The data in table IV are an attempt to establish peak height-yield relationships in some rough quantitative fashion. The column X/Y refers to the ratio of peak heights for the two peaks studied, and the ratio in the last column refers to the peak height of component X as a fraction of the pyrolyzable material of the starting film fragment (or oil sample in some cases), corrected for attenuation. The figures in the last column may be regarded as yield factors for peak X in arbitrary units. The results for X/Y show that the ratios are almost all within the range 3–4.5 for linseed oil type films, including the unsaturated triglycerides, but somewhat higher, at 5–6, for the saturated triglycerides, triolein, and olive oil (largely saturated triglycerides and oleic type triglycerides). There are significant differences, however, in the figures of the last column. The fresh oil films and the fresh triglycerides give high values in the range 12–22, with the exception of tripalmitin, which has a value of 8. The corresponding yield ratios for peak X for the pigmented aged films fall fairly well in the range of 2 to 7.5 units. The peaks X and Y appear to bear some relationship to the age or degree of deterioration of the film. This merits further investigation with many more samples.

Table IV

Assessment of selected peak heights in linseed oil film pyrograms*

Film sample	Weight, mg	X/Y	$\left[\dfrac{X \cdot \text{attenuation}}{\text{wt. organic}}\right] \cdot 10^{-3}$**
Tripalmitin	1.15	6	8
Tristearin	1.33	6	12
Triolein	0.99	5	17
Trilinolein	0.84	4	21
Trilinolenin	0.93	3	22
Fresh linseed oil	0.57	4.5	20
Olive oil	0.90	5	16
White lead/linseed oil stored under nitrogen	6.89	3	6
White lead/linseed oil naturally aged 4.5 yr	5.12	4	4
Iron oxide/linseed oil naturally aged 4.5 yr	4.85	4.5	7.5
Titanium dioxide/linseed oil naturally aged 4.5 yr	2.27	4.5	4
White lead/linseed oil U.V. exposed 4.5 yr	0.45	4.2	3.5
White lead/linseed oil Dutch 19th cent. painting	2.68	3.5	6.5
White lead/linseed oil 50 yr old (palette)	2.54	4.4	3
White lead/linseed oil Dutch 17th cent. painting	0.45	4.0	2
Linseed oil naturally aged 35 yr	1.22	4.4	4

* The usual conditions of pyrolysis, i.e., approximately 800° C furnace temperature and 20° C column.

** The ratio is made out by multiplying the peak height in millivolts, after correcting for base-line, times the attenuation, divided by the estimated organic content of the starting film. If the film is unpigmented the full weight of the film (second column) applies.

Conclusions

The results described above clearly indicate the usefulness of the technique of gas chromatography — as well as the modification of the technique in pyrolysis gas chromatography — to the study of the media of works of art. Not only can contributions be made to the study of ageing and deterioration phenomena in such films but also class differentiations can be made. The work undertaken here in pyrolysis gas chromatography can be developed much further. At the present time our approach is that of using the pyrograms as "fingerprints" of the medium in question. The need is now to identify the pyrolysis fragments and establish more clearly the chemical differences in the peaks shown in figs.11–14. The possibility for

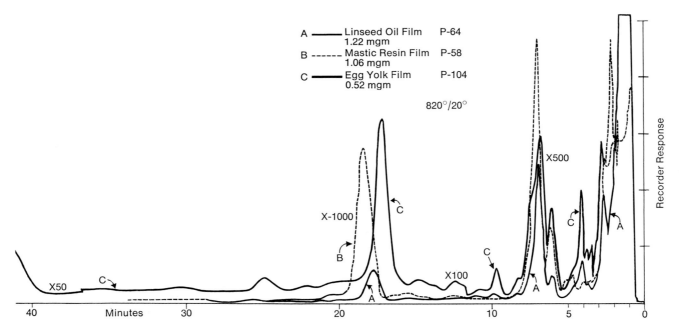

11. Pyrograms for linseed oil, mastic resin, egg yolk films.
A — linseed oil, 33 years aged normal conditions, diffuse light, approximately 50 μ thick.
B — mastic resin, 33 years aged as film in corked test tube, approximately 100 μ thick.

C — egg yolk, freshly prepared, aged 1 week 20° C, normal conditions, diffuse light, approximately 70 μ thick.
Pyrolysis and column conditions as in fig.10.

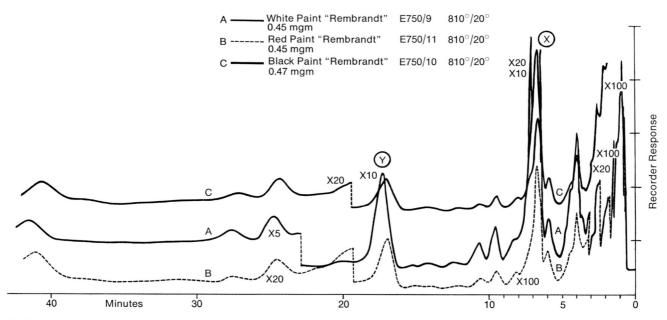

15. Pyrograms for three pigmented samples from Rembrandt painting ca. 1650. Pyrolysis and column conditions as in fig. 10.

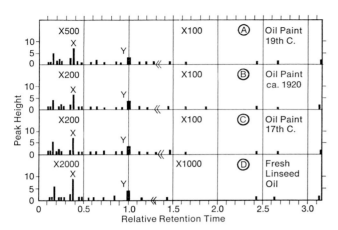

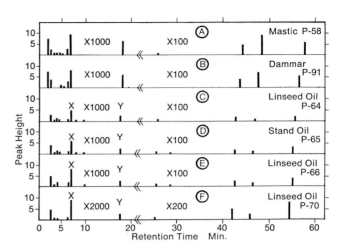

12. Reduced form pyrograms for various linseed oil paint samples —
peak heights versus relative retention times.
A — fragment of white lead-linseed oil from Dutch 19th century painting 2.68 mg.
B — fragment of white lead/linseed oil from artist's palette ca. 1920.
2.47 mg.
C — fragment of white lead/linseed oil from Dutch 17th century painting. 2.33 mg.
D — sample of fresh alkali-refined linseed oil, 1.00 mg.
All the peaks appearing on pyrograms are represented. Relative
retention times are with reference to peak Y, appearing very closely
to 17.8 minutes. Pyrolysis and column conditions as in fig.10.

14. Reduced from pyrograms for various unpigmented media — peak
heights versus retention times in minutes.
A — mastic resin, 33 years aged as film, in corked test tube, approxi-
mately 100 μ thick, 1.06 mg.
B — dammar, Singapore, lumps, 0.67 mg.
C — linseed oil, 33 years aged normal conditions, diffuse light, ap-
proximately 50 μ thick, 1.22 mg.
D — stand oil, 33 years aged normal conditions, diffuse light, approxi-
mately 50 μ thick, 1.02 mg.
E — linseed oil, 5 years aged normal conditions, diffuse light, ap-
proximately 35 μ thick, 1.18 mg.
F — sample of fresh alkali-refined linseed oil, 1.06 mg.
All peaks represented — pyrolysis and column conditions as in fig.10.

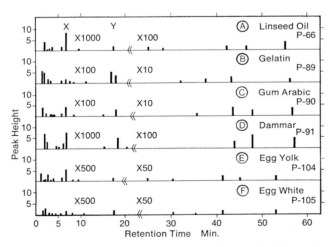

13. Reduced form pyrograms for various unpigmented media — peak
heights versus retention times in minutes.
A — linseed oil, 5 years aged normal conditions, approximately 35 μ,
1.18 mg.
B — gelatin, 0.38 mg.
C — gum arabic, 0.39 mg.
D — dammar, Singapore, lumps, 0.67 mg.
E — egg yolk, freshly prepared, aged 1 week 20° C, normal condi-
tions, diffuse light, approximately 70 μ thick, 0.52 mg.
F — egg white, as above, 0.65 mg.
All peaks represented — pyrolysis and column conditions as in fig.10.

doing so exists, fairly simple procedures having been described by Walsh and Merritt[18] and by Casu and Cavallotti[19] for identifying by chemical means the column effluents. Certainly the pyrolysis technique is very attractive from the experimental point of view in that small particles can be analyzed without preliminary chemical treatment and they produce a distinguishing pattern in a short period of time.

Acknowledgments

We should like to acknowledge the support and encouragement given in this research by the Director of the National Gallery of Canada, Miss Jean Sutherland Boggs; and to the following colleagues of this laboratory for advice or assistance: Dr. J. F. Hanlan for certain modifications to the pyrolysis accessory, to Mr. U. Dix for sampling of the painting *Job* by Lievens, and to Mr. J. MacG. Grant for the preparation and photomicrography of the cross-sections.

References and Notes

1. Stolow, N. "The Application of Gas Chromatography in the Investigation of Works of Art," Seminar on Application of Science in Examination of Works of Art, Boston, September 7–16, 1965, Boston, Museum of Fine Arts, pp.172–183.

2. The paint films were aged under strong ultraviolet illumination in a Hotpack environmental chamber kept at 20° C and 50 % R. H., at a distance approximately 20 inches away from the lamps. There were two high intensity quartz Hanovia 645 A, 200 watt mercury vapor lamps positioned above the sample plane at approximately 45° so as to give a fairly even illumination. The only filtration was by means of vycor heat-absorbing filters, generally transparent to the ultraviolet range 200–400 millimicrons. The strong mercury lines are at 366, 313, and 302 millimicrons. The incident illumination was measured in the ultraviolet range by a photometer with ultraviolet sensing head with appropriate filter absorbing the visible spectrum but transmitting the ultraviolet (Photovolt Electronic Photometer Model 501-M with sensor "B" responsive 200–600 millimicrons, Photovolt Corporation). The total spectral energy incident on the samples was also measured with the YSI-Kettering Radiometer Model 65 reading directly in energy units per square centimeter. Calculations showed that the light energy was divided approximately as 38 % ultraviolet, 44 % visible, and 18 % infrared – the ultraviolet portion (200–400 millimicrons) producing an incident illumination somewhat higher than 0.2 milliwatts per centimeter square. For samples immediately under the lamps the illumination in this range was about three times as high.

3. The ultraviolet reflectance was measured with the Bausch and Lomb Spectronic 505 spectrophotometer equipped with reflection attachment. By a special switchover device incorporating a deuterium and a tungsten lamp, it was possible to cover the range 220–450 millimicrons. A reference white standard of barium sulphate compressed into a flat block was run at the same time as the paint samples (see fig. 5).

4. Stutz, G. F. A. "Observations of Spectrophotometric Measurements of Paint Vehicles and Pigments," *J. Franklin Inst.* 200 (1926), 87–102.

5. National Gallery of Canada, 4093. Oil on canvas, 171.5 x 148.5 cm, given complete conservation treatment by Ursus Dix of this laboratory in 1968–69. The painting is signed IL 1631 on the middle right side.

6. Stolow, N., Hanlan, J. F., and Boyer, R. "Element Distribution in Cross-sections of Paintings Studied by the X-ray Macroprobe," *Studies in Conservation* 14 (1969), 139–151.

7. Zemany, P. D. "Identification of Complex Organic Materials by Mass Spectrometric Analysis of Their Pyrolysis Products," *Anal. Chem.* 24 (1952), 1709–1713.

8. Davison, W. H. T., Slaney, S., and Wragg, A. L. "Novel Method of Identification of Polymers," *Chem. and Ind.* 1954, no. 44, pp.1356–1357.

9. Ettre, Kitty, and Varadi, P. F. "Pyrolysis-Gas Chromatography Technique for Direct Analysis of Thermal Degradation Products of Polymers," *Anal. Chem.* 34 (1962), 752–775.

10. Ettre, Kitty, and Varadi, P. E. "Pyrolysis-Gas Chromatographic Technique – Effect of Temperature on Thermal Degradation of Polymers," *Anal. Chem.* 35 (1963) 69–73.

11. Cox, B. C., and Ellis, B. "A Micro-reactor – Gas Chromatographic Method for the Identification of Polymeric Materials," *Anal. Chem.* 36 (1964), 90–96.

12. Takeuchi, T., Tsuge, S., and Okumoto, T. "Identification and Analysis of Urethane Foams by Pyrolysis-Gas Chromatography," *J. Gas Chrom.* 6 (1968), 542–547.

13. Sadowski, F., and Kühn, Eva, "Gaschromatographische Untersuchung der Pyrolyseprodukte von Lackbindemitteln" (Gas Chromatography of Pyrolyzates of Paint Vehicles), *Farbe und Lack* 69 (1963), 267–274.

14. Cianetti, E., and Grottini, Anna, "La Gascromatografia dei Pirolizzati nel Riconoscimento delle Resine Naturali" – (Gas Chromatographic Examination of Pyrolyzates of Natural Resins), *Rassegna Chimica* no. 4 (July-August 1966), 166–181.

15. Jain, N. C., Fontan, C. R., and Kirk, P. L. "Identification of Paints by Pyrolysis-Gas Chromatography," *J. Forensic Science Society* 5 (1965), 102–109.

16. Levy, R. L. "Pyrolysis-Gas Chromatography – A Review of the Technique," *Chromatographic Reviews* 8 (1966), 48–89.

17. Brauer, G. M. "Pyrolytic Techniques," *J. Polymer Science* no. 8 (1965), 3–26.

18. Walsch, J. T., and Merritt, C. "Qualitative Functional Group Analysis of Gas Chromatographic Effluents," *Anal. Chem.* 32 (1960), 1378–1381.

19. Casu, B., and Cavallotti, L. "A Simple Device for Qualitative Functional Group Analysis of Gas Chromatographic Effluents," *Anal. Chem.* 34 (1962), 1514–1516.

KAZUO YAMASAKI

Recent Technical Studies of Works of Art in Japan

The Mural Painting of the Horyuji Temple, and Some Chinese and Japanese Glasses with High Lead and Barium Content

This paper consists of two parts, one on the mural painting of the Horyuji temple and the reproduction on paper which was undertaken recently, and the other on the Chinese and Japanese glasses with high lead and barium content which were studied by the fission track method.

The Mural Painting of the Horyuji Temple

There are about seventy mural paintings of the various periods now extant in Japan, mostly in Buddhist temples.[1] All of them are painted on wooden panels or doors except three: a mud wall painting of the Horyuji temple and two others on walls of lime plaster. The latter two are the painting of the Hokaiji temple, Kyoto, and that of the Hokuendo, Kofukuji temple, Nara, both of which are supposed to have been painted in the late 12th century.

The Horyuji temple in Nara is well known as a typical Japanese Buddhist temple, and it has numerous magnificent relics of the 7th and 8th centuries, among which the most famous was the mural painting of the Golden Hall. This painting consists of four large (310 x 260 cm) and eight small (310 x 160 cm) units. Each of the large walls represents a paradise of Buddha and the small wall a figure of Bodhisattva. These walls were situated in the outer sanctuary of the Golden Hall to surround the Buddhist statues placed in the center of the hall (figs. 1 and 2). Besides the main mural painting there were near the ceiling of the inner sanctuary twenty small walls on which were painted flying Buddhist figures (fig. 3). The latter painting was not so famous as the former, and they have never been studied extensively. Both mural paintings are supposed to have been painted sometime between the late seventh and early eighth century.[2]

Since the Golden Hall, one of the oldest wooden buildings in the world, showed signs of decrepitude, it was decided to repair it as a part of the repair project of the Horyuji temple which started in 1934. The actual repair of the Golden Hall began in 1940 at the last stage of the whole project. Before the hall was dismantled the murals had to be removed together with the walls of the hall. As it was feared that removal of the walls might cause damage to the painting on them, copying of the painting started in 1940. The copying work, however, made only little progress owing to various difficulties during and after the world war, and was not finished even after ten years. Consequently the repair work of the Golden Hall was also suspended, and the building was dismantled only halfway. Under these conditions a fire broke out in the Golden Hall in 1949 and the main mural painting suffered great damage and lost nearly all the colors. Fortunately the small mural paintings of flying angels in the inner sanctuary had been removed during the first stage of the repair work, and they have escaped the fire. The damaged main walls with the

1. Inside view of the Golden Hall of the Horyuji temple before the repair. The murals of the inner and outer sanctuaries are marked with x and o. (Reproduced from the report of the repair works of the Horyuji temple, 1956.)

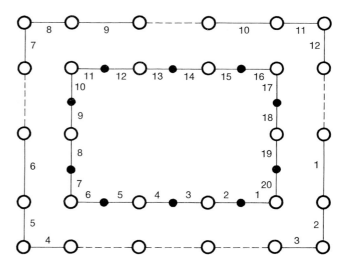

2. Wall numbers of the inner and outer sanctuaries of the Golden Hall.

3. The painting representing two flying angels on wall no.16 in the inner sanctuary. The shape of the scarf's end marked with *x* is different for walls nos. 5, 6, 7, 9, 10 and 11 from others. (Reproduced from the report of the repair works of the Horyuji temple 1956.)

painting were reinforced by synthetic resins and are now kept in a storehouse.

The Golden Hall itself was reconstructed in 1954 after the fire, but the new walls were plain white without any painting. In 1967 a plan to reproduce the lost mural painting materialized, and on this occasion the small mural paintings of flying angels were again studied. The results of studies carried out in collaboration with T. Yanagisawa of the Tokyo National Research Institute of Cultural Properties are presented in the following section.

Small Mural Paintings Representing Flying Angels

The small wall is about 75 cm x 140 cm and about 15 cm thick and is made of a mixture of mud and sand with bits of straw as a binder. The surface of the wall is coated with a thin layer of white clay[3] upon which are painted the flying angels with mineral pigments (fig. 4). The structure of the small wall is essentially the same as the damaged main walls in the outer

4. Details of the painting on wall no.16.

sanctuary. Each of these twenty small walls represents two flying angels which are almost identical in shape and size. The walls nos. 14, 15, 16, and 17 in the northeast corner of the Golden Hall have relatively well preserved colors. In some walls, for example, no. 7, concave lines are found on the wall surface along the outlines of the right-hand side angel (fig. 5), and this may indicate the use of a stencil for drawing outlines. Some hard pointed tools might have been used to press the stencil to the wall surface and copy the original drawing. This may provide a guide to the identity of the figures of twenty walls. The detailed part, however, seems to have done by free-hand drawing, for example, the shape of a scarf is different for

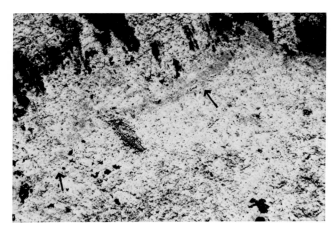

5. Concave lines on the face of the left angel of wall no. 7. Between hair and the forehead two concave lines marked with arrows are present.

6. Fingers of the right hand of the right angel of the wall no. 15. Enlarged.

several walls. Thus the end of a scarf of the left-hand side angel (marked with x in fig. 3) makes a circle in walls nos. 5, 6, 7, 9, 10 and 11, while it does not appear in the other walls. The pigments used in these small mural paintings were found almost the same as those of the damaged main mural paintings, as shown in table I, which I examined during the period 1940—1952.[4] Since the figures painted are simpler than those of the main mural painting, the numbers of pigments used are smaller. Although animal glue must have been generally used as an adhesive of pigments in the eighth century and there is documentary evidence that it was, it is difficult to prove its use in the walls now.

Table I

Pigments Used in the Mural Paintings of Japan

Horyuji temple (late 7th c.—early 8th c.)		Sliding doors (17th century)	Horyuji mural painting reproduced (20th century)
Main mural painting in the outer sanctuary	Small walls with flying angels in the inner sanctuary		
clay	clay	calcium carbonate	calcium carbonate
cinnabar	cinnabar	cinnabar	cinnabar
red ochre	red ochre	red ochre	red ochre
red lead	red lead	red lead	red lead
yellow ochre	yellow ochre	yellow ochre	yellow ochre
litharge	—	—	—
malachite	malachite	malachite	malachite
azurite	?	azurite	azurite
Chinese ink	Chinese ink	Chinese ink	Chinese ink

Reproduction of the Main Mural Painting of the Golden Hall

As described above the Golden Hall had only white walls without any painting after the reconstruction, and twenty years passed before a concrete plan materialized. The project[5] was undertaken in 1964 by the Asahi Shimbun (The newspaper *Asahi*) in collaboration with the Horyuji temple. After surmounting numerous difficulties the actual work of reproduction was started in March 1968 by fourteen of the best artists. Expenses were met by the contributions of the Horyuji temple, and the Asahi Shimbun and donations from the public, including commercial firms and the individuals. The emperor also made a contribution.

It was decided after much discussion to reproduce the paintings on paper as they had been just before the fire in 1949 and also that the whole process of reproduction should be limited to one year, from March 1967 to February 1968. As for the paper to be used a special hand-made paper was prepared from a Japanese plant, Kozo (Broussonetia Kazinoki Sieb.) in the Iwano paper mill, Fukui prefecture. To increase durability of the paper no bleaching agent was used in the preparation. The collotype plates were made from the life-sized photographs taken in 1935 by the Benrido Company, Kyoto, and the Buddhist figures were printed in black and white on the specially made paper. As the size of the walls was 310 x 260 cm for the larger and 310 x 160 cm for the smaller, paper large enough to cover the area could not be conveniently handled. Therefore the painting for a large wall was printed on 42 to 44 separate sheets of paper and for a small wall on 25 sheets. As the reproduction work progressed, separate sheets were pasted together successively until they finally made up the full size of each wall.

In making the reproduction, a thick ground coating of calcium carbonate was first made on paper and on this various kinds of pigments were applied along the outlines of the figures visible through the ground. The pigments used were prepared by the Ishida Hokodo Company, which had made the pigments used for the copying work in 1940–1949. The previously used pigments had been prepared on the basis of information obtained by examination of the original mural painting (table I). As is clear from table I, calcium carbonate is now used as the ground coating and also as the white pigment instead of the clay used in the original mural. This change in kinds of pigment with the historical period was first noticed by me. Replacement of clay by calcium carbonate seems to have taken place sometime in the period from the fourteenth to the fifteenth century. In and after the 16th century the palette of painters has been almost the same as that of modern painters.[6]

Fourtunately the work of reproduction proceeded according to schedule and was completed in February 1968. The reproductions made on paper were pasted on the specially made wooden panels 2.8 cm thick, and then these panels were placed just in front of the white walls of the Golden Hall and fixed. In addition to the reproduction of the main mural, that of the small mural representing flying angels has also been undertaken.

During the period of reproduction, May 1967–July 1968, the Tokyo National Research Institute of Cultural Properties studied the effects of light, temperature, humidity, dust, etc., in the Golden Hall on a test panel on which paper and pigments to be used for the reproduction were applied. A report[7] has been published where it was emphasized that the reproduced painting should be preserved with utmost care.

Some Chinese and Japanese Glasses with High Lead and Barium Content

In 1934 Beck and Seligman[8] first found high lead and barium contents in some Chinese glasses of pre-Han or Han period. Further Seligman, Beck, and Ritchie[9] published the results of semiquantitative spectrochemical analysis of more than 50 glasses of the same period, and barium was found together with lead in more than 20 specimens. They concluded that the ornamental glass of the pre-Han or Han period was for the most part a lead glass that also contained barium as a major component. In the glasses attributed to the periods following the Han period in no case was barium detected in more than a trace, and only glasses of soda-lime silicate or lead silicate were found. Since that time there has been no report on the discovery and chemical analysis of a barium-containing lead glass in countries outside China.

Specimens

In recent years archaeological investigations have been carried out on the sites of the Yayoi period (ca. 3rd century B.C.—3rd century A.D.) in Fukuoka prefecture, northern Kyushu, and in some tombs glass beads have been found together with other relics.[10] The glass bead reported here is one of them and is the first example of the high lead-barium glass ever found in Japan. This cylindrical glass bead was excavated from a tomb at Sugu-Okamoto, Fukuoka prefecture, the age of the tomb having been dated from about the first century B.C. from archaeological evidence. As more information was desired on the age of the bead itself, it and related Chinese and Japanese glasses were subjected to study by the fission track method in collaboration with M. Shima.[11] The details of the specimens which were analyzed earlier[12] are described in table II.

The Fission Track Method

In the fission track method initiated by Fleischer, Price, and Walker[13] the fission tracks formed by uranium in such specimens as minerals and glasses are counted. The numbers of tracks formed by the spontaneous fission of ^{238}U over a long period of time are counted under a microscope. The counting is made of the conical pits which were displayed after etching the surface of the specimen by appropriate chemicals. In the case of glasses hydrofluroric acid is generally used. Then the same specimen is put in a nuclear reactor and the numbers of tracks formed by the neutron-induced fission of ^{235}U are counted. From the data of these two countings the uranium content and also the age of the specimen are calculated on appropriate assumptions.

Table II

Japanese and Chinese Glasses Studied in the Present Investigation

No.	Glass
1	Fragment of a green cylindrical glass bead with a bore. The length, inner, and outer diameters are 23, 1.5, and 5 mm respectively. Lead-barium glass. The corrosion product was found by x-ray diffraction to be lead phosphate (ref. 12). Excavated from a tomb at Sugu-Okamoto, Fukuoka prefecture (ref. 10).
2	Fragment of a green Chinese ritual disc, pi. The date seems to be the Warring States period. The corrosion product was found to be a mixture of lead carbonate and sulfate (ref.12).
3	Fragment of a similar Chinese ritual disc, pi. Dark green. The corrosion product was lead carbonate.
4	Fragment of a brown glass bead with a diameter of ca. 8 mm. The same bead as sample no. 2 in table 6 of the article of Yamasaki, seminar, 1965, *Application of Science in Examination of Works of Art,* Boston, Museum of Fine Arts (1967), p.124. Made in Japan in the 8th century A.D.
5	Fragment of a similar bead with the above-mentioned no. 4 Dark green. Japanese bead made in the 8th century, A.D.

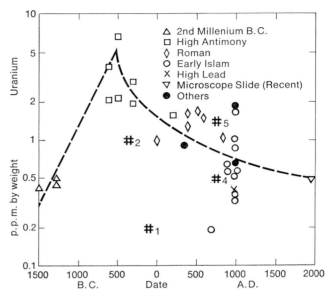

7. Uranium concentrations of glasses plotted against the probable dates of origin. The Far Eastern glass specimens are marked with # and number (cf. tables II and III).

Results and Discussion

This method of dating has been applied to man-made glasses by Fleischer et al.,[14] Brill et al.,[15] and Kaufhold and Herr,[16] and the ages of Western glasses containing uranium have been determined. There has been no report, however, on the Far Eastern glasses. Fleischer and Price[14] have determined the uranium concentrations of 34 ancient glasses by this method whose major components had been analyzed earlier by Sayre and Smith. When they plotted uranium concentrations of glasses as a function of the probable dates of the glasses, a curve showing a historical trend from initially low to high, and then to lower but widely scattered values of uranium concentration was obtained (fig. 7). These glasses were Egyptian, Roman, Islamic, and other Western glasses without a Far Eastern glass. Therefore the values of the Far Eastern glasses were quite interesting for comparison. Unfortunately the uranium concentrations of the specimens studied here were very low, as shown in table III, and the ages could not be determined by this method. When plotted in fig. 7 the values of the Japanese glasses seem to fit the curve drawn for the Western glasses, while the values of the high lead-barium glasses are quite apart from the curve. Many more data for the Far Eastern glasses may be necessary to deduce any conclusion on the historical trend, if any, of their uranium concentrations.

As is clear from table III the chemical composition of the high lead-barium glass bead excavated in Japan, no.1, is closely related to those of two Chinese ritual discs of the

Table III

Results of chemical analysis of the Japanese and Chinese glasses

	No. 1* (Japan)	No. 2* (China)	No. 3* (China)	Seligman and Beck (ref. 9) Cicada	No. 4** (Japan)	No. 5** (Japan)
	%	%	%	%	%	%
SiO_2	38	36	36	34.42	23.7	23.5
Al_2O_3	0.35	0.13	0.36	0.76	0.13	0.15
Fe_2O_3	0.29	0.07	0.13	0.16	0.97	1.15
CaO	1.1	0.01	1.6	0.12	0.26	0.34
BaO	14	13	14	12.58	–	–
MgO	0.15	0.08	0.16	0.34	0.57	0.15
Na_2O	3.90	1.96	1.65	4.32	0.10	0.15
K_2O	0.19	0.17	0.26	1.02	0.18	0.13
PbO	38.5	48.5	46.1	43.20	72.6	72.6
CuO	0.78	0.84	0.88	–	0.19	1.36
Ag_2O	0.01	0.05	0.05	–	–	–
U	0.2 ppm	1.0 ppm	Not determined	–	0.5 ppm	1.5 ppm

* Nos.1, 2 and 3 were analyzed by the spectrographic method except for Na, K, and Pb. Na and K were determined by the flame photometric method and Pb by the atomic absorption method. Duplicate analyses for the samples of ca. 30 mg.

** Nos. 4 and 5 were analyzed by the gravimetric and colorimetric methods. Duplicate analyses for samples of 0.2–0.4 gm.

Warring States period. As in no case such a high concentration of lead and barium was found in glasses except for the pre-Han glasses, it is highly probable that this bead, no.1, was made in the pre-Han period in China and then brought to Japan. There are two possibilities; one is that the bead itself was made in China into the present form, and the other is that an imported glass lump or glass object was re-melted in Japan to make the present cylindrical bead. The latter possibility seems to be more probable, because a mold made of sandstone for casting a comma-shaped bead (magatama), and a glass magatama with a high lead-barium content which fits in this mold have been found in the sites of the Yayoi period in Fukuoka prefecture.[10] Therefore the glass bead, no.1, might have been made by re-melting in Japan, in which case, the fission tracks formed by the spontaneous fission of ^{238}U contained in the original glass disappear by the applied heat, and afterward the tracks will be formed again in the period of time from the re-melting to the present day .Then the age of the bead determined will show the time of re-melting, not the age of the original glass melting. This is one of the reasons for subjecting this bead to age determination by the fission track method, but the result was unsatisfactory for deciding between the two possibilities.

In addition to this bead, no.1, several other glasses of similar high lead-barium concentrations have been found in the northern Kyushu, and they are now under investigation.[17] These facts indicate that trade might have been going on between Japan in the Yayoi period and China in the pre-Han period. Although there have been numerous archaeological and historical researches on the cultural relations between Japan and China, the present investigation of ancient glasses has offered direct chemical evidence of the traffic between two countries in this ancient time.

Acknowledgment

I am greatly indebted to Dr. R. L. Fleischer of the General Electric Research Laboratory for permission to reproduce fig. 7 from his paper and for supplying a copy of the original figure.

Notes and References

1. Yamasaki, K. *Archaeological Chemistry, A Symposium,* ed. Martin Levey. Philadelphia, University of Pennsylvania Press, 1967, p. 347; Yamasaki, K. *Studies in Conservation,* III (1957), 83.

2. The Golden Hall has never been studied by the radio-carbon method, but the five-storied pagoda of the Horyuji temple, which is situated quite close to the Golden Hall, gave the date of (1270–1450) $\pm$ 90 B.P. The tested samples were parts of the pillars. Kigoshi, K., Tomikura, Y., and Endo, K. *Radiocarbon,* 84 (1960), 4 (in English).

3. By the microscopic examination the main constituents of the clay used for the surface coating were found to be kaolinite mixed with quartz.

4. Shibata, Y., and Yamasaki, K. *Proc. Japan Acad.,* 24, (1948), 11 (in English); Yamasaki, K., *Bijutsu Kenkyu* (J. Art Studies), no.167 (1952), 32.

5. Details of the project are described in an article of T. Sakazaki, *Japan Quarterly,* 15 (1968), 466 (in English).

6. Yamasaki, reference 1. The presence of calcium carbonate can thus be used to distinguish paintings. Japanese painting in which calcium carbonate is used as the white pigment is later than the 14 to 15th century.

7. Sekino, M. *Hozon Kagaku* (Science for Conservation), no. 6 (1970), 1. In this article results of x-ray fluorescence and diffraction studies on the pigments used for reproduction which were carried out by Y. Emeto are included. Twenty-five pigments actually used are divided into the seven kinds shown in table I.

8. Beck, H. C., and Seligman, C. G. *Nature,* 133 (1934), 982.

9. Seligman, C. G., Beck, H. C., and Ritchie, P. D. *Nature,* 138, (1936), 721. Ritchie, P. D. *Technical Studies,* 5 (1937), 209. Seligman, C. G. and Beck, H. C. *Bull. Museum Far Eastern Antiques,* no.10 (1938), Stockholm.

10. Detailed reports on the excavations have not yet been published, and only a brief description of the glasses found has been given by S. Umehara, *Shirin,* 43 (1960), 1. I have been asked by Umehara to investigate specimens nos.1, 2, and 3. Since there has been no glass object found in the older Jomon period, these glasses found in the sites of the Yayoi period in the northern Kyushu (about 1st century B.C.) seem to be the oldest glass objects in Japan.

11. In a review article on the fission track method the uranium concentrations of these glasses have been cited without detailed description as examples. Shima, M. *Quaternary Research,* 6 (1967), 134.

12. The corrosion products of specimens nos.1, 2, and 3 were studied by x-ray diffraction. Yamasaki, K., and Saito, Y. *Proc. Japan Acad.,* 36 (1960), 503 (in English). Detailed descriptions of specimens nos. 4 and 5 are given in the article by Yamasaki in "The Glass Objects in Shosoin," *Nihon Keizai Shimbun,* Tokyo (1965).

13. Fleischer, R. L., Price, P. B., and Walker, R. M. *Science,* 149 (1965), 383, and and the references therein.

14. Fleischer, R. L., and Price, P. B. *Science,* 144 (1964), 841. Idem., G. E. Research Laboratory Report no. 64-RL-3634M (1964).

15. Brill, R. H., Fleischer, R. L., Price, P. B., and Walker, R. M. *J. Glass Studies,* 6 (1964), 151.

16. Kaufhold, J., and Herr, W. IAEA. Vienna, STI/PUB/152, (1967). p. 403.

17. Two glass beads have so far been studied which contained PbO 40, BaO 16 %, and PbO 43, BaO 8 % respectively. Both beads were excavated in sites of the Yayoi period.

G. STACCIOLI and U. TAMBURINI

Ageing of Wood: Preliminary Studies on Panel Paintings

In the current view, wood does not change in a normal climate, although it may be degraded by pests, chemicals, and fire. Thus we normally consider as wood decay the biological deterioration caused by fungi which are thought essential contributors to the degradation of wood.[1] It should be pointed out that fungi are responsible for the decay of the wood by degradation of cell wall material, while insects impair wood by boring throughout it. Much evidence supports this belief, since wood is essentially seen in its structural function, because clear specimens of ancient wood do not show any appreciable change in mechanical properties and also color changes do not involve at first sight alteration of the structure. Moreover, it was shown in the first studies about the absorption properties of wood that the equilibrium moisture content of ancient specimens falls within the normal distribution of modern ones. Mechanical tests were carried out with ancient material and showed no appreciable difference with respect to the mean rates for the wood of the same species and specific gravity. Mechanical tests have been carried out also by Giordano (Istituto del Legno, Florence) showing no differences in mean values,[2] and at present are being repeated with other timber from ancient houses. Such an analysis is very difficult since comparison between all chemical and physical properties causes a much greater spread of values than expected.

Wood should decay in a normal environment as do the high polymers which constitute it. Steaming and other heat treatments are very commonly practiced in wood technology with the aim of making it more plastic; on the other hand, timber is sometimes seasoned by first soaking it in water. Both procedures hydrolyzate to some extent the weaker constituents of the wood and may be regarded as an accelerated ageing process.

It should be pointed out that cell wall materials are formed by deposition of water-soluble monomers which join together, losing their solubility in water.[3] By alternate sorption during many centuries it is possible that weak bonds are saponified and fragments recover steadily their solubility in water. This naturally affects the structure of the cell wall material and explains the differences between ancient and modern wood. Differences are not too great, however, because wood constituents have similar absorptional properties and are also crosslinked to some extent.[4] It should also be noted that these changes depend on how wood has been stored. As a matter of fact such decay appears quite general to judge by japanese research carried out fifteen years ago on structural timber dating from six centuries ago.[5] Japanese work, however, uses a classical technique of investigation and does not afford an explanation for the decay of wood.

Our study deals with acetyl groups and hemicelluloses on the basis of our own research,[6] in connection with former work on the same subject.[7] We have found a striking decrease of acetyls and in connection with it an increase of hemicellulose extraction. Acetyl decrease is a linear function of the age of specimens that we have investigated. Hemicellulose extraction also shows a linear increase. This fact may be explained both by waterproofing imparted by acetyls to cell walls[8] and by the chemical bonds of hemicelluloses within the highly crosslinked lignin structure.[9]

The structure of hemicelluloses of wood has been lately investigated and consists of an O-acetyl-4-O-methyl-glucuron-oxylan.[10] Acetyls may be split off by saponification as pointed out in our former research.[6] In modern wood chemical bonds with lignin occur by esterification of the carboxyl groups and perhaps involve also some OH-group of the sugars. Decrease of acetyl groups favors the rearrangement of the bonds between hemicelluloses and lignin in this sense, but at the same time allows the cell walls to expand in the wet state by lack of bulking effect.[9, 11] This explains a faster moisture exchange rate and also higher dissolution of hemicelluloses when treated with concentrated alkalies.

Method of Specimen Collection

This work was carried out with the purpose of finding some characteristic change of wood due to differences in physical properties. Differences, as mentioned above, are not too great, but in ancient wood there is some disadvantage due to changes arising from shrinking and swelling of the specimen, and faster moisture exchange rate. Sampling requires a homogeneous history of the material within a six century period. This was accomplished by choosing the specimens from panel paintings from Florence churches. Samples were kindly donated by Professor L. Tintori and were selected from those whose age was certain. For this preliminary research we selected two specimens; the first is from 1380 by historical data, the second from 1525 by a label found on the back of the painting.

Such research does not require a great amount of wood so that we could use a few grams of chips selected in clear parts of the boards. The chips were pre-extracted with ethanol-benzene and water, thus eliminating any chemicals added for purposes of conservation. Comparison was made with a specimen from the workshop of our institute of the same species and similar density (*Populus nigra* L., 360 kg/m³). For chemical comparison density is not too important, but it should be pointed out that a slight change of density of the wood due to chemical degradation was observed.

Hemicellulose Extraction from Wood

Extraction was carried out with 24 % potassium hydroxide. Extractive-free poplar wood meal 40—60 mesh (2gm) was treated with 24 % (w/w) aqueous potassium hydroxide (14 ml) under vacuum at room temperature for 7 hours. Filtrate and washings were reduced in volume to 100 ml by freeze-drying, then poured in four times their volume of a mixture of acetic acid and ethanol (1/8 v/v) at −16° C. The precipitate formed was removed, washed successively with 80 % ethanol, ethanol and petroleum ether (bp 30−60° C), and dried in vacuum at room temperature. Percent yields were 13.67 for the control, 16.60 for 16th century, and 19.88 for 14th century wood at 9.5 % m.c.

Acetyl Extraction

The acetyl groups were readily split off by saponification with the same alkaline solution as above. The recovered liquor and washings were steam distilled after acidification with sulfuric acid to pH 1. After elimination of carbonates, the solution was potentiometrically titrated, with potassium hydroxide. The optimum conditions (especially the sulfuric acid concentration) may vary with different woods; the minimum amount of sulfuric acid was chosen which yielded the highest acetic acid content of the distillate.

Acetic acid yields were compared to air-dry weight of the wood (moisture content 9.5 %). Modern wood shows an acetyl content of 3.71 % while ancient wood has a much lower content, say 2.52 % for 16th and 2.02 % for 14th century wood. The above data are an average of five determinations. By plotting the data versus time we have a straight line.

Acetyl groups hinder the dissolution of hemicelluloses chemically bound to the highly cross-linked structure of lignin,[9] and the hemicellulose yield increases with the age of the wood, so that the plot of the acetyl to hemicellulose ratio versus time still appears linear. Both these results refer to a specific material (black poplar wood from panel paintings) and cannot be extended to other wood.

Results are in agreement, however, with the trend of research carried out by Kohara on Japanese structural timber some years ago.[5] In that work the chemical composition of wood was not studied with respect to its weak components, but by comparison of the data given for cellulose and lignin we suppose that the increases he has found correspond to the changes we could attribute to glucuronoxylans and acetyls. Checking the data will perhaps be troublesome because of the use of different techniques, but his work gives further support to promising research in this field.

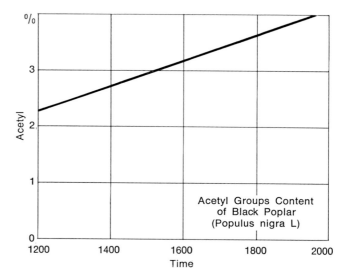

1. Acetyl content of wood from panel paintings versus time (years, Christian era). Corrected values are given for moisture content of the wood (about 9.5 %).

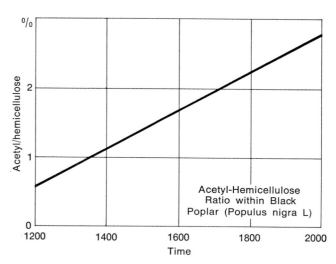

2. Comparison between acetyl and hemicellulose content of wood plotted against time (years, Christian era).

References

1. Kollmann, F. F. P., and Côte, W. A. *Solid Wood,* Berlin, 1968, chap. IV, p. 97.

2. Giordano, G. "Contributo sperimentale alla conoscenza mecanico-tecnologica del legname di castagno," *Riv. forestale it.* 5–6 (1943) 1.

3. Stamm, A. J. "Surface Characteristics of Wood and Cellulose" in *Surfaces and Coatings as Related to Paper and Wood,* R. H. Marchessault and C. Skaar, eds., Syracuse, Syracuse University Press, 1967, p. 387.

4. Christensen, G. M., and Kelsey, K. E. "Die Sorption von Wasserdampf durch die chemischen Bestandteile des Holzes, *Holz als Roh- und Werkstoff* 17 (1959), 189.

5. Kohara, J. "Studies on the Permanence of Wood," XV *J. Jap. Wood Res. Soc.* I (1955), 21.

6. Tamburini, U. "Alkaline Degradation of Wood," *Wood Science and Technology* 4 (1970), 284.

7. Klauditz, W. "Biomechanische Wirkung der Acetylgruppen im Festigungsgewebe der Laubhölzer," *Holzforschung* 11 (1957) 47.

8. Stamm, A. J. "Wood and Cellulose Science," New York, Ronald Press, 1965, chap. XIX, p. 312.

9. Nelson, R., and Schuerch, C. "Factors Influencing the Removal of Pentosans from Birch Wood," *J. Polymer Sci.,* 22 (1956), 435.

10. Timell, T. E. "O-Acetyl-4-O-Methylglucuronoxyloglycan from Birch," *J. Am. Chem. Soc.,* 80 (1958), 1209.

11. Timell, T. E. "Main Hemicellulose from Yellow Birch," *J. Am. Chem. Soc.,* 81 (1959), 4989.

ROBERT M. ORGAN

Examination of the Ardagh Chalice—A Case History

Ardagh now is scarcely more than a placename; it is in County Limerick in Ireland. In 1868, while a peasant named Quinn was digging potatoes in an earth fort, he found at a depth of about three feet beneath a thorn-tree some bronze objects and a silver chalice. These objects were taken to the convent at Limerick, where they were examined by the Bishop and by Lord Dunraven, an amateur antiquarian. Later, these objects passed to the Royal Irish Academy in Dublin. There they were cleaned and the chalice examined by a jeweler named Johnson. Johnson's report on it was incorporated into the report that Dunraven published in 1874 in "Transactions of the Royal Irish Academy." We are greatly indebted to his account for knowledge of the condition of the chalice at the time when it was found. Illustrations for his paper were drawn by Margaret Stokes, a writer on the antiquities of this period, who used photographs as the basis for her drawings. Through the exertions of Etienne Rhynne of the National Museum her photograph album was discovered a few years ago in a local bookshop. These have helped solve a problem that had arisen from observations made in the course of the examination to be described.

In June 1961 the chalice was taken to the Research Laboratory of the British Museum for repair because it had become loose at the joint between bowl and foot. This necessary work was also to provide a convenient occasion to study the chalice, both in order to discover how reliable for modern usage Dunraven's account had been and also to analyze its materials and construction.

The work proceeded alongside the normal activities in the laboratory (including moving to a new building) but became more and more complex as it developed. Nevertheless, because at least partial completion had been promised by the end of 1962 the chalice was actually placed on exhibition in the British Museum during December 1962 after it had been reassembled temporarily especially for this purpose. After the exhibition the examination recommenced and uncovered more and more problems. Eventually, details of the final reassembly were agreed with Dublin and the chalice was returned in December 1963. The following account itemizes some of the complexities encountered and gives an insight into the problems that can arise in a museum laboratory. The illustrations are from the two hundred or so photographs taken in the course of the examination.

Description

Fig.1 shows the chalice as received. It consisted essentially of a silver two-handled bowl joined to a silver foot through a gilt-bronze neck. The bowl is decorated with a rim, with two handle-escutcheons beneath the handles and with two roundels, one quite clearly visible at the front. It was decorated

also with a band of panels beneath the rim that is described here as the "bowl-girdle." The foot is decorated with an upper foot-girdle, in view when the chalice is at rest, and a lower foot-girdle, visible when the chalice is raised off a table.

Objectives

The objectives of treatment were as follows: first, to secure the loose neck; second, to check the accuracy of Dunraven's account and especially to confirm the existence of an iron bolt which Dunraven wrote "holds all together"; third, to determine the nature of the various materials employed. The results should be publishable. This objective of final publication had to be borne clearly in mind if the labor of preparation for publication was to be minimized. It influenced all of the work. The task of the scientific laboratory was considered to be to provide evidence in a form that could be interpreted by later generations of archaeologists using their own conventions. Dunraven's text was already proving unreliable although it was less than a century old. For this reason as much evidence as possible was to be recorded: not only evidence that could be understood now but also evidence that would have to be interpreted in the future, for example, the shape and the markings found on the chalice. For this reason the results of the work were to be recorded in graphic form which would in some degree be independent of words, whose meanings change with the passage of time. Records made included photographs and scaled engineering drawings. This account explains the methods used to make them and some of the discoveries made solely as a result.

The problems were attacked broadly as follows. First, study of whatever could be seen in the uncleaned condition of the chalice and of its components, followed by recording, as far as possible in a form suitable for immediate publication. Second, cleaning of a particular feature, recording anything newly revealed. Third, gathering together a number of these observations and making deductions. Emergence of a theory would then necessitate re-examination of the chalice with a view to confirming the theory. An example of this will be given later.

In accordance with the enormous value of the chalice, during the whole of the work extreme precautions were taken against risk of damage. Overnight it was stored in a strong-room. During the day it rested in a tray on a sponge support beneath a transparent protective cover so that nothing could fall accidentally against it. Throughout, precautions were taken against any kind of damage to any one part of it. According to Dunraven's account there were 354 parts!

Examination

As a preliminary, examination was directed toward discovering

1. The Ardagh chalice as received.

how the chalice was constructed. No single action was taken without thought. The chalice was laid on its side on its foam pad, its foot resting in a rubber ring to prevent it from rolling, as shown in fig. 2. This was one of the earliest of the photographs. Simply taken by daylight with a Leica camera, it is unclear because of the glare of light reflected from the multitudinous facets in the underfoot disc. The difficulty in taking a photograph was overcome later. Another feature of the photograph is a central dark patch in the crystal. It may be deduced from this that a reflecting surface beneath the crystal, probably metal foil, had been perforated. Perforation could have occurred at some earlier examination as a result of the

central crystal dome having been rotated carelessly in its mount against some sharp metal object lying beneath the foil.

The next stage of examination was to touch the underfoot disc, the component decorated with the five small circular studs, and to attempt to rotate it gently. The disc could rotate only through a small angle. From this it was deduced that the disc was mounted loosely upon a square bolt, or at least upon a bolt whose end was not circular in cross-section. The parts were next separated: first, the crystal was eased from its mount, shown at the bottom of the exploded view in fig. 3. Then the whole of the mount was lifted away from the under-foot disc. This then revealed inside the foot-cone the expected

2. The chalice laid on its side for preliminary investigation of its construction exposing the foot.

4. Removal of the foot-cone and the lower neck ring to reveal a mass of lead cast into the neck.

3. Exploded view of crystal mount, under-foot disc, and the end of the central bolt.

5. The neck assembly removed from the bolt.

square bolt. It also revealed two sharp tags projecting from the end of the bolt. The earlier two deductions now stood confirmed: here were the sharp projections that had torn the silver foil and the square bolt.

The next stage of exploration was to lift away the foot-cone. This revealed the lower of the three rings of the neck assembly and also exposed a mass of lead, fig. 4, that locked the bolt into the central ring of the neck. A loose stud that fell out of the foot-girdle during this work was immediately taped on to the appropriate position of the bowl, using pressure-sensitive tape, as a short-term precaution against loss or damage (see upper right-hand corner of fig. 4).

At this stage of examination it was believed that the lead in the neck had been inserted by Johnson, the jeweler who first examined and cleaned the chalice, and that it could there-fore be removed if need be because it was not original. In fact it was shown later to have been original, but removal now was essential, whatever its origin, because it was endangering the stability of the chalice: the lead had corroded — the crust of corrosion products on it is visible in the photograph — and had been forcing the foot away from the bowl. This turned out to have been the source of weakness in the neck that had ini-tiated the work.

The lead was removed very carefully. It was first channelled annularly with a rotary file with care that the file did not ap-proach any part of the chalice. Then the thin wall of lead that had been left against the central bolt was carefully levered back into the annular space made by the file. The neck could then be lifted away from the bowl. In fig. 5 it can be seen with its lead still within it, turned over and laid down alongside the place from which it came. Looking at the inside of the neck you may note that the lead that had lain against the silver bowl is white with corrosion products. Circular turning-marks in these suggest that a lathe had been used. In the periphery of the disc there is a greenish-white deposit that actually repre-sents corrosion products from the bronze of which the disc was made. On the silver bowl may be seen a circle of un-tarnished silver. This had been protected from the tarnishing gases in the atmosphere by the seal of corrosion products around the periphery of the disc. Toward the center of the clear circle of silver one or two patches of white material adhere firmly. These provide evidence that the expanding cor-rosion products of lead had been forced tightly against the silver at these places.

It has now been shown that the major components of the as-sembly consist of a foot-cone, a neck, and a bowl held to-gether by a bolt. Let us now consider separately the several minor components of the chalice, beginning with one of the two handles on the bowl, fig. 6.

6. One of the two handles on the bowl.

The Handles

This handle was secured to the bowl by two rivets at the top (invisible in this photograph) and two rivets at the bottom that are covered by small glass studs. For the moment let us ignore the decoration but consider how this handle has been made. Its shape suggests a curved sheet of silver having flanges, serving as stiffeners, attached to both sides. It was a question whether this handle had been cast in one piece or whether parts had been soldered together. This question could have been answered by making a metallographic cross-section in some portion but removal for such a purpose was not per-missible and preparation of a taper section in situ would have been very difficult.

Examination of the surface of the handle under a micro-scope at a magnification of about ten diameters suggested that the handles had been cast. This impression had to be con-

7. The side and exposed interior of one of the handles.

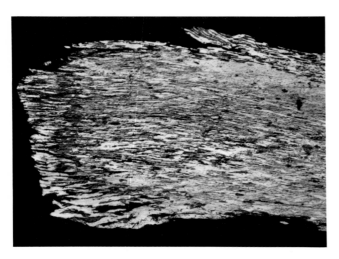

8. A prepared cross-section of a fragment of the silver liner of a handle.

firmed in some objective manner. It was confirmed by an examination of the curvature of the C-shaped flanges on the sides (see fig. 7). Here it can be seen that the "C" is not part of a circle — its radius of curvature varies from point to point. This was quite an important observation because if the handle is not circular, with a readily repeatable curvature, then there is a strong probability that one side of the handle will have a slightly different curvature from the other. It was decided to investigate this.

A very careful transfer was made of the curvature of the flange. The transfer was not made by tracing with a pencil: the handle was made to transfer its own curvature. This was done by placing a transparent sheet of "Kodatrace" backed with carbon-paper against the flange and then rubbing the Kodatrace in the region of the metal edge with the back of a fingernail held at a constant angle. By this means the line of the edge was transferred through the carbon-paper to the Kodatrace.

The trace was then laid against the other parallel flange of the same handle and it was observed that the two curvatures were different. In other words the handle was asymmetric. The trace from the left-hand flange of one handle was then laid against the left-hand flange of the other handle. It was found to fit perfectly throughout its whole length within the width of the traced line — within 0.1 millimeter ($^1/_{250}$ inch). A trace from the right-hand side of one handle was similarly found to match perfectly the right-hand side of the other handle. In other words it could be shown that the two sides of one handle differed from each other but were identical with the corresponding sides of the other handle. This implied that both handles were made from a single pattern by casting. It is most improbable that identical noncircular curvatures would have been achieved so precisely by any other method of fabrication. Other observations were made that rule out other possible forms of construction.

In the photograph the interior of the handle is shown exposed rather unpleasantly because the sheet of silver that covered it had been removed. The next photograph, fig. 8, illustrates the structure of this silver liner. It represents a cross-section through a fragment that has been examined metallographically: polished and examined at high magnification. The smaller dimension of the cross-section shown represents a distance of 0.3 mm ($^1/_{80}$ inch). The metal was examined in order to determine whether it was in fact as ancient as the chalice, about A.D. 800, or whether it represented a piece inserted by Johnson in 1869 — one of the liners appeared at first sight to be more recent than the other. The photograph shows a structure consisting of flattened dendrites. Clearly, the silver had been cast and then reduced in thickness by hammering. This is evidence for a primitive technique of fabri-

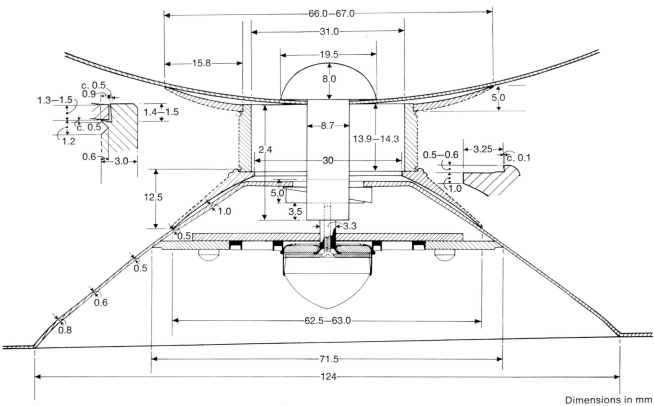

9. Dimensioned drawing of cross-section of central portion of the chalice.

cation: modern rolled silver has a quite different structure. Furthermore the silver has become enriched at its surface: the center area of the section appeared pink, consisting of an alloy of silver with much copper, whereas the peripheries of the section are white because they have lost copper and now consist of almost pure silver. The copper-rich phase has been converted during the centuries into the lines of dark mineral that may be seen in between the white crystals of the silver-rich phase, and even these have been lost from immediately beneath the surface at the edge of the fragment, leaving only the white silver-rich metal.

The Bowl

Next let us examine a diagram, fig. 9. This is an engineering drawing that has been very carefully scaled. This method of drawing was adopted deliberately because it ensured that the original was studied correspondingly carefully. The upper portion of the drawing shows a part of the bowl of the chalice. The detailed shape of the whole of this bowl was determined for the sake of precision by a mechanical method.

Obviously the bowl could not be cut across in order to determine its precise cross-section. Instead, a beam of light was used to make a shadowgraph (see fig.10). The source of light was a pointolite lamp. The bowl was inverted on a flat support immediately in front of a screen placed close against it and carrying a sheet of sensitized (bromide) paper. The essential precaution for the success of this kind of work is to position everything very carefully: the source of light has been placed exactly in the same plane as the rim of the bowl and rather far removed from it in order to cast a slightly enlarged shadow that truly represents the shape of the bowl.

Fig.11 shows the silhouette thus obtained. Dimensions have been added to it, showing that beneath the rim the silver is about one-half millimeter ($^1/_{50}$ inch) thick whereas at the center of the bowl the silver is a whole millimeter thick. From these measurements it can be deduced that the bowl was made by the process of raising. The silhouette also preserves evidence for posterity of the precision with which the light source was set in the same plane as the rim. These are in fact the four flanges, two to each handle, that appear exactly equal

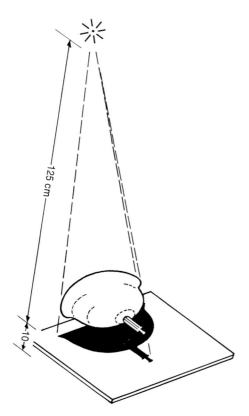

10. Arrangement of bowl and light source to yield an accurately proportioned shadow of the bowl.

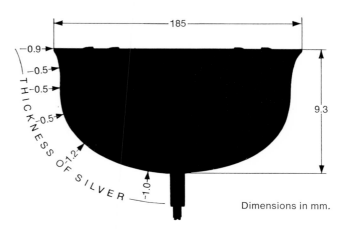

11. Silhouette of bowl and bolt with dimensions added.

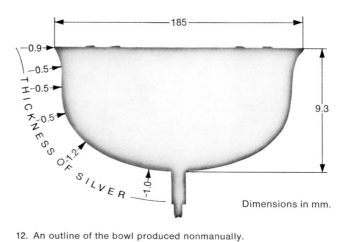

12. An outline of the bowl produced nonmanually.

in size only because the light-source was positioned correctly. The resulting black and white silhouette was not very convenient for publication: a simple black line is preferable. How was the transfer achieved? It was produced without risk of error in manual tracing by the simple expedient of Xeroxing the silhouette. The result, fig.12, became a sharp line edged by a grey border because of the special characteristics of the electrostatic process. In this way the beautiful curvature of the bowl has been presented without the falsification that manual copying could have introduced.

The Rim of the Bowl

The upper edges of the outline, representing the sharp rim of the bowl, were covered in the actual object by a rim made of gilt brass. This had a rounded upper surface and a groove beneath to fit over the edge of the bowl. It was held in place

by three tapered pins which were spaced around and passed through the rim and were bent over on the inside. All of this detail is shown very precisely in fig. 13. Unlike the bowl, the shape of the cross-section could not be obtained by use of the point-source of light because the outside of the complete ring would have shielded light from its inner surface. Furthermore, the groove itself was quite inaccessible to light. In this case the shape was determined with certainty by making an impression. A short length of the rim was laid in a channel, its ends stopped with wax. Ready-mixed fluid cold-setting silastomer was then poured into the space and allowed to cure. When hard the rubbery impression was slit and peeled away from channel and rim. Cross-sections were then made by cutting thin slices from the impression. These were laid on a glass plate in the photographic enlarger and the image projected on to bromide paper. From the silhouette thus obtained

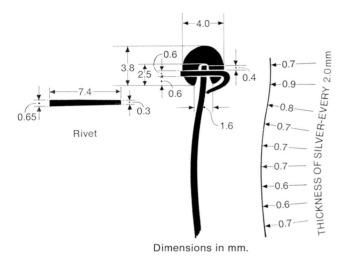

Rivet

THICKNESS OF SILVER-EVERY 2.0 mm

Dimensions in mm.

13. Scale drawing of cross-section of the rim of the bowl.

the dimensions could be scaled off, once the outside dimensions of the actual metal rim had been measured at the position from which the impression had been taken. The measurement of small dimensions, such as the 0.3 mm (twelve-thousandths of an inch) diameter of the end of the brass pin, was made by means of an eyepiece micrometer (a measuring graticule set in the focal plane of the objective of a low-power microscope).

The Neck-Assembly

Let us next return to our engineering drawing, fig. 9, and examine the neck. It can be seen to consist of three components, namely, the upper ring-mounting, lying immediately beneath the bowl; the cylindrical collar; and the lower ring-mounting sitting neatly on the foot-cone. The lower ring-mounting does not actually touch the foot-cone anywhere except along its lower border. The method of determining the dimensions of these components was quite straightforward, making use of a scale and calipers.

Fig.14 shows the details of the neck assembly. The three components have been decorated externally by the kerbschnitt technique. They fit very closely together: when properly assembled the three could be lifted together as one by grasping the upper ring-mounting alone. The black spot shown at the center of the periphery of the lower ring-mounting represents damage to the gilding. At this point the bronze has lost its protective gilding and has begun to corrode. Damage of this kind was turned to account, as will appear later.

Certain questions about this neck assembly required answers: how were the components made? How was the pattern formed?

14. The three components of the neck assembly fitted together.

15. The inner surface of the upper ring mounting.

Examination of their inner surfaces revealed that the components had been cast. Fig.15 shows the inner surface of the upper ring-mounting. At about three o'clock a casting flaw is visible, together with many blowholes. At about one o'clock there is also a tiny plug of copper metal that the bronze founder had inserted in order to fill a particularly deep blow-hole. In fact this plug was found to pass through the entire thickness of the metal to the other side, where it was obscured from casual inspection by the overall gilding. Clearly, this one of the three components has been cast and the other two show similar features. Furthermore, the inner surface has been either turned or stoned down: the circular markings from this process are clearly visible around the rim.

These observations of the inner surfaces do not answer the question of how the outer decorative pattern was made. It could have been cast or it could have been punched or chiselled. This problem was solved by examining the structure of the metal of one of the components. Preparation of a special taper-section by metallographic methods was found to be unnecessary because an area from which gilding had been lost some time ago was discovered on the basket-weave on the collar. From this spot the corrosion products that had formed during the centuries were carefully thinned by mechanical means and the final traces obscuring the metal were removed by a gentle chemical etching reagent. The area of metal exposed is shown in fig.16. In the elongated patch on the left-hand side there is a ladder-like pattern that represents the dendritic structure of cast metal. This confirmed that the metal had been cast. This conclusion had already been reached from other considerations but, in addition, because the straight lines of the dendrites pass quite up to the surface without deformation, it is difficult to believe that the metal could have been

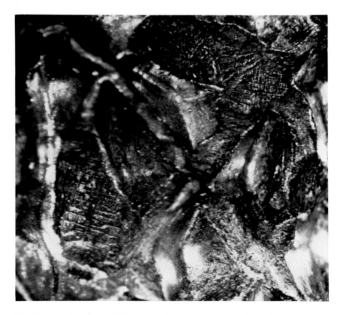

16. A corroded area of the basket weave on the collar, cleaned and etched to show structure of the metal.

either punched or chiselled. A chisel could scarcely have failed to deform the dendrites near the surface. Quite clearly here was a pattern that had been cast into the surface and, at least at the spot examined, had suffered a minimum of subsequent correction.

The Foot-Cone And Bolt

Next let us consider in the drawing, fig. 9, the silver foot-cone that supported the neck. In order to make the drawing the shape was determined by the shadow-casting method. Notice particularly the size of the aperture in the flat top of the foot-cone. In the plane of the drawing the foot-cone does not touch the bolt anywhere, but in a plane a few millimeters behind this the aperture fits the bolt closely. Let us now consider some of the problems posed by this bolt. It has a rounded head that lies inside the bowl and has been gilded. The bolt protrudes downward from beneath the bowl and holds all of the various components together. For the moment let us ignore the modern pair of wedges shown in the drawing passing through the bolt. Dunraven stated that the chalice was fastened together by an *iron* bolt "which secured all together." The bolt actually found was made of copper, not iron (fig.17). It was square in section with a hollow tubular extension at one end and a rectangular slot passing through the copper that could serve as a key-way. Next let us examine the aperture in the flat top of the foot-cone. Seen from above, fig.18, the aperture was square, fitting closely against the bolt, with additional slots cut on two opposite sides.

Now, although the copper bolt observed was not the iron bolt noted by Dunraven, an iron key was found that actually passed through the slot in the copper bolt and lay in the two additional slots found cut across the central square. The iron key lay there quite loose and served no useful purpose whatever. By close reasoning from a number of observations it was deduced that this was not the original key. On the bases of this theory, most important for the reassembly, a search was made for evidence that it was correct. Confirmation hinged on the fact that if the original key had been made of iron it should have rusted extensively because it would have lain underground in contact with a nobler metal, silver, for over 1000 years. The product of corrosion would have been iron oxide, of greater volume than the iron. This should have resulted in expansion of the key against the top of the foot-cone. Some evidence of such an expansion might have been preserved as a deformation of the silver at areas of contact with the key. Evidence of deformation was therefore sought on the flat top of the foot-cone. It was in fact found. We were next faced with the problem of recording this deformation in a form that would carry greater weight for posterity than mere words.

The resulting photograph is shown in fig.19, containing a grid of lines superimposed on the top of the foot-cone. The steps in

17. The copper bolt found in the neck. One of the two end tags has broken off.

18. View of the foot-cone, decoration removed, from above.

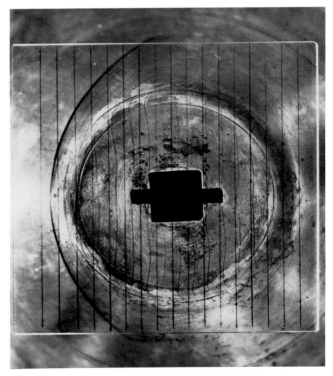

19. The deformed flat top of the foot-cone, illustrated by a family of curved shadows cast from a grid of straight lines.

producing it were as follows. Parallel lines were drawn as a grid on a glass plate (a 2 inch by 2 inch transparency cover-glass). The plate was laid on the top of the foot-cone with its lines across the axis of the deformation that had been observed. A point source of light was then set up on the left-hand side of the arrangement with the result that it cast shadows on the cone. In the photograph, on the left-hand side of the silver cone a black arc represents the shadow cast by the thick edge of the glass plate. This arc is the end member of a family of line shadows cast by the ruled grid. On the flat top can be seen both the straight lines of the grid and, between these, their shadows. The curves of these shadows indicate quite clearly that the slightly concave top has been deformed along the axis of the two side slots in which the iron key was discovered lying loose. It was also observed, in confirmation of this finding, that the whole foot-cone had been distorted slightly along this same axis. It had been "squeezed in." In fact, at the time when the chalice was reassembled temporarily for exhibition at the British Museum, at a time when the significance of this distortion was unrecognized, a pair of tiny pads had to be inserted between foot-cone and lower ring mounting in order to compensate for the distortion and to obtain a rigid structure. Those pads may be seen in fig. 25.

It was next argued that Johnson would have had to break away the original corroded iron key in order to dismantle the chalice and that when during reassembly he came to insert a replacement, the key actually found there, he would have been unable to do so because of the unsuitable simple shape he had given to it. Then, in the last-minute flurry to get it assembled in time for collection he had to cut out the side slots in order to admit the key. This was another theory for which confirmation had to be sought. It was found!

Fig. 20 shows the inside of the foot-cone. On the axis of the side slots, at the right-hand side, is a rather ragged line. It is believed that this was made at the time when Johnson was struggling to insert his key. The key slid down the side of the foot-cone, marking it because of a rough corner at its rear edge, and was then wiggled side to side in an endeavor to force it further. The impossibility of inserting such a key was checked by making a key and attempting to insert it. The fact that this experiment was made may suggest that the test caused the mark. Actually, photographs made of the inside of the foot-cone before the time of the theory revealed the mark already present, although it had not been noticed at that time. This alone was justification of the policy of taking careful photographs at all stages of the work. To summarize: there was now evidence to support the theory that Johnson cut away the rusted original key and replaced it with a new key and that he cut out the side slots in the top of the foot-cone in order to insert this new key.

Additional evidence was found that the side slots are actually different from the central aperture. Fig. 21 shows the central square aperture outlined in white lines because there is a burr on the edges. The two side slots are not outlined in white because they were made with a different tool at a different time, in accordance with the theory.

The Under-Foot Mounting
Let us turn again to the drawing, fig. 9, examining now the under-foot mounting in which the central crystal was set. Al-

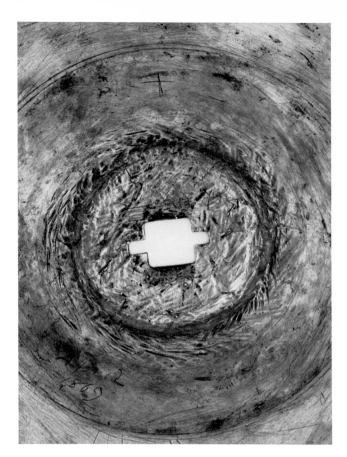

20. The interior of the foot-cone. The central area, normally hidden by the under-foot disc, remains marked by the silversmith's hammer and bears the date of Johnson's examination.

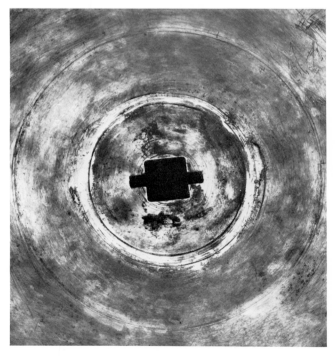

21. The exterior of the foot-cone in the uncleaned condition.

22. Detail of the under-foot disc without its central crystal.

23. The shadow cast by a steel straight-edge on the turned back surface of the catch-disc.

though this mounting was decorative it served to hide the central fixing-device and also served a structural purpose: it centralized the bolt on the axis of the foot-cone and made the whole structure rigid. We shall return to this point shortly. A detailed photograph of the under-foot mounting appears in fig. 22. The mounting is made of gilt bronze. In this view the crystal and reflective foil have been removed to expose the slotted so-called catch-disc in the center. The mount for the crystal itself is held against the back plate by means of this disc. Looking outward along any radius a number of features can be observed. First there is a gilt silver channel which contained fragments of malachite and amber. Outside the channel lies a circle of gold filigree interlace, zoomorphic in style. Outside this again lies another channel, silver-gilt, now empty. Beyond this is a double feature: a gilt bronze circle that contains five studs, and an outer circle of gilt bronze interlace. This outer circle is particularly important because it is evidence for a later argument.

The Catch-Disc

For the moment let us consider the problem presented by the central catch-disc: the one shown slotted that lay behind the crystal. This, when removed from behind the crystal, had exactly the appearance of having come from a modern clock: Its back had been lathe-turned. The problem was to decide whether this disc was indeed a modern introduction or whether it was the original ancient catch-disc. In order to solve the prob-

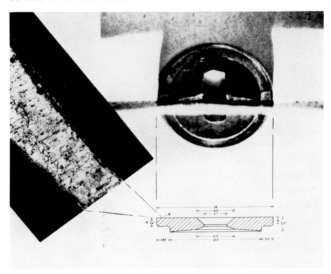

24. Scale drawing of cross-section of the catch-disc, derived from shadow casting, indicating the location of a metallographic section.

lem two methods of examination were used. The first was a superficial examination directed to discovering precisely the shape of the turned back of the disc. It was carried out as shown in fig. 23 by laying a straight edge along the back and then casting a shadow of this straight-edge upon the turned surface at a shallow angle. The side-view photograph shows clearly that the shadow of the straight-edge is curved. From a vertical photograph a diagram, fig. 24 was constructed, again a detailed scaled drawing. From this it can be seen that the original back has been turned off at an angle, leaving an edge that marks the limit of travel of the tool, and that the edge of the disc has also been rounded off.

The second method of examination involved making a minute metallographic cross-section along the line BB′ marked on the drawing. The cross-section reveals two thin broken white lines on the two surfaces of the disc. The lines represent gilding about 0.002 mm (less than $^1/_{10,000}$ inch) thick. It is believed that this gilding was applied at the time of Johnson's restoration because similarly thin gilding has been observed elsewhere on the chalice. This thin gilding was absent from the lathe-turned surfaces of the disc. From this it may be deduced that the lathe-turning followed gilding. Furthermore, the plane of turning has not been squared off nor has the tool been traversed fully before being withdrawn. This suggests that the work was being carried out in a great hurry — the ridge could have been removed in a matter of seconds by a few strokes of a file but it was not, and it may well have been carried out at the last moment of reassembly in order to make the crystal fit.

The metallographic section, viewed at a magnification of 50 diameters, contains numerous nonmetallic inclusions. This suggests that the metal is ancient. It therefore appears probable that the disc was the original catch-disc, regilded by Johnson (although it is not visible in the reassembled chalice) and altered by him at the last moment in order to allow the crystal to be fitted securely into its mount.

Design of the Assembly

Now let us turn our attention to fig. 9 again, in order to consider some evidence that tends to suggest that the original intention of the designer of the chalice was frustrated during actual construction. Considering the under-foot mounting as it lies within the foot-cone, it will be noticed that by raising it through a distance of about 3 mm it will lie neatly against the end of the solid bolt. This position would provide a much more rigid support than does the actual position in which it was found — part way up the hollow, thin tubular extension to the bolt. Furthermore, by raising this disc-shaped mounting by 3 mm — and to do so would involve making it smaller because it will then be seated higher up the walls of the cone — its edge would seat on the inside of the cone exactly level with the lower edge of the lower ring-mounting, which has already been noticed as the only portion of this mounting to make firm contact with the foot-cone. The disc can be reduced to the diameter needed for this arrangement, exactly, merely by taking away completely the outer element of ornament — the narrow outer interlace pattern that was mentioned above. Now, while

imagining the under-foot mounting in this new raised position, let us attempt to see the structure with the eye of an engineer. The foot-cone is made of comparatively thin sheet silver. In this new arrangement it would be clamped between a solid neck-mounting of cast bronze and a solid under-foot disc of cast bronze. The disc would be mounted very securely on the end of the stout solid copper bolt and the bolt would be located centrally in the strongest part of the foot-cone in a close-fitting square aperture. This arrangement could provide a very strong structure through which the bolt passes axially. There should have been no need for the mass of lead that was cast into the neck because a workman found himself unable to maintain the bolt in an axial position in the assembly. This and other evidence indicates that the designer of the chalice was much in advance of the means of construction that were available.

When the chalice was finally reassembled at the British Museum, the lead which, corroding, had endangered the security of the assembly was taken out of the neck and replaced by a spacer made of polymethyl methacrylate. This is obviously a 20th century fitting and could not be mistaken at some date in the future for work of the 8th or 9th century. An iron key was not replaced through the bolt because experiment had shown that one long enough to be secure beneath the slotted foot-cone could not in actuality be inserted. Instead a pair of brass wedges were inserted. These together ensured that the bolt remained perpendicular to the flat top of the foot-cone. Instead of allowing the whole weight of the under-foot mounting to be suspended on the two small tags of metal an 8 B.A. brass screw was inserted and a substantial brass disc was added beneath the crystal in order to support the load. The one completely detached tag was refitted with epoxy resin. Fig. 25 illustrates how the chalice was assembled temporarily in 1962.

The exploded view shows the crystal dome at the bottom. The silver foil is not shown here. Above this is the 8 B.A. screw centralized in the brass washer beneath the mount for the crystal. All of these were inserted into the under-foot mounting that was placed inside the foot-cone over the tubular extension to the bolt. Through the bolt passed the two new brass wedges that pulled the foot-cone tightly upward and compressed the neck-assembly rigidly against the underside of the bowl. At the neck, inside the lower ring-mounting can be distinguished a pair of white pads that at that time were inserted to compensate for the distortion of the foot-cone. In the final reassembly these were omitted because another method of insuring rigidity was found. The polymethyl methacrylate spacer is visible within the neck-collar.

The Decorative Plates beneath the Foot

The various decorative plates on the underside of the flange of found that the four plates of silver had indeed been made in this manner. Of the four plates, all have patterns that are identical in shape. They were shown to be identical by a number of methods. First of all they were compared visually side by side. Next, photographs were made of all of them under identical conditions of lighting and distance. The negative from one of them was laid in turn on contact prints made from the others. In each case the print was cancelled out — it became uniformly grey. This procedure yielded evidence that the negative of one was identical with positives of the other three. Finally, in order to confirm these findings an instrument called a synchrisi-scope was applied. This instrument is used by ballistic experts for comparing the marks on pairs of expended bullets. Again, it was found that all four silver "pressblech" plates were identical, all except the corner of one plate, on which a second misplaced impression of the pattern appeared, perhaps because the workman had mis-struck on the first occasion.

Next, in fig. 27, we see a small part of one of the copper plates, only 9 mm wide, that is patterned with swastikas. The pattern appears to have been formed by tracing with a punch. Quite clearly it has not been engraved. The line is shown partly filled with green material. This may consist of corrosion products or it may possibly be the remains of an original inlay. The evidence was uncertain, although the material has been examined by X-ray diffraction analysis.

Next let us consider the panels beneath the foot made of woven wire (fig. 28). The upper panel has a square pattern and the lower one has a herringbone pattern. Fig. 29 shows these same two panels turned over. It will be seen that the upper panel now has the herringbone pattern and the lower panel has a similar but rather rounded pattern. Fig. 28 represents the upper woven-wire panel as received in the chalice (square pattern). Fig. 29 shows the lower panel in the as-received aspect (rounded herringbone). In the final reassembly the sides to be exposed were selected so that both of them would exhibit the herringbone pattern. These photographs were made while the panels rested on a illuminated sheet of translucent glass in order to remove distracting shadows from between the finely spaced wires. As a result the photograph indicates clearly that two different kinds of wire are present. One was made of silver and the other of bronze.

Fig. 30 represents the inside of the lower foot-girdle after examination. At the stage shown it had been reassembled and the various components had been fixed permanently in position ready for replacement on the foot-cone. After replacement was complete, from stylistic arguments Etienne Rhynne raised certain questions concerning the arrangement of these panels. By this time it would have been exceedingly difficult to open up the girdle for reexamination. Nevertheless, it was possible to look at this photograph, examine it under the microscope

25. An exploded view to show how the components of the chalice were reassembled temporarily in 1962.

the foot-cone include one of silver, one of copper, and another made of woven wire (fig. 25). A combination of such plates made up the whole decorative scheme. Next, consider some interesting features of these panels. Fig. 26 shows the silver plate in detail. It was made of very thin silver, embossed into a pattern, supposedly, by the "pressblech" process, in which the silver was beaten down against a shaped die. Evidence was

26. One of the silver plates decorating the underside of the foot-cone.

27. A part of one of the copper plates decorating the underside of the foot-cone.

30. The inside of the lower foot-girdle after the panels were reassembled.

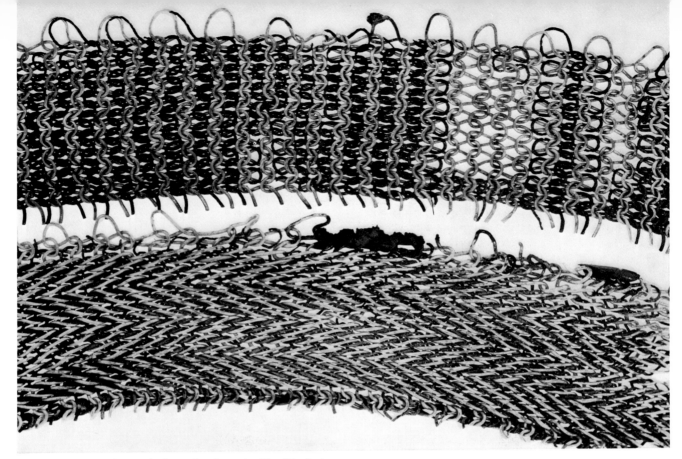

28. The two woven-wire panels decorating the underside of the foot-cone, arranged as received.

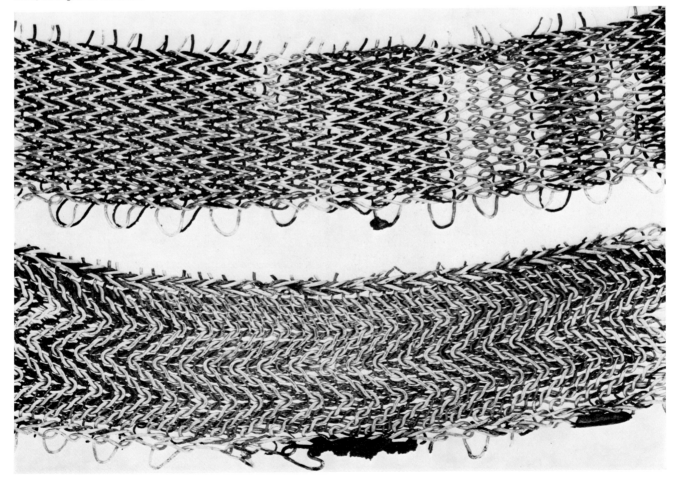

29. The two woven-wire panels shown in fig. 28, turned over to show their alternative patterns.

and to find at the ends of certain panels minute identification scratches, hitherto unsuspected, that ran off the ends of the panels onto the adjacent silver of the foot-girdle. In this way it could be shown quite conclusively that these panels had been in these particular positions at the time when someone else, perhaps Johnson, marked and dismantled it. This demonstration was further justification for the policy of making detailed photographic records of parts of the structure that would be hidden after reassembly.

Assembly of Decorative Elements around the Foot

Fig. 31 shows the assembly of the foot-girdles, of which the lower is shown in fig. 30. Above the lower girdle is shown a panel about to drop into place. A tiny flange had been formed on its two ends so that it could not drop quite through. Above lies a ring of lead and then the flange of the foot-cone. Fig. 32 shows the foot-cone itself viewed from above. The upper girdle

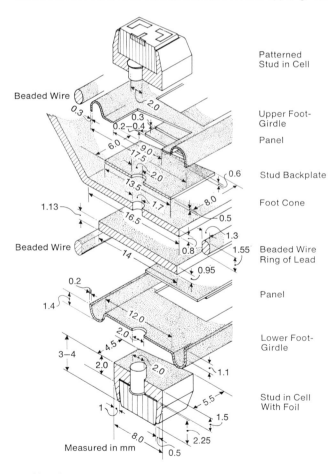

31. How the various components were assembled above and below the flange of the foot-cone.

32. The foot-cone, complete with upper foot-girdle, viewed from above.

33. A cross-section of a fragment of one of the gilt openwork bronze panels in the upper foot girdle, unetched. The length of the part of the fragment shown was about 0.9 mm.

lies around the flange. It is pierced by apertures for eight square studs and for eight intervening panels, of which four remain. These panels were made of cast bronze with openwork patterns that were gilded. They were backed with plates of mica, presumably with the object of making the panels gleam but in fact to little practical effect. The holes that are visible here through the apertures that lack panels were of

34. View of the interior of the upper foot-girdle after reassembly.

some interest. They were quite large, about 2 mm in diameter. They did not lie on the exact center-line of the panel apertures. In contrast the hole shown at four o'clock, at the center of the square aperture for a stud, is different in size from the others and lies exactly in the center of the square aperture. In fact there were eight of these smaller holes set on a circle of large radius, and there are eight of the 2 mm holes set on a circle of smaller radius. This observation proved valuable later. Let us return now to the open work panels. Had they been shaped by tooling or had they been cast?

Fig. 33 represents a cross-section of a fragment of one of the panels, a fragment found attached only by a thread of metal. The white area of the picture represents unetched polished metal. The upper area of darker material contains mineral corrosion products. These minerals no longer have the usual appearance of such corrosion crusts. The panel appears to have been cleaned by dipping in acid, presumably by Johnson, and to have been altered by this. Other points of interest are, first, the thick white line on the surface that appears at the bottom of the photograph — this is original gilding about 0.02 mm thick (less than $^1/_{1000}$ inch); second, a thin white line on the right hand side. This is newer gilding, perhaps by Johnson, 0.002 mm thick, similar in thickness to the gilding found on the catch-disc beneath the crystal shown in fig. 24.

The Plate of Lead in the Foot
Next let us turn back for a moment to fig. 31 and examine the

arrangement of the girdles above and below the flange of the foot-cone. This had presented a problem ever since the foot was dismantled. At that time it was discovered that the various components had been tacked together and onto a flat lead ring, which had been incorporated into the foot assembly, by means of lead-tin solder. Now the presence of this lead ring was not an essential feature of the design. It should have been quite unnecessary and probably had not been intended by the original designer. Again his design had been frustrated. He probably intended to rivet the lower studs directly on to the lower foot-girdle through the small holes made for this purpose on the circle of larger radius. The upper studs would have been riveted to the square back plates that appear just beneath them in fig. 31. These plates would have served as flanges to prevent the studs from leaving the apertures in the upper foot-girdle, through which they protruded. This was a general principle of the design. All the panels had flanges of corresponding purpose. He probably intended that the two girdles would be held together above and below the foot-cone flange by soldering along their outer edges. In this way they would secure the studs and panels.

Nevertheless, Dunraven's account refers to "plates of lead" in the foot — not to a single ring of lead such as was found but to multiple plates of lead. It seems likely that the designer's intentions had been frustrated by lack of skill on the part of the worker. He had had to insert lead packing plates into the foot because he had been unable to make his foot-girdles lie flat and sufficiently closely against the flange of the foot-cone to hold the various panels securely in position. When Johnson carried out his restoration he in turn made a whole ring instead of separate plates, and he tacked all his panels on to it by means of lead-tin solder. Nevertheless, it is probable that the chalice gained in stability as a result of the addition of weight to the foot.

In the British Museum reassembly, fig. 34, the foot was arranged more or less as the designer must have intended. The missing rivets were replaced by epoxy resin and the stud back-plates that were lacking were replaced by obviously modern transparent plates of cellulose acetate of similar thickness. In the photograph, at 12 o'clock and 3 o'clock, there can be seen all that remains of the original plates. A modern transparent replacement can be seen clearly at about 1:30 o'clock.

Construction of the Decorative Panels beneath the Rim
Next let us pass to the bowl girdle, the circle of panels below the rim. Fig. 35 is a drawing of its full length without either decorative panels or studs. It consists of an open-work silver frame passing around the bowl inside the handles. It is pierced alternately with circles for the studs to protrude through and

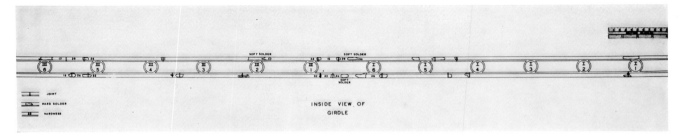

35. Drawing of the bowl girdle viewed from inside.

36. The ends of the bowl girdle, which do not meet, secured by means of soft solder beneath handle I.

with long apertures to display the panels. The numbers visible at certain positions represent the measured Brinell hardness of the silver. At the upper right-hand side of stud III 1 a particular short length of girdle is marked "18." This length is flanked on the left by a section of Brinell Hardness 32 and on the right by

a section of hardness 29. It would appear safe to assume that the short length of silver, so much softer than the silver on both sides, is an insertion. Further evidence to support this belief will be presented later. One of the questions asked about the girdle was whether it was made of solid silver. This was easily and early answered by pointing a camera into the space beneath a handle. Fig. 36 reveals clearly that the girdle was made of sheet silver that had been formed to the required hollow shape.

In fig. 37, in the upper length of a short portion of the girdle, there can be seen to the right of the left-hand stud, a length of inserted silver that is very much whiter than neighboring metal. In fig. 38 the same length of silver and its parallel fellow when seen from the back have clearly been soldered into place with hard solder. Next, consider the panels that were set in the long apertures in the girdle. They consisted of three types; one, shown here (fig. 39) and later described as of "C-pattern," was zoomorphic. The panel was made up in three layers, first the lines of the design ridged up in gold in the pressblech manner with the intervening background cut away; second, lying along the top of the ridges, soldered on, was a treble layer of beaded wires, only the top row being visible in the photograph at first sight but all three being clearly present on close examination; third, backing the open-work pattern was a plate of gilt copper, taken away for the purpose of making this photograph. Of especial interest in fig. 39, in the lower left hand quadrant, are two cones of twisted wires, the left-hand one broken off. Details of their method of construction will be presented later. Around the panel, beyond the bordering beaded wire, was left a narrow flange that would have prevented the panel from falling through the containing aperture in the original design. Although beaded wire was mostly used, certain details of the design have been filled in with twisted wire.

Fig. 40 present a view of part of the back of this same panel that supports the belief in a pressblech manner of construction. Even the sharp edges of the die against which the gold sheet was pressed can be discerned here along the lengths of the hollows. There is also visible a numeral, X, scratched at the top. This and similar numerals caused much perplexity, as

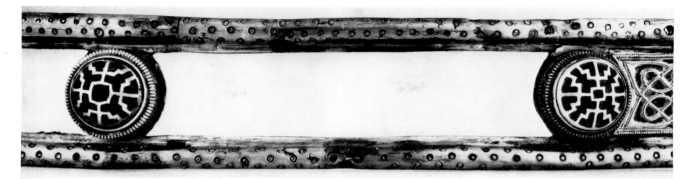

37. Frontal view of a short length of the curved bowl girdle between studs known as III 1 and I 6.

38. Interior view of same length as shown in fig. 37.

39. Detail of portion of zoomorphic panel from bowl girdle, type C.

40. Detail of the back of the panel shown in fig. 39.

41. Close-up view of the pair of cones shown in fig. 39.

will be discussed later. Fig. 41 is a close-up view of the pair of cones made of twisted wire described above. They have clearly been made by coiling up a pair of beaded wires. Fig. 42 shows another pattern of panel, one that has been described as type A — an ornithomorphic design. This is fabricated in a manner identical with that of the other panels. Notice also that the overall visual effect is very similar to that of the preceeding panel, type C. This observation became of considerable importance when the question of arranging the panels arose at the time of reassembly. The third design of panel, fig. 43, type B, consisting of knot-work, has a quite different visual effect and stands out quite clearly from a group of all three types.

Fig. 44 illustrates the back of the panel with its gilt back-panel in place. This particular back panel was gilded on its front face only. Clearly it has been held in place by tags, formed from the flange of the panel proper by snipping through and turning over. This is a simple but aesthetically unsatisfactory method of fixing that has been used extensively in making children's toys in recent times. Its use is not at all in keeping with the general concept of the design, and it is unlikely that the original designer intended to use it. He designed the

panels with end flanges to terminate behind the flanges of the two neighboring studs. These would secure it adequately. Notice also that the back of the left-hand stud is closed by a lead plug that is bordered by a row of punch-marks. These would serve to expand the plug into the inside of the cylindrical stud-mount and thus secure the mount tightly within its aperture in the girdle.

The Inscription around the Bowl

Next let us pass on to the inscription that runs around the bowl just beneath the girdle. Fig. 45 shows the one of the four quadrants that contains the names of Bartholomew, Thomas, and Matthew, three of the disciples. The clarity of the inscription as shown is solely the result of good photography. On the uncleaned chalice the inscription was almost invisible. Fig. 46 is a detail selected to illustrate how the inscription was made: freehand, scribed with a point, and the dotted background also impressed by a point applied almost vertically. In addition to inscribed names the bowl is decorated (fig. 47), with a set of four animals inscribed in the same manner. The illustration has been rendered so very clearly by the use of high-contrast photography. Indeed, it is more convenient to study this photograph than the bowl itself because the curved bowl has to be rotated to various angles in the available light in order to build up a mental impression of the whole animal, whereas here the image lies in a single plane.

The Two Roundels

Next let us examine the two roundels, which are located on the bowl between the handles. Fig. 48 shows that thick silver has been formed into an eight-lobed open frame. Within each aperture is a gold panel decorated with beaded wire and also faced with a decorative surface. These gold panels differ from the smooth gilded back plates in the bowl girdle by having a textured surface. The method of fabrication has not been discovered.

The roundel shown has four studs around its periphery. The two at 3 o'clock and 9 o'clock are made of blue glass and the two at 12 o'clock and 6 o'clock are made of red material that in fact now consists of wax. According to Dunraven this was originally amber, but no trace of amber was found remaining. These four studs hide the four rivets that attach the roundel to the bowl. One of these rivets, illustrated in fig. 49 and typical of all, is very interesting. The hidden interior end is shown. It is hollow and was made by folding copper sheet into a tube and then soldering it to the head of the rivet, a tiny convex disc made of silver in order to blend visually with the interior surface of the silver bowl on which it lay. This suggests that at the period in which the rivet was made labor was cheap and material was expensive, because a great deal of effort is re-

42. One of the ornithomorphic panels, type *A*, from the bowl girdle.

43. One of the knot-work panels, type *B*, from the bowl girdle.

44. The back of the open-work pressblech panel showing the plate
that covered the back.

45. One quadrant of the inscription around the bowl.

46. Detail of the inscription around the bowl beneath the bowl girdle, removed at the time of this photograph.

47. One of the four inscribed animals.

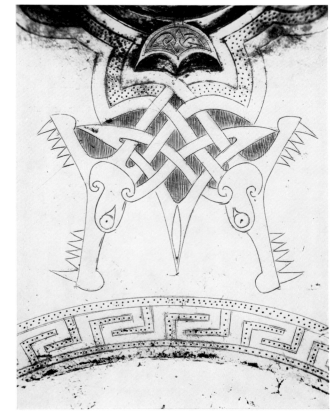

48. One of the two roundels.

50. The central stud in the other one of the two roundels.

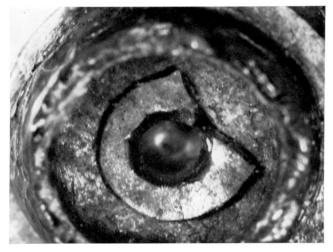

49. The end of one of the rivets hidden behind a stud in the roundel.

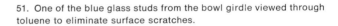

51. One of the blue glass studs from the bowl girdle viewed through toluene to eliminate surface scratches.

quired to make up a tiny rivet out of fragments of silver and of copper sheet.

Fig. 50 illustrates the central stud in the roundel on the other side of the bowl. A certain amount of damage had been done here, with the result that where the central silver grille had been torn away the glass of the stud had been exposed. The stud contains both red and blue glass. It could be seen that the red glass has been inserted into spaces in the grille and that the blue glass in a plastic condition has been pressed in behind it in order to fill all of the remaining cavities.

The damage here appears to have been done by someone in search of information. A less destructive method of examining a stud would have been to push it slightly forward in its mount so that the edge of the silver grille was exposed. The thickness of the exposed edge could then have been measured by means of a microscope. In fact, on preliminary examination a stud was found that had been pressed forward in this manner. Advantage was taken of this to measure the thickness of the grille, 0.1 mm ($^1/_{250}$ inch). There does exist, however, a general method of examination that is completely nondestructive. The next photograph, fig. 51, illustrates another stud, photographed while it was immersed in toluene so that the glass can be seen clearly without the confusion introduced by surface scratches. Here the actual thickness of the peripheral

53. One of the two escutcheons beneath a handle, before cleaning.

edge of the silver grille can be seen. In these circumstances it was not difficult to focus a suitable microscope first of all on the upper edge of the grille and then on the lower edge (fig. 52). By measuring the travel of the microscope between these two positions the thickness of the silver may be estimated. Details of the method are indicated in the illustration. A suitable factor has to be applied to compensate for the refractive index of the glass, but this need not be known very precisely.

The Handle Escutcheons

Next let us examine the handle escutcheons which provided some features of interest (fig. 53). The design is very elegant. It incorporates three subconical studs. The lowest stud has a central area decorated with gold granulation. Around its base

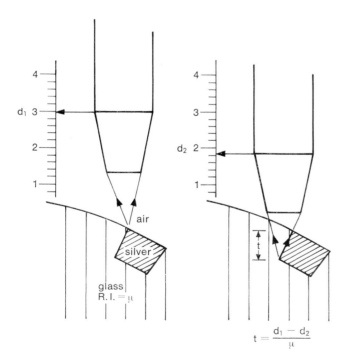

$$t = \frac{d_1 - d_2}{\mu}$$

52 Method of measuring the approximate thickness of the silver grille without damage to the stud.

54. Patterned silver foil for the underside of a stud in the under-foot girdle.

57. Some of the decorative studs in one of the handles.

55. A stud in the under-foot girdle photographed through immersion liquid in order to reveal bubbles and striae in the glass and the pattern of the foil beneath.

56. One of the four glass studs in the upper foot girdle.

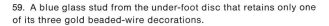

58. The silver foil backing of one of the transparent glass studs in a handle, and the method of attachment, photographed through a dental mirror.

59. A blue glass stud from the under-foot disc that retains only one of its three gold beaded-wire decorations.

is a partitioned ring filled now with malachite and originally decorated with roughly plano-convex cylindrical amber beads set upon the malachite. Before returning to this feature let us consider the studs generally.

The Studs in the Foot-Girdles

In the lower foot girdle there were eight studs of almost rectangular shape that supported the whole weight of the chalice on the table and were in consequence very much scratched. They were made of pale blue transparent material. One of the studs was missing, and a backing of patterned silver foil was in consequence exposed (fig. 54). We wanted to discover whether all of the studs were backed by similar silver foil. In order to establish this and to discover the pattern on the foil it became necessary to take photographs through the almost opaque scratched surface of each stud. To do this the stud was coated with an oil of suitable refractive index that would fill the scratches and give them optical properties similar to those of the mass of the material. Fig. 55 illustrates the result. Bubbles in the stud provide clear evidence that the stud was made of glass and not of some semi-precious stone. This photograph offers additional evidence that the stud is made of glass by showing the presence of striae. These are evidence of inadequate mixing of the molten glass. The pattern on the embossed foil is also visible. Not all of the foils had the same pattern. The one shown in fig. 55 is different from that in fig. 54.

The studs on the upper foot-girdle, of which fig. 56 presents an example, were never hidden by the foot while the chalice was standing: they were always in full view and were therefore made more ornate. The mass of the stud shown consisted of blue opaque glass. In its center was a red cross, and in each corner a yellow angle. Two of the four studs had this particular arrangement of colors. The other two had the colors reversed: yellow in the center and red in the corners. The various fields of color were separated by, not cloisons proper, but narrow strips of silver sheet that had been bent to shape and set on edge.

Fig. 57 presents the decorative studs set in one of the handles. Here a central vertical row of gold filigree panels is flanked on two sides by mirror-twin pairs of rectangular studs. All of the studs except those two across the middle of the field of view have silver grilles in their faces. The two exceptions have grilles made of red glass. Unfortunately the red has corroded extensively. Certain of the studs were made of pale blue transparent glass (two of these may be seen on edge on the curve of the handle). These were both backed by silver foil, but only one of the two foils was embossed. It was necessary to photograph this from inside the handle, for the benefit of posterity, while the silver liner of the handle that normally ob-

scured it had been removed. The photograph, fig. 58, was taken as shown here through a carefully aligned dental mirror.

The Studs in the Under-Foot Mounting

Fig. 59 shows yet another kind of stud: one of the five found in the underfoot mounting. Only two of the five still retained any of the gold beaded-wire decoration, and in this photograph only one of the coiled wires remains, but the shapes of the other two are retained in the glass stud. These indicate conclusively that the glass was pressed around the beaded wires while it was in a viscous condition. A little thought about this design will indicate that the shapes of these three coiled beaded wires were perfectly adapted to the method of construction of the stud. Placed back to back inside a hemispherical mold the three would slide to the bottom and align themselves symmetrically in contact while the viscous glass could be pressed in to fix them in place.

The Studs in the Bowl Girdle

Fig. 60 shows the silver grille and the blue-glass backing as seen by the naked eye. In fig. 61 all of the physical data concerning this stud have been incorporated in a single dimensioned drawing. It shows a cross-section through the stud accompanied by an exploded drawing that indicates how the panels and panel back plates were assembled in the bowl girdle. The mounted stud *B* was passed from the front into the hole in the girdle marked *C*. A lead plug marked *F* in the cross-sectional drawing was pushed into the back of the mount and was expanded by a series of punchings around its periphery. The adjacent panels with back plates, *D* and *E*, were dropped into place in the apertures in the girdle and the slit edges of the stud mount were turned over to hold them in position. The drawing shows the condition of the girdle as received. It would have been more in accordance with the concept of the design if the edge of the back plate, *E*, cut back by someone — possibly Johnson — had been left equal in length with the panel, *D*, and the two components had then been held together by the turned-over edge of the stud mount. All this and additional information is presented in this single drawing.

The Stud in the Handle Escutcheon

In fig. 62, the great subconical stud that was seen in the photograph of the handle escutcheon is shown illuminated with both frontal and back lighting while it was immersed in toluene. This illumination gave an impression of the transparency of the glass. As seen when mounted the glass appears to be opaque because no provision could be made in the design of the escutcheon for light to pass through it. The same stud is shown in the sectioned drawing, fig. 63, which was made to illustrate the details of construction of the mount.

60. A view of one of the blue glass studs in the bowl girdle that illustrates the beaded wire around it.

62. One of the subconical studs from a handle escutcheon photographed while it was immersed in toluene.

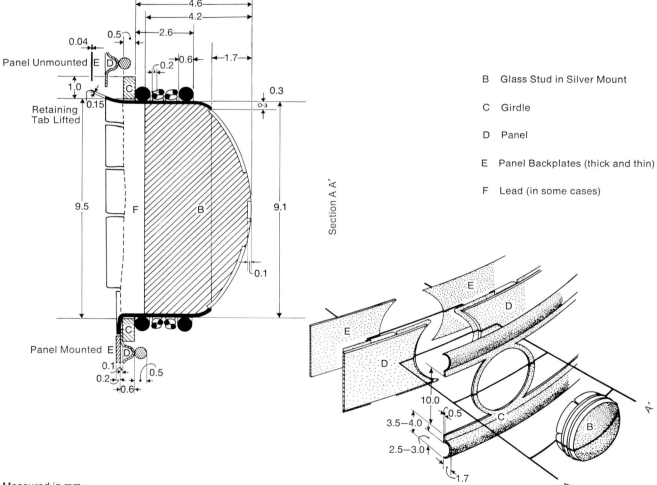

B Glass Stud in Silver Mount

C Girdle

D Panel

E Panel Backplates (thick and thin)

F Lead (in some cases)

Measured in mm

61. Cross-section and exploded view of a glass stud in the bowl girdle.

Beneath the stud can be seen three packing pieces made of cardboard. These pieces of card are part of a photographic print, possibly from the early 20th century, that must have been inserted at the time of some earlier examination.

The Malachite Paste beneath Inlays of Amber

The channel around the stud contained residues of green material that presented a problem. X-ray diffraction analysis indicated that it was made of malachite, but the shape of the filling indicated that it had been inserted while it was of a pasty consistency. If this were the case then the malachite may have been used in powder form, ground up with a medium such as glue, and inserted into the mounting to serve as a temporary packing and adhesive for the amber inlay. The fragments of amber inlay still remaining are plano-convex and are adequately held in position between the walls of the channel, under constraint by the lower beaded wire on the stud mount. It is suggested that the malachite mixture was applied as a temporary adhesive until such time as the stud mount should have been inserted as the final fixing device.

A question immediately arose from this study: why was a mixture of malachite employed? Why not make use of a gesso? A possible answer is that the particular mixture was already in use about the 9th century workshop for some other purpose and that it was pressed into service on this particular occasion. The mixture could have been in use for soldering fine granulation work (Maryon, H., *Metalwork and Enamelling,* London, Chapman and Hall, 1954, p.10). The partitions across the outer channel are secured in conical holes (fig. 63). The size of these holes was determined, even though they were on the back of an escutcheon that was firmly attached to the bowl, by a method shown in fig. 64. One of the two escutcheons was found to be separated from the bowl by a distance of about 1mm. A piece of reflective metallized cellulose adhesive tape was inserted into the gap and made to serve as a mirror in which the back of the escutcheon that contained the holes could be photographed. The diameter of the holes was measured by means of a microscope.

The Arrangement of Panels in the Bowl Girdle

The problem of the arrangement of the ten decorative panels in the bowl girdle may next be considered briefly. Their arrangement as received, unsymmetrical on both sides, had always worried the stylistic experts because it was said to be "aesthetically impossible" for the Irish craftsman. While sympathetic toward our colleagues of a different discipline, as scientists we were constrained to seek some objective evidence to justify some other arrangement of the panels. Etienne Rhynne of Dublin after considerable study proposed an arrangement that was based on aesthetic reasoning and that yielded a symmetri-

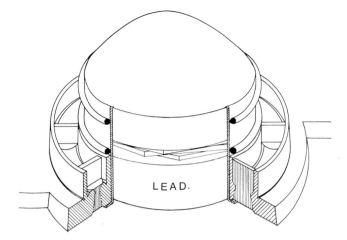

63. The construction of the subconical stud.

64. The use of reflective tape to view through a narrow gap details of the back of an escutcheon.

cal arrangement of the three types of panel. With the aid of this basic concept he was able to rationalize a number of difficulties that had arisen concerning the arrangement of several sequences of numerals that had been scratched on the backs of the panels. One of these, an "X," appears here in fig. 40. However, in search of additional objective evidence all of the data were now reviewed. First, the earliest documentary evidence that was available was examined. This was the photograph found in Margaret Stokes' album, fig. 65. After much study it became possible actually to identify the various panels not only by type — *A*, ornithomorphic; *B*, knotwork; *C*, zoomorphic — but individually. As a result it appeared certain that the

65. The photograph found in Margaret Stokes' album.

arrangement of panels shown in the photograph really belonged to the opposite side of the bowl as shown and had also been moved round by about the width of a panel. It could never have been actually as shown! The conclusion reached was that the girdle with its panels had been replaced temporarily during restoration only for the purpose of taking a photograph and it therefore did not provide evidence of much value for the purpose in view.

Another possible and historical arrangement for the panels was as they were received in the laboratory. This had in fact never been very satisfactory because as received the two ends of the bowl girdle, expanded by ill-fitting panels, had not come together as they should. The ends had been secured by solder to the bowl, with a gap between them, at a position obscured behind one of the handles.

Yet another historical arrangement of panels was found in a representation of the chalice that had been made by Johnson and was in the collections of the Victoria and Albert Museum in London. This arrangement was very close indeed to Etienne Rhynne's arrangement. It was so much more symmetrical than

the arrangement "as received" that it seemed rather odd that Johnson had not employed it when he himself replaced the panels in the chalice in 1869: he clearly held the same belief in aesthetically satisfactory arrangement as did the Early-Christian Irish!

The next attempt to resolve the difficulty ignored history: the actual physical fit of the various panels in the apertures in the bowl girdle was examined. Certain well-defined criteria that could be applied without any uncertainty in the answer were used. About a hundred trials were made of the fit of each panel into every aperture, extending over several days. The results were categorized in lists. They revealed that Rhynne's beautiful symmetrical arrangement was quite impossible in practice because all of the necessary panels just could not be inserted mechanically into the required apertures. It also showed that Johnson's arrangement as used in the representation in the Victoria and Albert Museum was not mechanically feasible in the present condition of the girdle. This explained why he had not used the arrangement in his own restoration. The result also showed that even the unsatisfactory arrangement in the

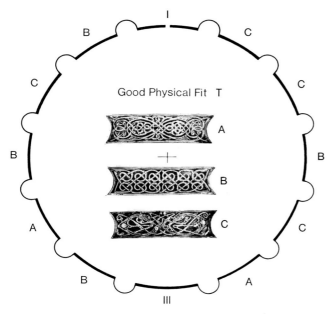

66. The arrangement of three types of panel between the studs in the bowl girdle.

chalice as received had only become possible because he had forced two panels into place. The question that then arose concerned what arrangement would be acceptable to Dublin, since neither perfect symmetry nor the Rhynne arrangement was physically feasible. From the new data it was discovered that there were two arrangements of panels that were physically possible and that contained maximum symmetry. Agreement on one of these was eventually reached and the panels were replaced as shown in fig. 66. Here the arrangements of panels are different on the two sides, but visually they appear symmetrical because panels of types C and A have similar visual impact although actually different in pattern. It is only fair to add here that some other arrangement was probably physically possible before the original restoration, at which time the bowl girdle was repaired by inserting silver and at least one panel aperture might have been shortened slightly during this operation. Finally, fig. 67 illustrates the chalice as received, grey and dull, with most of its detail invisible, and insecure at the neck. In contrast, fig. 68 shows one side of the chalice after the work and fig. 69 shows the other side, both views fully detailed and colorful and the chalice completely rigid to the touch.

Summary

The methods of observation used included the following: directly, by sense of touch; measurement with a scale, with calipers, with a slide gauge, by micrometer, by micrometer eyepiece in a microscope, by traveling microscope; direct visual observation; and microscope-assisted observation through air, through oil-films, and through immersion liquids. Observations have been made indirectly via silastomer molds, wax impressions, silhouettes, shadows cast by straight edges, and by grids of lines. Detailed comparisons were made visually, by superimposition of negative images from one component on positive images of another component, or by means of a synchrisiscope. Other comparisons of an essentially nondestructive nature have been made by measurements of Brinell Hardness. Metallographic observations have been made on naturally etched surfaces and on prepared and polished surfaces. Analyses on minute samples, barely mentioned above, were performed by spectrography and by X-ray diffraction analysis.

The recording of details, by no means the easiest part of the work, was carried out largely by photographic methods, lighting the subjects by daylight, by special arrangements of artificial light, by diffuse illumination, or using lighted backgrounds and supports in order to eliminate confusing shadows. A variety of cameras were used according to need: $3\frac{1}{4}$ by $4\frac{1}{4}$, $4\frac{3}{4}$ by $6\frac{1}{2}$ inch, 35 mm, ancient mahogany cameras, a modern all-movement Sinar, a Leica, and several models of single-lens reflex. In photomicrography a Vickers projection microscope was used. Objects were viewed either directly or through mirrors, even into crevices 1mm wide. In order to yield a good record, exploded views were made and Xerography was pressed into service to achieve a particular result. Pressure to record so precisely has been generated by the desire to produce detailed schematic drawings in which the objective data could be preserved precisely for the benefit of posterity. Preparation of these drawings often exposed our ignorance of some detail of the chalice and drove us continually to devise some means of recording features that were barely perceptible. The completed drawings brought to our attention certain formal relationships between components that would otherwise have escaped notice.

In conclusion it must be abundantly clear that no one person could have carried out all of the examination, recording, and reconstruction that has been outlined here. In fact eight or nine members of the staff of the Research Laboratory of the British Museum shared in the work in varying degrees. I served in the laboratory at that time, and this account is published with the permission of the Keeper of the Research Laboratory, Dr. A. E. Werner.

67. The other side of the chalice as it was received.

68. One side of the cleaned and reassembled chalice.

69. The other side of the cleaned and reassembled chalice.

DATE DUE
